Praise for *Slavery and Freedom in the Bluegrass State*

"The splendid essays in *Slavery and Freedom in the Bluegrass State* are most timely as we ponder how to remedy the racial injustices, misuses of history, and myths identified with the song 'My Old Kentucky Home.' Focusing on the racial tensions that have long plagued interactions between Blacks and Whites in Kentucky and in the nation at large, this collection is a heartfelt manifesto, a reckoning, for truth and respect in race relations and in history. Collectively the contributions offer a beacon of hope and change for racial equality in deed as well as in word." —John David Smith, coeditor of *The Long Civil War: New Explorations of America's Enduring Conflict*

"This volume reveals the profound racial limits of 'My Old Kentucky Home' as an iconic song and idea in the minds and hearts of most white Kentuckians and offers fresh new understandings of the ongoing African American fight (both inter- and intra-racial) for citizenship, freedom, and democracy. As such, this book suggests a model for activists, historians, and policy makers seeking a new history that is appropriate for the expanding postindustrial age among the other states of our fragile union." —Joe William Trotter Jr., author of *Pittsburgh and the Urban League Movement: A Century of Social Service and Activism*

"*Slavery and Freedom in the Bluegrass State: Revisiting My Old Kentucky Home* is history that matters. Smith's collection of superb scholarship on slavery, freedom, and civil rights is a crucial consideration of Black Kentuckians' centrality in shaping the history of the Bluegrass. It is an essential chronicle of Black life and humanity."—Luther Adams–Free Man of Color, author of *Way Up North in Louisville*

"Smith's scholarly compilation of melting pot–like perspectives on Kentucky's almost sacred-like state song tosses aside its shibboleths and casts more illuminating light on the song's contentious interpretations. A bodacious work."—William H. Turner, author of *The Harlan Renaissance: Stories of Black Life in Appalachian Coal Towns*

T0003217

Slavery and Freedom in the Bluegrass State

Slavery *and* Freedom *in the* Bluegrass State

• REVISITING MY OLD KENTUCKY HOME •

edited by **Gerald L. Smith**

UNIVERSITY PRESS OF KENTUCKY

Scholarly publisher for the Commonwealth, serving Bellarmine University, Berea College, Centre College of Kentucky, Eastern Kentucky University, The Filson Historical Society, Georgetown College, Kentucky Historical Society, Kentucky State University, Morehead State University, Murray State University, Northern Kentucky University, Spalding University, Transylvania University, University of Kentucky, University of Louisville, University of Pikeville, and Western Kentucky University.

Editorial and Sales Offices: The University Press of Kentucky
663 South Limestone Street, Lexington, Kentucky 40508-4008

www.kentuckypress.com

Library of Congress Cataloging-in-Publication Data

Names: Smith, Gerald L., 1959- editor.
Title: Slavery and freedom in the Bluegrass State : revisiting My Old
    Kentucky Home / edited by Gerald L. Smith.
Description: Lexington, Kentucky : University Press of Kentucky, [2023] |
    Includes bibliographical references and index.
Identifiers: LCCN 2022043808 | ISBN 9780813196152 (hardcover ;
    alkaline paper) | ISBN 9780813197111 (paperback ; alkaline paper) |
    ISBN 9780813196169 (pdf) | ISBN 9780813196176 (epub)
Subjects: LCSH: Foster, Stephen Collins, 1826-1864. My old Kentucky home. |
    African Americans—Kentucky—History. | Slaves—Kentucky—History. |
    Slavery—Kentucky—History. | African American women—Kentucky—
    History. | Kentucky—Race relations—History.
Classification: LCC E185.93.K3 S53 2023 | DDC 976.9/00496073—
    dc23/eng/20220923
LC record available at https://lccn.loc.gov/2022043808

For my wife, Teresa

Contents

Introduction

Gerald L. Smith

The time has come when the head will never bow
Wherever the Negro may go
A few more years and he'll show the nation how
He will thrive where the sugar canes grow.
A few more years and he'll shift the weary load
So that it will ever be light
A few more years and he'll triumph on the road
And sing, My Old Kentucky home's alright.
                    —Joseph S. Cotter, "My Old Kentucky Home"[1]

On March 13, 2020, at 12:48 a.m., Breonna Taylor died in the hallway of her Louisville apartment. She had been shot six times by police carrying out a no-knock warrant as part of a narcotics investigation. Taylor was a twenty-six-year-old Black emergency-room technician at Jewish and North Hospitals whose life was tragically snuffed out. A few hours after her death, protest erupted on the streets of Louisville, but that was just the beginning. Weeks later, the city witnessed a night protest in which seven people were shot. Demonstrations continued to gain momentum. Taylor's death amplified a worldwide cry for equal justice and police reform. The African American Policy Forum's Say Her Name Campaign and the Black Lives Matter movement elevated Taylor's killing among the Black women victims of anti-Black policing.[2]

Black Kentuckians counted for only 8 percent of the state's population in 2020. Louisville was home to the largest percentage of African Americans at 24 percent.[3] However, intergenerational and interracial marches, rallies, and protests took place throughout Kentucky much of the year. The movement became "bigger than Breonna." On June 11, Louisville's Metro

Council met and voted to pass Breonna's Law, which banned no-knock warrants.[4] On June 25, more than five hundred people participated in a rally at the Kentucky state capitol to advocate for racial justice. Four days later Black Lives Matter Louisville blocked the Second Street Bridge and hung a picture of Taylor's face with a message that read: "They tried to bury me. They did not know I was a seed."

Historically, much of the pain and suffering Black Kentuckians have experienced remains buried, but new studies are uncovering the state's past. African Americans came to Kentucky as slaves during the frontier years. They worked alongside whites, cutting through the wilderness, building cabins, planting crops, erecting forts, and fighting against the Indigenous peoples. Between 1790 and 1830, the enslaved population increased from 11,830 to 165,213 in number. That year, 24 percent of the state's more than 600,000 total residents were either enslaved or free Blacks. This would be the highest percentage of Blacks in Kentucky's history.[5]

Throughout the antebellum period, enslaved Blacks loaded boats and ferries on Kentucky docks and worked on hemp and tobacco fields and in cattle and sheep pastures. They labored in saltworks and iron manufacturing. Enslaved women toiled as domestic workers, cooking, cleaning, washing, and ironing for white families. Enslaved children weeded gardens and waited tables. From sweating in factories to serving as guides in Mammoth Cave, the state's enslaved people were the essential workers forced to build Kentucky's economy. "In essence," wrote the late historian J. Blaine Hudson, "enslaved African-Americans were the farm machines and the household appliances of this era which whites believed necessary both for their comfort and for the productivity of their lands and other enterprises."[6]

To maintain control over enslaved communities, white Kentuckians established slave patrols to monitor their activities by searching their homes, breaking up unlawful assemblies, arresting those without passes, and catching runaways. Enslaved African Americans despised them as "por [sic] white trash." In the eyes of one enslaved person, these white patrols were "the off-scouring of all things, the refuse, the ears, and tails of slavery, the wallet and satchel of pole-cats, the meanest and lowest and worst of all creatures."[7]

Because Kentucky's climate was not favorable to plantation labor, most enslaved people did not work on large-scale plantations but on small farms with an average of five workers. By 1860, the enslaved population had experienced a steady decline from year to year. In that year, there were 225,483 enslaved and 10,684 free African Americans living in the state. The next year the Civil War began, and Black men in Kentucky crossed into other states to join in the fight on the Union side. Three years into the war, President Abraham Lincoln permitted the recruitment of Black soldiers in Kentucky. Black men hurried to recruitment stations throughout the state. Marion Lucas writes about a former slave who as a child was "awakened late at night by his mother, who whispered for him to tell his uncles 'good-bye.' The startled child opened his eyes to see four of his uncles leaving to join the army, 'the light of adventure shining on their faces.'"[8]

White Kentuckians resented the presence of Black troops and the abolition of slavery. They refused to ratify the Thirteenth, Fourteenth, and Fifteenth Amendments during the Reconstruction period. They organized gangs known as "moderators," "guerillas," and the "Ku Klux Klan," intimidating, beating, and murdering African Americans who lived in rural communities. Anne Marshall writes: "In their efforts to shape a world where former slaves remained in a subservient status, thousands of Kentucky whites used intimidation to prevent African Americans from violating racial boundaries, or punished them when they did so." Between the years 1865 and 1874, eighty-seven Blacks were lynched. By the end of the century, there were 166 additional lynchings in the state; African Americans accounted for 110 of the victims.[9]

The African American population in the state dwindled to 13.3 percent by 1900. Kentucky became a geographic symbol for plantation literature that appealed to the North and South. Maryjean Wall writes that "travelers from the North found the Bluegrass more accessible than the Deep South. . . . Bluegrass Kentucky, with its slaveholding history, its large homes, and its pastures filled with horses, evolved as the Near South and, thus, as representative of the Old South." James Lane Allen, Annie Fellows Johnston, and John Fox Jr. were white Kentuckians who garnered national reputations in their works romanticizing the days gone by. "These writers peopled those of their works about the Bluegrass," argues Wall, "with kindly Confederate-supporting colonels, loyal slaves, and massive columned mansions that bespoke a social power and grace originating in a timeless connection to the land."[10]

The song "My Old Kentucky Home" symbolizes the misuse of history at the expense of Black people. It is an extension of the unfounded myth that Blacks and whites lived and worked together in Kentucky free of racial tensions. Generations of white Kentuckians have heard and sent out a resounding message that has sought to mute the realities of life in Black homes, churches, schools, and communities.

This book confronts the literature and historical narratives that have misrepresented Black voices. It examines three broad topics: slavery, freedom, and civil rights. It addresses unanswered questions about Black life in a border state between North and South. How did Blacks survive, resist, and persevere through slavery? How did slavery bolster Kentucky's economy? What were the interpersonal relationships between Blacks and whites outside of labor? How did Black men and women deal with violence at home and in the community after slavery? How did they engage in matters relating to politics and education?

The killing of Breonna Taylor placed racial violence, equity, justice, and, ironically, Kentucky in the global spotlight. It indirectly raised questions about Black history in Kentucky. In late August and early September 2020, protestors gathered outside the gates at the Churchill Downs site of the Kentucky Derby. The Derby had been rescheduled from May to September that year because of the coronavirus pandemic. Although the pageantry and crowds were not yet in full force, protesters still considered the Derby a cultural representation of race and class inequality. In the week prior to the Derby, they hung a banner with Taylor's picture over the top of the entrance gates and chanted, "No Justice, no Derby."[11] In an open letter to the CEO of Churchill Downs, Bill Carstanjen, the Louisville poet Hannah Drake wrote: "I question how horses running will be a progressive unifying force that can bring us together?" Moreover, in a blistering critique of one of the Derby's long-standing traditions, Drake asked: "Why is 'My Old Kentucky Home,' a song of a slave being sold down South, still sung at the Kentucky Derby? . . . Breonna Taylor and those in this city fighting for justice deserved more from this iconic institution."[12]

Stephen Collins Foster's song "My Old Kentucky Home, Good-Night" was published in 1853. The lyrics were likely inspired by Harriet Beecher Stowe's controversial antislavery novel *Uncle Tom's Cabin* (1852), with Kentucky as its backdrop. Stowe had visited Garrard and Mason Counties before finishing the book, which captured the cruelty of slavery through the value of human chattel. Stowe wrote in the novel, "Whoever visits some of the estates there, and witnesses the good-humored indulgence of some masters and mistresses, and the affectionate loyalty of some slaves, might be tempted to dream the oft-fabled poetic legend of a patriarchal institution, and all that; but over and above the scene there broods a portentous shadow—the shadow of *law*." In short, she pointed out that money "may cause [owners] any day to exchange a life of kind protection and indulgence for one of hopeless misery and toil."[13]

Stowe's influence on Foster was discovered in 1931 when his granddaughter sold the original draft of the song, titled "Old Uncle Tom, Good-Night," which pictures the separation of enslaved families in Kentucky, thereby revealing just how unlikely it was that Foster was inspired by a visit to Federal Hill. Foster wrote other southern melodies, including "Old Black Joe," "Camptown Races," and "Oh! Susanna," and had a Kentucky connection. He was a distant cousin of John Rowan, a nineteenth-century Bardstown lawyer and judge who served in the US Senate and was the owner and builder of the mansion Federal Hill. Enslaved people worked on the grounds and inside the home during the antebellum period. They constructed buildings, cleaned, cooked, and washed clothes. Rowan's will revealed in 1840 that several "negro" men, women, and children labored at the home.[14]

In a campaign to promote tourism and capitalize on the mythology of the Old South, Foster was said to have written "My Old Kentucky Home" while visiting Federal Hill. Without any conclusive evidence, it is claimed he "watched little Negroes playing in the sunshine and shadow" and wrote, "Tis the summer the darkies are gay."[15] Regardless of the lack of truth of such descriptions, private fundraising efforts and a state appropriation enabled the Commonwealth of Kentucky to purchase Federal Hill and name it "My Old Kentucky Home."

On July 4, 1923, flags and banners hung along the streets of Bardstown, Kentucky. By early morning a crowd was assembling for the dedication of Federal Hill. More than fifteen thousand people gathered east of Bardstown for the dedication ceremony. Four hundred and forty-one passengers arrived on a train from Louisville. Relatives of Foster and officials from his home city, Pittsburgh, Pennsylvania, were also on hand for the momentous occasion. The *Kentucky Reporter* reported, "It was truly a cosmopolitan crowd which gathered on the grassy slopes of Federal Hill. Old time Southern darkies walked around, their black countenances offering a curious mixture with their white clothing to pay tribute to a writer and the spot where he received inspiration." Federal Hill was "conceived as a 'shrine' to Foster and a symbolic 'home for all' Kentuckians that would welcome visitors from near and far," writes the historian Emily Bingham.[16]

The misrepresented generational symbolism of the site and song has been difficult to overcome. Not even a mass movement surrounding the death of an innocent Black victim was enough to shame leaders into silencing the distorted message engrained in "My Old Kentucky Home." Senate Majority Leader Mitch McConnell, in a telephone call to the president of Churchill Downs, "recommended that they play 'My Old Kentucky Home.'" "This is a song that goes back to the pre–Civil War period," said McConnell. "It used to have some language in it that I think could have been viewed as racially insensitive. That was dropped out what 30 or 40 years ago. It's very much a part of our culture and tradition and absolutely should be played at the Kentucky Derby." On September 5, 2020, at the 146th "running for the roses," there was no sing-along to "My Old Kentucky Home." Instead, there was "a moment of silence and reflection" and an instrumental rendition of the song. The following year, though, the original tradition continued when the song was performed.[17]

The song had been designated the official state song by an act of the state legislature in 1928. Eight years later, Federal Hill became part of the Kentucky Park system. The 150th anniversary of the erection of Federal Hill and Foster's 119th birthday were celebrated on July 4, 1945. The program, which was sponsored by the City of Bardstown, Division of Parks, Commonwealth of Kentucky, and the Honorable Order of Kentucky Colonels, also celebrated the 169th anniversary of the signing of the Declaration of Independence. Part of the celebration was broadcast over WGRC and the Mutual Broadcasting System. The Eighty-Second Army Ground Forces Band provided concert music. Mrs. A. B. Chandler, wife of the former governor A. B. "Happy" Chandler (in office 1935–1939), sang "My Old Kentucky Home." Lieutenant Governor Kenneth H. Tuggle addressed the crowd. He said: "'My Old Kentucky Home' stands as a symbol of home to our boys all over the world who are thinking about home today."[18]

Among the events was a tribute to the Kentucky enslaved people who had worked at Federal Hill. It involved the dedication of a monument marking what was said to be an old slave cemetery located on the southwest part of the property. However, to confirm the location of the burial ground, several involved in the commemoration chose to visit the site prior to the Fourth of July celebration. Mrs. Madge Rowan Frost, John Rowan's granddaughter and the last family member to reside at Federal Hill, had claimed that those who had been enslaved were "buried under a clump of trees not far to the southwest of the house." Catherine Barnes Tucker was curator of My Old Kentucky Home and had played on the grounds as a child when Frost was living there. She directed Anna Friedman, the secretary of the Honorable Order of Kentucky Colonels, and Lee S. Read, a Louisville realtor, to the group of trees on the golf course adjacent to the property as the site of the cemetery. According to J. F Conway, the mayor of Bardstown, "we just had to make it authentic."[19] Two graves were exhumed. A front-page article published in the *Louisville Courier-Journal* reported on June 19, 1945: "Nobody will quarrel with the arbitrary decision of a group of Bards-town leading citizens to designate the ancient grave yesterday at Old Kentucky Home as that of Old Black Joe. It could have been that of Uncle Ned, or Aunt Becky or any of the scores of slaves and retainers that lived at the famous Judge John Rowan home at Federal Hill. The important thing was that once and for all the site of the cemetery for the slaves has been determined." However, after one of the graves was exhumed, Tucker concluded that the casket was not Old Black Joe's and that "no can of money" was found in the grave. One of the witnesses present, J. M. Carothers, president of the Louisville Chamber of Commerce, commented that his "cook's father" was described as Old Black Joe's grandson. He had received Christmas presents and birthday recognitions. The children of visitors took pictures with him. "I guess he had a dozen harmonicas," stated Carothers. Despite the confusion of who was buried at the site, the tribute to enslaved people did take place.[20] The St. John African American Episcopal Zion Church and the First Baptist Church rendered two selections. A bronze marker was dedicated that read: "This Memorial Is Dedicated to the Faithful Retainers of Judge John Rowan Immortalized in the Songs of Stephen Collins Foster, Erected July 4, 1945 by the Honorable Order of Kentucky Colonels 'Well Done, Good and Faithful Servant.' Matthew 25 v. 21."[21]

After the program, controversy ensued regarding how the enslaved cemetery was to be designated. The issue was whether a marker would be erected to Old Black Joe or to the slaves who worked on the Rowan plantation. Friedman cleared up the matter in a letter to the *Louisville Times* editor. "There is no attempt to unhallow the ground of the State Park known as My Old Kentucky Home and never has been. . . . [O]ur feeble attempt is to enhance its glory for those of Kentucky who have lived and died and to preserve memories for those now living and those to come." Friedman noted that when the grave was exhumed, those present "said it was 'Old Black Joe' not because they believed it was but symbolically in memory of Foster's immortal song."[22]

Throughout the twentieth century and even into the twenty-first, tourists continued to receive the sanitized version of the slavery experience that had been created and perpetuated by whites. In 1999, a young male

Designated slave cemetery at My Old Kentucky Home (Federal Hill),
Bardstown, Kentucky. Photograph by Anthony Hartsfield Jr.

docent welcoming visitors at My Old Kentucky Home was told to refer to
enslaved persons as being "servants," not slaves. A few years later this
docent was given a script that accentuated the "positive" aspects of slavery
and noted that the enslaved people were "free to a certain extent there, and
that in some places the master had to ask permission to come into the
quarters or had to pay a fine if he didn't."[23]

On May 13, 2008, during a visit to Bardstown to give a presentation,
I visited the site with a student research assistant, who took pictures of the
cemetery. We heard the familiar reference to servants. But the most striking part of our visit was seeing the cemetery reserved for the enslaved that
was located in the field behind the house. As we approached the marked
burial ground, we first saw a wood fence around the area. The cemetery
was next to a golf course. There was no established path to the cemetery or
a sign to indicate the possible location of cabins where the enslaved lived
while they had labored on the grounds of Federal Hill. The cemetery consisted of the memorial marker and unmarked stones protruding out of the
ground. There was no list of names on the uneven row of fieldstones.

Designated slave cemetery at My Old Kentucky Home. Photograph by
Anthony Hartsfield Jr.

Deeply troubled about this visit, I began a personal crusade to draw
more attention to the Black experience at My Old Kentucky Home and
especially the cemetery. I met with the Kentucky State Parks commissioner at the time, Gerry van der Meer, who authorized an archaeological
survey of the burial ground. Archaeologists from the Kentucky Archaeological Survey conducted a geophysics study of the cemetery from March
30 to April 2, 2010. The report was revealing and yet unrevealing. It read:
"*KAS* archaeologists failed to locate any grave shafts in association with
any of the fieldstones at the slave cemetery. Based on these investigations
it appears that in fact this cemetery was created by a park employee to
acknowledge the enslaved African Americans who lived, worked, and died
at My Old Kentucky Home. This study did determine that there is a high
probability that structural remains that may be associated with former
slave cabins are located to the northeast of the cemetery and adjacent to
the service road." Basically, the study found that there was no evidence of
buried bones or caskets.[24] Benjamin LaBree had been curator of the Home
from 1922 to 1931. In his zeal to promote the Home for tourist attraction,

Pictured is Bemis Allen and young boys with their hats on the ground to collect money as they entertained visitors. His son, Richard Allen, is sitting on the fence post playing the harmonica near the entrance to My Old Kentucky Home in 1929. Photograph from the Caufield & Shook Collection, Photographic Archives, University of Louisville, Louisville, KY.

he was likely the "park employee" who had created the slave cemetery. LaBree was also key in developing the plantation atmosphere for those visiting the home.[25]

Beginning in the 1920s, a gray-haired, half-balding African American man named Bemis Allen portrayed "Old Black Joe" at Federal Hill and sat in a chair at the front entrance telling of "other days," as in Foster's song "Old Black Joe." Tourists were also entertained by African American boys dancing at the Home's gate.[26]

Emily Bingham offers an insightful contextualization of both Federal Hill and Foster's melody:

> The house museum known as My Old Kentucky Home became a sonic entryway into something much broader, what promoters called "the life-pulse of Kentucky—historic, tragic, and romantic." A song that

evoked various emotional meanings and associations was cemented to a mansion and its white owners. Tourists wanted more than shrines and memorials; they sought experiences that swept them into another world marked by reminders of another way of life. In the 1920s and for decades after, My Old Kentucky Home actively cultivated a plantation fantasy that pasted over the brutality of slavery, bathed the past in passive and happy blackface minstrel stereotypes, and reinforced racial prejudice.[27]

Kentucky African Americans have a long history of rejecting the song's lyrics. Joseph S. Cotter Sr. (1861–1949) was one dissenter. He was the Black principal of the Samuel Coleridge Taylor Elementary School in Louisville and a distinguished poet. He had family ties to Nelson County and Federal Hill. He was born in 1861 less than ten miles outside Bardstown in a log cabin owned by his great-grandfather. His grandmother, Lucinda, and her husband, Fleming Vaughn, owned a thirty-nine-acre farm. In 1853, Fleming hired out as indentured servants seven of their fifteen children, including Joseph's mother, Martha, who was a teenager at the time. Martha worked for the Rowan family, cooking, chopping wood, and attending to two of the Rowan daughters. She later settled in Louisville to work for the Cotter family. She was twenty years old when she gave birth to Joseph, whose father was his mother's sixty-year-old Scotch-Irish employer, who operated a local business.[28]

Joseph Cotter had heard about the Federal Hill mansion from his mother and chose to visit the site in 1921. His experience was published on the front page of the *Louisville Leader* on February 4, 1922. In "A Visit to Federal Hill, Bardstown, Kentucky," Cotter wrote how he "stood at the front door trying to think my mother's thoughts." Once the door opened, he met Madge Rowan Frost for a pleasant visit, who pointed out to him "the desk at which Steven [*sic*] Collins Foster wrote, 'My Old Kentucky Home.' I touched the desk lightly," wrote Cotter, "and seemed to hear the civilized world singing, 'The sun shines bright in the old Kentucky Home.'" At the end of his visit, Cotter recalled, "I thanked the spirit of Martha, my mother, for urging me to visit, 'Federal Hill and say a word about it.'" He wrote that as he left the mansion and traveled on "Spring field [*sic*] Pike" into Bardstown, "I found myself humming Foster's song and I said, 'Some of Foster's sentiments and wording do not suit the present day Negro, and unless there is a change he will cease tossing the song.

Joseph Cotter Sr. Photograph courtesy of the Filson Historical Society, Louisville, KY.

By doing so he will lose uplifting influence of a beautiful melody along with it a page of race history.'" Cotter believed in changing the word *darkies* to *Negroes*. He revised the song to reflect African American agency and *triumph*. "The time has come," he wrote, "when the head will never bow wherever the Negro may go."[29]

Cotter was somewhat prophetically correct. Kentucky African Americans did not always "bow." They would engage in demonstrations around the state in protest of segregation and discrimination. And they would protest against the song "My Old Kentucky Home." Civil rights organizations sought to remove the word *darkies* from the song through the court system but failed.[30] In April 1964, Black music instructors walked out of a luncheon meeting in Louisville as the president of the Music Educators' Association of the Kentucky Education Association asked those present to stand for the singing of the song. Harlan County native William (Bill)

Turner recalled, "I never went around humming the state song, 'My Old Kentucky Home,' as though the place was that charming, picturesque, and serene. We seemed to know, intuitively, that our Appalachian coaltown hollow was a temporary stopover to some other promised land." Turner further added: "We were taught it, we knew it, but we never sang the Kentucky state song . . . at the Lynch Colored School. Our eleventh grade English and Music teacher, Mrs. Mattie G. Knight, a Kentucky State College graduate, told us, 'I will wash your mouth out with soap if I ever hear you singing about how happy you were to be a slave.'"[31]

In the fall of 1968, the University of Kentucky Black Student Union protested the playing of the song "Dixie" at athletic events, noting that the issue was not the lyrics but their connotation. The next year Black students at the University of Louisville demanded the university address issues regarding Blacks on campus. They occupied university president Woodrow Strickler's office in Grawemeyer Hall before leaving after they met with him.[32]

On May 3, 1969, Derby Day, Black University of Louisville students picketed the entrance to Churchill Downs and carried signs that criticized President Strickler, Mayor Kenneth Schmied, Governor Louie Nunn, and President Richard Nixon, all of whom attended the Derby. A statement was prepared criticizing all four. One of the students, J. Blaine Hudson, provided the *Louisville Courier-Journal* with a statement on behalf of the Black Student Union questioning why money was "squandered" on "which animal will win a race." He argued that "the same amount of money" could be given to "black people that black people might help black people." The statement ended by proclaiming, "The darkies are not gay any longer."[33]

Blacks' protest for truth and respect within the context of the song "My Old Kentucky Home" has not been fully reckoned in Kentucky history. Carrie Allen Stivers, granddaughter of Bemis Allen, recalled that she "never gave" the song "much thought. It was not important to me whether they sung it or not." Sharon Shanks, also a longtime resident of Bardstown, said she "cringed" when she heard the song.[34] In the early 1970s, Reggie Warford, a University of Kentucky basketball player and the only Black man on the team at the time, was standing before a game when the crowd began to sing "My Old Kentucky Home." When they sang "Tis summer, the darkies are gay," he recalled that students yelled "the darkies" while laughing and pointing at him. He then told the team physician, V.

A. Jackson, "I can't do that," and sat down. Jackson was unable to get Warford to remain standing. "Doc, I can't, I can't do this," he responded. Fans began to boo throughout the coliseum as Warford sat on the bench. "After the game," recalled Warford, "they would not let anybody talk to me but the coaches and everybody wanted to know what happened." Assistant Coach Joe Hall told him, "Reggie, it's just a song."[35]

There was some inconsistency as to the whether the original lyrics would be sung at official programs and functions in the state. But disinterest and displeasure with the song among Kentucky African Americans became most public when Japanese students sang the song with the original lyrics during their tour of the Kentucky state capitol building in March 1986. The only Black Democrat in the House, Carl R. Hines Sr., protested. "It's the official state song. And when they got to the part and sang, it's summer and the 'darkies are gay' I just turned around and sat down. I didn't say a word. . . . And the next day Georgia Powers and I introduced legislation to make sure, make it official, that the words to that song would be changed." Carl noted that he was not angry with the students but "believed that if the Japanese are to have a presence in Kentucky with Toyota Motor Corporation they ought to understand the words."[36] Bardstown resident Sharon Shanks declared, however, that even after the change in lyrics in 1986, "I always think of the original words."[37]

This book is not about the song and the museum My Old Kentucky Home. It instead draws upon cultural and traditional tropes to expand the narrative of Kentucky history. Like the slave cemetery at Federal Hill, so much about Black life is buried in hidden places or even fabricated. Myths have been created, evidence destroyed, and stories forgotten. This work tears down a celebrated white heritage that has overlooked the myriad experiences of Black people in Kentucky. It captures the measures that whites employed to oppress, control, and marginalize African Americans in both slavery and freedom. It uncovers the struggles and hopes that encapsulated Black lives in the Bluegrass state. It explores the thoughts, motives, and desires of generations of African Americans whose story has not been told. Most important, it affirms their centrality in shaping how white Kentuckians had to adjust to various social, political, and economic issues facing the state.

In an essay titled "My Old Kentucky Home: Black History in the Bluegrass State," Luther Adams writes about his strong family ties to the state. He notes that many Louisville African Americans identified the South as home and sought to improve their lives and their hopes and dreams for future generations. "The idea of 'Home,'" writes Adams,

> resulted as much from placing black people at the center of their history, as it did from my family, which has lived in Kentucky for generations. . . . For well over 150 years, they raised families; they attended church, . . . they valued education no matter how much or little they had themselves; and they worked in tobacco factories, as janitors, postal employees, cafeteria workers, groomsmen, or joined the military to provide for their families. Some "ran the streets," drinking and gambling their paychecks and pain away—struggling with the violence of their lives. Yet they, and many more, worked and prayed for a better life for themselves and their children. Or at least to make ends meet.[38]

The groundbreaking scholarship in this book introduces readers to the work and sacrifices of both professionally trained and working-class Black people. Each essay opens windows and doors into Black homes and creates pathways into their communities for understanding themes on freedom, citizenship, identity, and public memory within the context of border-state dynamics and history.

Organized chronologically, this collection offers a vivid portrayal of Black humanity. These works capture the many nuances of Black life from a racial and intra-racial perspective while offering fresh insights into the complicated and twisted ideologies that whites espoused to promote white supremacy. Taken together, these works examine the strategies African Americans nurtured to negotiate *race* and *place* within the context of a border state.

Brandon R. Wilson examines the development of the slave economy in the state from the experiences and perspectives of the enslaved. He traces the domestic slave trade through Louisville, Lexington, and northern Kentucky and explains how slave capitalism financed the growth of businesses in the state. Jacob A. Glover's essay also explores the slave economy. However, he writes about the history of Shakers at Pleasant Hill and their antislavery beliefs within the context of an antebellum economy heavily dependent on enslaved labor. He offers insights into the lives of Black Shakers and the activities of enslavers and former enslavers who lived in the close-knit religious community that espoused egalitarianism.

James M. Prichard and Charles R. Welsko explore rebellion and racial violence prior to the Civil War. Prichard delves into an unsuccessful number of enslaved persons seeking to escape led by a young white Irish immigrant. He offers new details about the life of the participants and the court cases that followed. Welsko's essay explains how African Americans at times drew upon violence as means of resistance for survival and the preservation of their enslaved community. Both essays reveal the physical and psychological trauma enslaved persons experienced as they challenged the economic system that oppressed them.

African American life in the immediate years after slavery is a subject fertile for study. Giuliana Perrone's contribution delves into court cases involving the military, finances of slaveholders, and the Black family during Reconstruction. She addresses whites' resistance to accepting African Americans' freedom as well as various complexities and legal issues facing newly freed Blacks.

Despite the obstacles African Americans confronted, they pursued racial equality through education. Erin Wiggins Gilliam's and Le Datta Grimes's essays explore the independence and determination Blacks manifested to establish institutions that uplifted their communities and encouraged racial progress. Gilliam reveals how the Kentucky Normal and Theological Institute was an example of Black leadership and learning for the establishment of institutions in Arkansas and Virginia. Grimes highlights the commitment and creative endeavors of African American women who were at the forefront of making life better in their communities.

Yet, as Charlene J. Fletcher reveals in her essay, the life experiences of African American women in Kentucky made their call for racial uplift even more difficult to answer. Fletcher's study visits the "home" of two African American women confined by domestic labor and domestic violence. Her essay addresses the issues and circumstances Black women faced in search of a sanctuary of relief during the Gilded Age. Melanie Beals Goan documents African American women's engagement in social, political, and economic issues before and after the passage of the Nineteenth Amendment. They were organizers and reformers from rural and urban communities who worked in public and behind the scenes to pursue better schools and opportunities for Blacks. Their unrelenting work served as a beacon of hope and change.

My own essay captures an overlooked aspect of the Black freedom struggle during the 1960s. It examines Black protests led by students on the campus of the University of Kentucky. Exploring race, sports, and Black student activism, it chronicles how Black students were instrumental voices in the recruitment of Black athletes, students, and faculty on campus.

The last work in this volume offers a twist in understanding slavery and freedom in Kentucky through events of the twenty-first century. The killing of nine African American parishioners at Emanuel African Methodist Episcopal Church in Charleston, South Carolina, on June 17, 2015, sparked demonstrations and an undeterred movement to remove symbols and monuments that glorified slavery and the Confederate South. The decision to remove them has been filled with controversy and heated debates. With this background in mind, Alicestyne Turley addresses in particular the call to remove Freedom's Memorial in Washington, DC, which depicts President Abraham Lincoln and an enslaved man. She contextualizes the installation of this public monument and the hidden story of the enslaved man included in it, who, it turns out, has strong family ties to a Kentucky icon.

Each essay is sure to stimulate discussion on a range of topics. They set a new mark for the progression of scholarship on Kentucky African Americans. Moreover, they build on the progressive actions that local communities have taken to address Kentucky's Black past through tours, signage, and websites.

By 2018, information panels had been installed at My Old Kentucky Home to include the names of the enslaved who had worked there and the labor they were forced to carry out for the Rowan family. Yet the exact location of the slaves' cemetery has still not been determined.[39]

Like much of the state's racial past, the search is ongoing for truth and reconciliation. The killing of Breonna Taylor was an awakening for a state that had been lulled to sleep for generations by the melody of "My Old Kentucky Home." But now is the time to keep revisiting that past to better understand the present and to build and reshape our interpretation of Kentucky history.

Notes

1. Emily Bingham publishes these selected lines of Cotter's revision to the lyrics to "My Old Kentucky Home" in her article "'Let's Buy It!': Tourism and the My Old Kentucky Home Campaign in Jim Crow Kentucky," *Ohio Valley History* 19, no. 3 (Fall 2019): 45. Alex Lubet and Stephen Lubet include the new lyrics of the song Joseph Cotter proposed in 1921 in "The Complicated Legacy of 'My Old Kentucky Home,'" *Smithsonian Magazine,* September 3, 2020.

2. Tessa Duvall and Darcy Costello, "The Breonna Taylor Case Newsletter Takes You beyond the Headlines," *USA Today,* August 31, 2020, updated September 9, 2020; Tessa Duvall, "Breonna Taylor Shooting Fact Check: 9 Things People Often Get Wrong," *Louisville Courier-Journal,* June 16, 2020; "Say Her Name: How the Fight for Racial Justice Can Be More Inclusive of Black Women," in "Updates: The Fight against Racial Injustice," NPR, July 7, 2020.

3. "Kentucky Census 2020 Reveals Which Counties Are the Most Diverse," *Louisville Courier-Journal,* August 17, 2021; "Bigger Cities, Fewer Kentuckians in Rural Areas: What to Know about 2020 US Census Data," *Louisville Courier Journal,* August 13, 2021; US Census Bureau, "Louisville City, Kentucky; Louisville/Jefferson County, Metro Government (Balance), Kentucky," QuickFacts, population census, April 1, 2020, at https://www.census.gov//quickfacts/fact /table/louisvillecitykentucky,louisvillejeffersoncountymetrogovernmentbalance kentucky/POP010220.

4. "100 Days of Protests: Looking Back at Moments That Have Shaped the Breonna Taylor Movement," *Louisville Courier-Journal,* September 4, 2020; Richard Oppel Jr., Derrick Bryson Taylor, and Nicholas Bogel-Burroughs, "What to Know about Breonna Taylor's Death," *New York Times,* April 26, 2021, at https://www.nytimes.com/article/breonna-taylor-police.html.

5. Marion B. Lucas, *A History of Blacks in Kentucky,* vol. 1: *From Slavery to Segregation, 1760–1891* (Frankfort: Kentucky Historical Society, 1992), xiv–xvi.

6. Lucas, *A History of Blacks in Kentucky,* 1:xiv–11; J. Blaine Hudson, "Slavery in Louisville and Jefferson County, 1780–1812," *Register of the Kentucky Historical Society* 95 (1997): 126–27. The quotation from Hudson is also given in Gerald L. Smith, "Slavery and Abolition in Kentucky: 'Patter-rollers Were Everywhere,'" in *Bluegrass Renaissance: The History and Culture of Central Kentucky, 1792–1852,* ed. James C. Klotter and Daniel Rowland (Lexington: University Press of Kentucky, 2012), 78.

7. J. Winston Coleman Jr., *Slavery Times in Kentucky* (Chapel Hill: University of North Carolina Press, 1940), 98, quoted in Smith, "Slavery and Abolition in Kentucky," 88–89.

8. Elizabeth D. Leonard, *Slaves, Slaveholders, and a Kentucky Community's Struggle toward Freedom* (Lexington: University Press of Kentucky, 2019), 38, 44–45; Lucas, *A History of Blacks in Kentucky,* 1:xv–vi, 108, 155.

9. Wade Hall, *Passing for Black: The Life and Careers of Mae Street Kidd* (Lexington: University Press of Kentucky, 1997), 107, 124–25 (Mae Street Kidd represented the Forty-First District of Louisville in the Kentucky General Assembly and with Georgia Powers in the state Senate introduced a bill to pass these amendments in 1976); Anne E. Marshall, *Creating a Confederate Kentucky: The Lost Cause and Civil War Memory in a Border State* (Chapel Hill: University of

North Carolina Press, 2010), 58; George C. Wright, *Racial Violence in Kentucky, 1865–1940: Lynchings, Mob Rule, and "Legal Lynchings"* (Baton Rouge: Louisiana State University Press, 1990), 70–71.

10. Leonard, *Slaves, Slaveholders,* 78–79; Maryjean Wall, *How Kentucky Became Southern: A Tale of Outlaws, Horse Thieves, Gamblers, and Breeders* (Lexington: University Press of Kentucky, 2010), 204–6.

11. "'No Justice, No Derby' Is the Latest Cry in a Louisville Grappling with Racial Tensions," *Washington Post,* September 2, 2020.

12. Hannah Drake, "Let Them Eat Cake: An Open Letter to Bill Carstanjen, CEO of Churchill Downs Inc.," *LEO Weekly* (Louisville, KY), September 2, 2020.

13. In *Creating a Confederate Kentucky,* Anne E. Marshall discusses this passage from *Uncle Tom's Cabin.* The quotation is drawn from Harriet Beecher Stowe, *Uncle Tom's Cabin: Life among the Lowly* (New York: Cosimo, 2009), 9. See also Bingham, "'Let's Buy It,'" 28.

14. Bingham, "'Let's Buy It!,'" 48. See also J. Winston Coleman Jr., *The Rowan–Chambers Duel: An Affair of Honor in Nelson County, Ky, February 3, 1801* (Lexington, KY: Winburn Press, 1953), 1–11; Randall Capps, *The Rowan Story: From Federal Hill to My Old Kentucky Home* (Bowling Green, KY: Homestead Press, 1976), 102–3. Pen Bogert has written an excellent detailed summary of the buildings, crops, livestock, debts, and enslaved families at Federal Hill; see Pen Bogert, "Research Summary," 2011, in author's files and possibly in the My Old Kentucky Home collections in Bardstown, Kentucky.

15. Bingham, "'Let's Buy It,'" 46; "Stephen Collins Foster," in *The Kentucky Encyclopedia,* ed. John E. Kleber (Lexington: University Press of Kentucky, 1992), 349–50; Thomas D. Clark, "The Slavery Background of Foster's 'My Old Kentucky Home,'" in *A Kentucky Sampler: Essays from the* Filson Club Historical Quarterly, *1926–1976,* ed. Lowell Harrison and Nelson L. Dawson (Lexington: University Press of Kentucky, 1977), 107–16. See also *Louisville Courier-Journal,* July 3, 1977; and Charles Henry Prater, "The Home of 'My Old Kentucky Home,'" n.d., in file: "Architecture, Undated," Kentucky Historical Society, Frankfort.

16. *Kentucky Reporter* (Lexington), July 5, 1923; Bingham, "'Let's Buy It,'" 28.

17. "Kentucky Derby Will Play 'Old Kentucky Home' Despite Criticism," *NBC News,* September 5, 2020.

18. "Everyone Sings 'My Old Kentucky Home' at the Derby. Few Know Its Controversial Story," *Lexington Herald Leader,* April 27, 2018; *Kentucky Standard* (Bardstown), July 5, 1945; *Louisville Courier-Journal,* June 19, 1945.

19. *Kentucky Standard,* July 5, 1945; *Louisville Courier-Journal,* June 19, 1945.

20. *Kentucky Standard,* July 5, 1945; *Louisville Courier-Journal,* June 19, 1945.

21. *Kentucky Standard,* July 5, 1945; *Louisville Courier-Journal,* June 19, 1945.

22. Friedman's *Louisville Times* letter was reprinted in the *Kentucky Standard,* July 5, 1945.

23. Joanne Melish, "Recovering (from) Slavery: Four Struggles to Tell the Truth," in *Slavery and Public History: The Tough Stuff of American Memory,* ed. James Oliver Horton and Lois E. Horton (Chapel Hill: University of North Carolina Press, 2006), 115–18.

24. Philip B. Mink II, "An Electrical Resistance Survey and Subsequent Evaluation of the 'Slave Cemetery' at My Old Kentucky Home State Park, Nelson County, Kentucky," Kentucky Archaeological Survey jointly administered by University of Kentucky Heritage Council, Kentucky Archaeological Survey Report no. 188, OSA Registration no. FY10–6499, 2010, 2.

25. Emily Bingham notes that Young Allison, leader of the campaign to purchase and develop Federal Hill as a tourist attraction, had even criticized LaBree for "sullying the Old Kentucky Home with" tawdry myth and legend. She writes that LaBree "apparently installed the ersatz cemetery . . . to enhance the plantation mystique" ("'Let's Buy It!,'" 45–48).

26. See "African American Man and Children at Federal Hill, Bardstown, Kentucky," September 3, 1929, image no. ULPACS 104299, Caufield and Shook Collection, Photographic Archives, University of Louisville, Louisville, KY, at http://digital.library.louisville.edu/cdm/description/collectin/cs# conditions. See also "'My Old Kentucky Home' Netted Foster $1,372," *Kentucky Progress Magazine* 4, no. 1 (September 1931): 19, 42; Dixie Hibbs, *Nelson County: A Pictorial History* (Norfolk, VA: Dunning, 1989), 146. In an image in Hibbs's book, Bemis Allen appears to be the same man pictured in *Kentucky Progress Magazine* and the photograph from 1929.

27. Bingham, "'Let's Buy It!,'" 49–50. See also Emily Bingham, *My Old Kentucky Home: The Astonishing Life and Reckoning of an Iconic American Song* (New York: Knopf, 2022).

28. Ann Allen Shockley, "Joseph S. Cotter, Sr: Biographical Sketch of a Black Louisville Bard," *CLA Journal* 18, no. 3 (March 1975): 329–31. See also Emily Bingham, *My Old Kentucky Home: The Astonishing Life and Reckoning of an Iconic American Song* (New York: Knopf, 2022), 115–17.

29. *Louisville Leader,* February 4, 1922. See also Bingham, "'Let's Buy It!,'" 44–45; and Bingham, *My Old Kentucky Home,* 115–18, 226.

30. Bingham, "'Let's Buy It!,'" 45; *Louisville Courier-Journal,* March 12, 1986.

31. *Louisville Defender,* April 16, 1964; William H. Turner, *The Harlan Renaissance: Stories of Black Life in Appalachian Coal Towns* (Morgantown: West

Virginia University Press, 2021), 2; William H. Turner to Gerald L. Smith, email, August 7, 2021.

32. Emily Bingham, "A Race about Race: Looking Back at the Kentucky Derby of 1969," *Louisville Magazine,* May 2019, 61–63, 108–11.

33. Hudson's letter is quoted in Bingham, "A Race about Race."

34. Carrie Stivers, telephone interview by Gerald L. Smith, September 24, 2015; Sharon Shanks, telephone interview by Gerald L. Smith, September 24, 2015; both interviews are archived at the Louie B. Nunn Oral History Center, University of Kentucky, Lexington.

35. See Scott Brown, untitled memoir on the life of Reggie Warford, forthcoming from the University Press of Kentucky, Lexington.

36. *Louisville Courier-Journal,* March 12, 1986; Carl R. Hines Sr., interviewed by Catherine Herdman, June 28, 2006, Louie B. Nunn Oral History Center.

37. Shanks, interviewed by Smith, September 24, 2015.

38. Luther Adams, "My Old Kentucky Home: Black History in the Bluegrass State," *Register of the Kentucky Historical Society* 113, nos. 2–3 (Spring–Summer 2015): 385.

39. Darcy Costello, "My Old Kentucky Home State Park Addresses History of Slavery," *Louisville Courier-Journal,* August 7, 2018.

1

149 North Broadway

Slave Incarceration at the Foundation of Kentucky Finance

Brandon R. Wilson

On January 9, 2021, University of Kentucky basketball fans strode through downtown Lexington to watch the men's basketball team challenge the University of Florida in a much-anticipated game. As the first notes of the National Anthem echoed around the stadium, the team knelt on one knee in united support for the value of Black lives amid a national conversation about police brutality. Among those kneeling that night was Dontaie Allen, Kentucky's "Mr. Basketball," who was born forty miles north of Lexington in the town of Falmouth, a descendent of a notable enslaved woman who was herself enmeshed in the state's violent history against the Black body.

Blocks away from the arena, within earshot of the routine recitation of the National Anthem and singing of the state anthem "My Old Kentucky Home," fans paid $10 to park on the small paved lot at 149 North Broadway—the former site of Pullam's Slave Jail. Precisely there two centuries before Allen and his teammates knelt to protest the murders of Breonna Taylor and countless others, Allen's own great-great-great-great-grandmother had been imprisoned and sold into slavery. Kidnapped from Virginia in 1806, Allen's ancestor, Charity, was locked in one of William Pullam's jail cells before her forced journey north to Pendleton County, which Dontaie Allen calls home. In fact, hundreds of people were caged

The jailhouse belonging to William Pullam, which stood at 149 North Broadway in Lexington, Kentucky. Photograph courtesy of the Special Collections Research Center, University of Kentucky, Lexington.

at this site in downtown Lexington before enslavers, investors, and speculators forced them across the South along gradients of capital and finance.
The coffles of men and women, chained together with iron, marched past
the offices, hotels, churches, and banks built with the capital extracted
from their bodies. And just as the musical notes of the National Anthem
could be heard from the stadium in the quiet parking lot at 149 North
Broadway, the echoes of this history resound in the same sites. This chapter delves into that history—a history of the policing and incarceration of
Black Kentuckians for the purpose of profit, which is necessarily intertwined with the contemporary treatment of Black Americans. It is a chapter that uncovers the two centuries' old source of the echoes heard today
in the firing of police weapons and the clanging of prison bars. It argues
that the Commonwealth of Kentucky prisons were integral to the region's
slavery economy, forming the vital infrastructure to control a Black population bent on freedom. Furthermore, this chapter remarks on the tragic
continuities from this crucial history in the physical and social structures
that shape our contemporary world.

Seventy miles away from the game at Rupp Arena and less than two
centuries earlier, "My Old Kentucky Home" was sung under starkly different circumstances by a woman held captive in a Louisville prison.
When the renowned author Harriet Beecher Stowe toured sites of Kentucky slavery in the mid–nineteenth century, preparing material for *Uncle
Tom's Cabin,* she reportedly arrived on the Louisville waterfront to see
large coffles of enslaved people forced upon boats destined for Natchez.
Just one block from the river, on the corner of First Street and Main Street,
she found the jail belonging to Tarlton Arterburn, who later in 1876
recounted, "The pen was inclosed [*sic*] in high brick walls, and situated on
First, near Jefferson, east side of the street. We always had from ten to 100
negroes in the pen."[1] Stowe, who had spent significant time among abolitionist circles in Cincinnati, was no stranger to the slave trade. What she
witnessed in her long stints in northern Kentucky resembled the scene in
Louisville, with coffles of enslaved people and steamboats fueling commerce along the Ohio River. When she entered Arterburn's jail, she said
"she wished to purchase a likely woman to take East," an apparent alibi
to conceal her true investigative intent to document Kentucky's domestic
slave trade. Arterburn further recalled how "a bright mulatto girl . . .
[b]eing asked to sing, . . . delighted those present with—*The sun shines
bright in our old Kentucky home, in our old Kentucky home, far away.*"[2] The

thought of such a performance is haunting—an enslaved Black woman to be sold to the Deep South forced to sing a minstrel song written explicitly about Black separation and dislocation. The song, whose lyrics celebrated a nostalgia for blooming meadows and singing birds, was intended to echo abolitionist sympathies for the enslaved people of Kentucky. The song and the experience of the enslaved in Kentucky were intricately linked. Embedded in the lyrics are the thousands who were forced away from the state during the domestic slave trade and dispersed across the continent. It is important to point out, however, that if we are to accept Arterburn's account of an enslaved woman singing "My Old Kentucky Home" to Harriet Beecher Stowe, it must have happened years after Stowe's manuscript was completed. The song was published by Stephen Foster in 1853, the year after *Uncle Tom's Cabin* was published. Nonetheless, the juxtaposition of these two iconic symbols—"My Old Kentucky Home" and the slave jail—strikes at the heart of Kentucky's history and the history of America writ large: on the one hand a celebration of bucolic beauty and idyllic pasts, on the other the shrouded trauma of Black women ever present beneath the facade. In this way, "My Old Kentucky Home" brings the jailed enslaved woman and Dontaie Allen together in a crucial way as each forces a reframing of what that *home* really means—each contradicting the facade behind which Kentucky has long hidden its truest self.

Louisville, Lexington, and northern Kentucky formed a triad of slave-trading metropoles. In Lexington, Pullam's Slave Jail was just one of many points of incarceration across the city, which functioned as a node within a broad web of slave-trade infrastructure that stretched from the outskirts of Cincinnati to Bourbon Street in New Orleans.[3] At 520 West Short Street was the prison belonging to Lewis C. Robard, where enslaved women were incarcerated before sale into Kentucky's lucrative sex market.[4] At the corner of Short Street and Limestone stood "Megowan's Hotel," a euphemism for the slave jail operated by the Fayette County jailor Thomas B. Megowan. Just blocks away from that, enslaved people were traded at the infamous Cheapside Market. Along the roads coursing out from downtown, coffles of the enslaved were forcibly marched toward the Deep South to join an interconnected highway system necessary for the intranational exchange of human beings. Waterways were crucial to this network as well, with the Ohio and Mississippi Rivers serving to transport capital across the nation's midsection—human beings flowing southward, cash and cotton flowing northward. When Charity entered William Pullam's jail, crowded with enslaved people from across the Bluegrass, she would have seen firsthand the materiality of a national network of capital exchange. By interrogating this pivotal moment, when Charity gazed upon her shackled wrists, we can get a better scope of the basis of the Kentucky economy—the body of the Black person.[5]

William Pullam, who forced the shackles upon Charity's wrists, cared about capital, and the violent separation and caging of his victims were the means to financial solvency. In a phrase rooted in classical economics, Pullam can be considered a *rational actor:* his purpose was to maximize profits by any means. To centralize the rational aspect of the slave trade is to describe that violence as a function of finance so that it is recognizable and contextual in the long history of Western capitalism.[6] Enslavers like Pullam were ostensibly concerned with the flow of money and capital, and, thus, to understand the violence of his actions we must look to the business motivations that connected the ego to broader systems of global exchange. To Pullam and the majority of participants in the domestic slave trade, the pain experienced by people like Charity operated as both a tool of control and an unavoidable by-product of a necessary system for American progress. This pain, as expressed by the enslaved, required from white society a cognitive dissonance not wholly separate from the way carbon emissions are contemporarily ignored by many American consumers amid a global climate catastrophe. Within the Lexington slave jails of the nineteenth century, the chaining, whipping, and even sexual assaults wielded against Black captives were conceived as the means of acquiring and accumulating capital—mechanisms of power to transfer wealth from the labor of captives to the enslavers, cotton speculators, and financiers stretching from New Orleans to New York. As leading historians now argue, torture was a technology of slavery capitalism, and the jail was an essential infrastructure. Imagine the cries of Charity in a Lexington jail cell, heard from the sidewalk on North Broadway Street, no more significant to passersby than the casual stream of exhaust from a modern American automobile.

Pullam's work and Charity's trauma began long before the iron bars of his jail were built. The site was one node on a broad string of exchange. For Charity, the process began along the Potomac River outside of Washington, DC.[7] During the late eighteenth and early nineteenth centuries, Lexington maintained a close connection to the region surrounding the nation's capital. When the land that became Kentucky was seized from the Shawnee, Cherokee, Yuchi, and other Native groups, Euro-American migrants from Maryland, DC, and (eastern) Virginia pushed westward across the Blue Ridge Mountains to pursue the commercial success promised to landed white men. Along these same roadways, Black people were taken from their families and communities on the eastern seaboard to provide the labor necessary to develop the Bluegrass into a major player in the hemp industry. This first wave of migration was complex and included a diversity of people with varying relationships to the markets. Free Black people, for example, migrated along the Ohio River Valley to escape persecution after the American Revolution, when it became clear that slavery and white supremacy would remain central to the political structure of the new independent nation despite declarations to the contrary. Religious groups and utopian societies, including the Shakers and the burgeoning Evangelical movement, also joined the early American migration into the Bluegrass region, some harboring antislavery sentiment that would come to hold an important place in Kentucky abolitionism. Together, these various groups wove a complex social tapestry in the new territory, with varying moral responses to the institution of slavery. But for all their diversity, the majority linked themselves to the hegemony of the transatlantic economy, which held slavery at its core. Although small groups of subsistence farmers established themselves within mountain communities throughout the Appalachians, the Bluegrass, with its valuable soil and flat topography, was a haven for land speculation and commodity exchange, deeply connected to Washington and the broader political economy of the new nation.[8]

In the Chesapeake Bay region surrounding the nation's capital, newspapers carried advertisements aimed at potential migrants to the Bluegrass. Money was to be made in both the sale of lands in the West and the sale of enslaved people in the East, which formed a symbiotic relationship between the two regional economies. John Beckley, a Kentucky land speculator, advertised more than twelve thousand acres of Kentucky land in a DC newspaper in March 1806, "to be sold or exchanged for property in the city [of Washington]."[9] The advertisement joined dozens of posts listed in the first decade of the century, with speculators and private citizens connecting western and eastern markets. Another advertisement by a farmer named William Booth offered to sell his "four hundred and six acres in good repair" in Frederick, Virginia, to fund his move to Kentucky in 1802.[10] The advertisements posted in Virginia and Maryland were even more numerous than those posted in DC as inflated land prices along the tobacco-growing coast forced agricultural expansion to the west of the Appalachians. The corresponding migration of enslavers, speculators, and enslaved people to the West is a pivotal chapter in American history, setting the economic stage for the massive migration that would immediately succeed it—the Second Middle Passage, which forced millions of enslaved people from the Upper South to the Cotton Belt.

In the early 1800s, Charity found herself between these two migrations—the westward migration to what became Kentucky and the subsequent southwestward migration to what became the Cotton South. Shortly after her birth, she was sold to slave traders and forcibly transported west.[11] Following the roadways from northern Virginia through the Blue Ridge Mountains, Charity traveled the same routes of the enslaved people who had come before her to build the foundation of Kentucky's agricultural economy. When she arrived at Pullam's Slave Jail, she would have encountered some of the first people being taken from Kentucky to fuel the burgeoning cotton economy of the Deep South. Within the first decade of Charity's time in Kentucky, the economy of the region took a dramatic shift that would shape the course of her life.

Slavery's capitalism evolved as an integrated part of a more global, transatlantic economy that connected US markets with those of Europe, Africa, and the Caribbean. Thus, the tides of markets around the world directly impacted what happened at the local level, not least in the Bluegrass. As the British Empire expanded, connecting Western markets to regions such as Egypt, India, and China, international competition became one factor in a generally downward price pressure for American-grown tobacco. This meant that enslavers, whose profitability heavily depended on tobacco exports, saw decreasing returns, while at the same time the depletion of soil nutrients further curtailed tobacco's profitability.[12] Many producers diversified their businesses, centering on the lucrative markets for hemp and corn and using enslaved labor to stabilize production of these commodities. Yet, despite their adaptability, the regional economy eventually shifted against American tobacco profits, and Kentucky's internal demand for enslaved labor plummeted to an all-time low.[13] At the same time, the legal end to the importation of enslaved Africans through an act of Congress in 1808 led to a precipitous increase in the price of enslaved people in other regions of the United States.

In response, the Bluegrass region pivoted its economy beyond agricultural goods to one deeply vested in the exporting of enslaved people themselves. As enslavers faced headwinds in the international markets for their tobacco crop, the sale and leveraging of laborers became a profitable alternative. By midcentury, the sale of enslaved people to the Deep South became an entire industry unto itself, with bank lending, insurance, and the broader financial world intertwined with the trafficking of people. As agricultural profits became more difficult to stabilize, enslaved people functioned as more than unpaid labor in Kentucky; they were also the collateral that powered credit markets, and investors depended on the sustained value in enslaved people for backing a host of other investments. When slavery was under threat—when resistance and rebellion threatened to undermine the sale of a Black person—so too was Kentucky's broader financial system rendered unstable.[14]

In the years before the Panic of 1819, the Kentucky businessmen A. Morehead and Robert Latham submitted twenty enslaved people as collateral to cover nearly $16,000 in debt owed to the Bank of Kentucky. The value bound up in the bodies of the enslaved kept Morehead and Latham solvent for a time and gave the bank enough certainty to continue lending to the pair. This occurred many times over, so that one enslaved person, mortgaged between several financial institutions, could be repeatedly leveraged. According to one historian, "As Morehead and Latham continued to discount notes with the bank, these additional debts were just added onto the original mortgage using the same collateral."[15] In July 1819, Latham again mortgaged nineteen enslaved people through the Union Bank of Maryland to further renew debts owed.[16] This sort of relationship among financiers, enslavers, and enslaved formed an essential layer in the nineteenth-century American economy, intertwining slavery and finance into a powerful force of economic expansion.

In the late 1830s, American investors, financiers, and enslavers experienced the second major economic panic of the century, which undercut the value of their now most crucial asset—enslaved people. As tobacco profits waned, and as the Upper South's demand for enslaved labor diminished, the financial value of enslaved people required new and expanding markets. Amid the financial anxiety surrounding the Panic of 1837, the ingenuity of enslavers such as William Pullam transformed Kentucky's labor liability into a crucial asset. Between 1808, when America's transatlantic slave trade was abolished, and 1861, Kentucky's economy emerged as a leading exporter of enslaved people to the Deep South. The expanding cotton industry required intense labor power to clear old-growth forests, drain ancient swamplands, carve roadways, plow fields, and harvest cotton. By 1850, tobacco labor accounted for just 20 percent of the labor committed to cotton.[17] But the American cotton industry deeply depended on the flow of people, goods, and capital from Kentucky (as well as from the Chesapeake region) into and out of the Gulf states newly purloined from Indigenous groups.

In Kentucky, where enslaved labor was already in surplus, legislators aimed to limit the size of the state's Black population by banning the bringing of new enslaved people into the state in 1833. The effects of the "Non-importation Law" were both social and economic. On the one hand, a fear of abolitionist agitation swept the state: citizens protested the law in a number of newspapers, arguing that foreign agitators had forced the legislature to act against the well-being of the state.[18] On the other hand, the law had the effect of protecting the price of the enslaved by limiting supply. In a state whose economy was largely dependent on the price of enslaved people exported to the Deep South, the Non-importation Law's effect on the supply curve likely buoyed prices in the near term and cornered the state's domestic slave-trade market for large-scale enslavers.[19] For enslaved people, this changing Kentucky economy came with further tragic consequences. As enslavers sought to turn profits from their excess enslaved labor force, enslaved families were forcibly separated. Few were able to reclaim these kinship connections until years after the Civil War, if ever, and some—women such as Margaret Garner—would make harrowing escape attempts to protect family from the violence against them by Kentucky enslavers.

As Kentucky enslavers moved to profit from the state's labor surplus, they required the infrastructure of jailhouses to secure the slave trade at one of its most vulnerable points—the moment enslaved people were stripped from family and communities to be sold to the Deep South. The system worked through networks of credit and liquidity, with William Pullam and his ilk supplying the laborers necessary to transform the rich natural resources of the American South into marketable commodities on the global stage. Rising cotton prices gave enslavers the confidence to purchase land and people on credit, with liquidity most often supplied by northern banks. In exchange for human bodies from the Upper South, this liquidity then flowed from Mississippi, Louisiana, and Alabama into the Bluegrass and the Chesapeake regions. The amount of money brought into the state of Kentucky through the sale of Black bodies during this period was astronomical, estimated at $72 million between 1808 and 1860.[20] At an average inflation rate of 2 percent, this amount would equal nearly $2 billion in the twenty-first century. Such profits could then be diverted into a number of other industries, so that the state's economic vitality fully depended on the slavery industry. What made all this economic activity so lucrative, according to leading research in the history of slavery's capitalism, were the hands, feet, and backs of Black people working hectares of cotton.[21] The return on investment for a single enslaved person during one cotton harvest is estimated at 5 percent net yield, plus a 7 percent annual growth in the price of the individual, percentages that together far outpaced interest on borrowed funds.[22] Speculative and unstable as the cotton-slave economy could be, it made fortunes for many, seemingly overnight. It is no wonder that next to cotton the slave trade emerged as the most lucrative industry in the United States. The wealth that enslaved people were forced to extract from the Mississippi soil transformed the American economy forever, and the lives of particular people such as William Pullam and Charity were fully intertwined in this process.

The emerging cotton industry of the early nineteenth century was dependent on the movement of enslaved people from regions of surplus (Kentucky) to the Deep South, where labor demands were high, and this movement, inherently violent and forcible, met fierce resistance on the part of its victims. Margaret Garner became a particularly notable example, her act of filicide gaining national attention in 1856. At the same time, a wave of lesser-known acts of resistance swept the American South. Using networks of refuge houses stationed throughout the border states, enslaved people escaped the work camps of the South in droves. One research project has collected more than forty thousand advertisements about "runaways" in American newspapers between 1800 and the Civil War.[23] Historians have only partly uncovered the impact that escapees had on the slavery economy and community, with one historian noting that "runaways became so common in some sections that planters attributed the cause to a peculiar mental illness."[24] Escape as a form of resistance was particularly problematic for those whose finances depended on the exchange of enslaved people's bodies, threatening the flow of capital at critical junctures. For example, when Leonard Neale, president of Georgetown College in Washington, DC, met with college officials over the "Books of Proceedings" and the financial management of the college for 1805, he expressed a sense of urgency regarding the escape of one of the college's captives. In a letter updating other college officials, he wrote, "Spalding has runned [*sic*] away, but I expect that in virtue of an advertisement lately made, he will be soon lodged in the Washington jail."[25] Various solutions were imposed by enslavers and traders to quell the issue—that is to say, the escape attempts occurred so frequently and so impactfully that they fundamentally changed the system itself. Among the most prominent consequences was the passage of the Fugitive Slave Act of 1850, which extended the reach of Southern enslavers and the reach of jails for the enslaved into Northern states. This act transformed Kentucky's riverine border from a gateway to freedom into something more complex. On either side of the border, US marshals and everyday citizens could (and were legally required to) return Black people to Kentucky enslavers. As another major response to enslaved people's resistance, some enslavers and traders asserted their preference for intact families due in part to the consequential unrest from enslaved families' separation during sales. The State of Louisiana went as far as to outlaw the importation of separated mothers/children in part from pressure from the Catholic Church but also from pressure put on traders by enslaved people themselves, who made it clear that they would risk their lives to escape and reclaim family connections.[26]

Enslavers also deployed large teams of "night watches" or "slave patrols"—militia and police departments wholly dedicated to the surveillance and control of the nation's Black population.[27] These militarized groups often began with teams of volunteers, such as those in the state of Virginia who were legally required to serve a temporary stint in the night watch, with their primary concern being the behavior of the region's enslaved. Volunteering became a site of communal bonding—a way for white citizens to form community ties around the surveillance and othering of Black people. As communities grew and demands for surveillance expanded, Southern legislatures directed funds to formally organize police forces and construct jails to provide oversight and infrastructure to the duties of the night watch.[28]

The insurance industry also saw an opportunity to shore up risks in the domestic slave trade, offering policies for the death or escape of an enslaved person. Throughout the 1850s, for example, Aetna Insurance Company offered "slave policies" to enslavers across the South, covering the costs of injury or death. In one policy, an enslaver named Francis Fountain of Harrison County, Mississippi, agreed to a $26 insurance premium to cover $800 in damages to an enslaved person's body. In another policy, Aetna extended coverage to Charles Meyer of Missouri for $3,115 to protect his cash investments in the bodies of four enslaved teenagers worth an average of $1,100 each, but they were notably "not insured against smallpox." These policies were often purchased for short, three-month stints before an enslaved person was transported. In Meyer's case, the four individuals he held captive were to travel by steamboat from St. Louis. Such insurance policies were crucial for two reasons. First, they linked Southern and Northern economies, circulating the capital taken from Southern cotton fields throughout the transatlantic finance industry. The growth of northeastern finance firms, such as Aetna Insurance Co., heavily depended on the proliferation of slavery profits in the Deep South, where individuals such as Fountain and Meyer purchased insurance protection. Second, insurance companies were one of several key strategies to stabilizing a fundamentally unstable industry, where the deaths and escapes of enslaved people undermined profits throughout the Mississippi and Ohio River Valleys.

The legal and financial tools used to secure enslavers' profits—insurance companies, federal legislation, prison infrastructure—were centered around the enslaved person's body and how to control it in fixed locations. When Charity was brought to Pullam's Jail after arriving in Lexington from northern Virginia, she underwent a process referred to by enslavers as *safekeeping,* whereby an enslaved person could not escape while chained behind jail walls. From the street view, these sites of safekeeping appeared to be unimposing residential structures. If not for the sounds of the captives or the view of chained people entering and leaving, Charity would have had trouble discerning the jail from the buildings that surrounded it. From the outside, the jail blended with the townhomes and law offices that lined North Broadway and the rest of Lexington's downtown. Indeed, most slave jails of the era were designed in a similar way—decidedly unimposing with a domestic facade. As historians point out, this architectural choice was part of a rhetorical plan to appease local citizens and camouflage slavery's brutal reality. The need for appeasement was not that Lexingtonians, or most Southerners for that matter, had trouble with slavery prima facie. Rather, they had trouble acknowledging the truth of slavery—the scene of suffering that revealed their society's deep moral disregard for Black lives. Being forced to confront the ugly truth upon which their society was built pressured many cities to remove slave jails from residential areas.[29] An obstreperous building for confining the enslaved conflicted with the mythic gilt that lined Kentucky banknotes and shattered the carnival mirror that allowed most Americans to view themselves and their society as anything peaceful.[30] Thus, these structures of trauma were camouflaged by an unassuming, domestic aesthetic—an architectural manifestation of a broader cultural move to rebrand slavery as benign if not beneficial to the enslaved.

The domestic aesthetic of slave jails was common also beyond the city of Lexington. In Louisville, Tarlton Arterburn operated a slave jail downtown on the corner of First Street and Main Street. With proximity to the Ohio River, the location was ideal for the marketing and transporting of enslaved people destined for the Cotton South. But from the street view, the building blended with the rowhouses and businesses in this central part of the city. High walls blocked the view of the people in the jail yard, with "a long narrow frame cottage" functioning as the office space along First Street.[31] Much like the shallow, gilded beauty described in "My Old Kentucky Home," the jails presented a quaint imitation of benign domesticity. But peel back a layer, peer over the whitewashed prison walls along First Street in Louisville, and you would find the reality of the dozens of people caged there as forced labor to fuel the nation's agricultural dominance.

According to Tarleton Arterburn, the wish to peel back layers is precisely what brought Harriet Beecher Stowe to Louisville. In her notes on slavery, she took particular interest in the state of Kentucky and its role as an exporter of the enslaved to the Deep South. The particular slave economy of the state, dependent on family separation and short-term imprisonment, likely struck her as a site of the deep human trauma to be represented in her writings. In her notes, she took interest in a particular case reported from an Ohio River steamship: "At Louisville, a gentleman took passage, having with him a family of blacks,—husband, wife and children. The master was bound for Memphis, Tenn., at which place he intended to take all except the man ashore."[32] The note became significant to the plot of *Uncle Tom's Cabin* and to understanding slavery in the mid–nineteenth century. Beyond the trauma enslavers inflicted upon the individual, complex whole communities were also made victim to the *solipsistic speculative dance of capital*.[33] The domestic slave trade disintegrated families and communities in irreversible ways, and it was this crucial impact of slavery, affecting the Black community's social fabric, that grasped Stowe's interest. "These things *are*, every day, part and parcel of one of *the most thriving trades that is carried on in America*," Stowe wrote in 1853. "Instances have occurred where mothers, whose children were about to be sold from them, have, in their desperation, murdered their own offspring, to save them from this worst kind of orphanage."[34] The trauma of forced separation, most often permanent, inspired such daring acts of resistance. It was the role of prisons not only to restrain the enslaved during such moments of trauma but also to control slavery's public image writ large. If dramatic stories of women such as Margaret Garner captivated national audiences, prisons were built for the opposite effect: to muffle the cries of the enslaved so that they would not be heard by the surrounding society. In this way, slave jails were vital in maintaining Kentucky's errant self-image—that of an ordered society where, as Arterburn claimed, "slavery took a more amiable nature."[35]

The logic of prisons overlapped with their architectural aesthetic. Not apart from contemporary prisons, nineteenth-century slave jails worked to remove instances of dissonance and insubordination against the prevailing political economy. The *image* of public order was just as important to the perpetuation of slavery as the *process* of public order. Because slavery was neither a natural nor a seamless social state, it required work and rhetoric and propaganda to remain possible. When Harriet Beecher Stowe pursued her investigative journalism of Kentucky slavery, her work subverted this mythic gilt by looking beneath the state's deliberate efforts to conceal the violence engrained in the status quo. She uncovered the layers of trauma silenced by iron bars and high walls and brought them back onto the streets, challenging slavery by upsetting the status quo. But her work was just a small portion of the work performed by the enslaved themselves, whose daily decisions to escape, to fight, to commit suicide, to commit filicide, to murder their enslavers, or to take up arms rendered the rhetoric of slavery contradictory and the stability of the institution ultimately impossible. It was the resistance of the enslaved that necessitated prisons, forcing not just enslavers but also the state government itself to play a key role in slavery's perpetuation.

When Stephen Chenoweth became jailor for Jefferson County, Kentucky, he was charged with documenting and managing the many Black people incarcerated as suspected "runaways." This role positioned him at the nexus between slave trading in the private sector and the public infrastructure. As a government official and an active participant in the slave trade, Chenoweth embodied the intersection of state resources and enslaver profits. In Kentucky and a number of other states, particularly in the Upper South, state resources heavily funded prison construction and renovation. These buildings then went almost exclusively toward confining Black people presumed to be enslaved. In Washington, DC, Maryland, and Virginia, local jails were filled with the people advertised as "runaways." In contrast to jails in other regions, jails in the Upper South were in practice dedicated to the control of the Black population.[36]

Throughout the 1850s, Stephen Chenoweth purchased insurance policies on his captives: one for John Owen, an enslaved person forced to work as a firefighter. If Owen were to be killed risking his life on the job, Chenoweth would be compensated by the New York Life Insurance Company to cover the financial loss. He took out similar policies for others, including Tillman, a person forced to fight fires on a steamboat route between Louisville and New Orleans, and Jack, a "cabin boy" forced to serve steamboat crewmen and passengers.[37] The use of insurance policies to protect enslavers' capital underscores the financial risks undertaken by those investing in holding people captive. On riverboats, physical harm or escape could subvert enslaver profits at any time, and insurance was a practical solution to hedge against the uncertainty.[38] On land, prisons served as a similar hedge. Escape and injury were persistent financial threats, and jails were deployed at crucial moments in the investment cycle, when profits were most vulnerable and the presence of the enslaved most crucial. In an economy where human movement and transportation were essential to growth, jails served as vetting facilities against undocumented Black people.

In 1839, Stephen Chenoweth incarcerated Jim Allen, a man aboard the *New Albany* steamboat docked on Louisville's riverfront. Allen was among the many Black people working the transportation industry along the Mississippi and Ohio Rivers, a multimillion-dollar industry that depended on a mix of Black and immigrant labor to link much of Kentucky to urban nodes throughout the continent's interior. Allen was incarcerated under the suspicion of escaping slavery, which was particularly significant along the porous border between Louisville and the free soil of Indiana.[39] Along the Ohio's riverine corridors, steamboats were sites of tremendous ambiguity, where the line between freedom and slavery could be blurred behind the fog of anonymity. Riverboats became worlds of their own, microcosms of the broader United States where the callused racial code of nineteenth-century America split in small but consequential ways.

According to an account written in 1856, "A large proportion of the passengers on Western steamboats are persons from distant parts of the country, or emigrants, perhaps, from the old world, whose journeyings are unknown to their friends, and whose fate often excites no inquiry."[40] Rivers existed at the perimeter of state power, where local jails, night watches, slave catchers, and enslavers struggled to distinguish between "slave" and free person, even between Black and white. Enslaved people of light complexion found riverboats to be places of passing, where African ancestry could sometimes be feigned away, as in the case of Felix, who aboard the *Missouri* successfully passed as white to gain freedom denied him in the cities of New Orleans and St. Louis.[41]

At the edges of state control, riverboats gained reputations as sites of relative disorder, where the lines of the nineteenth-century racial code and Evangelical ideology blurred. On the Louisville riverfront, boats frequently docked to load cargo destined for the Deep South, including enslaved people to be transported for sale in Natchez and New Orleans. According to one nineteenth-century traveler, "The number of passengers which these boats carry, is very considerable; they are almost always crowded, although there are some which have two hundred beds. . . . On the downward voyage, their place is occupied by horses and cattle, which are sent to the South for sale, and by slaves."[42] As traders and boat workers loaded and unloaded cargo from the riverboats, masses of people gathered at the Louisville docks not only to board the vessels but also to observe the mechanical spectacle of steam power. It was a daily affair that gathered hundreds of people, travelers from across the country comingling with Louisville locals.[43] This mixing offered a level of anonymity to refugees from slavery as they were able to blend in with the crowds. For this reason, Chenoweth's arrest of Jim Allen encapsulated a consequential moment in the exercise of state power on behalf of enslaver interests. Allen's presence in Louisville as an unfamiliar Black person, slave or free, posed a threat to local systems of power, a breach between the anarchic world of the riverboat and the perceived racial order of nineteenth-century Kentucky. Enslaved people such as William Wells Brown sometimes breached the barrier between these worlds successfully, using capitalism's dependence on the rapid movement of people and goods against its callused structures of racial caste and identity. Brown escaped captivity in Louisville, where he "[took] up a trunk, went up the wharf, and was soon out of the crowd."[44] Men like Chenoweth were positioned to control men like Brown by arresting unfamiliar Black people they feared to be escapees. Jim Allen was one of these men who, despite legal free status, was captured in the prison system's broad-net suspicion of all Black people traveling through the state. With virtually no repercussions for false arrests or abuse of state power, men like Chenoweth, along with a chain of police and community watchmen, abducted Black people such as Jim Allen and held them until their freedom could be proven. For many, proof of freedom was difficult, if not impossible. Many people with free status were sold into slavery regardless. Fortunately for Allen, his freedom was proven, but the system nonetheless succeeded in vetting his identity as he crossed between the anonymity of the riverboat and the surveillance state of Kentucky's slaveholding society. When Allen was arrested again in a different location, Chenoweth could use the false record of Allen's identity from the Louisville jail to affirm that he lacked legal free status elsewhere. Chenoweth wrote to another jailor in 1841, "I received a letter from you concerning a negro man by the name of Jim Allen which you say you have in custody. All that I can say is that he was committed to this jail on 1st November 1839."[45] This moment, when different jails cross-referenced data on Black inmates, represents a crucial role that Kentucky jails played in the broader enslaving society. Not only did slavery require the confinement of people such as Jim Allen, but it also depended on the accurate tracking of people, too; slavery was a paradox that on the one hand depended on rapid mobility and transportation of goods and on the other was simultaneously undermined by the very presence of the Black people it actively displaced. Jim Allen, displaced by the slave trade in St. Louis, then threatened the slave trade by virtue of his displacement. For many states, the Sisyphean solution was prisons.

The system of enslavement upon which the Kentucky economy depended required innovation, and new technologies of power such as prisons were developed to maintain any semblance of stability because enslaved people constantly and ingeniously worked toward new ways of liberating themselves. By the time Charity was enslaved in Falmouth, Kentucky, vast networks for escape were established across the northern part of the state. Thousands of people fled captivity using safehouses and covert pathways through vast hickory forests to evade state-funded patrols, urban police, and self-deputized citizens seeking to maintain social order through the surveillance and restriction of Black movement. Enslaved people innovated in other ways, too. Through collaboration with abolitionists across the river in Cincinnati, many constructed legal arguments for freedom, wielding the state's own slave codes against it. In fact, Charity used this route to freedom, successfully suing for her freedom in the Pendleton County Court.[46] In this way, we find a powerful dialectic between the booming slavery economy and the people it exploited.

Separated by two centuries, Charity and her great-great-great-great grandson Dontaie Allen navigate the same city streets around downtown Lexington, where buildings once stood to imprison the enslaved.[47] The capital extracted from Charity's body, having been saved and invested decade upon decade, likely still circulates the city; indeed, it may ironically even help underwrite the current county jail itself. Gone though she is, the relics of her trauma can still be found in the structures left behind—in the technologies of power used to construct and protect "safety" and "property," which are imbued with racialized notions of criminality and exclusivity. The racial and gendered power wielded by Kentucky police against Breonna Taylor is not disconnected from the power wielded by William Pullam against Charity. The notion that Black people, especially those deemed new and unfamiliar, ought to be watched and monitored persists in the neighborhood watches in modern towns and suburbs. It is the inherited idea that public order is wholly dependent on the control and domination of the Black body—that the unmonitored and unchecked expression of Blackness inherently undermines safety and property precisely because Blackness has continually existed as a pivotal site for American property extraction. Allegorically, Charity's exploitation depended on the surveillance and containment of her body. The profits of major Kentucky industries were totally incongruent with her free movement if her labor and biopower were to be extracted. What of that dynamic was abolished, and what of that sort of power persists? If "My Old Kentucky Home" was first written about Black family dislocation and separation, if it was intended to echo the trauma of powerlessness against global industry—the tragic fate of those whose lives are overwhelmingly determined by state actors and financial interests—then perhaps the song speaks as much to contemporary African Americans as it did to those imprisoned in antebellum Kentucky slave jails. To really ponder the experience of women such as Charity—whose body was controlled with state resources *and* private capital, whose tragedy was written into Stephen Foster's lyrics, whose trauma had as much to do with financial greed as it did with surveillance and policing—is to better understand why her great-great-great-great grandson knelt with his teammates on the floor of Rupp Arena.

To reflect upon Charity and the power relations responsible for her condition is to awaken to the persisting forces of race, power, and finance no less embedded within capitalism today.

Notes

1. Tarlton Arterburn quoted in *"Uncle Tom's Cabin:* A House in Which Some of the Senes [*sic*] of the Story Were Laid, Torn Down," *Louisville Courier-Journal*, May 3, 1876, 4, Hoosier State Chronicles: Indiana's Digital Newspaper Archive, at https://newspapers.library.in.gov/.

2. Arterburn quoted in *"Uncle Tom's Cabin,"* 4. The first two lines in the original verse from 1853 are: "The sun shines bright in the old Kentucky home, / 'Tis summer, the darkies are gay."

3. Here, *incarceration* refers to those physically held against their will. But the term must be complicated by the changing nature of prisons over time. Enslaved people were "incarcerated" as a means of holding them and curtailing their resistance for the purpose of future sale, sexual exploitation, and/or continued labor extraction. This state differs from the "incarceration" of those processed by the judicial system, whose fates involved the rights of citizenship. Importantly, these two groups often found themselves overlapping in jails and penitentiaries. My forthcoming book expands on this history in the nation's capital.

4. For more on Lewis C. Robard's sex trafficking, see John Winston Coleman Jr., *Slavery Times in Kentucky* (Chapel Hill: University of North Carolina Press, 1940); and Sharony Green, "'Mr. Ballard, I Am Compelled to Write Again': Beyond Bedrooms and Brothels, a Fancy Girl Speaks," *Black Women, Gender, and Families* 5, no. 1 (Spring 2011): 17–40. For more on sex trafficking within the American slave trade, see Paula Giddings, *When and Where I Enter: The Impact of Black Women on Race and Sex in America* (New York: Harper Collins, 1984); Stephanie Camp, *Closer to Freedom: Enslaved Women & Everyday Resistance in the Plantation South* (Chapel Hill: University of North Carolina Press, 2004); Sharon Block, "Lines of Color, Sex, and Service: Comparative Sexual Coercion in Early America," in *Sex, Love, Race: Cross Boundaries in North American History*, ed. Martha Hodes (New York: New York University Press, 1999), 141–63; Kathleen Brown, *Good Wives, Nasty Wenches, and Anxious Patriarchs: Gender, Race, and Power in Colonial Virginia* (Chapel Hill: University of North Carolina Press, 1996); Melton McLaurin, *Celia, a Slave: A True Story of Violence and Retribution in Antebellum America* (New York: Avon Books, 1991); Joshua D. Rothman, *Notorious in the Neighborhood: Sex and Families across the*

Color Line in Virginia, 1787–1861 (Chapel Hill: University of North Carolina Press, 2003).

5. Brandon Wilson, "Carving Canaan from Egypt's Land: Free People of Color in Kentucky's Ohio River Valley, 1795–1860," master's thesis, University of Kentucky, 2014.

6. This is not to argue that the slave trade was entirely economically rational, though. It was built upon fundamentally irrational inspirations as well, including sexual predation, superiority complexes, and other exertions of gendered and racialized forms of power.

7. *Charity (by her next friend) vs. Palmer &al,* filed October 21, 1824, Att. W. C. Kennett, October term, 1825, Pendleton County Circuit Court, Kentucky State Archives, Frankfort.

8. John Alexander Williams, *Appalachia: A History* (Chapel Hill: University of North Carolina Press, 2002), 125–56.

9. "To Be Sold," *National Intelligencer & Washington Advertiser* (Washington, DC), March 31, 1806, 3, Chronicling America: Digital Newspapers Archive, Library of Congress, Washington, DC.

10. "For Sale!," *National Intelligencer & Washington Advertiser,* August 30, 1802, 2, Chronicling America: Digital Newspapers Archive.

11. *Charity (by her next friend) vs. Palmer &al.*

12. Allan Kulikoff, *Tobacco and Slaves: The Development of Southern Cultures in the Chesapeake, 1680–1800* (Chapel Hill: University of North Carolina Press, 1986), 78–116.

13. Kulikoff, *Tobacco and Slaves,* 396–415.

14. Within the past two decades, historians have taken significant interest in the role of slavery in the expansion of capitalism from the eighteenth to the nineteenth centuries. After decades of intensive research, it has by the 2020s become consensus that slavery was essential to capitalism's existence. The term *slavery capitalism* is used to describe the slave trade as an inherently capitalistic model to organize labor and privatize the human body as opposed to a precapitalistic agrarian system. For more on this topic, see Walter Johnson, *Soul by Soul: Life inside the Antebellum Slave Market* (Cambridge, MA: Harvard University Press, 1999); Walter Johnson, *River of Dark Dreams: Slavery and Empire in the Cotton Kingdom* (Cambridge, MA: Harvard University Press, 2013); Edward Baptist, *The Half Has Never Been Told: Slavery and the Making of American Capitalism* (New York: Basic, 2014); Sven Beckert, *Empire of Cotton: A Global History* (New York: Random House, 2014); Sven Beckert and Seth Rockman, eds., *Slavery's Capitalism: A New History of Economic Development* (Philadelphia: University of Pennsylvania Press, 2016); Calvin Schermerhorn, *The Business of Slavery and the*

Rise of American Capitalism, 1815–1860 (New Haven, CT: Yale University Press, 2015); Joshua D. Rothman, *The Ledger and the Chain: How Domestic Slave Traders Shaped America* (New York: Basic, 2021); Joshua D. Rothman, *Flush Times and Fever Dreams: A Story of Capitalism and Slavery in the Age of Jackson* (Athens: University of Georgia Press, 2012).

15. Sharon Ann Murphy, "Banking on Slavery in the Antebellum South," presentation at the Yale University Economic History Workshop, May 1, 2017, 5.

16. *Bank of Kentucky v. Vance's Adm'rs,* 4 Litt. 168 (1823).

17. J. D. B. Debow, *Statistical View of the United States (Compendium of the Seventh Census)* (Washington, DC: A. O. P. Nicholson, 1854), 94, Digital Collections, US National Library of Medicine, Bethesda, MD, at https://quod.lib .umich.edu/cgi/t/text/text-idx?c=moa;idno=AJB5448.0001.001. It is suggested that in 1850 about 400,000 slaves lived in cities and towns and that 2,500,000 slaves of all ages worked in agriculture: 1,815,000 in cotton, 350,000 in tobacco, 150,000 in cane sugar, 125,000 in rice, and 60,000 in hemp.

18. Jennifer Cole, "'For the Sake of the Songs of the Men Made Free': James Speed and the Emancipationists' Dilemma in Nineteenth-Century Kentucky," *Ohio Valley History* 4, no. 4 (Winter 2004): 27–48.

19. Benjamin Lewis Fitzpatrick, "Negroes for Sale: The Slave Trade in Antebellum Kentucky," PhD diss., University of Notre Dame, 2008, 90.

20. This figure was calculated from the estimated 6,000 enslaved people annually sold to the Deep South at an average price of $400 per person. Figures taken from T. D. Clark, "The Slave Trade between Kentucky and the Cotton South," *Mississippi Valley Historical Review* 21, no. 3 (December 1934): 331–33.

21. Baptist, *The Half Has Never Been Told.*

22. Richard Sutch, "The Profitability of Ante Bellum Slavery: Revisited," *Southern Economic Journal* 31, no. 4 (1965): 365–77.

23. See "Freedom on the Move," a digital project compiling advertisements for fugitives from slavery, at freedomonthemove.org.

24. Loren Schweninger, "Counting the Costs: Southern Planters and the Problem of Runaway Slaves, 1790–1860," *Business and Economic History* 28, no. 2 (1999): 270.

25. Leonard Neale to Francis Neale on the management of the Missions, 1805, Slavery Archive, Georgetown University Library, Washington, DC.

26. See Louisiana's Code Noir (1865), implemented under French (and Spanish) rule beginning in 1685: *Le Code Noir ou recueil des reglements rendus jusqu'a present,* trans. John Garrigus (Paris: Prault, 1767; reprint, Guadaloupe, French Antilles: Societé d'histoire de la Guadeloupe, 1980).

27. For more on refugees from slavery and their interaction with patrol units and police, see Gerald L. Smith, "Slavery and Abolition in Kentucky: 'Patter-rollers Were Everywhere,'" in *Bluegrass Renaissance: The History and Culture of Central Kentucky, 1792–1852,* ed. James C. Klotter and Daniel Rowland (Lexington: University Press of Kentucky, 2012), 75–92.

28. Sally Hadden, *Slave Patrols: Law and Violence in Virginia and the Carolinas* (Cambridge, MA: Harvard University Press, 2001).

29. Marion B. Lucas, *A History of Blacks in Kentucky,* vol. 1: *From Slavery to Segregation, 1760–1891* (Frankfort: Kentucky Historical Society, 1992), 92.

30. Walter Johnson, *Soul by Soul: Life inside the Antebellum Slave Market* (Cambridge, MA: Harvard University Press, 1999).

31. "*Uncle Tom's Cabin,*" 4.

32. Harriet Beecher Stowe, *A Key to* Uncle Tom's Cabin: *Presenting the Original Facts and Documents upon Which the Story Is Founded. Together with Corroborative Statements Verifying the Truth of the Work* (Boston: J. P. Jewett, 1853), 50.

33. Slavoj Žižek coined the phrase "solipsistic speculative dance of capital" to describe the irreverent movement of capital over human and natural geographies. See Slavoj Žižek, "With Hegel beyond Hegel," *Criticism* 53, no. 2 (2011): 295–313.

34. Stowe, *A Key to* Uncle Tom's Cabin, chap. 11. Stowe is referring to the infamous case of Margaret Garner, who escaped slavery in Boone County, Kentucky. When cornered by enslavers, she killed her daughter, Mary, and attempted to kill herself and the other escaped slaves to avoid a life blighted by sexual abuse, labor exploitation, and family separation.

35. Arterburn quoted in "*Uncle Tom's Cabin,*" 4.

36. Brandon Wilson, "Safekeeping: Slavery, Capitalism, and the Carceral State in Washington, D.C., 1830–1863," PhD diss., Washington University, St. Louis, 2020. "Slavery Era Insurance Registry," n.d., California Department of Insurance, Sacramento.

37. Aetna Life Insurance Company, "Register of the Slave or Slaves Insured in This Policy," Exhibit 3, n.d., at https://insurance.illinois.gov/Consumer/Slavery Information/SlavePoliciesReports.pdf.

38. Jonathan Levy, *Freaks of Fortune: The Emerging World of Capitalism and Risk in America* (Cambridge, MA: Harvard University Press, 2012).

39. Levy, *Freaks of Fortune.*

40. Quoted in Johnson, *River of Dark Dreams,* 114.

41. Johnson, *River of Dark Dreams,* 114.

42. Guy Stevens Callender, *Economic History of the United States, 1765–1860* (Boston: Ginn, 1909), 363.

43. John Edward Heller, "A History of the Ohio River Trade at Louisville from Its Beginning until 1840," PhD diss., University of Louisville, 1922.

44. Johnson, *River of Dark Dreams,* 144.

45. "ALS S. R. Chenoweth, Louisville, to an Unspecified Recipient," March 18, 1841, American Slavery Collection, Digital Collections, Eastern Kentucky University, Richmond.

46. *Charity (by her next friend) vs. Palmer &al.*

47. Dontaie Allen traces his roots to Charity Southgate through his mother's ancestry. His mother, April, is the granddaughter of Mae Ayers. Mae was the daughter of Betty Ayers (a graduate of Wilberforce University and a pioneer for Black education in the state) and Robert Lee Ayers. Robert (b. 1866) was the son of Lucinda Southgate, and Lucinda (b. 1836) was the daughter of Charity Southgate. The author of this chapter is also a descendant of Charity, and many other descendants still reside in the Ohio River Valley today.

2

Race Matters in Utopia

The Shakers and Slavery at Pleasant Hill

Jacob A. Glover

On May 16, 1849, the Shaker community at Pleasant Hill in Mercer County convened for the funeral of Brother Anthony Chosen. Although the Shakers did not fear death and faithfully looked forward to an eternal, spiritual existence after their life on earth, the funeral was nonetheless a serious occasion intended to mark a life well lived. Born near Port Royal, Virginia, in August 1782, Chosen had been brought to the Commonwealth of Kentucky as an enslaved person in the early 1790s. Engaged mainly in boat building throughout central Kentucky, Chosen came to spend most of his time in Mercer County, and he was a member of a Baptist church at Shawnee Run before the outbreak of the Kentucky Revival. In July 1806, Chosen "confessed his sins" and received the Shaker gospel. For the next forty-one years, Chosen remained a committed member of the Shaker community, regularly walking the three miles from the residence of his enslavers to Pleasant Hill on Sundays and other holy days to practice his faith. In July 1847, at which time he was "now feeble and in the 64th year of his age," Chosen's enslavers sold him to Shaker trustee Rufus Bryant. The Shakers swiftly emancipated Chosen and brought him to equal legal status with the rest of the Pleasant Hill community. For the last twenty-three months of his life, then, Chosen lived as a free man among his fellow Believers.[1]

Attended by members of the Church of Christ as well as by several outsiders, the funeral proceedings for Chosen began with a "solemn song without words," followed by "a regular and very edifying sermon" that was intended for the "serious reflection of those unbelievers present." It was at this point that events took a rather dramatic, although not unprecedented, turn. According to one Shaker observer, another member of the community became "inspired" by the deceased and commenced relaying a message from Chosen from beyond the grave. Chosen had received "a cordial reception in the eternal world," the medium began, and he had been "crownd [sic] and robed with everlasting brightness." Later, another "messenger" conveyed a "Farewell Poem" from Chosen that described the joys of paradise and the importance of laying "up treasures in heaven above" during one's life on earth. His message thus sufficiently relayed, Chosen left the assembled Shakers in peace. After singing their "common funeral hymn," the community "went on to do our last duty to his lifeless remains" and brought the ceremony to a close.[2]

Often utilized as moments of instruction for living Shakers, funerals at Pleasant Hill regularly followed the basic outline described at Anthony Chosen's death. To conclude that the events of this May morning were business as usual, however, would be far from the mark. Predictably, it was Chosen's former status as an enslaved person that presented the rather unique circumstances attending to his service. It was not unheard of for outsiders to attend Shaker funerals at Pleasant Hill, but it was remarkable that on this day the group contained "some of [Chosen's] former young Masters and Mistress's [sic] it being their own request." One can only wonder what the family members of Chosen's former enslavers expected to gain from attending the ceremony. Whatever it was, their expectations were likely shattered. Not only did the medium convey Chosen's apparent eternal bliss, but there were also reports of "numbers bound in chains and cast in prison, there weeping wailing and gnashing their teeth." Among these imprisoned masses "had been [Chosen's] old master for many years," although Chosen communicated that his master had been released recently "and had asked for my forgiveness for all the harshness and opposition he showed to me while on earth, in preventing me from serving God according to my faith, light and understanding." The Shaker scribe did not record any apparent reaction from the "outsiders" in attendance, but it is not hard to imagine the shock and consternation they felt at being castigated so brazenly and publicly for the wicked and sinful practice of slavery.[3]

Given Pleasant Hill's origins and the religious beliefs of its members, such a staunch antislavery stance is hardly surprising. Founded in 1806 amid the religious enthusiasm of the Kentucky Revival, Pleasant Hill was a communal, Christian settlement established upon the precepts of the United Society of Believers in Christ's Second Appearing.[4] Originating in Manchester, England, in the 1760s as the followers of Ann Lee, the "Shakers," so-called by detractors because of their energetic, frenzied worship services, adopted a spiritual message that was entirely unique. According to Lee, the second coming of Christ had already occurred, and the Millennium had commenced. For the Shakers, God was both male and female, and thus women were empowered to preach and act with the same authority as men in all matters. People of any color or creed could confess their sins, share their resources with other believers as the first Christian church had done, and join the group as equals. Although only eight Shakers departed England for America in 1774, their number grew quickly in the American ferment. After Lee's death in 1784, eleven villages were established throughout the Northeast in the next two decades. Reports of the Kentucky Revival encouraged the Shakers to send missionaries to central Kentucky in early 1805. By December 1806, the first local converts in Mercer County had signed a "Family Covenant" and had consecrated themselves and their possessions to the pursuit of the Shaker ideal—a perfect, sinless existence that involved, among other things, celibacy, confession of sin, and isolation from the sinful "World" outside their communal borders.[5]

By 1849, the Shakers at Pleasant Hill had developed into a rather mature community that had been living out the precepts of their faith for more than four decades. Although no surviving records from Pleasant Hill elaborate further on the events of Anthony Chosen's funeral and the forceful antislavery message conveyed that day, the timing of such a statement is intriguing. The Shakers at Pleasant Hill infrequently commented on matters outside of their community in their journals and correspondence, but they were certainly aware of the bubbling antislavery movement in Kentucky that peaked in the summer of 1849 before it was repelled by the decidedly pro-slavery state constitution of 1850. One Shaker brother noted that he attended an antislavery speech given by John C. Young of Centre College in June 1849, and it was in nearby Madison County, after all, where Cassius M. Clay and Squire Turner had their infamous debate that same month that ended in Clay's stabbing and killing one of Turner's sons while fending off attacks from a pro-slavery mob.[6] News of important events and developments from nearby towns such as

Harrodsburg, Danville, and Lexington filtered into the community regularly, and many Shakers traveled throughout the local area on various personal and family matters.[7] Thus, although the medium's antislavery message at Chosen's funeral was rooted in the specific context of the Shakers' faith and experience, it was also part of Kentucky's cultural milieu and should be considered within the broader history of antislavery in central Kentucky.

There were many other connections between Pleasant Hill and the rest of Kentucky as well. The community's economic ties with the outside world ensured that Shaker trade deacons regularly traveled throughout central Kentucky and the southern United States, while the portion of the Lexington-Harrodsburg-Perryville Turnpike that ran through Pleasant Hill brought outsiders into the community on a daily basis.[8] Furthermore, the Shakers at Pleasant Hill were clearly aware of the slave economy that powered growth throughout mid-nineteenth-century America, and at times it is apparent that they were repulsed by their own complicity in the system. In fact, the first sorghum crop in Kentucky was harvested at Pleasant Hill in 1857 at least in part to reduce the Shakers' reliance on purchased sugar, which was produced by enslaved labor.[9] On other occasions, however, the Shakers evinced apathy or feigned oblivion as slave coffles were driven along the turnpike through Pleasant Hill; they traded in markets where enslaved persons were regularly bought and sold; and they even hired enslaved laborers at various times. Simply put, the isolation from the "World" that Shaker communities so highly prized was often rather tenuous at Pleasant Hill.

In many ways, then, Pleasant Hill provides a unique lens through which to examine slavery in Kentucky. The community was, to put it bluntly, a society that was established on the principals of human equality but that coalesced in the midst of a slave state—a state that premised its economic, legal, and political systems on the value spectrum of white-supremacist patriarchy.[10] Of course, reality was often much more complicated than broad statements can easily convey. This essay examines the lives of Black Shakers and other Black persons at the Pleasant Hill community to reveal the complicated intersection between slavery and the Shakers' commitment to racial egalitarianism. Whereas some Black Shakers spent nearly their entire lives as free people of color at Pleasant Hill, others, such as Anthony Chosen, had to carefully navigate between the freedom of the community and the reality of their continued enslavement outside of it. At other times, the white Pleasant Hill leadership paid for the labor of enslaved persons and engaged freely with the wider economy of antebellum Kentucky that was built upon enslaved labor, actions that reinforced and legitimized slavery and racial inequities while economically supporting white enslavers who lived in the area. The legacy of Pleasant Hill is thus more complicated with the history of slavery and racial exploitation in Kentucky than is often remembered.[11]

This essay explores three major "developments" in the history of Pleasant Hill to examine this complicated legacy. The first development was the founding of the community amid the Kentucky Revival and related religious fervor. In this upheaval, several enslavers joined the Shakers, emancipated their enslaved persons, and lived as equals alongside them. These revolutionary decisions were unique to the earliest years of the Pleasant Hill community, and after the 1810s no more white enslavers would become Shakers at Pleasant Hill. Nevertheless, the firm commitment to equality of persons that was embedded within the community during this time allowed for racial equality in living spaces, work, and access to Pleasant Hill's resources for all covenanted members that would persist throughout the Society of Believers' existence in Mercer County.

The second development was the maturation of the Pleasant Hill economy in the mid–nineteenth century and the flourishing of the Shaker community within the state's slave economy. Although the Shakers were decidedly antislavery in their beliefs, they continually found themselves enmeshed in a capitalistic whirlwind whipped up by slavery. The third development was the Shakers' emancipationist worldview in the 1850s and 1860s and their decidedly antislavery views during and after the Civil War. Although the Shakers were not abolitionists and only rarely spoke out against slavery outside of their own borders, their views and practices were well known in the broader community in which they lived, and they sometimes became targets of the Ku Klux Klan and other regulator groups in post–Civil War Kentucky. Viewed as a whole, these developments shed light on both the Shakers' radically progressive and inclusive views in regard to slavery in Kentucky and the ways in which even the Shakers found it impossible to completely separate from the influence of slavery.

Between 1806 and 1814, the Shakers at Pleasant Hill legally defined their relationships with each other by drafting and signing three "covenants."[12] Each of these covenants marked a significant step in the community's evolution, demonstrating continued spiritual growth, the desire for increased separation from the outside world, a stated goal of union among all community members, as well as the dedication and consecration of individual property for the use of the society at large in the manner of the first Christian Church. These testaments were hardly lip service to an unrealistic ideal; the covenant of 1810, the second of the three from this period, specifically addressed "a greater inequality and separation in our temporal possessions" among the community members as one of the driving forces for restating the society's goals. Due in large part to the rapid increase in the number of Believers at Pleasant Hill, the Shakers came "to a mutual determination to rectify such separation and inequality as far as circumstances and our present situation will admit."[13]

Like the initial covenant from 1806, the updated version in 1810 specifically required all members who owned property before they came to Pleasant Hill to draft a detailed inventory so that they might be reimbursed if they chose to leave the community in the future. By 1814 and the execution of the first true "Church Covenant," however, any remaining freedom to retain individual right to possessions was forfeited by those who covenanted together. "A full and entire union in all things, in perfect imitation of the primitive gospel Church[,] . . . [being long] contemplated," the Shakers later explained, it was determined that "each individual should make an irredeemable surrender of his personal or private interest, his time and talents."[14] In the Shakers' own words: "And the joint interest of the Church thus formed and established by the free will offerings of the members respectively . . . shall be held and possessed by the whole body jointly as their natural and religious right; that is, all and every individual of or belonging to the church, shall enjoy equal rights and privileges in the use of all things pertaining to the church."[15] If any detractors wanted an example of how radical the physical manifestation of the Shakers' faith could become, here was a prime candidate.

Although such a drastic leveling of socioeconomic status is not unique to the Shaker movement in world history, the Shakers' commitment to an egalitarian version of communism that recognized no distinctions of gender and race in central Kentucky in the 1810s was remarkable. Only a few years earlier, the Kentucky General Assembly had drafted the Commonwealth's slave and marriage codes in such a way that provided broad protections for the rights of white men and legally reinforced patriarchy.[16] At the same time, the strain of republicanism percolating throughout the new United States prized white men as sources of moral authority and virtuous independence. In this sense, the Shakers' notion of dependence—of men upon women, of the previously rich upon the formerly impoverished, of white Shakers upon Black Shakers, of everyone on everyone else— codified in these early covenants is one of the most jarring reminders of how different their political, social, and economic worldview was from mainstream American thought in the early nineteenth century.

•   Although former enslavers and their former enslaved persons composed only a very small fraction of the early Shaker converts in Mercer County, their presence in the Pleasant Hill community was notable. Many early records have been lost, but it is certain that at least four enslavers lived at Pleasant Hill for a considerable amount of time: James Congleton, John Bryant, Tobias Wilhite, and Namon Roberts. Of these four heads of household, Roberts was the last to join in 1812—and, coincidentally, the first to leave Pleasant Hill in 1815. Congleton, Bryant, and Wilhite, therefore, were the only three white enslavers who became full covenant members at Pleasant Hill.[17] It is unsurprising that these three white men and their families joined the community when they did, between 1806 and 1810, because this period represents the height of the religious impulses associated with the Kentucky Revival and the democratizing features of the various "New Light" congregations that proliferated throughout the Commonwealth. Whereas other denominations debated the morality of slavery, the Shakers restricted full acceptance to those who had disavowed the institution entirely.[18]

At least nine people of color, among whom at least eight were enslaved at the time of their arrival, ultimately came into contact with the Shakers at Pleasant Hill through the actions of these former enslavers. The variety of experiences among these nine individuals is instructive, and in many ways they mirrored the experiences of white Shakers from the same period. Although some of these individuals lived the rest of their natural lives among the Shakers, others departed the community for one reason or another and rejoined the "World." Such a decision would have been weighted with significance, although on most occasions there is no explanation given for their so doing. Like the majority of the white Shakers at Pleasant Hill, most of the formerly enslaved persons who remained there appear only occasionally in the historical record. One individual, however, became an accomplished songwriter and was celebrated broadly for her personal accomplishments—as odd as that may seem in the Shaker context. In other words, it is apparent that these formerly enslaved persons were well and truly presented with the same opportunities for personal growth and freedom of movement accorded to their white Shaker brethren and sisters.

Tobias Wilhite, a Revolutionary War veteran who had been born in Virginia, came to "believe," along with his family, in 1806, and they later moved from Bullitt County to Pleasant Hill in November 1808. Wilhite remained a Shaker until his death in 1839. In addition to the white members of Wilhite's family, four persons of color were brought to Pleasant Hill through this conversion. One woman, referred to only as Daphne or Daphna or Daphay, lived for nearly five years among the Shakers before passing away in November 1813. Although the only known description of Daphne notes at her time of death that "she was a colored woman that Tobias Wilhite brought among Believers," she is listed in the church roll books as a member of the "Society but not of the Church." This indicates that Daphne maintained an association with the Shakers without ever signing the covenant, something that was not entirely unusual—Tobias Wilhite, for instance, did not sign the covenant until 1814.[19] Whether Daphne continued to be enslaved during her time at Pleasant Hill remains unclear, but it is certain that Tobias Wilhite did retain legal ownership of at least three other enslaved persons even after he signed the covenant in 1814. On May 7, 1821, Wilhite emancipated Suckey (Sukey) and two of her children in the Mercer County Court.[20] Although many early Pleasant Hill records no longer exist, the fact that none of these three individuals appear in any extant material raises questions as to how involved they were with the Shaker community. At the very least, they were present in Mercer County in 1821 on the day they were legally emancipated.

Like Wilhite, John Bryant remained committed to Shakerism for the remainder of his life after his conversion in 1809. Arriving at Pleasant Hill in 1810, Bryant brought many white family members as well as Adam Baty and Clary Baty Bryant, two individuals who were likely enslaved persons. John Bryant quickly became a respected leader within the community and was appointed as the first trustee when the Church Covenant was signed in 1814, a position he filled until his death in 1823. No written records survive that indicate whether Adam Baty and Clara Baty Bryant were legally emancipated before or after their arrival at Pleasant Hill, but it is apparent that they were afforded the full benefits of community membership. In the late winter of 1825, Clara Baty Bryant was one of several

Shakers who died from fever or consumption, the Shaker ministry noting that "all these we believe were good Believers and had their union with the rest of the faithful when they left this world."[21] Adam Baty, however, chose to exercise his independence and departed Pleasant Hill in June 1827. The Shakers did not record a specific reason for his withdrawal from the community, but this absence of a recorded reason was common for many other defaulters from this period as well.[22] In any event, it is apparent that Shakerism had once again profoundly changed the relationships between enslaver and enslaved and severed the physical control that John Bryant once had over Adam Baty and Clara Baty Bryant.

If the experiences of the individuals who came into contact with Shakerism through the actions of Tobias Wilhite and John Bryant offer a reassuring narrative of the progressive and liberating aspects of the community's faith, James Congleton and Namon Roberts present a different dynamic that illustrates the continued stranglehold of slavery in early nineteenth-century Kentucky. Born in North Carolina, James Congleton and his family were residing in Bourbon County when they accepted the Shaker faith in 1809 before removing to Pleasant Hill the following year. James Congleton remained an active member of the community for the remainder of his life, serving as an elder in various families and helping to spread the gospel until his death in 1837.

Sarah Foster and Robert Foster, likely a mother and son, were two enslaved persons whom Congleton brought to Pleasant Hill at that time. By early 1813, both Fosters were living in "a two story hew, d [sic] log house" on an outlying piece of land referred to as the Lebanon Farm with James Congleton and other Shakers. Although Congleton, Sarah, and Robert had become covenanted members of the society, it was apparently accepted by the community that Congleton retained legal ownership of the mother and son. In practical terms, however, it does not appear that Congleton exercised any restrictive rights of ownership in regard to the Fosters because both moved from the Lebanon Farm to different spiritual families in the main village by the spring of 1815. By the next year, both Fosters were on the move again—Robert departing the community and going "to the world" in January, while Sarah relocated to the "grainery" along the Kentucky River in June with several other Shakers. Sarah would also eventually depart Pleasant Hill in May 1823. According to all remaining official church records, James Congleton opposed none of these actions.[23]

There is striking evidence, however, that Congleton did retain legal ownership of Robert Foster at the time of Robert's departure from Pleasant Hill in January 1816. According to an early history recorded by the Shakers, Robert Foster was "a colored man; formally own, d [*sic*] by James Congleton," and "[was] about 19 years of age" when he left Pleasant Hill.[24] This seems to be the last reference the Shakers made to Robert Foster in any surviving material except for one startling exception. In a journal kept by a Shaker brother that covered the years 1816 and 1817, Robert Foster is mentioned in an entry dated January 22, 1816—the exact date as Robert's noted departure. "Note this Robert Foster," the short description begins, "went to Madison to subistute [substitute] a molatoae [mulatto] girls place formaly [formally] the property of [N]aman Roberts ___ see page 46 letter A ___ in my book of 1815."[25]

With no other context or information provided in any Shaker records, and because the "book of 1815" mentioned here is not known to exist, this revelation leads to more questions than answers. One certainty is that "naman roberts" is the same Namon Roberts who accepted the Shaker faith in November 1812 and lived at Pleasant Hill for a short time before departing with most of his family in January 1815. The Robertses had moved from Rockingham County, North Carolina, to Madison County, Kentucky, in the early 1800s, and likely attended many of the revival meetings that were occurring throughout central Kentucky at the time. Two white female members of the Roberts household, in fact, had believed and moved to Pleasant Hill by January 1809. Around this same time, another member of the Roberts household, Patsy Williamson, had also believed. Because she was enslaved by Namon Roberts, however, she did not arrive at Pleasant Hill until November 1812 with the rest of the family. Patsy Williamson was the only person of color associated with Namon Roberts's household at this time. It is nearly certain that she is the individual referred to as "a molatoae girl" in the January 1816 journal entry.[26]

There is no doubt that Namon Roberts retained legal ownership of Patsy Williamson during his time as a Shaker. According to church records and multiple journals kept by various Shakers, Williamson was enslaved at the time of her arrival and was "purchased" and "set at liberty" by the Shakers in 1815 after the departure of Namon Roberts with the majority of his family. All of these sources, however, are dated to August 1860 and coincide with Williamson's death after she had lived the last fifty-one years of her life at Pleasant Hill. In addition to composing a number of beautiful hymns, Williamson was remembered as someone who had "continued zealous into the cause, according to her understanding till death."[27] With no evidence to contradict these recollections from 1860, we are left to conjecture as to the exact nature of the transactions in 1815 and 1816 that resulted in the departure of Robert Foster and in Williamson remaining with the community for the remainder of her life. Perhaps Foster wanted to leave Pleasant Hill, and he agreed to move to Madison County to secure the release of Williamson from bondage? Had Foster himself become free by 1823 and sent for Sarah Foster to leave Pleasant Hill at that time? Or were other motives at play? It was not coincidental surely that both Foster and Williamson were referred to as "formally" the property of separate white enslavers, an apparent recognition of both the legalities of slavery and its practical abandonment within the community. Did the Pleasant Hill leadership, then, dictate that Foster leave the community and take Williamson's place as an enslaved person in the World? This seems unlikely, but it is without question that the pernicious and cancerous effects of slavery remained in play in the Shaker community.

In addition to the individuals brought to Pleasant Hill by white enslavers, other persons of color joined Pleasant Hill during these early years. Alley and Jane Hyson accepted the Shaker faith in 1806 and 1807, respectively, and both later signed the Church Covenant and remained with the Society of Believers for the rest of their lives. Alley was born in Virginia around 1760, and Jane was born in Mercer County, Kentucky, in 1801. It is likely that they were free at the time of their arrival at Pleasant Hill, and it is possible that they were a mother and daughter. Jane Hyson, in fact, would go on to become a kitchen deaconess in the East Family, the only known Black Shaker to hold a titular position of leadership at Pleasant Hill.[28] Daniel Montgomery, another early Black convert, supposedly had visions of the Shakers before they even came to Kentucky, and when he met the first missionaries to the area, he "immediately embraced the gospel, which was in the early part of 1807. He deceased a few months afterwards firm in the faith, and much lamented by all his acquaintances."[29] Yet another Black man, Robert Lamb, believed in 1815, but it would be another decade before the Shakers freed him from his enslaver, and he was able to move from Fayette County and live alongside the Shakers. Interestingly enough, Lamb never officially signed the covenant, although he retained an association with the Shakers until his death in 1841.[30]

Although many photographs exist of Pleasant Hill from the late nineteenth century, group photos such as this one are rare. Taken in the 1870s or 1880s, this photo includes thirty Shakers standing near the East Family Brethren's Shop. On the far right is a Black Shaker sister. Photograph courtesy of Shaker Village of Pleasant Hill, KY.

Although the number of Black Shakers continued to be fairly modest in the first decades of life at Pleasant Hill, their presence was noted by outsiders, who regularly visited the community to witness the Shaker's peculiar religious habits. One particularly descriptive visitor in 1825 reported that he lingered outside the Meeting House, fearful of the pandemonium within, before finally deciding to enter: "There were about an hundred and thirty worshippers including both sexes, black and white. The females were drawn up in the west end of the Church in ranges of eight abreast and seven or eight deep. The men were drawn up in like manner in the opposite end[;] . . . the blacks of each sex, were arranged indiscriminately in the same ranks, and attired in the same manner with the whites."[31] Although only one account, this visitor's experience speaks to the integrated, inclusive nature of Shaker worship that occurred at Pleasant Hill on a consistent basis throughout the community's existence. If the number of Black persons who found a sense of belonging and community at Pleasant Hill was limited, the meaning and value given to each individual were decidedly profound.

Any assessment of the formative years at Pleasant Hill must recognize the revolutionary decisions undertaken by all who joined the community to level distinctions and live equally as brothers and sisters in the faith. The Shakers' intentional choice to enshrine dependence on one another into their foundational covenants stood in stark contrast to developments in Kentucky and America outside of Pleasant Hill in the early nineteenth century. Again, the particular conditions of the Kentucky Revival provided the context in which a few white enslavers made the decision to forsake the prerogatives of mastery. As slavery tightened its grip on Kentucky and the nation throughout the first half of the nineteenth century, and as white Southerners increasingly defended the institution as a "positive good," it was exceedingly rare that a white enslaver would even consider joining Pleasant Hill. Although many records have been lost, on only one other instance was this known to have occurred. In March 1855, certainly a very different time and place in history, one Archibald Weatherford arrived at Pleasant Hill "with his wife Rachel and four children, namely, John, William, Nancy Ann and Mary Elizabeth, also two black persons, Simon and Nancy," and all their household furniture. What exactly had befallen Archibald Weatherford was never made clear. A short four months later he departed the North Lot and "took his two blacks from the West Lot, Simon and Nancy."[32]

In 1871, Sister Hortency Hooser, a Believer who had joined the community in 1809, offered a rather operatic explanation of the village's evolution and growth throughout the nineteenth century. "I have watched the rise and progress of Pleasant Hill from my childhood up, for sixty-two years," Hooser began. She continued: "I saw the brethren, with their own industrious hands, fell the sturdy oaks and maples, right here, where our large and commodious dwellings now stand and have stood for many long years . . . and then, by giving their hearts to God and putting their hands to work, they wrought wonders in this land."[33] If Hooser can be forgiven for waxing poetic about the beauty and awe-inspiring faith required by the Shakers to build their utopia in the face of impending decline, other observers throughout the years have similarly been impressed by the community's industriousness and productivity. Thomas Clark, writing in the late 1960s, noted that whatever "their Kentucky neighbors thought about the strangeness of Shaker religious practices and social philosophy, they were thoroughly convinced that the Believers were industrious, ingenious, and orderly." More recently, scholarship on the "Shaker fever" that gripped America during the mid–twentieth century has explored how notions of thrift, independence, and self-sustainability came to be ingrained in conceptions of Shaker industry and economy. Without a doubt, these notions are thoroughly ensconced in traditional narratives of Shaker history that have not changed a great deal since Clark wrote. Pleasant Hill "proved itself a thrifty, progressive, agricultural body," he concluded. "For the area the society was an excellent farm demonstration community as well as a religious society."[34]

These conceptions of Pleasant Hill's economic development are not so much incorrect as they are myopic. The tendency to focus on individual exertions, thriftiness, and ingenuity fit well within a constellation of ideas that recognizes the Shakers' unique contributions and qualities that allowed them to transform a small patch of central Kentucky into "heaven on earth." Situating the genius of their rapid industrial and economic growth in the first half of the nineteenth century as somehow distinct from the larger development of Kentucky and America also contributes to a sense of "otherness" that has long characterized how the Shakers have been portrayed. In other words, the Shakers are seen as exceptional and somehow apart from and above the economic concerns that dominated life for other Kentuckians in the early to mid–nineteenth century.[35] In the case of Pleasant Hill, however, this "exceptional" representation does not withstand close scrutiny. The community, in fact, was closely interested and involved in most of the important economic developments of the day: internal improvements and transportation networks; expanding markets in the US South and West; the mechanization of trades and industrial pursuits; and, notably, the exploitation of enslaved labor.

At first glance, such a portrayal might seem to contradict one of the Shakers' core philosophical underpinnings—the commitment to communal ownership of all Shaker property. Although there certainly were some exceptions and small amounts of personal property were maintained by individual Shakers on occasion, all covenanted members of Pleasant Hill enjoyed a share in the community's wealth. The desire for individual gain and profit, therefore, was uncommon at Pleasant Hill, and it was rare for Shaker brothers and sisters to exchange currency or other goods with one another. Without question, this rejection of the stockpiling of individual and familial wealth placed the Shakers squarely at odds with the vast majority of Kentuckians in the mid–nineteenth century. The same cannot be said, however, regarding the community's economic relationship to the outside world. It is apparent that the Pleasant Hill Shakers understood and in many cases mastered the market dynamics of capitalism in early nineteenth-century America. The community appointed trustees to oversee legal contracts and conduct business in the name of the Society of Believers, and trade deacons were appointed to sell an assortment of goods in distant markets. At the same time, the community celebrated the profits realized from their agricultural and industrial pursuits, and the accumulation of large amounts of land and the construction of immense dwellings were sources of great pride.[36]

Like many other central Kentucky agricultural communities in the mid–nineteenth century, Pleasant Hill was intimately concerned with the networks of rivers and roads that connected the Bluegrass to the eastern seaboard and the markets of what was considered the US Southwest at the time. Pleasant Hill's economic growth, especially its flourishing in the 1840s and 1850s, was closely linked to the community's ability to efficiently transport its wares to distant markets along the Kentucky, Ohio, and Mississippi Rivers. By 1825 at the latest, the community had sent trustees to the Crescent City laden with goods. By the mid–nineteenth century, these expeditions had become annual voyages, and Pleasant Hill established a well-known reputation throughout the Deep South. In 1856, a newspaper from East Feliciana Parish, Louisiana, advertised forty-eight varieties of garden seeds, "all warranted fresh and genuine . . . by the Society of Shakers, Pleasant Hill, Ky."[37] In addition to trading in New Orleans, the Pleasant Hill Shakers also frequented markets in St. Louis, Memphis, and Natchez, all along the Mississippi River, a route that unquestionably placed them squarely within the burgeoning slave economy of the old Southwest.

One specific item that caused the Shakers some level of apparent consternation because of its connection to enslaved labor was cane sugar. In 1858, for instance, the community produced at least two hundred gallons of molasses to replace their reliance on purchased sugar. Although a substantial beginning, this was a pittance compared how much sugar Pleasant Hill consumed: during the spring of 1856, the community partitioned 6,788 pounds of sugar among its 222 residents. Molasses could replace some purchased sugar in the Pleasant Hill diet, aligned with Believers' antislavery beliefs, and provided a small chance to reduce their dependence on the products of enslaved labor, but, in the end, any lasting uneasiness was often wiped away by economic necessity. Writing in September 1857, the farm deacon at Pleasant Hill noted that the community was producing fruit preserves, another pillar of the Pleasant Hill economy, so quickly that it constantly ran out of sugar. We "are making preserves so fast," he noted, "that we are difficulted [*sic*] to keep ourselves in sugar this is the 3rd trip we have had to Lexington for sugar in the course of one week."[38]

As evidenced by the purchase of sugar in Lexington, it was not necessary for the Shakers to travel to distant markets to interact closely with the hallmarks of slavery. Trips to markets in Harrodsburg, Danville, Louisville, and Lexington were made weekly, if not daily, in the mid–nineteenth century as the Shakers expanded their commercial ties throughout central Kentucky. By the 1840s and 1850s, Pleasant Hill was well known throughout the region for its fruit preserves and other commodities, and it also sold fresh fruit on occasion as well. A publication at the end of the nineteenth century recalled that prior to the 1860s the Pleasant Hill Shakers were one of the select few who "had been pretty large growers of berries." In fact, three Shaker brothers were fixtures of the Lexington market who "always stopped their wagon on Cheapside in front of Wm. Wilson's drug store." At least one of them was "an inimitable story-teller . . . [who] could always sell berries and amuse the crowd."[39] With such a reputation in a city housing a notorious slave market, it is obvious that the Shakers were aware that involvement in the larger regional economy, even if they did not explicitly note its influence, was impossible to separate from tacit and implicit acceptance of slavery in those same circles.

In any event, the suffocating closeness of slavery in nearby Lexington would hardly have come as a shock to the Pleasant Hill community. In October 1836, an elder visiting Pleasant Hill from the Mount Lebanon community described a scene for other eastern Shaker leaders "which may be interesting to some of my good friends who have never witnessed such things." After a number of horses and mules had passed along the turnpike through the village one afternoon, an altogether different scene met his eyes the next day:

> I turned my eyes to the window and discovered another drove coming; but it was not a drove of mules, nor of horses. Neither was it a drove of hogs, sheep or goats, nor any kind of fowls. But it was a drove of human creatures, whose color subjects them (as the laws of this State are) to perpetual bondage, and to be sold as horses, mules or cattle. The number of this drove I did not think to count, until the fore end had proceeded past the meetinghouse, and out of my sight; but I learned that

there were between 50 and 60, composed of men, women and children; some tied or chained together. Such a sight is sufficient to shock human nature, and is a striking evidence of the depravity of the human race.

Within a week, this scene would be repeated: "Again on the next Sabbath afternoon, after the public meeting was over, another drove appeared— the fore part was composed of 15 female slaves, and one male that was loose, and 5 males that were chained together. Connected with these was a large covered waggon, drawn by 5 mules, probably loaded with Negros and their rations &c."[40] Although the regularity with which slave coffles passed through Pleasant Hill can only be hinted at in this account, it is striking that no other known sources by Pleasant Hill Shakers mention these two coffles or any others that passed their doors.

The Pleasant Hill Shakers' failure to directly confront the implications of their involvement in the national slave economy or the presence of enslaved human beings in their midst is both confounding and frustrating. There are several possible explanations for the absence of such commentary, although all of them are speculative. First and foremost, it is certainly possible that material with such content has been lost or remains to be uncovered. As discussed later in this essay, there certainly were moments when Pleasant Hill Shakers commented on the inhumanity of slavery in the abstract and chastised outsiders for how they treated the enslaved and profited from slave trading. Another possibility is that the authors of Shaker letters and journals considered the institution of slavery to be such an intrinsic part of larger society that it hardly warranted mention. These Shaker men and women, after all, were products of Kentucky and surrounding states and had been raised in a time and place where the trappings of slavery were ubiquitous. A third and far less pleasant explanation is that the Shakers themselves were more involved in the institution than has often been portrayed.

In April 1868, Shaker brother James Levi Ballance included a rather stunning entry in his immaculately detailed personal journal. Last "Thursday Charles Crutcher quit tending our grist mill and moved over in Jessamine Co.," Ballance noted, a rather surprising turn since Crutcher "has been tending the mill for a great many years." "We hired him in 1833 to work on the farm and drive a 6 horse team," Ballance continued. He "followed farming some 10 or 12 years [and] the most of the time since that he has tended our grist mill." The practice of hiring additional farm labor would become more common in the late nineteenth century as Pleasant Hill's population declined, but in the early decades of the nineteenth century it was also an option the community utilized to complete specific work projects, especially those that required special skills. Shockingly, however, Ballance concluded his entry for the day: Crutcher "is a yellow man, formally belonged to Thomas Croucher [*sic*], he was a good miller and with all and [*sic*] honest man, that is said to be uncommon for a miller."[41] It appears that Charles Crutcher was one of several enslaved persons whom Pleasant Hill had been in the habit of hiring from white enslavers. In April 1857, Ballance hinted at the broader pattern of slave hiring at Pleasant Hill. "Last Saturday . . . Sally Croucher [*sic*] departed this life," he wrote. "She lived over Jessamine County for the last 24 years. We have been in the habit of hireing her black men. We have 4 of them. She is 65 years of age."[42] While most of his journal is written in this matter-of-fact tone, the casual nature with which Ballance recorded this fact is revealing, and it is possible that more enslaved persons were hired at Pleasant Hill than just those enslaved by Sally Crutcher.

The practice of slave hiring was a fact of life in central Kentucky and a favorite tactic of white enslavers looking to turn a quick profit, but it is striking that the Pleasant Hill community participated in this endeavor.[43] Scattered references to "hirelings" and "hired Negroes" appear in Shaker writings, although often with little further explanation than to relate that a task was completed. Pleasant Hill's existing account books are also incomplete, and in some cases it is not clear whether payment for services was rendered to the laborer or to a white enslaver.[44] In any case, by at least as early as 1816 the Pleasant Hill Shakers were relying on hired Black laborers to perform tasks that were often quite dangerous. In September 1816, "a hired black man [was] blasting out our mill race" before "the blast took fire unexpectedly to him and hurt him badly."[45] Charles Crutcher also suffered severe injuries in 1853 while tending the grist mill. Crutcher "whirled around the shaft with the velocity of mill gearing and [was] horribly mangled and bruised," the Shakers noted, "tho not killed, before the mill could be stopped."[46] Although the extent of slave hiring at Pleasant Hill remains unclear, it is certain that the community benefited from and exploited the labor of enslaved persons throughout the early and mid–nineteenth century—much the same as other white Kentucky agriculturalists.

Viewed in totality, Pleasant Hill's engagement with the state and national slave economy in the mid–nineteenth century is difficult to reconcile with the Shakers' avowed commitment to equality enshrined in the covenant. John Rankin, a South Union Shaker writing early in the nineteenth century, posed a series of questions regarding slavery that undoubtedly also were debated by the Shakers at Pleasant Hill. "Shall money or property which has been obtained by the sale of Negro slaves be refused or accepted by the Church of Christ?" It was a difficult question, but not one that long plagued Pleasant Hill because very few white enslavers joined the community. The more difficult choice to make, Rankin assumed, would involve the use of such things as coffee, sugar, and the other products of enslaved labor: "How far removed from the sweat and blood of the slave must money or property be, in order to render such money or property acceptable to the Church?"[47]

In May 1857, several Pleasant Hill Shakers noted what surely must have been one of the rarest things that they witnessed during their lives. "A company of Negroes, thirty four in number . . . passed thro' this place," the East Family deaconess and several others recorded. Although the Shakers had certainly seen slave coffles pass through their midst, this procession was different. According to the Shaker writers, "Wm. Thomson, one of our near and best neighbors had manumitted [them] for the purpose of sending them to Liberia . . . that happy land of freedom, which they could not find in the renowned state of Kentucky which boasts so highly [of] liberty and human rights!"[48] Perhaps more than anything, this brief lamentation of the limits of freedom in Kentucky reminds us of two important facts. First, the antislavery sentiment that did exist in Kentucky in the 1850s was quite limited, and ideas such as colonization still held sway over many prominent figures from the era.[49] Second, for all of the Pleasant Hill community's compromises with the economics of slavery, at heart it detested slavery and did include Black Shakers as full and equal members throughout its existence. One Pleasant Hill journalist remembered upon the death of one formerly enslaved man that they had hired for years that he "was a slave, and being hired by Believers received faith . . . and confessed his sins on the 15th of Oct 1839. . . . [W]e continued to hire him, that he might have the opportunity of spiritual instruction, and obey his faith."[50] As Kentucky and the nation moved closer to a war that would be fought over slavery, Pleasant Hill would have many more chances to prove exactly where it stood on the issue of slavery and its aftermath.

To be clear, it would be incorrect to label the Pleasant Hill Shakers as abolitionists. As should be obvious, they fully participated in the state's slave economy and of their own accord did essentially nothing to end the institution of slavery within Kentucky. This can be explained largely through the Shakers' conscious decision to remove themselves from the "World" and to abrogate involvement in the political sphere. Although there were many exceptions, and this isolation was hardly total, the Shakers for the most part focused on improving life within the community and pursuing the path of their faith. From this perspective, Pleasant Hill committed itself to perfecting life only within the community; reformation of the "World," then, was something that would come through the dissemination and acceptance of the Shaker faith instead of through a radical transformation of the political, social, cultural, and economic systems that dominated life outside of Pleasant Hill.[51] Perhaps just as important, the Pleasant Hill Shakers defined equality within their community through an individual's dedication to the Shakers' interpretation of Christianity. This equality was open to all who believed, as evidenced by the diverse individuals who called Pleasant Hill home, but there was never a conscious effort to proselytize specific racial or ethnic groups simply because they were oppressed in the "World."[52]

It would be more apt to characterize the Pleasant Hill community as *emancipationists,* a term often applied to those who accommodated the evils of slavery but still spoke out against the institution for one reason or another.[53] Given their removal from the "World" in so many aspects of their life, it is unsurprising that the Pleasant Hill Shakers made few public proclamations against slavery. In private journals, however, scattered references recognized the inhumanity of the institution. In January 1884, one Shaker brother reported the death of a local Harrodsburg merchant, Albert Roberts, in stark terms: "He was once an awful Negro Buyer & trader. He will now get the reward of his doings."[54] Beyond these occasional mentions, however, far and away the strongest example of the Shakers' emancipationist worldview was the manner in which they lived within the community. After all, the Shakers at Pleasant Hill did emancipate enslaved persons and live alongside them and free people of color as equals. When considered alongside other Kentuckians who manumitted enslaved persons and sent them out of state or out of the country entirely, clearly the Shakers were a people apart.

In 1844, one travel writer clearly noted this difference when he reported that other "Kentuckians speak evil of them [Shakers] without cause" due to this interracial harmony at Pleasant Hill. The Shakers, he continued, "in their midst, all free, wealthy and happy, are an everlasting reproach upon them and their accursed slavery system."[55] This equality, it is apparent, was well and truly felt by Black Shakers at Pleasant Hill. Charlotte Tann, a free Black woman who joined another Shaker community in 1810 before later settling at Pleasant Hill, delivered a powerful testimony in 1841 regarding her membership within the Society of Believers: "And I am thankful I was called into the gospel when I was a child, and I am also thankful I can say, that I never turned my back on the way of God although I have had some very trying scenes of trouble and distress to pass through, yet I have been able, by the mercy and charity of God and the help of my good Ministry and Elders, to hold and keep my relation to the people of God thus far."[56] Tann would remain a dedicated Shaker at Pleasant Hill for more than three decades after providing her testimony, ultimately passing away an honored sister in 1875.

Although it was rare for the Shakers to speak out publicly against slavery, one noted exception occurred in October 1858 when Brother James Levi Ballance spent "5 days . . . attending court as a witness for the commonwealth against Samuel Bayley for the abuse of his slaves." The very fact that Bayley was even brought to trial suggests that his behavior must have been uniquely abhorrent, and there must have been some level of community support for the legal actions taken against the enslaver. Nevertheless, Ballance's participation in the trial should not be taken lightly, and such actions undoubtedly would have placed the community at odds with many of their slaveholding neighbors, especially as the national crises over slavery deepened, war crept closer, and violent outbursts over the institution occurred more regularly. On October 18, Ballance reported that "this evening it was decided they gave [Bayley] the Negro man Charles, the Commonwealth took the woman Melinda and her child. Last July Court he [Bayley] was indicted before the grand jury and the slaves taken away from him and hired out until court."[57] The outcome likely pleased Ballance because he had previously recorded his thoughts about how the courts in Kentucky were largely prejudiced against Black Kentuckians. Commenting on the hanging of five men in June 1854, the Shaker brother opined that "another negro . . . has not had his trial yet. I suppose he will be hung as sure as he has his trial."[58]

As the nation moved toward the Civil War, the Pleasant Hill Shakers' emancipationist outlook placed them at odds with most of their white neighbors in central Kentucky, who either sympathized with the South or evinced a peculiar brand of pro-slavery Unionism.[59] Much like other Kentuckians at the time, the Shakers were keenly aware that slavery was at root the cause of the sectional conflict. As early as 1856, one Shaker brother worried that the election that year would "terminate in social war before it is settled. There has been considerable blood shed in the territory of Kansas already on the slavery question," he concluded.[60] As dedicated pacifists, the Shakers abhorred any act of violence, but they seemed especially distraught by the possibility of a war that threatened to destroy civil society. "The whole country is at present greatly agitated from one end to the other, on the question of negro slavery," commented one Shaker in August 1861. It "is certainly the most singular and sad spectacle that has ever been witnessed since the creation of the world." By the end of 1861, the same individual decried the "uncivil war that has broken out in this most favored land" because of the South's "plea [that] their cherished institution of slavery" was endangered by the election of 1860.[61] After the exhausting events surrounding the Battle of Perryville, James Levi Ballance was even less forgiving and denounced the Confederacy as the "wickedest and most ungodly rebellion that ever took place. . . . It is nothing but demagodism [sic]."[62]

The building sense of dissatisfaction and anger toward the Confederacy evinced by the Shakers was in stark contrast to the feelings of the majority of white Kentuckians, who chafed under federal policies that increasingly came to focus on emancipation as a chief war aim. In March 1862, Pleasant Hill celebrated a letter from the South Union Shaker community that gave an "account of their deliverance by the Federal Army, from the dominion of the Southern Confederacy by whose armies they had suffered much affliction and oppression." By October, Pleasant Hill would feel the effects of feeding and supplying of Confederate troops that were making their way to Perryville, an action the Shakers undertook out of Christian charity—but also out of obligation. To "refuse it [forage and meals] we lay ourselves liable to arrest and punishment," the Shakers noted. "And there is danger of arousing the lion of Secessia, which would be like carrying firebrands over a magazine that is under our feet. Ho! For Southern Rights! Liberty! and Freedom!" Although major Confederate armies would not occupy Kentucky after 1862, widespread guerilla violence still sometimes plagued the Shakers. In October 1864, "a band of five [Confederate] guerrillas one of whom was a runaway Shaker boy (Sam Berry) attacked and robbed the stage at the bridge by our mill dam . . .

[and] carried off two of our best horses that happened to be in the crowd."[63] By war's end, therefore, the Shakers were well prepared for the waves of racial violence perpetrated by irregular units and Southern sympathizers that would wreak havoc on central Kentucky.

The campaigns of racial terror carried out in the aftermath of the Civil War by enraged whites against Black Kentuckians and their white supporters in pursuit of white supremacy are well documented.[64] Given Pleasant Hill's known emancipationist beliefs, the fact that Black Shakers had lived and worked within the community as equals to whites for decades and that a number of Blacks who were not Shakers were hired and compensated for their labor, it is unsurprising that the Shakers were targeted by these marauding whites. Yet although the Shakers were threatened fairly regularly to fire their Black laborers, it was rare that any white Shakers suffered actual violence from these brigands. In April 1865, "a band of highway robbers 6 in number" broke into the community's post office and wantonly fired at anyone they saw before being chased off, but this was the exception to the rule. Black laborers, however, often faced much worse violence. In March 1866, two Black laborers hired by the West Lot Family were shot by "some drunken outlaws and villains." In July 1868, "18 or 20 scamps called at Theopheles['s] house and took him and his wife out of their beds and whipped them" because the Black couple refused to admit knowing who burned a white man's property. Theophclcs was a "black man we have hired here to carry on blacksmithing and a very honest man."[65] These nighttime visits would continue well into the 1870s, and the Ku Klux Klan was a well-known presence at Pleasant Hill for many years.

Despite the very real threats that the community faced at the hands of these bands of whites intent on enforcing a strict interpretation of white supremacy in which Black people had no rights, Pleasant Hill continued to hire and support Black laborers in the decades after the Civil War. In September and December 1869, threats were left at the Shaker Post Office "stating among other things that if we did not dismiss our Negroes he would burn us out by G—d—, we shall see." As "barking dogs seldom" bite, the Shakers responded, "we shall wait before sending them away."[66] Throughout the remainder of the nineteenth century, hired Black Kentuckians remained an important part of the workforce at Pleasant Hill. In March 1884, Brother Henry Daily sadly reported that "John Acew a yellow man [mulatto] departed this life about 2 o'clock this morning." According to

Daily, Acew had "been working for the Shakers for about 50 years or more. He was a carpenter. He was a good clever hand who we might trust."[67] As the population of Shakers declined, in fact, the percentage of individuals living at Pleasant Hill who were Black likely increased in the final decades of the nineteenth century. By 1890, one Shaker brother's census reported that roughly 20 percent of the non-Shakers who resided at Pleasant Hill as tenants and laborers were Black.[68] The emancipationist worldview that set the Shakers apart from their neighbors during the Civil War and Reconstruction continued to be a strong influence within the community to the very end of its existence in the early twentieth century.[69]

No Pleasant Hill Shaker's life better illustrates the conundrum of slavery within the society than that of Jonah Crutcher. Born an enslaved person in Hardin County in 1817, Crutcher first came to Pleasant Hill in the 1830s around the same time as Charles Crutcher. While both men were enslaved by Sally Crutcher, it is unclear if they were related. After his arrival at Pleasant Hill, Jonah would spend the next twenty-three years of his life as a hired hand whose labor was worth approximately $75 annually paid to his white enslaver. Census records and various Shaker sources noted that Crutcher served as both a farmer and a teamster at Pleasant Hill, common occupations within the community that were filled by Shakers and non-Shakers alike throughout the nineteenth century. Shaker account books regularly noted the payments made to Sally Crutcher and later to Polina Campbell after Sally's death in January of each year for Jonah's services. In 1859, however, Campbell decided that Jonah would be "sold south" instead of hired out by the year. The Shakers quickly took the opportunity to purchase Jonah from Polina Campbell for the sum of $875, an action that on the surface appears strange. "He was a slave," one Shaker recounted, "and being hired by Believers, received faith in their testimony and confessed his sins on the 15th of October 1839." And as he "continued to be a faithful Believer, we continued to hire him, that he might have the opportunity of spiritual instruction and obey his faith" until he was purchased in early 1859. For the last two years of his life, Crutcher would "enjoy a privilege in the gospel on equal terms with the rest of us, which he did & continued faithful until the day of his decease."[70]

The portrait of Pleasant Hill and its relationship to slavery that has emerged in this essay, encapsulated in the experience of Jonah Crutcher, is likely confusing and confounding to twenty-first-century Americans. It seems rather simple to delineate a binary between the immorality and evil of slavery and enslavers, on the one hand, and the hopeful promise of individual freedom and self-autonomy that are inherent rights of all human beings, on the other. Pleasant Hill's history, however, complicates this comparison and provokes a host of questions that do not have easy answers. Founded upon the principles that all Shakers enjoyed an equal standing within the Society of Believers, Pleasant Hill was undoubtedly one of the earliest and longest-lasting biracial communities to form in early Kentucky.[71] It was also a place where the formerly enslaved and their enslavers lived alongside each other as equals—something that was unprecedented in Kentucky. At the same time, Pleasant Hill fully participated in the state's economy, which was powered and driven by the institution of slavery at every turn. When Charlotte Tann provided her moving testimony, the Shakers were paying Sally Crutcher annually for the labor of Jonah Crutcher. The claims made by the Shakers in 1859 that they had hired Crutcher for so many years so that he might continue in the faith are touching, but they must be considered alongside the hire of other individuals who never joined the community, such as Charles Crutcher. And yet despite their obvious economic connection to slavery through the hiring of enslaved persons and the regular trading trips to markets in the old Southwest, the Shakers were unabashed emancipationists who consistently decried the existence of slavery and the demoralizing effect it had on individuals, Kentucky, and the nation. Seemingly at odds with themselves, the Shakers provide yet another example of how insidious and parasitic slavery was and of its ability to infiltrate and taint seemingly every aspect of life in Kentucky.

Acknowledgments

The author acknowledges the work of Larrie Curry, Randy Folger, Vickie Cimprich, Aaron Genton, Christian Goodwillie, Carol Medlicott, Rebekah Roberts, Holly Wood, and Sarah Porter, whose tireless research and dedication to the Shaker legacy in central Kentucky have been invaluable and continue to inspire.

Notes

1. For a brief overview of Anthony Chosen's life, see Pleasant Hill Journal, July 1, 1846–March 14, 1853, Harrodsburg Historical Society (HHS) Collection,

Harrodsburg, KY, p. 163. Credited to Zachariah Burnett, the entries for May 15 and 16, 1849, in this journal are mainly about Anthony Chosen. For more detail on the emancipation of Anthony Chosen, see Family Journal, Book A, Kept by Order of the Deaconess of the East House, January 1, 1843 October 19, 1871, vol. 4 of Bohon Shaker Collection (hereafter Shaker Collection), p. 60, Filson Historical Society, Louisville, KY.

2. For a complete description of Chosen's funeral, see Spiritual Journal, November 3, 1846–May 4, 1867, vol. 6 of Shaker Collection, pp. 137–39.

3. Spiritual Journal, November 3, 1846–May 4, 1867, vol. 6, of Shaker Collection, pp. 137–39.

4. John Meacham, Benjamin Seth Youngs, and Issachar Bates were the three missionaries tasked with taking the Shaker gospel to the western states in early 1805 in response to reports of ongoing revivals and camp meetings filled with embodied religious experiences. The charged religious atmosphere they found in Kentucky proved to be fertile ground for their message. For the most influential Shaker text on these revivals, see Richard McNemar, *The Kentucky Revival; or, A Short History of the Late Extraordinary Outpouring of the Spirit of God in the Western States of America* (New York: Edward O. Jenkins, 1846). On the development of Shakerism amid competing denominational elements, see the following articles by Douglas L. Winiarski: "Shakers and Jerkers: Letters from the 'Long Walk,' 1805, Part I," *Journal of East Tennessee History* 89 (2017): 90–110; "Shakers and Jerkers: Letters from the 'Long Walk,' 1805, Part II," *Journal of East Tennessee History* 90 (2018): 84–105; and "Seized by the Jerks: Shakers, Spirit Possession, and the Great Revival," *William and Mary Quarterly* 76, no. 1 (January 2019): 111–50. In general, historians have written widely about the Second Great Awakening. For specific works related to Kentucky and the Shakers, see Carol Medlicott, *Issachar Bates: A Shaker's Journey* (Hanover, NH: University Press of New England, 2013); John B. Boles, *The Great Revival: Beginnings of the Bible Belt* (Lexington: University Press of Kentucky, 1972); Dickson D. Bruce Jr., *And They All Sang Hallelujah: Plain-Folk Camp-Meeting Religion, 1800–1845* (Knoxville: University of Tennessee Press, 1974); Diane Sasson, *The Shaker Spiritual Narrative* (Knoxville: University of Tennessee Press, 1983); and Richard C. Traylor, *Born of Water and Spirit: The Baptist Impulse in Kentucky, 1776–1860* (Knoxville: University of Tennessee Press, 2015).

5. Quite a bit has been written about the Shakers in America. For foundational works produced by the Shakers themselves, see Benjamin Seth Youngs, *The Testimony of Christ's Second Appearing; Containing a General Statement of All Things Pertaining to the Faith and Practice of the Church of God in This Latter-Day* (Lebanon, OH: Press of John McLean, 1808); Rufus Bishop and Seth Youngs

Wells, comps., *Testimonies of the Life, Character, Revelations, and Doctrines of Our Ever Blessed Mother Ann Lee* (Hancock, MA: J. Talcott and J. Deming, 1816); John Dunlavy, *The Manifesto; or, A Declaration of the Doctrine and Practice of the Church of Christ* (1818; reprint, New York: Edward O. Jenkins, 1847); and Richard McNemar, *A Review of the Most Important Events Relating to the Rise and Progress of the United Society of Believers in the West* (Union Village, OH, 1831). For the most important and influential scholarly account of the sect, see Stephen J. Stein, *The Shaker Experience in America: A History of the United Society of Believers* (New Haven, CT: Yale University Press, 1992). Other works that have influenced this essay include Edward Deming Andrews, *The People Called Shakers: A Search for the Perfect Society* (Mineola, NY: Dover, 1963); Thomas D. Clark and F. Gerald Ham, *Pleasant Hill and Its Shakers* (Harrodsburg, KY: Pleasant Hill Press, 1968); Julia Neal, *The Kentucky Shakers* (Lexington: University Press of Kentucky, 1983); Priscilla J. Brewer, *Shaker Communities, Shaker Lives* (Hanover, NH: University Press of New England, 1986); Priscilla J. Brewer, "'Tho' of the Weaker Sex': A Reassessment of Gender Equality among the Shakers," *Signs* 17, no. 3 (Spring 1992): 609–35; Suzanne R. Thurman, *"O Sisters Ain't You Happy?": Gender, Family, and Community among the Harvard and Shirley Shakers, 1781–1918* (Syracuse, NY: Syracuse University Press, 2002); Glendyne Wergland, *One Shaker Life: Isaac Newton Youngs, 1793–1865* (Amherst: University of Massachusetts Press, 2006); Glendyne Wergland, *Sisters in the Faith: Shaker Women and Equality of the Sexes* (Amherst: University of Massachusetts Press, 2011); Carol Medlicott, *Issachar Bates: A Shaker's Journey* (Hanover, NH: University Press of New England, 2014); and Joseph Manca, *Shaker Vision: Seeing Beauty in Early America* (Amherst: University of Massachusetts Press, 2019).

6. For Zachariah Burnett's attendance at an antislavery speech, see the entry for June 16, 1849, in Pleasant Hill Journal, July 1, 1846–March 14, 1853, HHS Collection. For more information on the antislavery movement in Kentucky, see Lowell H. Harrison, "The Anti-slavery Career of Cassius M. Clay," *Register of the Kentucky Historical Society* 59, no. 4 (October 1961): 295–317; Lowell H. Harrison, *The Antislavery Movement in Kentucky* (Lexington: University Press of Kentucky, 1978); Stanley Harrold, "Violence and Nonviolence in Kentucky Abolitionism," *Journal of Southern History* 57, no. 1 (February 1991): 15–38; Gerald L. Smith, "Slavery and Abolition in Kentucky: 'Patter-rollers Were Everywhere,'" in *Bluegrass Renaissance: The History and Culture of Central Kentucky, 1792–1852*, ed. James C. Klotter and Daniel Rowland (Lexington: University Press of Kentucky, 2012), 75–92; and Harold D. Tallant, *Evil Necessity: Slavery and Political Culture in Antebellum Kentucky* (Lexington: University Press of Kentucky, 2003).

7. The fluidity and mobility of the population at Pleasant Hill are rather surprising given the Shakers' desired separation from the outside world, but by the mid–nineteenth century individuals were coming and going regularly. The consistent influx of new Shakers from across Kentucky and from other states as well as the visits by Shakers from other communities kept Pleasant Hill apprised of local, regional, and national developments. For a detailed list of arrivals and departures during this era, see Gathering Journal, January 6, 1851–October 24, 1868, vol. 8 of Shaker Collection.

8. For a rather fascinating early history of Kentucky roads originally published in 1935 that includes a discussion of the turnpike that ran through Pleasant Hill, see J. Winston Coleman Jr., *Stage-Coach Days in the Bluegrass, 1800–1900* (1935; reprint, Lexington: University Press of Kentucky, 1995). For more recent works, see Neal Owen Hammon, "Early Roads into Kentucky," *Register of the Kentucky Historical Society* 68, no. 2 (April 1970): 91–131; and Karl Raitz and Nancy O'Malley, *Kentucky's Frontier Highway: Historical Landscapes along the Maysville Road* (Lexington: University Press of Kentucky, 2012). The Shakers themselves paid to complete the section of the turnpike through Pleasant Hill, and they were very happy with the end result—even if at times a little wary of the close nature of interactions with outsiders. See Freegift Wells to Ministry at New Lebanon, New York, August 19, 1839, and Benjamin Dunlavy to Isaac Newton Youngs, April 9, 1852, series IV: A, folders 54 and 55, Shaker Manuscripts, Western Reserve Historical Society, Cleveland, OH.

9. M. J. Daviess, "A Familiar Essay on the Cultivation, Uses, &c., of Chinese Sugar Cane," in Robert W. Scott, *Report of the Kentucky State Agricultural Society to the Legislature of Kentucky for the Years 1856 and 1857* (Frankfort, KY: A. G. Hodges, 1857), 287–91.

10. For overviews of slavery in Kentucky, see J. Winston Coleman Jr., *Slavery Times in Kentucky* (Chapel Hill: University of North Carolina Press, 1940); Marion B. Lucas, *A History of Blacks in Kentucky,* vol. 1: *From Slavery to Segregation, 1760–1891* (Frankfort: Kentucky Historical Society, 1992); Tallant, *Evil Necessity;* and James A. Ramage and Andrea S. Watkins, *Kentucky Rising: Democracy, Slavery, and Culture from the Early Republic to the Civil War* (Lexington: University Press of Kentucky, 2012).

11. This essay explores mainly the connections between slavery and Pleasant Hill, but many Black individuals came into contact with the Shaker community as free persons. For a succinct account of all persons of color who were Shakers at Pleasant Hill, see Vickie Cimprich, "Free and Freed Shakers and Affiliates of African Descent at Pleasant Hill, Kentucky," *Register of the Kentucky Historical Society* 11, no. 4 (Fall 2013): 489–523.

12. Shaker covenants were inspired by biblical precedent, and they detailed the Shakers' relationship to God and one another in the new dispensation brought about by the return of the Christ Spirit to the earth. Although most early Shaker covenants were strictly legal documents meant to clarify rights regarding the communal ownership of property, they evolved over time to include a theological explication of the Shaker worldview. For a brief overview of these developments, see Stein, *Shaker Experience in America,* 92–94. Early Shaker publications also spoke to the importance of covenants and their relevance within the larger context of Christian history. For an example from one of the most influential Shaker texts, see Youngs, *Testimony of Christ's Second Appearing,* 505–7.

13. Much of the early history of Pleasant Hill is contained in three manuscript Church Record Books, denominated A, B, and C, which were originally compiled by the community in 1845 to provide a more succinct and readable account of the founding, development, and membership of the Society of Believers in Mercer County. For the texts of the 1806 and 1810 covenants, see Church Record Book B, pp. 7–15, HHS Collection. The quote here is from Church Record Book B, p. 10.

14. Church Record Book A, pp. 23–24, HHS Collection.

15. Church Record Book B, p. 22, HHS Collection. For the text of the 1814 covenant, see Church Record Book B, pp. 16–26, HHS Collection. After the adoption of the Church Covenant in 1814, circumstances required the Shakers to update and strengthen their covenant in 1830 and again in 1844 in response to changing Kentucky laws and a barrage of lawsuits from apostates. Despite these updates, the theological foundation of the covenants remained the basis for communal ownership of property and order within the Society of Believers.

16. James C. Klotter and Craig Thompson Friend, *A New History of Kentucky,* 2nd ed. (Lexington: University Press of Kentucky, 2018), 56–63, 81–83.

17. It was not uncommon for individuals and families to live at Pleasant Hill and other Shaker communities for extended periods of time without officially signing the covenant. In fact, the Shakers established "gathering orders" as early as 1800 in New Lebanon, New York, to assist in the education and cultivation of new and potential converts. These family orders, or groups, allowed for individuals to become more acquainted with Shaker orders and rules to determine whether they truly wanted to sign the covenant and partake in the joint interest. For a succinct overview, see Stein, *Shaker Experience in America,* 54–55, 63, 165, 172, 209–13, 247.

18. For two works that explore links between religion and slavery in the antebellum South, see John Patrick Daly, *When Slavery Was Called Freedom: Evangelicalism, Proslavery, and the Causes of the Civil War* (Lexington: University

Press of Kentucky, 2002); and Lacy K. Ford, *Deliver Us from Evil: The Slavery Question in the Old South* (New York: Oxford University Press, 2009). For some regional examinations of the ties between religion and slavery, see Charles Irons, *The Origins of Proslavery Christianity: White and Black Evangelicals in Colonial and Antebellum Virginia* (Chapel Hill: University of North Carolina Press, 2008); Jewel L. Spangler, *Virginians Reborn: Anglican Monopoly, Evangelical Dissent, and the Rise of the Baptists in the Late Eighteenth Century* (Charlottesville: University of Virginia Press, 2008); and Randolph Ferguson Scully, *Religion and the Making of Nat Turner's Virginia: Baptist Community and Conflict* (Charlottesville: University of Virginia Press, 2008).

19. Another important manuscript that contains some of the earliest surviving records of activity at Pleasant Hill is "The Origin and Progress of the Society at Pleasant Hill." In the Harrodsburg Historical Society Collection, it contains information on early construction, the first families to settle at Pleasant Hill, and more. For references to Daphne in Shaker records, see "The Origin and Progress of the Society at Pleasant Hill," p. 93, HHS Collection; Church Record Book A, p. 83, and Church Record Book C, p. 65, HHS Collection.

20. Deed of Emancipation for Sukey [Wilhite] and Children, May 7, 1821, Archive of Mercer County, KY, Court Records, HHS Collection.

21. Pleasant Hill Ministry to New Lebanon, New York, Ministry, April 12, 1825, series IV: A, folder 53, Shaker Manuscripts.

22. See Church Record Book B, p. 26, HHS Collection. Adam Baty is listed as having signed the Church Covenant in May 1815, with an X marked next to his name to signify that he had departed the community by the time the document was originally compiled in 1845. Baty can also be found among the list of defaulters "prior to Nov. 1845" contained in Church Record Book C, p. 472, HHS Collection. No reason is given for any of the departures in this section of Church Record Book C.

23. "Origin and Progress of the Society at Pleasant Hill," pp. 92, 93, 98, 101, 107, 112; Church Record Book B, pp. 15, 26; Church Record Book C, p. 474: all in HHS Collection.

24. "Origin and Progress of the Society at Pleasant Hill," p. 107, HHS Collection.

25. Maurice Thomas Journal, January 1, 1816–December 31, 1817, vol. 2 of Shaker Collection, p. 97.

26. "Origin and Progress of the Society at Pleasant Hill," pp. 80, 92, 95–96, 103, HHS Collection; Church Record Book C, pp. 69, 71, 81, HHS Collection. See also Cimprich, "Free and Freed Shakers and Affiliates of African Descent," 499–501.

27. See Church Record Book A, p. 106, HHS Collection; Family Journal, Book A, vol. 4 of Shaker Collection, p. 215; and Journal of James Levi Ballance, April 1, 1860–December 31, 1866, vol. 12 of Shaker Collection, p. 23.

28. Family Journal, Book A, vol. 4 of Shaker Collection, p. 79; Church Record Book A, p. 96, and Church Record Book C, pp. 63, 79, HHS Collection.

29. Church Record Book C, p. 87, HHS Collection.

30. Church Record Book C, p. 54, HHS Collection; Edmond Bryant and Micajah Burnett to Elders at Watervliet, NY, August 30, 1841, series IV: A, folder 54, Shaker Manuscripts.

31. "Letters on the Condition of Kentucky," *Richmond (KY) Enquirer,* May 3, 1825.

32. Gathering Journal, January 6, 1851–October 24, 1868, vol. 8 of Shaker Collection, pp. 38–40.

33. Hortency G. Hooser, "Retrospection," *Shaker* 1, no. 10 (October 1871): 78.

34. Clark and Ham, *Pleasant Hill and Its Shakers,* 21, 34; William D. Moore, *Shaker Fever: America's Twentieth-Century Fascination with a Communitarian Sect* (Amherst: University of Massachusetts Press, 2020).

35. For a general and brief discussion of how the "Shaker myth" developed in the mid–twentieth century and its lasting influence, see Stein, *Shaker Experience in America,* 422–32. Although not specific to Pleasant Hill, Stein's analysis sheds light on how the Shaker "ideal" is a "romantic . . . sentimental projection" that contemporary Americans have created for themselves but that falls apart in the face of close examination of the historical record the Shakers left behind.

36. For a few works that have considered the economic development of the Upper South and the interplay between slavery and capitalism, see Jonathan Daniel Wells, *The Origins of the Southern Middle Class, 1800–1861* (Chapel Hill: University of North Carolina Press, 2004); Tom Downey, *Planting a Capitalist South: Planters, Merchants, and Manufacturers in the Southern Interior, 1790–1860* (Baton Rouge: Louisiana State University, 2006); L. Diane Barnes, *Artisan Workers in the Upper South: Petersburg, Virginia, 1820–1865* (Baton Rouge: Louisiana State University Press, 2008); and L. Diane Barnes, Brian Schoen, and Frank Towers, eds., *The Old South's Modern Worlds: Slavery, Region, and Nation in the Age of Progress* (New York: Oxford University Press, 2011).

37. "Catalogue of Garden Seeds at the Clinton Drug Store," *Feliciana Democrat* (Clinton, LA), February 16, 1856.

38. Journal of James Levi Ballance, April 1, 1854–March 31, 1860, vol. 11 of Shaker Collection, p. 204.

39. "History of Strawberry Raising in Central Kentucky," *Lexington Morning Herald,* May 24, 1899. The Shakers' records are packed with references to

raising strawberries. For one example, see Centre Family Journal, 1839–1860, Shaker Village of Pleasant Hill Collection, Harrodsburg, KY. See also Julius P. Bolivar MacCabe, *Directory of the City of Lexington and County of Fayette for 1838 and '39* (Lexington, KY: J. C. Noble, 1838).

40. Mount Lebanon Ministry to Harvard Ministry, October 19, 1836, series IV: B, vol. 8, Shaker Manuscripts.

41. Journal of James Levi Ballance, January 1, 1867–October 31, 1871, vol. 13 of Shaker Collection, p. 53.

42. Journal of James Levi Ballance, April 1, 1854–March 31, 1860, vol. 11 of Shaker Collection, p. 182.

43. On slave hiring in Kentucky, see Lucas, *History of Blacks in Kentucky,* 1:101–17; Keith C. Barton, "'Good Cooks and Washers': Slave Hiring, Domestic Labor, and the Market in Bourbon County, Kentucky," *Journal of American History* 84, no. 2 (September 1997): 436–60.

44. For an example that includes a recorded payment to Sally Crutcher, see Pleasant Hill Account Book, 1842–1849, vol. 26 of Shaker Collection, p. 64.

45. "Origin and Progress of the Society at Pleasant Hill," p. 115, HHS Collection.

46. Family Journal, Book A, vol. 4 of Shaker Collection, p. 42.

47. John Rankin quoted in Andrews, *The People Called Shakers,* 214–15.

48. Family Journal, Book A, vol. 4 of Shaker Collection, p. 171. Such a scene was undoubtedly unusual, and it seems that news of the emancipation of these individuals had spread within the local area before the group passed through Pleasant Hill. Another Shaker brother recalled that these thirty-four individuals had been freed two months earlier "upon the condition of their going to Liberia." He also noted that the group was traveling through "Lex. Cin. Baltimore, etc." on their way to Liberia. See Zachariah Burnett Temporal Journal, September 17, 1853–October 7, 1864, vol. 10 of Shaker Collection, p. 203.

49. Tallant, *Evil Necessity,* 27–68; Smith, "Slavery and Abolition in Kentucky," 87; Klotter and Friend, *A New History of Kentucky,* 104–6.

50. Family Journal, Book A, vol. 4 of Shaker Collection, p. 233.

51. By the late nineteenth century, the Shakers had more directly involved the Society of Believers in reform conversations of the day, but this lessening of sectarian separation represented a different era in Shaker history than the period considered in this essay. See Stein, *Shaker Experience in America,* 304–19.

52. The one exception to this general pattern at Pleasant Hill involved efforts to proselytize and convert a group of Swedish individuals in the mid–nineteenth century. Driven in large part by a Swedish man who came to Pleasant Hill from Bishop Hill, an unrelated communal society in Illinois, Pleasant Hill expended

quite a bit of time and energy in these efforts. Although more than one hundred Swedes initially immigrated to Pleasant Hill, very few stayed permanently. See Clark and Ham, *Pleasant Hill and Its Shakers,* 70–72, 86.

53. See Smith, "Slavery and Abolition in Kentucky," 88.

54. Henry Daily Journal, March 1, 1881–April 30, 1885, vol. 20 of Shaker Collection, p. 351.

55. John Finch to Editor, *New Moral World* (London), February 10, 1844. Finch also noted, incorrectly, that Pleasant Hill had only one Black community member.

56. Charlotte Tann, testimony, in "Declarations or Testimonies of the Inspired Instruments at Pleasant Hill, Ky," series VI: B, vol. 49, Shaker Manuscripts.

57. Journal of James Levi Ballance, April 1, 1854–March 31, 1860, vol. 11 of Shaker Collection, p. 260.

58. Journal of James Levi Ballance, April 1, 1854–March 31, 1860, vol. 11 of Shaker Collection, pp. 11–14.

59. On the secession crisis in the border South, see Michael D. Robinson, *A Union Indivisible: Secession and the Politics of Slavery in the Border South* (Chapel Hill: University of North Carolina Press, 2017). On pro-slavery unionism, see Patrick A. Lewis, *For Slavery and Union: Benjamin Buckner and Kentucky Loyalties in the Civil War* (Lexington: University Press of Kentucky, 2015).

60. Journal of James Levi Ballance, April 1, 1854–March 31, 1860, vol. 11 of Shaker Collection, p. 154.

61. Family Journal, Book A, vol. 4 of Shaker Collection, pp. 230, 236–37.

62. Journal of James Levi Ballance, April 1, 1860–December 31, 1866, vol. 12 of Shaker Collection, p. 92.

63. Family Journal, Book A, vol. 4 of Shaker Collection, pp. 240, 253, 281.

64. For two important studies that have shaped the narrative here, see George C. Wright, *Racial Violence in Kentucky, 1865–1940: Lynchings, Mob Rule, and "Legal Lynchings"* (Baton Rouge: Louisiana State University Press, 1990); and Aaron Astor, *Rebels on the Border: Civil War, Emancipation, and the Reconstruction of Kentucky and Missouri* (Baton Rouge: Louisiana State University Press, 2012).

65. Family Journal, Book A, vol. 4 of Shaker Collection, p. 288; Journal of James Levi Ballance, April 1, 1860–December 31, 1866, vol. 12 of Shaker Collection, p. 217; Journal of James Levi Ballance, January 1, 1867–October 31, 1871, vol. 13 of Shaker Collection, p. 65. Ballance further noted regarding the March 1866 shooting, "I suppose they would have killed both of them but the one that shot through the brest picked up a gun that set near by and broke the stock over them and made them leave the other one was slightly wounded."

66. Ministerial Journal, 1868–1880, vol. 16 of Shaker Collection, pp. 54, 60; and Journal of James Levi Ballance, January 1, 1867–October 31, 1871, vol. 13 of Shaker Collection, pp. 114–15, 122.

67. Journal of Henry Daily, March 1, 1881–April 30, 1885, vol. 20 of Shaker Collection, p. 376.

68. Journal of Henry Daily, May 16, 1889–December 2, 1890, vol. 22 of Shaker Collection, pp. 75–76.

69. It is beyond the scope of this essay to discuss the decline and closing of the Pleasant Hill community by the early twentieth century, although Black laborers remained an important part of the workforce at Pleasant Hill to the very end of the Shaker experience in Mercer County. For general accounts of the last decades at Pleasant Hill, see Clark and Ham, *Pleasant Hill and Its Shakers,* 82–92; Neal, *The Kentucky Shakers,* 78–93; and David Marsich, "'And Shall Thy Flowers Cease to Bloom?': The Shakers' Struggle to Preserve Pleasant Hill, 1862–1910," *Register of the Kentucky Historical Society* 109, no. 1 (Winter 2011): 3–26.

70. Family Journal, Book A, vol. 4 of Shaker Collection, p. 233.

71. For examples of how enslaved persons forged a sense of belonging in the frontier days in Kentucky, see Ellen Eslinger, "The Shape of Slavery on the Kentucky Frontier, 1775–1800," *Register of the Kentucky Historical Society* 92, no. 1 (Winter 1994): 1–23; and Marion B. Lucas, "African Americans on the Kentucky Frontier," *Register of the Kentucky Historical Society* 95, no. 2 (Spring 1997): 121–34.

3

"This Priceless Jewell—Liberty"

The Doyle Conspiracy of 1848

James M. Prichard

In the late summer of 1848, Edward James Doyle, a twenty-two-year-old Irish immigrant, engineered one of the largest slave escape attempts in Kentucky history. More than forty-two of Lexington's "finest slaves" slipped away on the night of August 5 in a desperate bid for freedom. The fugitives rendezvoused at nearby Russell Cave, where Doyle distributed pistols and knives. After declaring "Victory or Death" as their watchword, he led the party northward toward the Ohio River.[1]

News of the escape created intense excitement throughout the Bluegrass region, and a reward of $5,000 was offered for the capture of the runaways. The *Lexington Observer and Reporter* warned, "There are abolitionists in our midst—emissaries from this piratical crew—whose business is to tamper with and run off our slaves."[2] A mass meeting swiftly convened at the courthouse to determine the best method for the "detection and punishment of abolitionists and others in enticing slaves from their owners."[3]

The fugitives were soon being hotly pursued by swarms of armed riders. At least one owner, John Wilmot, was among the party. After marching all night, the fugitives rested in a cornfield before resuming their flight at dawn. The only food they found was raw corn, and some runaways began to tire. Two of them, desperate for food, gave themselves up at Claysville in Harrison County on the morning of August 7 and revealed the whereabouts of the main party. Shortly after that, two other armed runaways were captured nearby.[4]

A ten-man posse led by Dr. Benjamin F. Barkley overtook the remaining runaways on the Germantown Road later that night. Shouting "Charge" and "Fire," the fugitives turned on their pursuers and drove them off after a brisk firefight. John Wilmot later stated that it felt like a "continuous blaze" of gunfire. Elliott Roberts afterward related that the posse faced "a furious attack," while another slave catcher claimed they "fought well & fired often." One pursuer, Charles H. Fowler, was carried away, gravely wounded.[5]

Two fugitives later stated that Doyle attempted to abandon them after the first clash but was forced to remain. The runaways soon made another stand at Walker's Mill in Bracken County. Joseph Duncan, a member of Barkley's party, ordered the fugitives to surrender. They rose from behind a thicket and opened fire. The slave catchers were quickly surrounded by the fugitives but shot their way to safety.[6]

However, these were hollow victories for the runaways, whom Doyle left to their fate. By the dawn of August 8, between three and four hundred pursuers were scouring the woods along the Licking River, while others guarded nearby Ohio River crossings. The remaining runaways soon found themselves completely surrounded. When Presly Coleman and three companions were seized, he shouted, "Victory or Death," and urged his comrades to fight "or all is lost!" After four days of desperate flight, it was all over. One fugitive was killed, and the rest never made it across the Ohio.[7]

Doyle, who had threatened to shoot any deserters, now only thought of saving himself. Posing as a Methodist Circuit Rider, he aroused the suspicions of three pursuers because of his muddy shoes and clothing, and he was seized in present-day Robertson County. Protesting his innocence, he claimed the fugitive slaves had beaten and robbed him. However, numerous captured runaways identified Doyle as their leader. Not long after he was confined in Cynthiana, an angry lynch mob surrounded the Harrison County jail.[8]

Samuel F. January, who commanded the jail guards, armed himself and kept the mob at bay. Although the Kentucky militia had not been activated, General Lucius B. Desha had assumed authority over the pursuit. With the assistance of Dr. Barkley, Desha arranged for Doyle's swift and secret transfer to the Lexington jail.[9]

On August 17, Doyle appeared before two magistrates in Lexington. The witnesses' testimony focused primarily on Doyle's arrest and his identification by the captured fugitives. Jeptha Dissure of Bracken County stated that Doyle "had a down looking countenance when brought before the (captured) negroes."[10]

One Lexington witness revealed that he had seen Doyle conversing with enslaved men in the vicinity of Lexington as early as June. Doyle, who was permitted to cross-exam the witnesses at his arraignment, impressed a *Louisville Morning Courier* journalist by "manifesting not a little quickness of apprehension and smartness in detecting any . . . injustice or error upon the part of the prosecuting attorney or witnesses."[11]

On the night of August 19, Doyle was caught attempting to escape by cutting a hole through the wall of his cell. He was promptly clapped in irons and made no further attempts. He afterward appeared before Judge Richard A. Buckner Jr. in the Fayette Circuit Court on October 9. Ironically, Buckner had presided over the criminal trial of the noted abolitionist duo Reverend Calvin Fairbank and Delia Webster in 1844. Doyle was represented by Samuel Redd Bullock and John C. Breckinridge. Although both men were talented young lawyers, they were also part of the local slave-owning aristocracy. Furthermore, Bullock was the legal agent charged in the recovery of one of the runaways, and Breckinridge's paternal grandmother had five bondsmen in Doyle's party.[12]

Doyle's trial and conviction were swift and sure. After Commonwealth attorney Alexander H. Robertson questioned several witnesses, the case was submitted to the jury without argument. After a few minutes, the jury handed down a verdict of guilty. On October 24, Judge Buckner sentenced Doyle to a twenty-year prison sentence for "Enticing Slaves to Run Away."[13]

By the time Doyle was sentenced, most of the fugitives had been returned to their owners for punishment. However, three fugitives, who were regarded as Doyle's lieutenants, were later tried and convicted of "Insurrection" in the Bracken County Circuit Court. In virtually all accounts of the incident published since then, young Doyle has been portrayed as an abolitionist martyr. At the same time, the three rebel slaves died on the gallows as an "example" to other would-be fugitives.[14]

However, an examination of original court records, the papers of Governors William Owsley and John J. Crittenden, as well as contemporary newspaper accounts tells a different story that, among other key details, places Doyle's motives in a different light. Equally as important, these sources provide a glimpse of how slaveholders viewed both themselves and their human property. They also reveal that enslaved people were able to compel members of the slaveholding elite to recognize their common humanity by demonstrating both their courage and their desire for freedom.

It is doubtful whether the real Edward James Doyle will ever be known because from the moment he arrived in Kentucky, the young Irishman became the subject of controversy. In 1844, Doyle settled in Springfield and requested to be accepted as a candidate for the Dominican Order at nearby St. Rose Priory. Members of the parish originally from Zanesville, Ohio, informed the prior, Father Nicholas Dominic Young, that Doyle had been employed as a hotel waiter in Zanesville. They also reported that Doyle's application for admission to St. Joseph's near Zanesville had been rejected. Nevertheless, it was decided to give the young wanderer a chance. It was here that he apparently adopted the spiritual name "Patrick."[15]

Father Young later recalled that Doyle soon became unpopular with the other novitiates. He claimed that due to Doyle's poor scholarship and propensity for lying, he was dismissed from the order in 1845. Doyle made his way to Bardstown and studied at St. Thomas Seminary, but, Young relates, he was dismissed again for the same conduct.[16]

Alone in a new country that largely scorned Irish immigrants, Doyle apparently attempted to turn the ongoing tensions between American Protestants and Catholics to his advantage. He made his way to Danville, announced that he had rejected the Catholic faith, and applied for admission to Centre College, a Presbyterian institution. He claimed to be the nephew of the late Bishop James Warren Doyle of Ireland. This was a coup that Centre leadership could not resist, and Doyle was duly enrolled in the grammar school.[17]

Doyle was also given a comfortable room in a small dwelling just behind the home of Alexander Sneed, a Presbyterian elder.[18] The president of Centre, Reverend John C. Young, regarded him as a "quiet and inoffensive" student. Soon Doyle began to tell classmates that during a visit to Lexington he had received threatening letters from Catholic priests as well as verbal death threats from individuals who had accosted him on the street. He also claimed that two men had chased him for a considerable distance.[19]

On the evening of March 29, 1846, he informed Mr. Sneed that someone had attempted to break into his room. Later that night the

Sneeds were startled by the sound of a gunshot and ran to Doyle's room. They found the young Irishman in a daze with a bullet hole in the left pocket of his waistcoat. Doyle declared that someone had shot at him through the open window while he was seated at his writing desk.[20]

The incident sparked a lengthy war of words between the Catholic and Presbyterian press. Doyle swore that he was the target of a Catholic assassination attempt not only for his apostasy but because he knew the actual fate of Milly McPherson. This statement would have electrified his Presbyterian benefactors because McPherson, a Kentucky Catholic, had disappeared in 1836 after she charged a priest with seduction.[21]

Reverend Young of Centre College fired the opening shot with his exposé of the "Papal Outrage" in the *Louisville Presbyterian Herald* on May 7, 1846. He declared, "It seems almost incredible that such an outrage should be attempted in a Protestant community." He closed his diatribe by stating: "The Roman priests boast of their authority over their followers. If they choose that the life of a young man shall be safe from assassination, it will be safe; if he shall fall victim to his change of religion, mankind will know who are to be held responsible."[22]

In its responding volley, the *Louisville Catholic Advocate* repeatedly ridiculed Young's charge and hinted the incident was staged by the "Little Shot At." On May 30, the *Advocate* published a letter from Prior Young at St. Rose Priory that described Doyle as an "Irishman of the lowest class" who had been dismissed at St. Rose. He also described Doyle's visit to Springfield not long after the Danville affair. Accompanied by a Centre professor, Doyle had intended to visit St. Rose before May 30 but lost his nerve. He and his companion went instead to the Dominican convent of St. Magdalene and requested that a message be sent to St. Rose.[23]

After a friar arrived at the convent, Prior Young met with Doyle, who declared he was still a Catholic. He also told one of the sisters that he was shot at by Presbyterians because of his Catholic background. Young also claimed that Doyle declared in the Presbyterian professor's hearing that he was a Presbyterian for "only a while."[24] In a letter published in the *Louisville Presbyterian Herald,* Professor Ormond Beatty acknowledged that he had accompanied Doyle to Springfield but denied that Doyle claimed to be a reluctant Presbyterian convert.[25]

Doyle was soon spirited out of Danville and given the position of a colporteur at Versailles. The *Catholic Advocate* sneered at Doyle's new role as a peddler of anti-Catholic tracts and published a letter reportedly from

Doyle to Father James (Vincent) Bullock of St. Rose dated May 15, 1846, at Lexington, where Doyle declared that he remained a devout Catholic who acted as a "mole" to obtain the Protestants' secret code.[26]

Doyle's dual claims to both sides of the controversy might have merely been the result of fear. However, his subsequent conduct increasingly bordered on criminal activity. On April 12, 1848, he was indicted in the Franklin County Circuit Court for stealing a small amount of banknotes and silver in Frankfort. He was found not guilty on April 16 reportedly because he claimed to be temporarily deranged when he committed the theft.[27]

He next appeared in Louisville accompanied by a free man of color. He was soon arrested for attempting to sell his companion back into slavery and confined in the city workhouse on a charge of "Evil Fame"—a charge that testifies to his growing reputation as a criminal or con man. He feigned illness and was transferred to the infirmary, from which he escaped on May 20. The *Louisville Morning Courier* afterward reported that a Louisville official encountered Doyle in Cincinnati, where Doyle boasted about his escape and claimed he now worked as a "Slave Catcher" for Kentuckians seeking to recover their human property.[28]

After reviewing Doyle's conduct since he had come to Kentucky, the *Louisville Morning Courier* concluded on August 14, 1848, after the slave escape that Doyle, had he succeeded, would probably have returned to Lexington and reported the fugitives' whereabouts in order to claim the reward for their capture. The *Courier* declared that "the anti-slavery men should not claim Mr. Doyle as a martyr to their cause."[29]

Ironically, Frederick Douglass would have agreed with this proslavery editor. On August 25, 1848, Douglass declared in his antislavery paper the *North Star:* "In charging the escape of these people to the Abolitionists, those Kentucky wretches breathe an infamous lie. The slaves are not headed by white men, but by themselves—black men. . . . Brave fellows!"[30]

This depiction is further supported by the fact that as Doyle fled through Bracken County, he offered his services as a "slave catcher" to a local resident whose bondman had fled to Ohio. Furthermore, when captured, Doyle was carrying a letter by a free woman of color from Cincinnati that contained instructions to purchase the freedom of her enslaved son. At the same time, he possessed $228 in gold, silver, and banknotes—the fees he had collected from the fugitives.[31]

From the moment the Irishman had stepped foot in Kentucky, he had witnessed slavery on a daily basis. Both priories, St. Rose and St. Magdalene, owned slaves. Alexander Sneed of Danville was, by Kentucky standards, a large slave owner.[32] Based on his conduct in 1848, Doyle apparently sought to increase his income by preying equally on the enslavers, the enslaved, and free persons of color. As Andrew Delbanco notes in *The War before the War,* "Like generations of illegal immigrants, fugitive slaves were both dependent on and exploited by those who aided them."[33]

Doyle's motives were thus far from pure, so the fugitives themselves were the only parties who sought to strike a blow against slavery. Generally speaking, their mass flight was nothing new as large groups of runaways had become common by the 1830s.[34] The fact that the Lexington fugitives armed themselves and clashed with their pursuers was also common with other runaways, whether they were traveling alone or in groups throughout the South.[35] One factor that did place these rebel slaves in a unique light was the fact that several of the owners who claimed them belonged to Lexington's leading families.

Foremost among them was Mary Hopkins Cabell Breckinridge, the matriarch of one of Kentucky's foremost families. The blind, seventy-nine-year-old widow of Senator John Breckinridge, she lived at the family estate, Cabell's Dale. In 1848, she owned forty-four slaves, including five of the fugitives: Wilson, Phillip, Carey, Harry, and Reuben, whose ages ranged between forty-three and seventeen.[36]

Two other fugitives, Jerry and Walker, were owned by Benjamin Gratz, a leading member of Lexington's Jewish community who resided on North Mill Street. A War of 1812 veteran, he was a graduate of the University of Pennsylvania who had settled in Lexington in 1819. In the years that followed, Gratz grew wealthy by engaging in the hemp industry. His bale rope and bagging factory became the largest in the city.[37]

This fifty-six-year-old businessman who served on the board of trustees for Transylvania University was a staunch Whig and well acquainted with Senator Henry Clay. More than thirty-seven slaves labored at his home and hemp factory. An additional thirty-four worked his lands in the neighboring Woodford and Clark Counties.[38]

Gratz's hemp industry rivals, David Lawson and Lawson's business partner John Adolphus Erdman, also had slaves among the fugitives.[39] Other hemp factory owners, Stark Taylor and William Frazer, learned that their slaves Washington and Henry Washington, respectively, were among those confined in the Bracken County jail. So, too, was Anderson, who was claimed by Andrew Caldwell, a Fayette County steam mill operator.[40]

Other prominent Lexington residents enmeshed in the Doyle incident included Henry T. Duncan, a wealthy businessman who owned sixty-six slaves,[41] and Dr. Samuel Annan, a member of the Transylvania Medical College faculty, whose slave T. Myers also languished in jail.[42] A friend of Henry Clay and member of the American Colonization Society, Matthew Thompson Scott, who was a cashier at the Northern Bank of Kentucky, also claimed human property that had been "enticed away" by Doyle.[43]

A valuable house servant, thirty-year-old Harry Slaughter, fled from the residence of Miss Sidney Edmiston, another member of Henry Clay's social circle. She was the forty-nine-year-old niece of Esther Montgomery Morrison, the widow of Colonel James Morrison, one of the wealthiest and most influential residents of early Lexington. Slaughter later recalled that the spinster had very specific qualifications for her male house servants—they must be tall and powerfully built.[44] Slaughter was legally owned by Edmiston's nephew Richard H. Pindell, a young attorney who had helped convict the notorious "slave stealers" Reverend Calvin Fairbank and Miss Delia Webster in 1845. A grandnephew of the Widow Morrison, Pindell was a staunch Whig and friend of Henry Clay. When Miss Sidney caught sight of the six-foot-two Slaughter, she begged her nephew to lend him to her to act as her dining-room servant.[45]

Ironically, another of Doyle's victims was the controversial antislavery advocate Cassius Marcellus Clay. At the time of his father's death, Clay had inherited seventeen slaves. As his antislavery views matured, he set them free in 1844. At the same time, to keep Black families together, he purchased and freed an additional thirteen enslaved people. These steps instantly made him a hero to Northern abolitionists.[46]

However, although Clay was regarded as a firebrand in Kentucky, he was in reality an antislavery moderate who championed a gradual, legal approach to ending the "peculiar institution." At White Hall, his Madison County estate, he still controlled a number of estate slaves held in trust for his children by his brother Brutus. Under Kentucky law, he did not have the legal right to free them.[47] When Clay moved to Lexington around 1839, several trust slaves, including Jack, apparently went with him to serve as his personal servants. Clay gained further national attention when he founded the antislavery newspaper the *True American* in the heart of

Cassius M. Clay Sr. Drawing courtesy of the Filson Historical Society,
Louisville, KY.

the Bluegrass region. A group of Lexington's leading citizens, including Henry T. Duncan, Samuel R. Bullock, and John C. Breckinridge, suppressed the "incendiary" journal in 1845.[48]

With the outbreak of the Mexican War in 1846, Clay raised a company of volunteers and served as a captain in the First Kentucky Cavalry. "Trusty Jack" accompanied Clay to Mexico as an officer's servant and may have been present with the regiment at the celebrated battle of Buena Vista in 1847. Within a matter of months after Clay's return from Mexico, "Trusty Jack" would slip out of Lexington to join Doyle's runaways.[49]

Without question, the wealthy enslavers involved in the Doyle incident were clearly stunned by the "inexplicable behavior" of their once "faithful servants." Convinced that these members of their "black families" had been deluded by Doyle, they took immediate steps to secure their release and return. On August 17, before the ringleaders were formally indicted, four of the fugitives—Bob Walker and Jerry, the property of Ben Gratz; William Frazer's Henry Washington; and Marshall, claimed by the Fayette County farmer Thomas E. Boswell—were released on bail.[50]

On August 21, Gratz and Frazer petitioned Governor William Owsley to pardon their slaves. Both men described Doyle as the only culprit in the affair, and they denied that their fugitives, who had previously been well behaved, had participated in the two armed clashes. Gratz reported that all four were currently confined in Lexington, adding that if his and Frazer's request was granted, they would send the slaves "out of state." As a result of their owners' efforts, Bob, Jerry, Henry, and Marshall were pardoned before the trial began.[51]

On August 25, Henry Clay Pindell, whose brother Richard was out of town, petitioned Governor Owsley on behalf of Harry Slaughter. He contended that Harry had been persuaded to run away in part by Stark Taylor's man Wash, "of notorious bad reputation," who had turned state's evidence and had claimed Harry was a one of Doyle's lieutenants.[52]

Pindell stated that he interviewed several of the released fugitives in jail and that they denied Wash's allegations, claiming that Slaughter, rather than leading the column, had lagged behind because of sore feet. The slave Henry Washington revealed that Harry took no active part in the first skirmish and was not seen during the second.[53]

Pindell confessed that his aunt, Miss Sidney, "was the worst manager of servants in the world," but Harry was the only member of her household who "never gave her a word of impudence." Furthermore, he continued, "it may be proper to add that no negro has ever sustained a higher character than Harry, and he has been especially marked for his respect and deference toward white men—poor as well as rich." He concluded that Doyle had beguiled Slaughter with "such overwrought pictures of the blessings of liberty as few men in bondage could resist."[54]

Slaughter himself later recalled that "I had a good home. Miss Sidney treated me as well as she did her own nephews but there was something lacking—I wanted to be free. I felt that I was a man and that I ought not continue [to be] the chattel of another man. At the same time I had no complaint of my master and mistress, but I wanted to marry my sweetheart as a free man and not a slave."[55]

Slaughter's recollections reflect James Oakes's conclusions in *The Ruling Race:* "Many slaves acknowledged the existence of a good master," but "they preferred freedom to slavery." In his account of his flight for freedom, Slaughter made it clear that he was determined to reach Ohio or die. He related that after he and Shadrack were surrounded by the posse, he shouted, "I will not be taken. The man that kills me is my friend. I'd rather die here and now than go back to slavery."[56]

The reward placed on Slaughter's head proved his shield from serious violence. The big Kentuckian knocked down every man who tried to physically subdue him. Finally, a dignified old gentleman rode up and ordered the fighting to halt. He calmly assured Slaughter that no one would harm him if he came along quietly to Brooksville.[57]

Suddenly a big white man struck Slaughter from behind, and the old man, known as "the Major," drew his pistol. Slaughter related that the Major declared "that if any man attempted to do me [Slaughter] harm while I was his prisoner he would make daylight shine through him." Nearly fifty years later, Slaughter stated, "I never saw a man show more bravery and more true manhood than did the old Major at that moment."[58]

Pindell's petition was supported by a second from George B. Kinkead, a Lexington attorney; a third from Charles W. Castleman, a prominent farmer; and a fourth signed by twenty-one Lexington citizens. Another petition dated August 26 was submitted by Benjamin F. Graves and his sisters, Maria K. Thomas, Fanny C. Hanbro, and Eliza A. Walker. Graves related that Slaughter had originally been owned by their late father, John C. Graves, and they all were raised together. He declared that Harry was never whipped, adding, "We can safely say . . . that we have never known a negro so honest, upright and truthfull [sic]."[59]

Graves stated that he had inherited Harry from his father's estate, that he had employed him in the "hatting trade," and that Harry had been so trusted that he was permitted to travel alone on business to northern Kentucky, Indiana, Virginia, North Carolina, and Tennessee. He also stated that when Harry fled, he left more than a thousand dollars' worth of household silver untouched. In his recollections, Harry revealed that Graves had been forced to sell him to Pindell after Graves's hat factory went out of business.[60]

Ominously, Governor Owsley decided that "the case in my opinion is one not proper for executive interference before trial." He added, "After trial the circumstances may be more fully understood so as to make the executive do what may seem proper in the case."[61]

On August 28, 1848, Slaughter, John Chism's Bill Griffin, Samuel R. Bullock's Jasper, Alexander Prewitt's Anderson (there were two fugitives named "Anderson," the other claimed by Andrew Caldwell), Cassius M. Clay's Jackson Clay, Thomas Christian's Shadrack, and James Wordlaw's Presley Coleman were indicted for "Conspiracy, Insurrection and Rebellion" and "Shooting with Intent to Kill." On September 2, the jury found Shadrack, Slaughter, and Coleman guilty of the first charge. The three were condemned to death by hanging on October 28. Although four of the defendants were acquitted of the first charge, they and the other three still faced a trial on the second charge.[62]

The close of the first trial was followed by a flood of petitions to Governor Owsley and his recently elected successor, John Jordan Crittenden, seeking executive clemency for the "Brooksville seven." In a letter to Crittenden dated September 5, 1848, Cassius M. Clay wrote:

> My trusty slave, Jack, was among the late runaway slaves. . . . It is possible that he may be found guilty of being in the crowd where shooting was done—but no more.
>
> I have raised him and know him to be eminently pacific—he was in Mexico and had every means of escape and did not and now I believe he was enticed away without thought or knowledge of the liabilities which he incurred by being with armed men. . . .
>
> I think public justice ought to be satisfied with the hanging of the four [sic] now condemned, and spare the rest.[63]

Given the severity of the charges, there was every reason to believe that Slaughter and his two companions would die on the gallows. However, Owsley, after reviewing the September 2 trial transcript, pardoned Harry Slaughter on September 6, the governor's last day in office.[64]

On September 7, twenty-four Fayette County citizens petitioned Governor-elect Crittenden on behalf of Thomas Christian's Shadrack. They contended that Shadrack had "heretofore always been considered honest and faithful" and was so trusted that he was once permitted to travel alone to Cincinnati on business for Christian. Without question, they contended, Doyle had led the once faithful servant astray.[65] On September 28, Christian himself petitioned Crittenden and assured him that Shadrack, if pardoned, would be sold out of state.[66]

On September 8, Samuel R. Bullock, one of Doyle's defense attorneys, petitioned Crittenden in his capacity as agent for the T. P. Satterwaite estate. He contended that there was no strong evidence against nineteen-year-old Jasper, whom Bullock owned. He maintained that the youth was regarded by local citizens as "a boy of fine character." If pardoned, he assured the governor that Jasper would be "sold out of the state, never to return."[67]

A petition on behalf of William "Bill" Griffin[68] was submitted to Crittenden by his owner, John Chism, on September 9. The Lexington tailor claimed that Griffin was the only servant he ever owned and that he had been raised from boyhood. He added that Griffin had never misbehaved, and he blamed Doyle for Griffin's conduct.[69]

Chism also enclosed a letter dated September 2 from William R. Fowler, Charles H. Fowler, John B. Fowler, and Elliott Roberts. The father of the gravely wounded Charles, the elder Fowler stated he was instrumental in bringing criminal charges against the fugitives. However, he, his sons, and Roberts stated Griffin was too weak and exhausted to have participated in the fighting, and so they asked that he be pardoned.[70]

On September 11, Alexander E. Prewitt, a Fayette County farmer, submitted a plea for clemency on the prisoner Anderson's behalf. The growing number of petitions and increasing public sympathy for the prisoners brought further results. On September 19, Commonwealth attorney Harrison Taylor dismissed the remaining "Shooting" charge against Jackson Clay, Bill Griffin, Jasper, and Anderson. The four prisoners were ordered to be released into the custody of their respective enslavers.[71]

Additional petitions crowded Crittenden's desk in Frankfort as Presley and Shadrack remained in the shadow of the gallows. Reverend John A. McClung, a Maysville clergyman and historian, acted as the leading defense counsel for the fugitives. On September 22, he advised Crittenden that the Brooksville seven had been randomly selected from the total group of fugitives largely because their masters were slow to reclaim them. He described Presley as a "mere lad" who was undoubtedly influenced by older, more intelligent runaways. He added that the real ringleaders were Harry Slaughter, the five Breckinridge bondsmen, and Gratz's Jerry and Walker.[72]

McClung related that Doyle had promised the fugitives that they would be quietly and safely guided to Ohio. However, many of the fugitives had expressed their concern when the Irishman armed them because they were promised there would be no fighting. McClung also claimed that it was Doyle who gave the command to open fire on their pursuers.[73]

He related that Shad and Presley had made moving appeals to the court before the death sentence was pronounced and that there was widespread sympathy for them throughout Bracken and adjoining counties. McClung reported that between six and seven hundred people, including the presiding judge and the Commonwealth attorney, had just signed petitions requesting clemency for both runaways.[74]

John S. Finley, a wealthy Harrison County farmer, also petitioned the governor on Presley's behalf on September 27. He stated that Presley had been captured with Gratz's and Frazer's runaways. He pointed out that even though all four had resisted capture, Governor Owsley had pardoned all except young Coleman. He also enclosed a letter from his uncle, James Wordlaw, Presley's seventy-two-year-old master. The Fayette County farmer stated that Presley had been his slave for twenty years and had never committed a crime.[75]

Wordlaw also stated that Presley "has been a good slave all the time and appeared satisfied with his condition," adding, "I have never whipped him or caused him to be whipped." He contended that Presley fell under bad influence while visiting his wife in Lexington. The old gentleman declared that he had a "strong desire that [Presley] shall not be hung" and promised that he would "send [Presley] out of the state" if he were pardoned. Wordlaw's petition was supported by another from fourteen Fayette County men.[76]

To one Kentucky historian, the numerous petitions merely revealed that the enslavers were concerned only about preserving the monetary value of their unfaithful servants. However, since 1798 Kentucky law had provided that any master whose human chattel was executed for crime would be reimbursed the full "market value" from the state treasury.[77] Research by John Hope Franklin and Loren Schweninger indicate that the petitioners' motives were undoubtedly more complex and that the comments they made in their pleas reflected the views of many if not most slave owners throughout the South.[78]

Generally, enslavers were surprised, saddened, and angry when members of their "black family" broke faith with them, especially when their trusted servants fled when there had been no "unjust or injurious treatment" of them.[79] A plantation mistress was stunned when her favorite female slave "deserted" her. She lamented that the woman was "so honest, so faithful, so truthful, so devoted to my interests that I trusted everything to her and now I have to depend on those so entirely different from her."[80] Runaways, most enslavers believed, were never motivated by mistreatment and therefore had to have been "enticed" by "evil minded persons."[81] Jesse Williams, a Kentucky farmer, was convinced that his runaways "were conducted [away] by some villain to be sold" for his personal profit.[82]

Virtually all enslavers, according to Franklin and Schweninger, "considered themselves kind, God fearing, humane masters. Admittedly, it was sometimes necessary to sell black children away from parents, wives away from husbands and older slaves away from friends and kin. Admittedly, it was necessary to correct recalcitrant slaves as one would discipline one's own children. These actions, however, were done not out of malice or caprice but out of necessity. . . . Invariably owners looked upon themselves as decent, compassionate and well-meaning men and women."[83]

Evidence indicates that this self-image may have been particularly intense among Kentuckians. Although Cassius M. Clay condemned slavery as an evil, he conceded that Kentucky slave owners were the most humane. Incredibly, Frederick Douglass's antislavery newspaper the *North Star* reprinted a description of Kentucky slavery that contended, "Perhaps in no State of the Union has the institution existed under milder auspices." Although this view has been strongly challenged by modern scholarship, it was still current in the twentieth century.[84]

The importance of one's image among fellow slave owners in the community no doubt played a role in the petition drive as well. Clay's Jack was not the first (trust) slave to disrupt Clay's Lexington home. In early 1845, Jim had run away but was recaptured in Jessamine County. In 1843, Clay's son, Cassius Jr., had died under mysterious circumstances. When a second child became gravely ill in early 1845, Clay suspected that Emily, their Black nursemaid, had poisoned both. Emily was subsequently acquitted of murder charges, but Clay sold Emily "down the river" anyway.[85]

Former governor Thomas Metcalfe, a staunch defender of slavery, ridiculed Clay in an open letter: "My negroes never run away from me. . . . They do not poison my children, nor are they ever falsely charged with poisoning as an apology for their imprisonment and sale of their innocent relatives."[86]

Henry Clay Pindell's observations about his aunt Sidney also indicate that slave owners passed judgement on each other's management skills or lack thereof. To her nephew, Miss Sidney was a terrible manager because she allowed her servants to be impudent.[87] Therefore, it is likely that in the Doyle case slaveholders sought to save face by petitioning the governor. By reclaiming their unfaithful servants from the grip of the law, the wealthy owners were regaining their authority, control, and right to determine a fitting punishment.

As noted earlier, Reverend John A. McClung, the leading defense counsel, advised Crittenden that the cry for clemency for Presley and Shad was also widespread in Bracken and surrounding counties. In fact, large numbers of local citizens sought clemency for all seven prisoners at various times. Prior to Owsley's last day in office, on the day the verdict against Slaughter, Shad, and Presley was handed down, an unsigned petition from Brooksville contained the following plea: "We want no blood shed here because of the demoralizing effects on the coming generation. I could see Doyle suffer death even but who of us would not have run away to taste the sweets of Liberty. . . . I think . . . the verdict just but I look more to the abolitionist then [sic] the victims."[88]

McClung also enclosed a separate petition that contained the signatures of ten of the jury. Containing more than 104 names, the petition was also signed by three posse members, who beside their names scrawled "who they shot at."[89] Five additional petitions for clemency dated September 2 were submitted to the governor. The first group contained more than 386 names. One contained 18 signatures from the village of Germantown in neighboring Mason County.[90] Another bore the signatures of eight women with the notation, "On this some ladies' names are put down but none of the rest." The concluding lines indicated that many more women would have signed had they been permitted to.[91] A sixth petition, dated September 3, contained 110 names, including the signatures of four additional women. In all, more than 419 signatures for clemency were obtained in the immediate aftermath of the trial.[92]

At the same time, McClung and fifty-four others petitioned Governor Owsley to pardon Bill Griffin, Jasper, Anderson, and Jack Clay before they could be tried on the second charge of "Shooting with Intent to Kill." The signatures included not only those of eight jury members but that of Joseph Duncan, a posse member who served as a prosecution witness.[93] All the petitions reflected a common theme. The slaves had been "most shamefully deceived" or "seduced" by Doyle and should not suffer a "ruthless" execution. Others argued that Doyle's imprisonment was sufficient to satisfy justice, while four of the petitions requested pardons on the condition the prisoners were sold away from Kentucky.[94]

Two additional petitions submitted on September 2 added another dimension to the effort to save the fugitives from the hangman. In the first petition, Commonwealth attorney Harrison Taylor contended that he was convinced that the "negroes were deluded by the scoundrel Doyle by inducements which he held out to them which it was not in their nature to resist."[95]

The second petition was submitted by John N. Furber, who assisted Taylor in the prosecution. He contended that based on his own conversations with the prisoners and statements made during the trial, Doyle exhibited the "most arch stratagem and base villainy ever invented by the human mind to induce the slaves to accompany him across the Ohio River." Because of Doyle's threat to shoot anyone who deserted him, Furber claimed, the fugitives were forced to obey him.[96]

After Harry Slaughter was pardoned on September 6, two additional petitions were submitted on behalf of Shad and Presley. Both used virtually the same language; the condemned men were "seduced . . . by the villainy of the white man," and it was best to sell them beyond Kentucky. These petitions bore a total of 145 signatures.[97]

On or about September 19, another petition began to circulate in Bracken County that stated, "We believe that [Shad and Presley] were no guiltier then [sic] the others who have been discharged," and "we think that clemency is warmly called for by the public opinion of the community." The petitioners included posse member Elliott Roberts, a prosecution witness, Reverend McClung, and Harrison Taylor.[98]

By far the most notable of the 257 petitioners was the presiding judge, Walker Reid. The appearance of his name would not have surprised Governor Crittenden because the sixty-three-year-old jurist had previously expressed his views on the case both to Crittenden and his predecessor.

Described as "one of the ablest judges of northern Kentucky," the Mason County Democrat had been in office since 1832. Given the fact that his circuit, which stretched from the Virginia line to Covington, bordered the Ohio River, he presided over numerous fugitive-slave cases.[99]

The owner of forty-one slaves valued at $8,000, Judge Reid defended the institution with biblical passages as well as with historical comparisons to the classical civilization of Rome. He regarded abolitionists as common "negro thieves" who enticed slaves to run away in order to collect the rewards offered for them. He dismissed the rhetoric of Northern antislavery ministers as "mere twaddle."[100]

Not surprisingly, Reid initially sought to make an example of Doyle's followers. If the law was not upheld, he argued, abolitionists "would swarm into Kentucky, with arms to furnish our deluded slaves." In another letter, he stated, "we are losing our slaves . . . we may as well emancipate as to let them all be stolen or aided away."[101]

Reid balked at sending all seven to the gallows, though. On September 2, the day Jackson Clay, Bill Griffin, Jasper, and Anderson were acquitted of the first charge, Reid wrote to Governor Owsley with the recommendation that all four be pardoned before they were tried on the "Shooting" charge. He regarded the four as the most innocent and felt that further prosecution was not necessary.[102]

However, he bristled at newspaper reports that claimed he sought clemency for all seven. In a letter to Crittenden on September 12, he denied the reports. "I think," he wrote, "as Gov. Owsley did, that an example ought to be made of the ringleaders." It is interesting to note, however, that he quickly added that he would not be opposed to possible pardons.[103]

Having firmly expressed his determination to make an example of Shad, Presley, and Harry, Reid retired for the night. The next day he sent the following to Crittenden: "I could not sleep after writing last night about the slaves. I thought of 'Rebellion' and 'treason' . . . and the innocent blood collected in one great reservoir sufficient to swim in by false and unjust decisions. I begin to think I have a conscience too, but far different from that ascribed to the Preachers and negro thieves."

After launching into a spirited defense of slavery, Reid continued:

Yet with death staring me in the face, I could not rest for thinking what a century might bring forth and exchanging places. . . .

We know their object was to get away and become free contrary to law. They have no rights . . . they are *property*. And yet they are men. And when I think of what History may say. I almost wish this trial had never come before me. I know I must say what the law is, not what I would have it to be.

. . . Although it first seemed to me proper to have an example made, I had rather you pardon all . . . [and] I shall have a good conscience, because after doing my office to my best skill and Judgement I have begged for mercy.[104]

On September 19, the day Judge Reid sentenced Shad and Presley to death, he sent another, deeply emotional plea to Crittenden, "I have been sorely vexed at the great weight of trouble the *slave* business threw upon me." He added, "I should never think of it more if I could believe that the majority of the law had been *honored* and the *poor wretches pardoned*."[105]

Upon learning that Crittenden had requested the trial records, Reid made a final appeal on October 9:

In the general, I have been satisfied upon discharging my duties as Judge. Yet in this instance I am not so. There is something in the *name* of the *crime* itself, which will make part of History in time to come that I cannot get over.

We know very well that all the gang of 42 wanted was *liberty*. . . . They armed and resolved to *resist masters* & the *laws* of the State in search of this priceless Jewell Liberty.

After reminding the governor that the spirit of the law had been honored, Reid concluded: "Now, sir, you know your constitutional prerogative and if you exercise it in the pardon of the *two* slaves, the only *two* remaining *not* pardoned or acquitted of the *whole* number. It will add to your well-acquired fame for humanity which has been witnessed in many instances—and to your character as a statesman."[106]

Reid's effusive praise of Crittenden was no longer necessary. On the very day the venerable judge penned these words, Shad and Presley were pardoned. There would be no "blood shed" in Bracken County.[107]

In one sense, Reid's change of heart is not surprising. The Kentuckian was not the first member of the "ruling race" to recognize the fundamental injustice of slavery. The eccentric Virginian John Randolph of Roanoke, a noted defender of slavery in the early republic, once listened to a Southern lady's passionate support of Greece's struggle to be free from Turkish oppression. When she concluded her remarks, Randolph pointed to the enslaved children of her household and solemnly declared, "Madam, the Greeks are at your door!"[108]

Yet some scholars of slavery and the law contend, as abolitionists had in the past, that slaves were people without rights. As the historian Andrew Fede has concluded in *People without Rights,* the law, as far as the slave was concerned, was nothing more than a "compact between his rulers." To Fede, all references to "humanity" in Southern court decisions were mere judicial rhetoric.[109]

Fede regards any evidence of fairness or humanity in criminal procedures of the antebellum South as nothing more than a means to protect the enslavers' economic investment. Any appearance of concern for a slave's "rights," he contends, "must be looked at critically." Fede maintains that Southern criminal law "epitomized the oppression of slavery" and that "a slave felony trial was the functional equivalent of a civil forfeiture proceeding."[110]

Yet Fede fails to recognize the impact of Enlightenment ideals on enslavers as well as of the republican spirit of the age.[111] Other scholars of slavery and the law have pointed out that many Southern jurists were "driven by conscience" as well as by republican values and Judeo-Christian ethics. Indeed, Mark V. Tushnet argues in *The American Law of Slavery* that the "appeal to humanity cannot be dismissed as high irony or reduced to the protection of interest."[112]

Tushnet's work reveals that Reid was not the only Southern jurist confronted by the humanity of enslaved people. Judge Eugenius Nesbet of Georgia in 1851 declared that although slaves "are, in law and in fact, property, they are recognized as human creatures."[113] As the Alabama Supreme Court decreed in 1861, enslaved people were recognized as being "endowed with intellect, conscience and will."[114] However, as chattel, they had no legal rights in civil lawsuits. Yet the high court decreed that in criminal proceedings they must be considered persons capable of committing acts that are punishable by law.

It is difficult to discern the depth of Reid's religious faith or whether Judeo-Christian values influenced his decisions in the courtroom. However, there is ample evidence that the jurist, like many Southerners, based his defense of slavery on the Bible. Reverend John G. Fee, perhaps Kentucky's most radical antislavery advocate, described Reid as "the noted defender of slavery." After Fee was physically assaulted in 1844 for his antislavery stance, he filed a civil suit for damages in the Lewis County Circuit Court.[115]

Years later Fee recalled Reid's closing remarks at the hearing: "Gentlemen, Mr. Fee is an Abolitionist, and if slave-holding is sinful, the Abolitionists are right. They say, repent of sin immediately; and you would not say to pickpockets, quit your sins gradually." Reid then called for a Bible, opened it, and declared, "Slavery is not sinful; the Bible sanctions it." Fee recalled that Reid then referred to the "case of Abraham, and the instruction of Moses to buy the heathen round about and of Paul returning Onesimus, a runaway slave." Despite this view, Reid ruled in Fee's favor, stating "free speech must be had."[116]

On another occasion, when Reid presided over a public meeting in Mason County, many of those present clamored that Fee be ejected for his antislavery remarks. Reid flatly refused and in a stentorian voice told Fee, "Speak on, speak on!"[117]

An old, slim Judge's Docket Book in the Bracken County Courthouse appears to contain Reid's thoughts as he prepared to render his decision in Fee's Lewis County case. He mentions Fee by name and counters his antislavery views by referring to the Apostle Paul's Letter to Philemon. This New Testament passage, in which Paul instructs Christian slaves to obey their masters, was apparently the bedrock of Reid's pro-slavery defense.[118] In his letter to Crittenden on September 13, Reid praised Southern clergymen for instructing the enslaved to heed Paul's teaching and obey their masters.[119] Little wonder that former slaves often referred to their days in bondage as "Paul's Time."[120]

The key to Reid's emotional plea for clemency was no doubt rooted in the Enlightenment values embraced by the Founding Fathers. Furthermore, the year 1848 witnessed republican revolutions throughout Europe. Ironically, given Doyle's role in the affair, the plight of Ireland also influenced the Brooksville proceedings. During his final argument for the defense, Reverend McClung cited *The Queen vs. Daniel O'Connell,* which resulted in the Irish statesman's conviction for sedition and subsequent imprisonment in 1844.[121]

Reid informed Crittenden that he did not feel the decision in *Queen* was pertinent to the case. But in an earlier letter, Reid wrote that the prisoners "make the same figure as Robert Emmet and Smith O'Brien made."[122] These Irish patriots were household names in antebellum America. O'Brien, a prominent leader in the recent rising of 1848, was sentenced to banishment in Tasmania. Emmet, who took up the sword of Irish liberty in 1803, was captured and hanged by the British.[123]

Reid was also deeply impressed by the bearing, intelligence, and courage of Harry Slaughter and Shad. He wrote, "They are brave men, sensible and capable as any white man of doing business which does not require pen and figures."[124] Contrary to Slaughter's recollections, courtroom testimony made no mention of violent resistance to their captors. Rather, when the fugitives were surrounded by their white pursuers, they boldly asked permission to fire their pistols into the ground before surrendering. Their noble gesture was worthy of any brave Southern gentleman.[125]

"What Chivalry," Reid exclaimed in one of his many letters. "Bravery like it," he continued, "seldom takes place among the *anglo-saxon* [sic] race." Observing that the fugitives would not surrender without the "honors of war," he added, "True Knights, they would first break a steele [sic]."[126]

Although the runaways escaped death, the majority of them undoubtedly suffered the tragic fate of being "sold down the river." Indeed, Brutus Clay sold off twenty-year-old "Trusty Jack" on September 11, eight days before he was released from the Brooksville jail.[127] The five Breckinridge bondsmen shared a similar fate. In a letter dated August 15, 1848, Reverend William L. Breckinridge informed his brother Robert J., who was also a Presbyterian minister, that he had shared Robert's recent letter with their mother. The matriarch of the family was away from Cabell's Dale at the time of the Doyle affair. William promptly expressed her wishes about the matter: "She had not previously heard of the elopement of the negroes. . . . [H]er wish is that all of them may be sold with the obligation of taking them out of the country [state] . . . & that she is determined that in no case not one of them can come on her farm while she lives."[128]

On September 7, Robert informed his brother: "I have sold the six negroes to Richard Higgins to be taken to his cotton lands over the Mississippi. . . . [T]he price of the 5 negroes, excluding Mike, is $2,300. I would much have preferred not selling him at all, but Moma's desire that I do so, and the difficulty of selling the two older men, Philip and Rueben without him, induced me to let him go with the rest."[129]

The sale was facilitated by William A. Pullam, a Lexington slave trader whose jail would eventually hold Harry Slaughter after his pardon. Slaughter later recalled that he angered Pullam for refusing to allow a passing trader to examine his teeth and limbs. Pullam attempted to flog him, but Slaughter physically kept him at bay. John Graves heard about the incident and intervened. Shortly afterward, Miss Sidney instructed the slave trader to send Slaughter to her home. Slaughter related that after a long talk Miss Sidney told him "how sorry she was that I had not let her know that I wanted to be free."[130]

At this point, Slaughter offered to purchase himself, and Miss Sidney loaned him $200. With loans from four other white Lexington residents, he purchased his freedom and married his sweetheart. He later boasted that he repaid the loans within five years and six months. He ended his story as follows: "All the other boys who went with me during that memorable struggle for liberty are dead. I don't suppose I will last much longer, but thank God I have lived for forty-six years a free man." The big Kentuckian died at the age of eighty-eight in Lexington on June 14, 1906.[131]

The Doyle affair was overshadowed by the scheme of Daniel Drayton carried out a few months earlier. More than seventy-six slaves attempted to escape from Washington, DC, aboard Drayton's schooner, the *Pearl*, but were overtaken and captured in Chesapeake Bay. Drayton was convicted of "Slave Stealing" and sentenced to prison.[132]

Edward James "Patrick" Doyle enjoyed some notoriety in the years after his confinement. According to an account in the *Louisville Courier-Journal* in September 1887, he received numerous letters, apparently from those who regarded him as an antislavery "martyr." On November 14, 1863, he died of typhoid fever in the Kentucky State Penitentiary. A forgotten man, he was buried in Frankfort's potter's field.[133]

Given the excitement and fear sparked by the Doyle affair, it was a miracle that the trials did not result in multiple executions. Had John Wilmot, the slaveholder who pursued the fugitives, been killed or if Charles Fowler had died of his wounds, the cries for vengeance would have drowned out any pleas for mercy. The lives of the African American ringleaders were spared in part by good fortune and their status as the "trusted house servants of Lexington's most socially prominent families."[134]

But another important factor was revealed during the incident. Despite the anger and fear that the fugitive-slave "problem" caused Kentucky slaveholders, some in that class were not blind to the humanity of the runaways and at least in some cases understood their motives. The willingness to fight for their freedom and their noble bearing in the courtroom reflected the constant struggle of all enslaved people to compel the "ruling race" to recognize their common humanity.

Harry Slaughter's account of his fight for liberty reflects current scholarship that describes the pre-1861 antislavery struggle as the opening shots of the Civil War. In *Border War: Fighting over Slavery before the Civil War*, Stanley Harrold identifies the Doyle affair as a significant event in the struggle.[135] In many ways, the shots fired by the rebel slaves were the distant thunder of a coming storm.

Notes

1. J. Winston Coleman, *Slavery Times in Kentucky* (Chapel Hill: University of North Carolina Press, 1940), 89–92; "Commonwealth vs. Harry Slaughter et al.," John A. McClung's Trial Transcript, box 27, folder 575, Governor William Owsley Papers, Public Records Division, Kentucky Department for Libraries and Archives (KDLA), Frankfort (hereafter cited as Trial Transcript).

2. *Lexington Observer and Reporter*, August 9, 1848.

3. William H. Townsend, *Lincoln and the Bluegrass: Slavery and the Civil War in Kentucky* (Lexington: University of Kentucky Press, 1955), 154.

4. Coleman, *Slavery Times in Kentucky*, 89–92; Trial Transcript, KDLA.

5. Trial Transcript, KDLA.

6. *Louisville Morning Courier*, August 12, 1848; Trial Transcript, KDLA.

7. *Louisville Morning Courier*, August 21, 1848; Trial Transcript, KDLA.

8. *Louisville Morning Courier*, August 12, 1848; Trial Transcript, KDLA.

9. *Louisville Morning Courier*, August 12, 1848; Trial Transcript, KDLA; obituary of Samuel F. January, *Lexington Daily Leader*, September 9, 1900.

10. *Louisville Morning Courier*, August 21, 1848.

11. *Louisville Morning Courier*, August 21, 1848.

12. *Lexington Daily Atlas*, August 22, 1848; Randolph Paul Runyon, *Delia Webster and the Underground Railroad* (Lexington: University Press of Kentucky, 1996), 47–54. Breckinridge would serve as US vice president and a Confederate major general. See William C. Davis, *Breckinridge: Statesman, Soldier, Symbol* (Baton Rouge: Louisiana State University Press, 1974), 29–30, 178–79, 288–90.

13. *Lexington Daily Atlas*, October 10, 1848; Fayette County Circuit Court Order Book 34, p. 304, Public Records Division, KDLA.

14. J. Blaine Hudson, *Encyclopedia of the Underground Railroad* (Jefferson, NC: McFarland, 2006), 82. See also Stanley Harrold, *Border War: Fighting over Slavery before the Civil War* (Chapel Hill: University of North Carolina Press, 2010), 131.

15. *Louisville Catholic Advocate*, May 30, 1846.

16. *Louisville Catholic Advocate*, May 30, 1846.

17. *Louisville Presbyterian Herald*, May 7, 1846.

18. Obituary of Alexander Sneed, *Louisville Daily Journal*, October 19, 1867.

19. *Louisville Presbyterian Herald*, May 7, 1846.

20. *Louisville Presbyterian Herald*, May 7, 1846.

21. *Louisville Presbyterian Herald*, May 7, 1846. See also C. Walker Gollar, "The Alleged Abduction of Milly McPherson and Catholic Recruitment of Presbyterian Girls," *Church History* 65, no. 4 (December 1996): 596–608.

22. *Louisville Presbyterian Herald*, May 7, 1846.

23. *Louisville Catholic Advocate*, May 30, 1846.

24. *Louisville Catholic Advocate*, May 30, 1846.

25. *Louisville Presbyterian Herald*, July 9, 1846.

26. *Louisville Catholic Advocate*, May 30, 1846.

27. *Commonwealth vs. Edward James Doyle*, April 12, 1848, Franklin County Circuit Court Case Files, bundle 719, and Franklin County Circuit Court Order Book 8, p. 334, KDLA.

28. Louisville City Court Minute Book, December 7, 1846–March 30, 1849, Collections Department, Filson Historical Society, Louisville, KY (this record is not paginated); *Louisville Morning Courier*, May 13 and 22, 1848.

29. *Louisville Morning Courier*, August 14, 1848.

30. *Rochester (NY) North Star*, August 25, 1848.

31. *Rochester North Star*, August 21, 1848. Detailed information regarding Doyle's money can be found in *Henry Coffman vs. E. J. Doyle*, Fayette County Circuit Court Case Files, box 131, bundle 1168, KDLA.

32. Slave Owners Census for Washington County, KY, 1850, KDLA; Slave Owners Census for Boyle County, Kentucky, 1850, KDLA. Standard works on Kentucky slavery such as Marion B. Lucas's *A History of Blacks in Kentucky*, vol. 1: *From Slavery to Segregation, 1760–1891* (Frankfort: Kentucky Historical Society, 1992), and Harold D. Tallant's *Evil Necessity: Slavery and Political Culture in Antebellum Kentucky* (Lexington: University Press of Kentucky, 2003) do not address the Catholic Church and slavery in Kentucky.

33. Andrew Delbanco, *The War before the War: Fugitive Slaves and the Struggle for America's Soul from the Revolution to the Civil War* (New York: Penguin, 2018), 112–13.

34. Merton L. Dillon, *Slavery Attacked: Southern Slaves and Their Allies, 1619–1865* (Baton Rouge: Louisiana University Press, 1990), 144–45, 185, 232.

35. John Hope Franklin and Loren Schweninger, *Runaway Slaves: Rebels on the Plantation* (New York: Oxford University Press, 1999), 83–84, 112. See also Harrold, *Border War*, 129–30.

36. James C. Klotter, *The Breckinridges of Kentucky* (Lexington: University Press of Kentucky, 1986), 39–41; John B. Castleman, *Active Service* (Louisville, KY: Courier-Journal Job Printing, 1917), 31. For Mrs. Breckinridge's totals, see the Fayette County Tax Assessment Book, 1848, KDLA. The names and ages of the Breckinridge fugitives are found in Robert J. Breckinridge to William L. Breckinridge, Lexington, KY, September 7, 1848, box 132, Breckinridge Family Papers, Manuscript Division, Library of Congress, Washington, DC.

37. Robert Peter, *History of Fayette County, Kentucky* (Chicago: O. L. Baskin, 1882), 612–14; James F. Hopkins, *A History of the Hemp Industry in Kentucky* (Lexington: University Press of Kentucky, 1998), 135.

38. Peter, *History of Fayette County*, 612–14; Fayette County Tax Book, 1848, and City of Lexington Tax Book, 1848, KDLA.

39. Fayette County Manufacturing Census, 1850, KDLA. Erdman's birthplace is listed in the Fayette County Population Census, 1850, KDLA. Erdman's full name can be found on his tombstone inscription via www.findagrave.com.

40. Taylor and Frazer's hemp factories as well as Caldwell's steam mill are enumerated in the Manufacturing Census for Fayette County, 1850, KDLA. The names of the fugitives that these business owners claimed are given in the *Lexington Observer and Reporter*, August 12, 1848.

41. See Duncan's obituary in the *Lexington Transcript*, March 23, 1880. For the number of slaves he owned, see Fayette County Tax Assessment Book, 1848, and City of Lexington Tax Assessment Book, 1848, KDLA.

42. Robert Peter, *The History of the Medical Department at Transylvania University*, Filson Club Publication no. 20 (Louisville, KY: John P. Morton, 1905), 138–39; *Lexington Observer and Reporter*, August 12, 1848.

43. Peter, *History of Fayette County*, 700–701.

44. An abstract of Colonel James Morrison's will is found in Michael L. Cummings Cook and Bettie L. Cummings Cook, *Fayette County Kentucky Records*, 5 vols. (Evansville, IN: Cook, 1986), 5:296–300. See also Henry Clay, *The Papers of Henry Clay*, 11 vols., ed. James Hopkins (Lexington: University Press of Kentucky, 1959), 3:416 n. 2. Harry Slaughter's recollections were published as an interview in the *Lexington Morning Herald*, July 20, 1897.

45. Webster was impressed by the force and eloquence of Pindell's closing argument (Runyon, *Delia Webster and the Underground Railroad*, 52). For the Morrison connection, see Clay, *Henry Clay*, 3:538 n. 5, and *Lexington Morning Herald*, July 20, 1897. It should also be noted that Pindell's paternal grandmother, Eliza, was the sister of Lucretia Hart, the wife of Henry Clay. See G. Glenn Clift, *Remember the Raisin! Kentucky and Kentuckians in the Battles and Massacre at Frenchtown, Michigan Territory, in the War of 1812* (Frankfort: Kentucky Historical Society, 1961), 149.

46. Lowell H. Harrison, *The Anti-slavery Movement in Kentucky* (Lexington: University Press of Kentucky, 1976), 50.

47. Harrison, *The Anti-slavery Movement in Kentucky,* 50. When challenged by the Reverend John G. Fee, a noted Kentucky abolitionist, about the slaves he held in trust, Clay replied, "I feel it is my duty to keep my children's slaves together and control them" (quoted in James Rood Robertson, *A Kentuckian at the Court of the Tsars: The Ministry of Cassius Marcellus Clay to Russia* [1935; reprint, Berea: Kentucky Imprints, 1976], 31).

48. H. Edward Richardson, *Cassius Marcellus Clay: Firebrand of Freedom* (Lexington: University Press of Kentucky, 1976), 51–55; *Historical Record of the Proceedings of Lexington and Vicinity in the Suppression of the* True American (Lexington, KY: Virden Press, 1845), 3, Special Collections, Margaret I. King Library, University of Kentucky, Lexington.

49. David L. Smiley, *Lion of White Hall: The Life of Cassius M. Clay* (1962; reprint, Gloucester, MA: Wadsworth, 1969), 113–14; Samuel E. Hill, Adjutant-General of Kentucky, *Roster of the Volunteer Officers and Soldiers from the State of Kentucky in the War with Mexico* (Frankfort, KY: Public Printer, 1889), 10.

50. Bracken County Circuit Court Order Book H, August 17, 1848, pp. 212–13, Bracken County Circuit Court Clerk's Office, Brooksville, KY.

51. Bracken County Circuit Court Order Book I I, pp. 212–13.

52. H. C. Pindell to Governor William Owsley, August 25, 1848, box 27, folder 573, Owsley Papers, KDLA.

53. Pindell to Owsley, August 25, 1848.

54. Pindell to Owsley, August 25, 1848.

55. Harry Slaughter's recollections in *Lexington Morning Herald,* July 20, 1897.

56. James Oakes, *The Ruling Race: A History of American Slaveholders* (New York: Norton, 1998), 183; Slaughter's recollections in *Lexington Morning Herald,* July 20, 1897.

57. *Lexington Morning Herald,* July 20, 1897.

58. Slaughter's recollections in *Lexington Morning Herald,* July 20, 1897.

59. All of these petitions are found in box 27, folder 573, Owsley Papers, KDLA.

60. Slaughter's recollections in *Lexington Morning Herald,* July 20, 1897.

61. Owsley's endorsement in Trial Transcript, KDLA. See also H. C. Pindell to Governor William Owsley, August 25, 1848, box 27, folder 573, Owsley Papers, KDLA.

62. Bracken County Circuit Court Order Book H, p. 235.

63. Cassius N. Clay to Governor John J. Crittenden, September 5, 1848, box 27, folder 575, John Crittenden Papers, KDLA.

64. Executive Journal, p. 235, bound volume, Owsley Papers, KDLA.

65. Richard Dowling et al. to Governor John J. Crittenden, September 7, 1848, box 1, folder 15, Crittenden Papers, KDLA.

66. Thomas Christian to Governor John J. Crittenden, September 28, 1848, box 28, folder 581, Crittenden Papers, KDLA.

67. Samuel R. Bullock to Governor John J. Crittenden, September 8, 1848, box 1, folder 15, Crittenden Papers, KDLA.

68. Both "Griffin" and "Griffen" are given in various documents.

69. John Chism to Governor John J. Crittenden, September 9, 1848, box 1, folder 15, Crittenden Papers, KDLA.

70. William R. Fowler et al. to Governor John J. Crittenden, September 2, 1848, box 27, folder 574, Crittenden Papers, KDLA. See also Fowler's deposition, box 27, folder 572, Owsley Papers, KDLA.

71. Bracken County Circuit Court Order Book H, p. 249.

72. John A. McClung to Governor John J. Crittenden, September 22, 1848, box 1, folder 16, Crittenden Papers, KDLA.

73. McClung to Crittenden, September 22, 1848.

74. McClung to Crittenden, September 22, 1848. McClung had sent a similar request to Crittenden's predecessor on September 2 (box 29, folder 574, Owsley Papers, KDLA).

75. John S. Finley to Governor John J. Crittenden, September 27, 1848, box 29, folder 574, Crittenden Papers, KDLA.

76. James Wordlaw to Governor John J. Crittenden, enclosed in Finley to Crittenden, September 27, 1848.

77. J. Blaine Hudson, *Fugitive Slaves and the Underground Railroad in the Kentucky Borderland* (Jefferson, NC: McFarland, 2002), 138; see also William Littell and Jacob Swigert, *A Digest of the Statute Law of Kentucky*, 2 vols. (Frankfort, KY: State Printer, 1882), 2:1154–55.

78. Franklin and Schweninger, *Runaway Slaves,* 248, 250.

79. Franklin and Schweninger, *Runaway Slaves,* 169.

80. Quoted in Franklin and Schweninger, *Runaway Slaves,* 165.

81. Franklin and Schweninger, *Runaway Slaves,* 250.

82. Quoted in Franklin and Schweninger, *Runaway Slaves,* 250.

83. Franklin and Schweninger, *Runaway Slaves,* 248.

84. Cassius Marcellus Clay, *The Writings of Cassius Marcellus Clay* (New York: Harper, 1848), 254; *Philadelphia Weekly Bulletin* quoted in *Rochester North Star,* May 18, 1849; Coleman, *Slavery Times in Kentucky,* 54–56; Tallant, *Evil Necessity,* 62–65. The origins of the description of Kentucky slavery as "mild" have never been fully explored. Speaking to the American Anti-Slavery Society

before the Civil War, James A. Thome of Lane Seminary declared, "It is well known that in Kentucky, slavery wears its mildest features" (quoted in *Liberator* [Boston], May 17, 1834).

85. *Lexington True American,* July 22, 1845.

86. Thomas Metcalfe quoted in *Lexington True American,* July 22, 1845. See also Smiley, *Lion of White Hall,* 71.

87. H. C. (Henry Clay) Pindell to Governor William Owsley, August 25, 1848, box 27, folder 573, Owsley Papers, KDLA.

88. McClung to Crittenden, September 2, 1848 (date inserted by the unidentified court recorder), box 27, folder 574, Owsley Papers, KDLA.

89. John Downing et al. to Governor Owsley, September 2, 1848, box 27, folder 574, Owsley Papers, KDLA.

90. McClung to Crittenden, September 2, 1848; Martin Dodson et al. to Governor, September 2, 1848, KDLA.

91. John H. Sellers et al. to Governor, September 2, 1848, box 27, folder 575, Owsley Papers, KDLA.

92. McClung et al. to Governor, September 2, 1848, KDLA.

93. Downing et al. to Owsley, September 2, 1848, and other multiple petitions mentioned in the text, box 27, folder 574, Owsley Papers, KDLA.

94. H. Taylor et al. to Governor, September 2, 1848, box 27, folder 574, Owsley Papers, KDLA.

95. Harrison Taylor to Governor, September 2, 1848, box 27, folder 574, Owsley Papers, KDLA.

96. John N. Furber to Governor, September 2, 1848, box 27, folder 574, Owsley Papers, KDLA; Trial Transcript, KDLA.

97. John N. Furber to Governor, September 2, 1848, box 28, folder 583, Owsley Papers, KDLA.

98. Furber to Governor, September 2, 1848.

99. H. Levin, *Lawyers and Lawmakers of Kentucky* (Chicago: Lewis, 1897), 699–700; Coleman, *Slavery Times in Kentucky,* 236–37.

100. Mason County Tax Assessment Book, 1848, p. 22, KDLA; Walker Reid to Governor William Owsley, September 2, 1848, box 27, folder 574, Owsley Papers, KDLA; Walker Reid to Governor John J. Crittenden, September 12, 1848, box 1, folder 15, Crittenden Papers, KDLA.

101. Reid to Owsley, September 2, 1848.

102. Reid to Owsley, September 2, 1848.

103. Reid to Crittenden, September 12, 1848.

104. Walker Reid to Governor John J. Crittenden, September 13, 1848, box 28, folder 581, Crittenden Papers, KDLA, emphasis in original.

105. Walker Reid to Governor John J. Crittenden, September 19, 1848, box 1, folder 16, Crittenden Papers, KDLA, emphasis in original.

106. Walker Reid to Governor John J. Crittenden, October 9, 1848, box 1, folder 17, Crittenden Papers, KDLA, emphasis in original.

107. Executive Journal, October 9, 1848, p. 13, bound volume, Crittenden Papers, KDLA.

108. Robert Dawidoff, *The Education of John Randolph* (New York: Norton, 1979), 63–64.

109. Andrew Fede, *People without Rights: An Interpretation of the Fundamentals of the Law of Slavery in the U.S. South* (New York: Garland, 1992), 6, 94.

110. Fede, *People without Rights,* 40, 193.

111. Peter Karsten, *Heart vs. Head: Judge-Made Law in Nineteenth Century America* (Chapel Hill: University of North Carolina Press, 1997), 5.

112. Mark V. Tushnet, *The American Law of Slavery, 1810–1860* (Princeton, NJ: Princeton University Press, 1981), 5.

113. Quoted in Tushnet, *American Law of Slavery,* 19.

114. Quoted in Tushnet, *American Law of Slavery,* 214.

115. Lucas, *History of Blacks in Kentucky,* 1:54.

116. John G. Fee, *The Autobiography of John G. Fee* (Chicago: National Christian Association, 1891), 45–46.

117. Fee, *Autobiography of John G. Fee,* 51.

118. Judge's Docket Book, Miscellaneous Volumes, c. 1845, Bracken County Circuit Court Clerk's Office.

119. Reid to Crittenden, September 13, 1848. See also Laura L. Mitchell, "'Matters of Justice between Man and Man': Northern Divines, the Bible, and the Fugitive Slave Act of 1850," in *Religion and the Antebellum Debate over Slavery,* ed. John R. McKivigan and Mitchell Snay (Athens: University of Georgia Press, 1998), 146–49.

120. Eric Foner, *Reconstruction: America's Unfinished Revolution, 1863–1877* (New York: Harper & Row, 1988), 94.

121. Reid to Crittenden, September 19, 1848.

122. Reid to Crittenden, September 12, 1848.

123. S. J. Connolly, "Robert Emmett," in *The Oxford Companion to Irish History,* ed. S. J. Connolly (Oxford: Oxford University Press, 2002), 180; Peter Grey, "Smith O'Brien," in *The Oxford Companion to Irish History,* ed. Connolly, 417.

124. Reid to Crittenden, September 12, 1848.

125. Trial Transcript, KDLA.

126. Reid to Crittenden, September 12, 1848.

127. Bill of sale, box 7, folder 49, Clay Family Papers, Special Collections, University of Kentucky, Lexington.

128. William Breckinridge to Robert J. Breckinridge, August 15, 1848, box 132, Breckinridge Family Papers.

129. Robert J. Breckinridge to William Breckinridge, September 7, 1848, box 132, Breckinridge Family Papers.

130. Slaughter's recollections in *Lexington Morning Herald*, July 20, 1897.

131. Slaughter's recollections in *Lexington Morning Herald*, July 20, 1897; Harry Slaughter, City of Lexington Death Certificate no. 420, 1906, KDLA.

132. Franklin and Schweninger, *Runaway Slaves*, 14.

133. *Louisville Courier-Journal*, September 4, 1887; *Report of the Keeper and Lessee of the Kentucky Penitentiary* (Frankfort, KY: State Printer, 1865), 10.

134. Runyon, *Delia Webster and the Underground Railroad*, 123.

135. Harrold, *Border War*, 131.

4

Necessary Violence

African American Self-Preservation, Violence, and Survival in Civil War–Era Kentucky

Charles R. Welsko

On May 25, 1859, a gunshot cut through a peaceful Caldwell County, Kentucky, morning. Edmund Stevens, a local farmer who worked alone in his field, was the target of the assassin's bullet. Stevens's killer escaped unobserved, though authorities found two sets of footprints at the murder scene. Despite the lack of witnesses, it did not take long for local suspicion to fall on Jesse Williams, another Caldwell County farmer. Williams and Stevens had a well-known and lingering rivalry. Caldwell County residents also knew Williams as a cruel man who "had not been sober for any length of time for three years" and whose family had a violent history. Williams was therefore the logical start of any investigation. Authorities quickly determined that such suspicions were partially correct—the killer had come from Williams's property, yet Jesse Williams was not the man who had pulled the trigger. Instead, the authorities arrested Wesley, one of Williams's twenty-three enslaved people.[1]

As the authorities led Wesley away from the Williams property, the enslaver might have congratulated himself for orchestrating the removal of a rival and shifting the blame onto Wesley. If only Jesse Williams understood how Wesley's desire for self-preservation would prove the enslaver's undoing. After his arrest, Wesley confessed to the county jailer that he had killed Stevens. Yet according to a petition on his behalf, Wesley added that he had acted "through *fear* compulsion and constraint of his Master Jesse Williams and from no wish or will of his own." Wesley explained that Williams had ordered him to kill Stevens under the threat of physical harm, including death, if he failed to comply. That confession prompted Williams's arrest. Perhaps Williams had anticipated such a development but relied on his status as a white man to protect him. In antebellum Kentucky, as was the case across much of the South, enslaved individuals could not testify in court. Thus, any official legal proceeding would have heard only from Williams, not from Wesley. If the legal system protected Williams, so did the pro-slavery ideology of the South. White Southerners abhorred acts of violence by enslaved people, especially when those acts intersected directly with the lives or material interests of white citizens. Williams likely expected that local authorities would accept his version of events and hold the Black man solely responsible for the murder of Stevens. Wesley might have suspected this would happen as well—Williams had placed the enslaved man in an unwinnable situation as dictated by the legal, social, and cultural structures of nineteenth-century Kentucky. Yet Wesley's actions before and after the killing directed events in ways that neither man had anticipated.[2]

In August, "a mob" of local citizens apprehended Jesse Williams and lynched him. That mob was the result of a long countywide history of sociopolitical divisions and irregular violence. In the late 1850s, Caldwell County officials had little success staunching local civic disorder. In response, white residents pulled on their shared history of vigilante justice and formed bands of "regulators to police the county." Although "regulators" rose to postwar prominence in Kentucky and the South as paramilitary organizations to enforce white supremacy and curb Black freedom, in antebellum Caldwell County they policed everyone. The mob that executed Williams in the summer of 1859 were "regulators" who dragged Williams either from his home or from jail. Despite the contradiction between different reports—that Williams was taken from his jail cell or dragged from his home—the end result was that his body was found the next morning "hanging to the limb of a tree." Local "regulators" lynched Williams for upsetting the racial and social order of the county.[3] Although whites owned a monopoly of power over enslaved Blacks and could apply violence as a form of punishment at their discretion and usually without interference from others, it was anathema for Black individuals to wield violence on their own or at the behest of a white master. In the latter, the thinking went, lay the possibility for chaos and social upheaval. This meant that Wesley would have to go on trial for murdering Stevens—after all, he had killed a white man. Yet his case offers more than just a stunning tale of white violence enacted through a Black body. It provides an opportunity to contextualize how Black Kentuckians labored to survive their enslavement and in doing so shaped life in Kentucky before and during the Civil War.

Any examination of the survival of the enslaved must start with a clear understanding of the cultural and legal landscape of the slave South. By the middle of the nineteenth century, white Southerners had formalized a society built on white supremacy and the extractive labor of enslaved people. Southern white enslavers as well as white nonslaveholders constructed legal and social systems that controlled Black Americans. This control directed most aspects of enslaved people's lives—it denied them formal education, dictated their working hours, restricted their travel, determined their living accommodations, influenced their worship, and directed their marriages. Disobedience, tardiness, slackened production, or an enslaver's whim could result in the application of punishment—physical, mental, and/or sexual—against Black bodies. Although there were regional differences that granted African Americans opportunities for extra work, income, or increased movement, the system of slavery at its heart constrained options for the enslaved, leaving Black Southerners with little control over their lives.[4]

White Southerners cast this manipulation in a pro-slavery ideology that glorified the subversion of Black people. They argued that their ownership of African Americans was a righteous cause that civilized enslaved Blacks out of their "natural" backward condition. This argument was merely an excuse, of course. In reality, white Southerners had built definitions of freedom and independence that relied on Black subjugation, equating mastery over others with their independence and exhibiting a shallow regard for the souls and lives of those they supposedly were elevating. White supremacy not only influenced how whites thought about themselves, providing illusions of grandeur, but also allowed for their opulent wealth and acted as a means of social control. Their view of the world subjugated the enslaved to the bottom rung of the South's social ladder and presented the opportunity for poor or middling whites to rise in social standing based on their control over others or simply on their race. Kentucky, like the other Southern slave states, modeled itself as a paragon of benevolent white power that concentrated wealth at the upper levels of society for the benefit of citizens farther down the rungs of society. Though pro-slavery ideology created a grossly imbalanced system, the power of enslavers was far from complete.[5]

We might be tempted to classify Wesley's actions as an enslaved man's resistance against Williams. It might be more accurate to claim that he tried to survive by adapting everyday forms of undermining the restrictions of enslavement to his unique situation. African Americans challenged their enslavement and social limitations in a variety of ways that stretched from the small to the grand. Everyday methods or what we might consider hidden forms of resistance occupied the safest and most frequent challenges to enslavement. Although *safe* is a relatively fraught word when others owned the bodies and lives of Black individuals, these actions allowed African Americans to assert a measure of control over their lives. Some enslaved individuals challenged their enslavers by slowing down their work, breaking tools, and feigning illness. Others skirted the physical and temporal boundaries of their owners' property through their social relations. Some started their own families on or off an owner's property (abroad marriages), built communities around religious life, hosted their own holiday celebrations or "illegal" parties in remote locations, or temporarily ran away to visit family or to escape punishment. Although these measures were small, they denied enslavers absolute control over the bodies, spaces, and lives of enslaved people. They also allowed the enslaved opportunities to build communities or "neighborhoods" on adjoining plantations, across farms, or in urban spaces. These communities varied depending on location and concentration of the enslaved, but enslaved individuals used these social connections to enrich their lives outside the direct purview of their enslavers.[6]

Beyond hidden, everyday actions that were not openly confrontational, other enslaved Blacks took a more direct approach. As J. Blaine Hudson summarizes in his study of the Underground Railroad in Kentucky, Black Kentuckians had two paths to freedom before the Civil War: legal and extralegal actions. Some attempted to earn their own or family members' freedom through self-purchase by hiring out their labor or selling homemade crops and products. Other enslaved African Americans embarked upon bolder and, according to nineteenth-century laws, less than legal means of emancipation. These freedom seekers threw off the shackles of their enslavement and attempted to escape to gain their freedom. In Kentucky, this meant they would have to cross the Ohio River into the southern Midwest. Escape provided enslaved individuals—often men—with the greatest opportunity to gain control of their lives by forcibly ending their relationship with white enslavers. Such potential for Blacks' greater control over their own lives challenged the pro-slavery ideology of white Southerners. Any escape attempt brought the possibility of retribution on the escapees, if caught, or their families. This punishment could come as physical violence, the dismemberment of a family through sale, or dogged pursuit by slave catchers. Self-emancipation and overt challenges to white supremacy thus put freedom seekers into direct conflict with the visions of white Kentuckians, and those contradictions could transcend into other, spontaneous, and more dangerous means of resistance.[7]

As Wesley's case demonstrates, enslaved individuals often found themselves in precarious situations, forced to act with limited options. Although infrequently deployed, violence was one recourse Black Kentuckians used to assert control over their lives. Kentucky's antebellum history offers several examples. In 1848, Edward James Doyle, a Centre College student, led forty to seventy-five enslaved men on a march for freedom. Doyle's motives might not have been pure, and the band met fierce resistance from a white posse, who engaged and captured the would-be freedom seekers. Similarly, when Margaret Garner, her husband, Robert, their children, and her in-laws attempted to flee Archibald Gaines's property for Ohio in 1856, the enslaver and Cincinnati authorities caught up with the family within hours of their escape. When Robert Garner failed to fend off their captors, Margaret tried to kill her children to spare them the horrors of enslavement. In the spring of 1861, Jim Brown from Henderson County fled his enslaver after she refused to let him visit his wife. As Brown raced toward his wife, Dr. Walter A. Norwood cornered him in a barn. Brown killed Norwood and fled but was unwilling to abandon his wife, perhaps fearful that the looming secession crisis would keep them apart. Brown concealed himself near his wife's enslaver. Local whites, enraged by Norwood's death and inflamed by sectional tensions, hunted down Brown and slew him in a shootout. The Garners, the enslaved men with Edward Doyle, and Jim Brown represent examples of enslaved Kentuckians who wielded violence in calculated or desperate moments to enact their own vision of community and familial relationships.[8]

Wesley's actions offer a glimpse into how enslaved Kentuckians navigated and attempted to survive their enslavement through violence. Few enslaved individuals regularly turned to violence as a means of challenging their station in life. For every instance of an enslaved individual striking a white individual and living to tell about it (as when Frederick Douglass did so in 1834), there are many more stories of excessively brutal punishment, such as in response to Nat Turner's rebellion in 1831 or even to the rumor of enslaved rebellion in Mississippi in the 1840s. White Southerners freely wielded violence to punish Black individuals. Historians, however, are increasingly focusing on the moments when African Americans, enslaved or free, used violence to push back against the constraints of slavery. Although Black Americans could not freely wield violence, there are moments when they deployed violence as a necessary survival tool.[9]

If violence was occasionally necessary to survive in slaveholding Kentucky, what does that say about slavery in the state? Nothing good. This chapter complicates slavery and Black action in Kentucky. Violence used to preserve one's life might not have been intentional resistance to slavery on par with the actions of the Black men who followed Nat Turner, but it did challenge the institution by exposing its contradictions nonetheless. For enslaved individuals, wrapped in a system of racism and brutal oppression, sometimes violence was necessary to live. To advance that narrative, this chapter pulls examples from the *Civil War Governors of Kentucky Digital Documentary Edition,* a project that uses documents produced during the administrations of Kentucky's five wartime governors to explore how ordinary people appealed to the governors as a means to arbitrate their lives in the throes of civil strife. Using Wesley's story, this essay frames how enslaved Kentuckians used violence when necessary to navigate an oppressive system. In addition to Wesley, the chapter pulls from the examples of John and Jourdan, enslaved men who also lived in Caldwell County; Caroline Dement, an enslaved woman from Tennessee who sought freedom with the US Army; and other Blacks in military service during the war. From these examples, we can glimpse the intersection of agency, force, self-preservation, and community maintenance in the lives of enslaved Kentuckians throughout the mid–nineteenth century.[10]

When Jesse Williams handed Wesley a gun and instructed him to murder Stevens, the enslaver operated from a worldview where white men held all the power. Williams likely believed that he had designed the perfect crime: Who would believe the word of an enslaved man set against that of his white owner in pro-slavery Kentucky? To some degree, Williams was partially correct: the Caldwell County Circuit Court would in fact convict

Wesley and sentence him to hang for murder. Yet in the end Williams was not alive to see that development because he was wrong on a much deeper level. By ordering Wesley to kill Edmund Stevens, Williams had undermined the foundation of a society built on a pro-slavery ideology.[11]

Two petitions from Caldwell County attorneys provide the background for Wesley's case. One came from William H. Calvert, an attorney and enslaver in Caldwell County who handled the disbursement of Jesse Williams's estate after his death. The other petition came from Edward P. Campbell, the Commonwealth's attorney, who likely led the prosecution of Wesley. Both petitions noted the rivalry between Williams and Stevens and the petitioners' belief that Wesley had acted through manipulation by his enslaver. Yet neither attorney directly intimated why they might have written on Wesley's behalf. Another, undated letter from Calvert to the governor's office provides a potential motivation behind the petitions. In the aftermath of Jesse Williams's death, he notes that Williams's older sons—John and James—fled the state "in order to save their lives and were persued [sic] with an armed force to the state line." Not only had Jesse Williams concocted the murder of a rival, but also between 1858 and 1859 the father and sons had received several indictments in the Circuit Court for assault and another for attempted murder. Calvert suggests that the Williams family had consistently upset the local community through violent actions. The murder of Stevens at the hands of an enslaved man, used as a weapon to deflect suspicion, went too far. The two petitions also cut across a wide section of Caldwell County society. Campbell's petition includes the signatures of a judge, the county clerk, a sheriff, a deputy sheriff, and a jailor, while Calvert's petition pulls from local residents, including painters, farmers, and wealthy enslavers. Although the petitioners could not condone Wesley's actions, they could sustain their pro-slavery ideology by blaming a violent white family as the primary instigators of the murder of Stevens. In turn, they asked for leniency on Wesley's behalf. Such a defense was interested less in securing justice for Wesley than in preserving social order, stripping Wesley of agency, and shifting blame solely onto Williams.[12]

Yet, despite the desire to condemn Williams and preserve order, these petitions do recapture the enslaved man's actions. Ironically, by using those actions to demonstrate how Williams manipulated Wesley, the petitioners revealed how enslaved individuals wrested a modicum of control over their lives from the intent and will of their enslavers. The petitions on

Wesley's behalf argued that after he received Williams's murderous instructions, he went "time and again under the order of his master to kill Stevens, of nights that he would not leave the farm of his master and would come in in the morning and tell his master he could not get a chance to kill Stevens." On the surface, Wesley wielded an important tool of the enslaved arsenal—he slowed down his work. Taking multiple trips and reporting his failure to an increasingly frustrated Williams, Wesley delayed killing Stevens. Before he stretched such delays too far, he also informed Williams of a dog that guarded the Stevens property, which made a stealthy approach impracticable. To remedy this hindrance, Jesse Williams provided the enslaved man with strychnine to poison the dog. Unwilling to slay the canine, Wesley discarded poison-laced meat in a nearby tree that the dog could not reach.[13] Again, Wesley demonstrated how he and other enslaved Kentuckians challenged their enslavers' control. Throwing away the poison, Wesley adapted how other enslaved individuals challenged their enslaver's will by breaking tools or damaging crops subtly but not openly to assert control and undermine their owners through the waste of resources.

Such challenges by enslaved individuals often pitted white enslavers and Black people in competitions over space: a social configuration that Stephanie Camp terms the "rival geography" of enslaved life. Enslavers depended on strict visions of space and time to control their human property. As Camp argues, enslavers built "geographies of containment" that divided farms or plantations into well-cultivated, legitimate spaces and the wild, unmaintained areas between white properties. The latter swamps and forests represented wilderness or, more precisely, illegitimate spaces not to be used by Black or even white Southerners. Such geographical development dually marked the end of a white man's property and thereby the point where the world of enslaved Blacks should, according to whites, cease. Yet enslaved individuals often extended these boundaries on their own accord or in performing duties for their enslavers. Armed with passes that permitted their travel, enslaved people (most often but not exclusively men) served as carriage drivers, visited families on other properties, and attended religious services. Whites intended that the physical boundaries of their properties and a pass system would contain enslaved individuals to their will and vision of Southern society. Black men and women, however, reworked those boundaries, moving without passes or their master's permission to hold illicit parties, to visit family without permission, or to temporarily run away. Wesley shared in this process by his use of space to undermine Williams's intent.[14]

Ultimately, despite all his attempts to evade his task, Wesley had to kill Stevens as a practical if desperate step to ensure his own temporary survival. None of the petitions speculates as to why Wesley worked to thwart his master other than a short note that he was waiting for the release of John Williams (Jesse's son) from the county jail on a charge of "Striking with the intent to kill." It is possible that Wesley hoped the return of the other Williams would allow him to appeal for some form of intervention. The fact that Jesse escorted Wesley to Stevens's property on the morning of John Williams's release from jail lends some credence to this explanation. But why did Wesley kill a man for whom he harbored no ill will? The simple answer is survival. Faced with Jesse Williams on one side, threatening to "cut his back to pieces," and the act of pulling the trigger on the other, Wesley took the safest course he saw: to kill Stevens. Wesley's use of violence was a last resort geared toward preserving his life in the moment. The key here is that an enslaved man first used traditional forms of resistance against Jesse Williams, but when forced to confront his own mortality, Wesley resorted to "necessary" violence. This was a rare and dangerous venture, but one that was strategically deployed by African Americans and that blended both open and hidden forms of resistance. Violence was a bold move, but in Wesley's case it protected him from summary execution by Williams. More subtly, it protected other enslaved people on Williams's property because any danger fell on one person rather than on the whole. Wesley's confession after his arrest lends credence to the fact that he tried to control his life and save it for as long as he could.[15]

Other enslaved individuals wielded violence as a means of protecting themselves or their communities in antebellum Kentucky. On January 17, 1860, Thomas Wadlington, his son William, and two enslaved men, John and Jourdan, made their way down the road to cut lumber for firewood. When the Wadlingtons' slaves chopped down a tree later that afternoon, the resounding crash ignited tensions between Thomas and his neighbor, Milton Cartwright. For months, the Wadlingtons and Cartwright had argued over timbering rights on their adjoining properties. Not long after the tree fell, Cartwright arrived with John Prince and James Blalock, two white laborers he employed, to confront the Wadlingtons.[16]

Conflicting reports distort what happened next, but the role of violence and enslaved individuals intersected as Wadlington and Cartwright's words came to blows and then to the use of weapons. Prince and Blalock testified that Thomas Wadlington fired first, unloading his shotgun into Cartwright's chest. Thomas and his son William unsurprisingly challenged that Milton Cartwright started the melee after drawing a concealed pistol and firing at Thomas. Regardless of the conflict's origin, both Wadlington and Cartwright exchanged gunfire. After the first volley, Wadlington closed the distance between them and bludgeoned Cartwright. As they struggled, Prince attempted to intervene, but at least one of the enslaved men stopped Prince from interfering in the deadly clash— although clear details are illusive. Blalock later testified that when Prince went to separate Cartwright and Wadlington, William Wadlington interfered, and the slave "Jourdan ran up and drew his axe on Prince and told him if he attempted to interfere he would slay him." When the fighting concluded, Cartwright was dead, pierced by bullets and bludgeoned across his face and back, and Wadlington had suffered a bullet wound to his leg. In the aftermath of the confrontation, Wadlington, his son William, and Jourdan were arrested for their roles in the affair.[17]

Jourdan's involvement in the Wadlington–Cartwright affair was minor, but we should consider why he would have interceded at all. According to the Slave Schedule for 1860, Mary Wadlington, Thomas's wife, owned seven enslaved persons: three men (ages thirty-five, fifteen, and one) and four women (ages twenty-three, eighteen, seventeen, and thirteen). It is unclear if the two older enslaved men are Jourdan and John, but it is clear that an enslaved family unit existed on or near the Wadlingtons' property. The violent clash between Thomas Wadlington and Milton Cartwright could have threatened that Black family. Mary Wadlington reported that Cartwright had besieged their home for months—throwing verbal abuse at the family and, on at least one occasion, shooting at their home. While Mary and Thomas Wadlington slept in fear, their enslaved people, ranging from young children to adults, would have also sensed the danger from Cartwright's actions. Allowing the white men to resolve their difficulty, especially in a manner that seemed to favor Wadlington, would afford the Wadlingtons' slaves a modicum of protection against a person they might have viewed as a threat to their own or their community's safety.[18]

Alternatively, other practical concerns about their community might have also influenced Jourdan and John. One of the greatest threats against enslaved communities was their enslavers' ability to sell individuals as property. Enslavers used the sale of African Americans as a means of both profit and control. The selling of individual family members either "down river" to the Deep South or to another enslaver farther away separated Black families and disrupted their communities in Kentucky and across the South. John and Jourdan likely realized that if the fight did not go well for Thomas Wadlington, they or members of their community could suffer. If Thomas died in the fight, the Wadlingtons could experience financial troubles and in turn could sell some of their enslaved people to ease economic burdens. Alternatively, Mary Wadlington could have blamed John or Jourdan for not protecting her husband, which could have led to physical punishment or the dismemberment of their enslaved community. Thomas also could have ordered the enslaved individuals to assist him, and if they failed to do so, they could have also faced punishment. Jourdan never provided evidence about why he interceded, but his actions—threatening violence to keep the white men Prince and Blalock out of the affair yet not actually attacking the two men—again indicates a calculated deployment of violence by enslaved Kentuckians to assert liminal control and to guard themselves or their community.[19]

As we have seen from the examples of Wesley, Jourdan, and Jim Brown, Black Kentuckians could and did wield violence on select occasions to protect themselves or to gain temporary control over their lives. Although these violent acts were rare, they also allow us to reframe the longer history of African Americans' challenges to enslavement in Kentucky. Black Kentuckians did not passively accept the shackles of enslavement. Rather, they used various strategies to contest those constraints. The Civil War amplified those opportunities for African Americans across the South. In Kentucky, the ability to challenge enslavers came unevenly, but as it did, Black individuals adapted prewar methods to wartime circumstances.

When the war began in 1861, Kentucky fractured along political, geographical, and regional lines. In the presidential election of 1860, white Kentuckians had voted for John Bell, advocating for the continuation of the United States as it was—a united nation built upon the back of Black enslavement, which ignored racial inequity and looked forward to a prosperous future. Abraham Lincoln's victory, made possible mostly by Northern voters—in Kentucky, for example, he received double-digit votes in only a handful of counties—and his membership in the Republican Party, which opposed the expansion of slavery, prompted white Southerners to respond with vitriol. Eleven of the slaveholding states eventually inaugurated open warfare against the federal government to build their own slaveholding republic. Kentuckians, with social and economic ties to both the North and the South as well as a politically nurtured fondness for compromise, charted a neutral course that demanded the preservation of slavery. When Confederate troops preemptively moved into the state in September 1861, and neutrality failed, the war came to Kentucky. Whereas white Kentuckians were divided in their responses, enslaved residents had no reservations about the conflict.[20]

Black Kentuckians saw in the presence of the United States Army new opportunities to challenge their enslavement. As the army moved into Kentucky, occupying cities and building camps across the state, Union soldiers became the focus of attention for enslaved African Americans. Black Kentuckians turned the Confederacy's rallying cry—that Lincoln would destroy slavery—into an ironic self-fulfilling prophecy. Black men and women looked to urban centers and US Army outposts as sites of their emancipation. The allure of freedom no longer rested solely beyond the Ohio River but rather came into Kentucky with the US Army.[21]

In their attempts to assert control in the wake of civil war, enslaved people in Kentucky and throughout the South found uneven success. When the war began, most white Northerners and even the Lincoln administration did not intend to dismantle slavery. This is especially true in Kentucky, where white residents predominately supported the preservation of the Union *and* slavery. The Lincoln administration aided these efforts early in the war: ordering soldiers to return freedom seekers and designing policies that did not target enslaved Blacks in Kentucky. Yet as Amy Taylor notes in her recent work on emancipation and Black refugees, African Americans persisted in their challenges to slavery despite these restrictions. Freedom came slowly, and its success depended on time as well as place. In Kentucky, enslaved African Americans found success at places such as Camp Nelson and in urban centers. Throughout the wartime South, some white Union soldiers grew resentful of slavery, viewing the institution as a bulwark of Confederate strength and an ill that needed to be remedied to prevent future conflict. These men helped enslaved individuals escape from their masters, hiding them in camps, extracting them across the Ohio River, hiring them as camp servants, and refusing to return them to their owners. White Kentuckians increasingly resented these acts and grew hostile to emancipation as well as to the federal government as a result.[22]

Wesley again provides an example of how Black slaves challenged white pro-slavery ideology during the war, despite white Kentuckians' animosity to emancipation. In April 1861, as the conflict began, Wesley escaped from the county jail while he awaited sentencing. There is little information about what exactly happened next; a newspaper article noted that he escaped, but there is no information other than the fact that someone recaptured him before his sentencing in June. However, his timing is important. Wesley fled around April 15, 1861, mere days after the attack on Fort Sumter and the inauguration of open hostilities between the United States and the Confederacy. Although Wesley might not have known directly about the start of the conflict, rumor networks informed Black Americans about the looming possibility of war following Lincoln's election. Regardless of his knowledge, Wesley escaped from jail in another bid to control his life and prevent the looming death sentence. Despite his unsuccessful attempt to escape, his gambit is instructive for how the war presented Black Kentuckians, male and female, with greater opportunities to break away from the institution of slavery.[23]

Although Black men often appeared to be the sole or primary challengers to enslavement, in recent years historians have reframed the gendered dynamics of enslaved resistance and survival to highlight how Black women also challenged their masters. Nineteenth-century Americans framed their world around gendered ideologies according to which men operated publicly through political activities, military service, and business transactions, whereas women maintained domestic spaces that privileged home and family. Enslavers attempted to impose a similar structure on their enslaved peoples. Black men more often worked in the fields, and enslaved women operated as cooks or domestic laborers in the home. Of course, the size and location of enslavement influenced these conditions because larger plantations could divide enslaved labor along gendered lines. On smaller slaveholding farms, which were common in Kentucky, enslaved men and women worked side by side in the fields with one another. In urban settings, enslaved men could often earn extra work as laborers, while enslaved women might serve as domestic servants. In addition, Black men could work as carriage drivers or receive passes to visit families on adjoining property if they were part of an abroad marriage. Each of these responsibilities, although framed within the control of white owners, permitted Black men opportunities to step beyond the sight of their enslavers. These few moments could allow Black men the opportunity to learn more about local geography or forge networks with other slaves and sympathetic whites. All of these advantages could help an enslaved man to escape. Yet enslaved women also attempted to control their lives and challenge their enslavers.[24]

To many observers, including contemporaries and early historians, such challenges by Black women often went unmarked, leaving many to think of resistance as a male prerogative. However, Black women did participate in those obscured but everyday forms of survival. Marion Lucas's history of African Americans in Kentucky from 1760 to 1891 highlights a variety of forms of Black female resistance. Some enslaved households, like that of Joseph Cotter's mother near Louisville, served as a hiding place for freedom seekers looking to cross the Ohio River. Lucas notes how one enslaved woman used domestic activities, such as selling goods at a market in Cincinnati, to sneak her family to freedom. Black women also used their access to the kitchens and the stomachs of their white masters as a means of poisoning their enslavers. Other historians have noted how Black women and their homes served as locations of resistance to enslavement. Some enslaved women provided food—either grown by themselves or acquired from their masters' larders—for private social gatherings for the enslaved or for freedom-seeking enslaved individuals. In addition, like Lucas's examples, the homes of enslaved individuals, often under the stewardship of women, could also serve as temporary hiding places for enslaved persons who attempted to evade their enslavers, as in Wesley's navigation of space to avoid killing Stevens. Any enslaved Black man (or woman) who fled from slavery had to rely on networks of individuals to assist them in their escape. Last, an enslaved person's home could serve as a site of information exchange. Black Americans, who worked in the homes of their owners and overheard conversations between whites, shared that information with one another in their own private spaces. By sharing information, supporting social events, aiding freedom seekers, or escaping themselves, enslaved women participated in resistance against white elites.[25]

Women's role in reproduction and thus in the continuation of the system of slavery created another space of resistance at the intersection of Black bodies, reproductive rights, and childcare. Enslaved peoples could enact small measures of resistance, but whites maintained control over four million Black bodies in 1860. This control was never clearer than in the reproductive rights of Black women. Enslavers determined the status of Black children by the condition of their mother—a free mother bore free children, whereas an enslaved mother brought into the world slave children. Thus, any children born by enslaved women, regardless of the fathers' condition, were born as slaves. Economically, the birth of enslaved children sustained the wealth and power of enslavers, making childbearing an essential element of Black female slave labor. Emotionally, for enslaved women, their children represented the balance of hope and horror within the institution of slavery, where they strived to survive and lived with hope that freedom would come for their children.[26]

Some African American women looked to prevent their children from experiencing the crushing toll of slavery. One option was to extricate whole families from the horrors of enslavement—by escape or, more seriously, by death. A few enslaved women, such as Margaret Garner, would rather kill their children than allow them to grow up in the oppressive institution of slavery. The act of infanticide emerged as an option for enslaved women to resist their enslavers and challenge the role of sexual violence in the institution of slavery. White owners could and did rape enslaved women. These women rarely had the ability to prevent their white masters' violence against them. This is not to suggest that Black women passively accepted such actions. Rather, the imbalance of power favored the white men's control and authority and left Black women with minimal control over their own bodies. Although some white men might face scorn or disapproval from other whites for their sexual exploitation of Black women, this did not prevent sexual violence. Instead, rape and sexual assault remained a form of white social control of Black women from the antebellum years to well into the twentieth century. Yet if sexual violence functioned as a means of controlling Black women, it also held out a space of resistance. Some women would attempt to flee from their abusive owners or report the illicit acts to other whites, and others used violence. This violence could be carried out directly in the form of physical resistance against their attackers or indirectly by infanticide to stop the horrors of slavery and abuse from spreading to their children. Through infanticide, Black women used violence to challenge white authority.[27]

One example of infanticide and Black female resistance found in the *Civil War Governors of Kentucky Digital Documentary Edition* concerns the actions of an enslaved woman by the name of Caroline Dement in 1862. Late that summer, Caroline followed the Union army out of Tennessee as it raced to defend Kentucky from Confederate invasion. She followed

Union forces away from her enslaver, John Dement, around the same time that the US government had begun to tacitly if incompletely embrace emancipation as a tangential goal of the war. The current of potential freedom thus pulled Caroline (and possibly her husband) north to Louisville. Kentucky and its largest city denied Black people freedom of movement without the permission of their masters or proof of their freedom. When a slave patrol in the city inquired as to Caroline's status, they determined she was an escaped slave and arrested her. From there, the Jefferson County sheriff remanded her to the custody of Willis and Annie Levi until her owner could collect his property. In the meantime, Caroline would live with the Levi family and take care of their young child, Blanche.[28]

At first, Caroline seemed to have found a precarious if acceptable position in Louisville, removed from her enslavement: the Levis treated her well, and she was able to spend time with her husband. Yet she was neither free nor entirely secure. The relationship with the Levis eventually soured as they criticized Caroline's relationship and late-night rendezvous with her husband. The identity of Caroline's husband is unclear, but their late-night meetings angered Annie Levi. Further, Willis accused Caroline of leaving a gate open that allowed local livestock to damage several fruit trees. Neighbors also noted a tense exchange after Caroline threw trash on a freshly painted fence. Tensions were thus high when Willis departed Louisville on a business trip to Tennessee. Annie Levi continued to reprimand Caroline during Willis's absence, and the discord only grew. Tensions reached a critical point one morning when Annie fell ill. Not long after Annie went to take a nap, Caroline burst into the room claiming that Blanche was acting strangely, and within a few moments the two were with the child as she died from strychnine poisoning.[29]

It is little surprise that, prompted by whites' fears of being poisoned by their slaves, the strained relationship between Caroline and the Levis, and the trauma of Blanche's death, Annie and Willis accused Caroline of murdering their daughter. Willis Levi had acquired the strychnine to rid the neighborhood of annoying animals, although he conveniently left out the fact that those animals were his neighbors' domesticated pets. The Levis had also left the poison in an unlocked chest in their home. Annie Levi would testify that a few days prior to Blanche's death, she had seen that very chest disturbed, though Caroline denied any knowledge of the chest. Annie Levi's testimony also noted that her own illness had come on after she had consumed a cup of coffee prepared for her by Caroline. Based on this testimony from the Levis, the Jefferson Circuit Court sentenced Caroline to die.[30]

Not all Louisvillians were convinced of Caroline's guilt, and some individuals rallied to her defense. Local antislavery advocates, a few lawyers, Black religious leaders, and some of Willis Levi's neighbors appealed the writ of execution to Governor Thomas E. Bramlette. The defense centered on the relationship between Willis Levi and his neighbors. Put in the best of terms, they despised him. Willis, for instance, had tried to poison the neighbors' pets. If Willis had strewn poison-laced meat around his property with murderous zeal, they argued, how likely was it that Blanche had accidentally grabbed one of those tainted pieces of meat? The defense worked, and Governor Thomas Bramlette pardoned Caroline in September 1863. Bramlette himself was an enslaver and an opponent of Black freedom, so his leniency in this case might have been the result of evidence on the enslaved woman's behalf, but it could also have been a politically practical decision. By late 1863, Kentucky had continued to divide over the war and the scope of emancipation. Bramlette could have pardoned Caroline to bury the story and prevent conflict over the execution of an enslaved Tennessee woman in Louisville as tensions between the Commonwealth and Washington roiled. Regardless of his motivations, Caroline, once pardoned, slipped out of the historical record.[31]

Yet as Carole Emberton argues in her essay on Caroline Dement in the *Register of the Kentucky Historical Society,* historians can use "disciplined imagination" to reconstruct and interpret the lives of individuals such as Dement who barely appear in written records. The charge of infanticide both highlights the enslavers' fear that their enslaved people would wield poison against them and calls attention to the fact that enslaved women could and at times did use violence as a means to resist the institution of slavery. Context is important here—most discussions of infanticide in enslaved communities concern enslaved mothers who killed their children rather than allow them to exist in a world that would destroy them physically, emotionally, and spiritually. The murder of a white child would have been a drastic attack against the family that kept Caroline chained in quasi-enslavement. According to the notion of disciplined imagination, it would have been possible for Caroline to access the poison in the Levi household. If she had attempted to poison both Annie Levi and Blanche, she could have removed a barrier to her confinement in Louisville, joined her husband, and attempted to escape from the city while

Willis Levi was away on business. However, Caroline did not attempt to secure her freedom after the child died. Nevertheless, the conversation around the child's poisoning highlights how enslaved women challenged their enslavement in spaces and ways subtly different from those of their male counterparts.[32]

Regardless of Caroline Dement's guilt or innocence, her attempt to wrest control of her life away from a society bent on enslaving her was possible because of the Civil War. The conflict fundamentally rearranged boundaries on the border of slavery and freedom, and in Kentucky it provided enslaved individuals with the opportunity to flee toward freedom. Enslaved Blacks throughout the South forced Union authorities to consider the meaning of slavery in a war that pitted masters against the Union. Free Black orators and publishers extolled the service of African Americans during the American Revolution and the War of 1812 as well as the immorality of slavery as arguments for why the United States should embrace emancipation. Confronted by an increasingly difficult war and the actions of enslaved African Americans, by late 1862 a growing number of Northerners had come to see the destruction of slavery as instrumental to a successful conclusion of the war. When Lincoln announced and the government later implemented the Emancipation Proclamation, the Civil War became a conflict for the preservation of the Union *and* the destruction of slavery.[33]

As the war loosened the constraints of slavery elsewhere, white Kentuckians tried to tighten their hold over the vestiges of a slaveholding republic. As Black Kentuckians attempted self-emancipation, seizing on the proximity of the US Army as a liberating element, white enslavers responded harshly, increasing slave patrols to hunt down and punish the freedom seekers. White Kentuckians beat, tortured, and murdered Black men and women to prevent them from acquiring any semblance of freedom during the war. Nevertheless, Black Kentuckians persisted in their attempts to escape from their enslavers. Some went to Union outposts as laborers hired out by their enslavers to aid the Union cause. Others arrived at those outposts as fugitives who hoped the army might shield them from vengeful masters. Eventually, around US outposts such as Camp Nelson in Jessamine County, Black women and children built temporary refugee communities. Despite white enslavers' resistance to emancipation and the federal government's desire to placate an important border state, the pull of freedom overwhelmed the institution of slavery in Kentucky. Starting in 1864, Black Kentuckians were able to enlist in the United States Colored Troops (USCT) within Kentucky instead of having to make the perilous journey to Ohio, Illinois, Indiana, or Tennessee, as they previously had to do. Many enlisted enthusiastically. By war's end, more than twenty-three thousand formerly enslaved Kentuckians would serve in the USCT—roughly 56 percent of the eligible Black male population (ages twenty to forty-five) in the state. In comparison, approximately eighty thousand white Kentuckians served in the Union army, while another twenty to forty thousand joined the Confederate army. Those enslaved Kentuckians worked to ensure that their military service would help secure their freedom and extend protection to their families.[34]

If we reframe the use of violence by Black Kentuckians as a mechanism to assert control over their lives, then the Civil War provides an opportunity to understand how enslaved people expanded their prewar acts of resistance to their wartime experience. In essence, it offers an opportunity to show continuity between their struggles before, during, and after the war. The idea that African Americans used extreme means, if necessary or in desperation, to protect themselves or their families leads to a logical conclusion for the war: service in the US military presented a path that promised the destruction of slavery and the possibility of freedom. Freed from slavery's shackles, Black Kentuckians could gather their families, build their own communities, and determine their own lives. This grand idea, however, met practical challenges. Early enlistments only freed enslaved men from their masters and offered little in the way of protection to their families. Whereas some Union officials supported the freeing of all enslaved individuals, others returned Black family members to their owners, even while formerly enslaved husbands, fathers, brothers, and sons fought in the Union army. Despite the obstacles posed by both Southerners and some Northerners, Black Kentuckians saw military service as a means of asserting control over their lives in an unprecedented way and of protecting the nation. They would also push for greater control of their lives by demanding that military authorities shield their families in exchange for service. In short, through military service Black Kentuckians legally wielded violence against the Confederacy and the institution of slavery.

If Black Kentuckians extended antebellum means of asserting control over their lives, enslavers also continued their prewar methods of forcing compliance. If enslaved men ran away to join the Union army and enslavers could not stop them, the enslavers turned their malice on Black families. In early 1865, the case of a formerly enslaved woman named Lennie testifies to the extent of protection that military service could offer enslaved Kentuckians. A letter penned by H. H. Hadley of the 119th USCT extended protection to Lennie, formerly enslaved by Parker Bryant of Lexington. Lennie claimed that her escape was supported by an order "issued by Maj Gen'l Palmer freeing the wives of C'd Soldiers—She says that she is the wife of a colored Soldier." The letter also extended protection to Daniel Engles, who sheltered Lennie from persecution by Lexington authorities. Although the letter provides no information as to the identity of Lennie's husband other than that he served in Captain Hall's company, that omission matters little. Rather, his service enabled Lennie to choose her fate by running away from her enslaver.[35]

Black soldiers from Kentucky reinforced the idea that military service was more than just patriotic duty; it was a means to use state-sanctioned violence to gain control over their lives and, they hoped, to protect their families. Enlistment and freedom for Black men thus offered new opportunities to assert control but also risked endangering their families. Black soldiers would push for the government to protect their families in exchange for their service. Aaron Oats, a Black private, appealed to Edwin Stanton, the US secretary of war, in early 1865 to assist him in the recovery of his wife. Oats claimed that Jerry Smith, his wife's enslaver, had captured her after Oats enlisted in the USCT. Oats argued that as he was "a *Soldier.* willing to loose [*sic*] my life for my Country and the liberty of my fellow man," so the government should assist him in the protection of his family. Similarly, John Burnside of the 124th USCT noted the threat presented by his wife's enslaver and military policy in Kentucky. When the son of William Royster returned home after serving with John Hunt Morgan in the Confederate army, Royster blamed Burnside's wife for alerting the provost marshal of the Confederate soldier's presence. Burnside secured the promise of a Colonel Sedgwick to protect his family and was thus able to bring them to Camp Nelson. In November 1864, Speed S. Fry, commander of Camp Nelson, evicted hundreds of enslaved refugees from the installation, including Burnside's family, and thrust them into the harsh winter with little protection. Burnside and other Black soldiers complained that while they served the nation, their families suffered, despite assurances for their protection. In the minds of Oats and Burnside, they had extended that action of service to the national government and in exchange for the violence they enacted upon enemies of the government, they expected a modicum of control that would reward their families with protection.[36]

Other Black soldiers drew upon the concept of military service, violence, and support of the government as the linchpin in their arguments for Union protection of the Black community. When Charles W. Singer of the 107th USCT recruited Black volunteers in Louisville, he argued that if Confederate troops had penetrated as deep into the North as the Union army had into the South, "our homes would have been burned to the ground, and our aged and defenseless parents barbarously treated." Singer pledged to fight for the rest of his life if necessary and reminded Black soldiers, "We are fighting a great battle for the benefit not only of our country, but for ourselves and the whole of mankind." If enslaved men failed to take part in the war, they would "lose the best opportunity that has ever been afforded to us to show the whole world that we are willing to fight for our rights." Singer's rhetoric tied together the threat of enslavement and, for the vast majority of Black Kentuckians, their hitherto denied rights. In a letter to the *Weekly Anglo-African,* William A. Warfield also noted the connections between service and Black community on the Fourth of July in 1865. As Black Kentuckians gathered in a former slave state to celebrate their newfound freedoms, Warfield argued that to secure their rights the formerly enslaved "must *strive* for them" and be willing to "pay the same price that other people [have] been compelled to pay. By laboring for our own cause we show, in the first place, that we understand and appreciate what our rights are; in the second place, that we have the courage and manhood to ask for them; in the third place, that we are determined, sooner or later, to have them." Warfield portrayed military service and active vigilance against whites as necessary steps to allow Black Kentuckians to maintain control of their lives. This juxtaposition between the celebration of slavery's destruction and the work that remained before them signified the continual struggle for control among Black Kentuckians carried from antebellum resistance into wartime service. It also poignantly signaled the work that remained after the Civil War.[37]

It did not take long for Warfield and other Black Kentuckians to realize these long-term challenges. When Governor Thomas Bramlette presented his annual message to Kentucky's General Assembly in December 1865, he articulated a vision of the state that reflected antebellum race relations. Although the war had destroyed slavery and made freedom a natural condition protected by the Constitution, Bramlette argued, "Franchises other than freedom are political, not natural, and are left to the States respectively to regulate each for itself." The war may have ended slavery, but it did not alter white Kentuckians' expectation of control over Black Kentuckians. Bramlette pledged the full might of the state to prevent Black Kentuckians from acquiring political rights.[38]

Bramlette did not lie about white Kentuckians' intention to restrict the rights and opportunities of African Americans after 1865. White Unionists such as Bramlette and former Confederates, including the state's second provisional Confederate governor, Richard Hawes, worked to constrain Black Kentuckians in the years after the war. Some historians have argued for the benevolence of Kentucky race relations during Reconstruction, but in doing so they are denying the reality of racial violence throughout the state. Other historians such as George C. Wright, Aaron Astor, Patrick Lewis, and Anne Marshall have demonstrated how white Kentuckians bitterly repressed African Americans in their newfound freedoms. Their tactics were numerous: intimidation, violence, legal codes that controlled movement, redistricting after African Americans earned the right to vote by means of the Fifteenth Amendment in 1870, and race baiting. In short, racial violence and oppression were an integral part of Kentucky's postwar history.[39]

A return to the stories of Wesley, Caroline, and Jourdan is instructive regarding the legacies of African American violence, survival, and struggles for control in the long nineteenth century. After the pleas from local officials on Wesley's behalf, Governor Beriah Magoffin commuted the enslaved man's death sentence to life in the Frankfort State Penitentiary. Wesley lived there for two years until his death in January 1863. It remains unclear how he died. Perhaps it was from an outbreak of disease. Thomas Wadlington, who likewise had his sentence commuted by Magoffin to life in prison for killing Milton Cartwright, also died in the state penitentiary two months after Wesley's death. Aside from his entry in the penitentiary's records, Wesley disappears from the historical record after Magoffin reduced his sentence. Similarly, Caroline Dement and Jourdan also disappeared from historical narratives. The absence of these three Black individuals who tried to survive the institution of slavery is a reflection on the social circumstances of mid-nineteenth-century American *and* archival practices that eschewed Black voices. Yet with a careful reading of documents and contemporary digital practices that pull together previously scattered documents, it is possible to capture how African Americans in Kentucky survived their enslavement through both subtle and visible actions.[40]

After the war, despite limitations and silences, African Americans in Kentucky continued to resist the control of whites who had once enslaved them and who attempted to remodel the state in the veneer of the antebellum racial landscape. As they had before the war, Black Kentuckians offered a variety of responses to white control. Some built communities; others left Kentucky or moved to urban settings in the state, where they built or expanded Black neighborhoods. Others used new avenues available to them—they voted in elections, appealed to state and governmental officials, and cited their loyalty to the federal government during the Civil War. A select few would defend their homes or property with violence. The destruction of slavery in Kentucky was an unexpected extension of the actions of enslaved people and the contours of the Civil War itself. Yet, much as the rest of the nation has noticed in recent years, the end of the Civil War in Kentucky did not resolve the lingering issues of racial oppression and conflict. Kentucky was still a state dominated by white individuals who had fought for a nation—whether it was the United States or the Confederacy—that would have maintained the institution of slavery.[41]

Exploring how Black Kentuckians attempted to survive their enslavement and how they used violence when necessary before and during the Civil War helps us recenter how the antebellum and wartime experiences of African Americans were part of a continual contest over civil rights and a persistent fight to protect their own lives, their families, and their communities. In that context, what we see is a continual struggle over their place in American society. Black men and women might have earned their freedom during the Civil War, but they would have to continue to fight to keep it.

Notes

1. This essay uses the name "Wesley" because it is used in court documents, although this person is also referred to as "West" in some petitions. See Edward P. Campbell et al. to Beriah Magoffin, June 16, 1861, Office of the Governor, Beriah Magoffin: Governor's Official Correspondence File, MG8-120 to MG8-121, Apprehension of Fugitives from Justice Papers, 1859–1862, Kentucky Department for Libraries and Archives, Frankfort, accessed via *Civil War Gover-*

nors of Kentucky Digital Documentary Edition (Frankfort: Kentucky Historical Society, n.d.), at http://discovery.civilwargovernors.org/document/KYR-0001-021-0033 (hereafter cited as *CWGK* with the appropriate web address to the document being cited); W. H. Calvert et al. to Beriah Magoffin, July 16, 1861, *CWGK,* at http://discovery.civilwargovernors.org/document/KYR-0001-021-0035; W. H. Calvert et al. to Beriah Magoffin, n.d., *CWGK,* at http: //discovery .civilwargovernors.org/document/KYR-0001-020-0713.

2. Calvert et al. to Magoffin, July 16, 1861; Edward P. Campbell et al. to Beriah Magoffin, June 16, 1861, *CWGK,* at http://discovery.civilwargovernors .org/document/KYR-0001-021-0033; Jeff Forret, "Slave–Poor White Violence in the Antebellum Carolinas," *North Carolina Historical Review* 81, no. 2 (April 2004): 139–67.

3. Two letters highlight the different narratives of Jesse Williams's lynching: Calvert et al. to Magoffin, n.d., and James R. Howlett et al. to unknown, n.d., *CWGK,* at http://discovery.civilwargovernors.org/document/KYR-0001-020-2380. For discussions of "regulators," racial violence, and Caldwell County, see George C. Bronaugh to Beriah Magoffin, January 30, 1860, *CWGK,* at http://discovery .civilwargovernors.org/document/KYR-0001-020-0004; Edward L. Ayers, *Vengeance & Justice: Crime and Punishment in the 19th-Century American South* (New York: Oxford University Press, 1984), 4–5, 11, 131–33; Laura Edwards, *The People and Their Peace: Legal Culture and the Transformation of Inequality in the Post-revolutionary South* (Chapel Hill: University of North Carolina Press, 2009), 5, 25, 188–89, 192–96, 240–44; Libra R. Hilde, *Slavery, Fatherhood, & Paternal Duty in African American Communities over the Long Nineteenth Century* (Chapel Hill: University of North Carolina Press, 2020), 18–19; Christopher Waldrep, "Opportunity on the Frontier South of the Green," in *The Buzzel about Kentuck: Settling the Promised Land,* ed. Craig Thompson Friend (Lexington: University Press of Kentucky, 1999), 156; and Christopher Waldrep, "Rank-and-File Votes and the Coming of the Civil War: Caldwell County, Kentucky, as Test Case," *Civil War History* 35, no. 1 (1989): 59–72.

4. Stephanie M. H. Camp, *Closer to Freedom: Enslaved Women & Everyday Resistance in the Plantation South* (Chapel Hill: University of North Carolina Press, 2004), 2–7; John Hope Franklin and Loren Schweninger, *Runaway Slaves: Rebels on the Plantation* (New York: Oxford University Press, 1999), 1–16; Steven Hahn, *A Nation under Our Feet: Black Political Struggles in the Rural South from Slavery to the Great Migration* (Cambridge, MA: Belknap Press of Harvard University Press, 2003), 16–61; Anthony E. Kaye, *Joining Places: Slave Neighborhoods in the Old South* (Chapel Hill: University of North Carolina Press, 2007), 4–12; Stephanie McCurry, *Confederate Reckoning: Power and Politics in the Civil War*

South (Cambridge, MA: Harvard University Press, 2010), 218–62; Christopher Phillips, *The Rivers Ran Backward: The Civil War and the Remaking of the American Middle Border* (New York: Oxford University Press, 2016), 27–42, 47–48.

5. J. Blaine Hudson, *Fugitive Slaves and the Underground Railroad in the Kentucky Borderland* (Jefferson, NC: McFarland, 2002), 7; Marion B. Lucas, *A History of Blacks in Kentucky,* vol. 1: *From Slavery to Segregation, 1760–1891* (Frankfort: Kentucky Historical Society, 1992), 51–53; Stephanie McCurry, *Masters of Small Worlds: Yeoman Households, Gender Relations, and the Political Culture of the Antebellum South Carolina Low Country* (New York: Oxford University Press, 1995), 171–207; Alicestyne Turley, "Spirited Away: Black Evangelicals and the Gospel of Freedom, 1790–1890," PhD diss., University of Kentucky, 2009, p. 15, at https://uknowledge.uky.edu/gradschool_diss/79.

6. Camp, *Closer to Freedom,* 60–79; Kaye, *Joining Places,* 4–12, 22–26, 32–44; Lucas, *History of Blacks in Kentucky,* 1:33–39. See also Kenneth W. Goings and Gerald L. Smith, "'Unhidden' Transcripts: Memphis and African American Agency, 1862–1920," in *The New African American Urban History,* ed. Kenneth W. Goings and Raymond A. Mohl (Thousand Oaks, CA: Sage, 1996), 142–66, as a conceptual framework for the idea that African Americans resisted inequality before, during, and after the Civil War through both open and hidden means of resistance.

7. Camp, *Closer to Freedom,* 15–16, 28, 35–44, 47–48; Franklin and Schweninger, *Runaway Slaves,* 17–48; Hilde, *Slavery, Fatherhood, & Paternal Duty,* 59, 112; Hudson, *Fugitive Slaves and the Underground Railroad,* 4–5, 11–12, 32–35; Lucas, *History of Blacks in Kentucky,* 1:63; Charyl Janifer LaRoche, *Free Black Communities and the Underground Railroad: The Geography of Resistance* (Champaign: University of Illinois Press, 2014).

8. For a larger discussion on Edward Patrick Doyle, see James Prichard's essay in this volume (chapter 3) as well as Hudson, *Fugitive Slaves and the Underground Railroad,* 136–37; Lucas, *History of Blacks in Kentucky,* 1:73; and James A. Ramage and Andrea S. Watkins, *Kentucky Rising: Democracy, Slavery, and Culture from the Early Republic to the Civil War* (Lexington: University Press of Kentucky, 2011), 249. For Margaret Garner's story, see Steven Weisenburger, *Modern Medea: A Family Story of Slavery and Child-Murder from the Old South* (New York: Hill and Wang, 1998), 5–11, 62–65; and Hudson, *Fugitive Slaves and the Underground Railroad,* 144–45. Jim Brown's story comes from Matthew C. Hulbert, "Wanted, Dead or Alive: The Fugitive Jim Brown and the Price of Loyalty," January 13, 2016, *CWGK,* at https://civilwargovernors.org/wanted-dead-or-alive-the-fugitive-jim-brown-and-the-price-of-loyalty/; Alex H. Major to Beriah Magoffin, April 3, 1861, *CWGK,* at http://discovery.civilwargovernors.org/document/KYR-0001-021-0029; Emily Moses, "On the Border of Free-

dom," *CWGK,* at https://civilwargovernors.org/on-the-border-of-freedom/#_ftn6; Robert T. Glass to Beriah Magoffin, April 4, 1861, *CWGK,* at http://discovery.civilwargovernors.org/document/KYR-0001-021-0028. In addition, Lucas provides an overview of numerous examples of enslaved resistance in chapter 3, "Resistance to Slavery," of *History of Blacks in Kentucky,* 1:51–83.

9. David Blight's biography of Douglass relays a singular clash between the overseer, Edward Covey, and Douglass in August 1834. Both Blight and Douglass cite the event as an important moment in the enslaved man's maturation, but the fight also represents a rare moment in which a Black man fought a white overseer, drew blood, and lived to write about the event years later. See David Blight, *Frederick Douglass: Prophet of Freedom* (New York: Simon & Schuster, 2018), 55–66. See also Vanessa M. Holden, *Surviving Southampton: African American Women and Resistance in Nat Turner's Community* (Champaign: University of Illinois Press, 2021), 2, 5–7, 10; Kellie Carter Jackson, *Force and Freedom: Black Abolitionists and the Politics of Violence* (Philadelphia: University of Pennsylvania Press, 2019), 3–6, 17–20, 25–26, 60, 62, 96; Joshua D. Rothman, *Flush Times & Fever Dreams: A Story of Capitalism and Slavery in the Age of Jackson* (Athens: University of Georgia Press, 2012), 91–156; and Stanley Harrold, *Border War: Fighting over Slavery before the Civil War* (Chapel Hill: University of North Carolina Press, 2010), 36–39.

10. Colin G. Calloway, *White People, Indians, and Highlanders: Tribal Peoples and Colonial Encounters in Scotland and America* (New York: Oxford University Press, 2010), 24–30; Forret, "Slave–Poor White Violence in the Antebellum Carolinas"; Stanley Harrold, "Violence and Nonviolence in Kentucky Abolitionism," *Journal of Southern History* 57, no. 1 (February 1991): 15–38; Hilde, *Slavery, Fatherhood, & Paternal Duty,* 16–21; Lucas, *History of Blacks in Kentucky,* 1:58; Ramage and Watkins, *Kentucky Rising,* 242.

11. For a discussion on other examples of enslaved individuals ordered to commit violence against white Southerners, see Craig Buettinger, "Did Slaves Have Free Will? *Luke, a Slave, v. Florida* and Crimes at the Command of a Master," *Florida Historical Quarterly* 83, no. 3 (2005): 241–57.

12. Calvert et al. to Magoffin, July 16, 1861; Campbell et al. to Magoffin, June 16, 1861; both letters deal with Wesley's case. Calvert to Magoffin, n.d., covers the death of Jesse Williams and the crimes and flight of his two sons, John and James.

13. Calvert et al. to Magoffin, July 16, 1861; Campbell et al. to Magoffin, June 16, 1861.

14. Camp, *Closer to Freedom,* 6–7, 14–16, 36–48; Franklin and Schweninger, *Runaway Slaves,* 98–103.

15. Calvert et al. to Magoffin, n.d.; Campbell et al. to Magoffin, June 16, 1861. This concept of open and hidden resistance comes from Goings and Smith, "'Unhidden' Transcripts."

16. *Commonwealth of Kentucky v. Thomas B. Wadlington,* January 1861, transcript, *CWGK,* at http://discovery.civilwargovernors.org/document/KYR-0001-020-0001; Mary A. J. Wadlington, affidavit, January 29, 1861, *CWGK,* at http://discovery.civilwargovernors.org/document/KYR-0001-020-0023.

17. *Commonwealth of Kentucky v. Thomas B. Wadlington,* January 1861, transcript; "The Wadlington Case," December 1860, *CWGK,* at http://discovery .civilwargovernors.org/document/KYR-0001-020-0079.

18. Jourdan was released on bail from the Princeton jail in time to return home for the census in June 1860. It is possible that this would make him the thirty-five-year-old enslaved man and John the fifteen-year-old belonging to Mary Wadlington—possibly explaining Jourdan's arrest. See extract from the *Princeton (KY) Bulletin* published in the *Louisville Daily Courier,* February 10, 1860; *Eighth Manuscript Census of the United States* (1860), Slave Schedules, Kentucky, Caldwell County, Princeton Division, pp. 221B–222A, accessed via Ancestry.com; Mary A. J. Wadlington, affidavit, January 29, 1861.

19. Camp, *Closer to Freedom,* 36–37; Hilde, *Slavery, Fatherhood, & Paternal Duty,* 58–62; Hahn, *A Nation under Our Feet,* 50–55; Hudson, *Fugitive Slaves and the Underground Railroad,* 55–56.

20. Patrick A. Lewis, *For Slavery and Union: Benjamin Buckner and Kentucky Loyalties in the Civil War* (Lexington: University Press of Kentucky, 2015), 55; James C. Klotter, "Kentucky, the Civil War, and the Spirit of Henry Clay," *Register of the Kentucky Historical Society* 110, nos. 3–4 (Summer–Autumn 2012): 243–63; Phillips, *The Rivers Ran Backward,* 105–8; Elizabeth Varon, *Armies of Deliverance: A New History of the Civil War* (New York: Oxford University Press, 2019), 6–15; Kenneth H. Williams and James Russell Harris, "Kentucky in 1860: A Statistical Overview," *Register of the Kentucky Historical Society* 103, no. 4 (Autumn 2005): 743–64.

21. Berry Craig, *Kentucky Confederates: Secession, Civil War, and the Jackson Purchase* (Lexington: University Press of Kentucky), 5–7 and chap. 6; Hahn, *A Nation under Our Feet,* 14, 82–89; Victor B. Howard, *Black Liberation in Kentucky: Emancipation and Freedom, 1862–1884* (Lexington: University Press of Kentucky, 1983), 4–5; Elizabeth D. Leonard, *Slaves, Slaveholders, and a Kentucky Community's Struggle Toward Freedom* (Lexington: University Press of Kentucky, 2019), 40–41.

22. Lewis, *For Slavery and Union,* 90–96; Lucas, *History of Blacks in Kentucky,* 1:148–49; Anne E. Marshall, *Creating a Confederate Kentucky: The Lost*

Cause and Civil War Memory in a Border State (Chapel Hill: University of North Carolina Press, 2010), 16–31; Amy Murrell Taylor, *Embattled Freedom: Journeys through the Civil War's Slave Refugee Camps* (Chapel Hill: University of North Carolina Press, 2018), 54–57, 180–81, 186. For examples of Kentuckians' disdain for emancipation, see Thomas E. Bramlette, "Message of the Governor T. E. Bramlette to the General Assembly of Kentucky, at Their Adjourned Session of 1863–4," January 4, 1865, *CWGK,* at http://discovery.civilwargovernors.org/document/KYR-0001-008-0001; and P. J. Honaker to James F. Robinson, July 23, 1863, *CWGK,* at http://discovery.civilwargovernors.org/document/KYR-0001-0031-0318.

23. *Commonwealth of Kentucky v. Wesley (a Slave),* judgment, no date given, *CWGK,* at http://discovery.civilwargovernors.org/document/KYR-0001-021-0032; *Louisville Daily Journal,* April 15, 1861; Hahn, *A Nation under Our Feet,* 15, 57–60.

24. Camp, *Closer to Freedom,* 36–38; Hilde, *Slavery, Fatherhood, & Paternal Duty,* 50–66; Thavolia Glymph, *Out of the House of Bondage: The Transformation of the Plantation Household* (Cambridge: Cambridge University Press, 2008), 2–4, 36–37, 63–64; Hudson, *Fugitive Slaves and the Underground Railroad,* 34–35; Kaye, *Joining Places,* 86; Lucas, *History of Blacks in Kentucky,* 1:51.

25. Camp, *Closer to Freedom,* 38; Glymph, *Out of the House of Bondage,* 85–93; Hahn, *A Nation under Our Feet,* 28–29; Kaye, *Joining Places,* 24; Lucas, *History of Blacks in Kentucky,* 1:58, 64, 68; Turley, "Spirited Away," 3, 113–14, 131–32.

26. Hilde, *Slavery, Fatherhood, & Paternal Duty,* 2, 13, 40, 226–53.

27. Wilma King, "'Mad' Enough to Kill: Enslaved Women, Murder, and Southern Courts," *Journal of African American History* 92, no. 1 (Winter 2007): 37–56. Black female bodies were often the site of contest over freedom and control before, during, and after slavery. See Danielle L. McGuire, *At the Dark End of the Street: Black Women, Rape, and Resistance—A New History of the Civil Rights Movement from Rosa Parks to the Rise of Black Power* (New York: Vintage, 2010); Tera Hunter, *To 'Joy My Freedom: Southern Black Women's Lives and Labors after the Civil War* (Cambridge, MA: Harvard University Press, 1997); Hannah Rosen, *Terror in the Heart of Freedom: Citizenship, Sexual Violence, and the Meaning of Race in the Postemancipation South* (Chapel Hill: University of North Carolina Press, 2009).

28. Matthew C. Hulbert, "Part 1: Incidents in the Life of a Contraband," January 27, 2016, in *The Caroline Chronicles: A Story of Race, Urban Slavery, and Infanticide in the Border South, CWGK,* at https://civilwargovernors.org/the-caroline-chronicles-a-story-of-race-urban-slavery-and-infanticide-in-the-border-south-part-i/; R. F. Baird and J. H. Price to James F. Robinson, August 12, 1863,

CWGK, at http://discovery.civilwargovernors.org/document/KYR-0001029-0503. This chapter refers to Caroline Dement predominately as "Caroline" because of conflicting reports of her last name as either "Dement" or "Denant." In addition, Caroline mentions her enslaver as James Dement, yet no James Dement who owned enslaved individuals fits her story. *CWGK* has identified a John Dement in Rutherford County, Tennessee, who might be Caroline's enslaver. See Caroline Dement to Thomas E. Bramlette, n.d., *CWGK,* at http://discovery.civilwargovernors .org/document/KYR-0001-004-0134; *Ninth Manuscript Census of the United States* (1870), Population Schedules, Tennessee, Cannon County, District 1, pp. 113B–114A, accessed via Ancestry.com.

29. Hulbert, "Part 1: Incidents in the Life of a Contraband"; Dement to Bramlette, n.d.

30. John L. McKee to Thomas E. Bramlette, September 3, 1863, *CWGK,* at http://discovery.civilwargovernors.org/document/kyr-0001-004-0127; Carole Emberton, "Searching for Caroline: 'Disciplined Imagination' and the Limits of the Archive," *Register of the Kentucky Historical Society* 117, no. 2 (Spring 2019): 345–56.

31. Emberton, "Searching for Caroline," 352; Dement to Bramlette, n.d.; John G. Barrett to Thomas E. Bramlette, September 2, 1863, *CWGK,* at http:// discovery.civilwargovernors.org/document/kyr-0001-004-0129; Josephine Lynch, affidavit, September 17, 1863, *CWGK,* at http://discovery.civilwargovernors.org /document/kyr-0001-004-0133; L. A. Civill et al. to Thomas E. Bramlette, September 3, 1863, *CWGK,* at http://discovery.civilwargovernors.org/document /kyr-0001-004-0132; Raymond Lynch, affidavit, September 19, 1863, *CWGK,* at http://discovery.civilwargovernors.org/document/kyr-0001-004-0128.

32. Emberton, "Searching for Caroline," 346–47; King, "'Mad' Enough to Kill."

33. Lucas, *History of Blacks in Kentucky,* 1:146–54; Taylor, *Embattled Freedom,* 138–39; Brian Taylor, *Fighting for Citizenship: Black Northerners and the Debate over Military Service in the Civil War* (Chapel Hill: University of North Carolina Press, 2020), 17–19, 33. See also Chandra Manning, *What This Cruel War Was Over: Soldiers, Slavery, and the Civil War* (New York: Vintage Press, 2007).

34. Leonard, *Slaves, Slaveholders, and a Kentucky Community's Struggle,* 36, 47; Howard, *Black Liberation in Kentucky,* 27–28, 51–52, 57–67; Lucas, *History of Blacks in Kentucky,* 1:156–59, 166; Marshall, *Creating a Confederate Kentucky,* 2; Taylor, *Embattled Freedom,* 200–203, 225; Williams and Harris, "Kentucky in 1860." See also William F. Bishop to Major Brown, September 25, 1865, *CWGK,* at http://discovery.civilwargovernors.org/document/KYR-0001-003-0127; and Brutus J. Clay to Thomas E. Bramlette, January 15, 1864, *CWGK,* at http://discovery.civilwargovernors.org/document/KYR-0001-003-0050.

35. H. H. Hadley to unknown recipient, n.d., *CWGK,* at http://discovery .civilwargovernors.org/document/KYR-0001-004-1795.

36. Private Aaron Oats to Hon. Ed. M. Stanton, January 26, 1865, enclosing "Lucrethia to Dar husban," December 22, 1864, and [Jerry Smith] to Aaron Utz, January 10, 1865, O-6 1865, Letters Received, series 360, Colored Troops Division, Adjutant General's Office, Record Group 94, National Archives, Washington, DC, accessed via the Freedmen and Southern Society Project, at http://www.freedmen.umd.edu/Oats.html; John Burnside, affidavit, December 15, 1864, enclosed in Captain E. B. W. Restieaux to Major General M. C. Meigs, December 16, 1864, "Camp Nelson, Ky.," Consolidated Correspondence File, series 225, Central Records, Quartermaster General's Office, Record Group 92, National Archives, accessed via the Freedmen and Southern Society Project, at http://www.freedmen.umd.edu/Burnside.html.

37. Charles W. Singer, Louisville, Kentucky, to the *Christian Recorder,* September 18, 1864, in *A Grand Army of Black Men,* ed. Edwin S. Redkey (Cambridge: Cambridge University Press, 1992), 213–15; William A. Warfield, Nelson, Kentucky, July 7, 1865, to *Weekly Anglo-African,* in *Grand Army of Black Men,* ed. Redkey, 187–88, emphasis in original.

38. Thomas E. Bramlette, "Message of Governor Thos. E. Bramlette, to the General Assembly of Kentucky, December Session, 1865," December 4, 1865, *CWGK,* at http://discovery.civilwargovernors.org/document/KYR-0001-008-0002.

39. Aaron Astor, *Rebels on the Border: Civil War, Emancipation, and the Reconstruction of Kentucky and Missouri* (Baton Rouge: Louisiana State University Press, 2012), 135–45, 237–41; Charles L. Davis, "Racial Politics in Central Kentucky during the Post-Reconstruction Era: Bourbon County, 1877–1899," *Register of the Kentucky Historical Society* 108, no. 4 (August 2010): 347–81; Lewis, *For Slavery and Union,* 157–86; Marshall, *Creating a Confederate Kentucky,* 58–70; George C. Wright, *Racial Violence in Kentucky, 1865–1940: Lynchings, Mob Rule, and "Legal Lynchings,"* paperback ed. (Baton Rouge: Louisiana State University Press, 1996), 1–5, 19–60.

40. Matthew C. Hulbert, "Part IV: The Decision," February 17, 2017, in *The Caroline Chronicles, CWGK,* at https://civilwargovernors.org/the-caroline-chronicles-a-story-of-race-urban-slavery-and-infanticide-in-the-border-south-part-iv/; Register of Prisoners, 1855–1861, in *Kentucky State Penitentiary–Frankfort,* Film no. 7009891, Kentucky Department for Libraries and Archives; Lauren F. Klein, "The Image of Absence: Archival Silence, Data Visualization, and James Hemings," *American Literature* 85, no. 4 (December 2013): 661–88.

41. Wright, *Racial Violence in Kentucky,* 56–59.

5

Unfinished Freedom

The Legal History of Reconstruction in Kentucky

Giuliana Perrone

After the Civil War, the courts of every former slave state, whether it had seceded or not, addressed unanticipated legal questions raised by the end of slavery. When did the federal government gain the legal authority to emancipate enslaved people? Were contracts for the sale or hire of enslaved people still enforceable? Were debts incurred in those purchases still owed? Did marriages between enslaved people become legally valid once husband and wife were free? By answering these questions, judiciaries engaged in broader discussions about Reconstruction and the emergence of a fully free nation. They debated the status and rights of freedpeople, the lasting legacies of previous enslavement, whether antebellum law and legal culture would shape postbellum life, and, most important of all, what it meant to be—or become—a citizen of the United States.

This essay investigates cases brought by white and Black petitioners and explains how Kentucky's resolutions in postemancipation litigation shaped the prospects for freedom and equality for the formerly enslaved. The Kentucky Court of Appeals heard nearly eighty postemancipation cases related to slavery, the second highest of any former slave state (only the Tennessee Supreme Court considered more).[1] The significant number of cases reflects Kentucky's fierce resistance to any wartime attempts to weaken slavery and its centrality to the state's economy. (In 1860, Kentucky's enslaved population totaled more than 225,000.) The number of suits involving Black litigants reveals both their determination to exercise new rights and sometimes their distinct level of comfort with and understanding of American legal procedure.[2]

Since the publication of Eric Foner's influential work *Reconstruction: America's Unfinished Revolution* in 1988, scholars have largely accepted the argument that emancipation and subsequent enfranchisement constituted a "radical development"—"a massive experiment in interracial democracy without precedent."[3] Further, though Reconstruction failed to deliver Black equality in the mid–nineteenth century, federal and constitutional reforms instituted during the era "redefin[ed] . . . the American body politic" and "created a vehicle" for the future realization of equal rights in the twentieth century.[4] Legal historians have similarly maintained that freedpeople's acquisition of rights constituted a profound transformation in American law that underlay the eventual realization of equal citizenship.[5]

An examination of judicial activity in state courts complicates this view. Kentucky's postemancipation legal history reveals a particularly complex picture. State court judges worked to repress any "experiment in interracial democracy" from succeeding and never relieved freedpeople of the burdens of their former bondage. Instead, they charted a conservative judicial path. Although they begrudgingly accepted that the Thirteenth Amendment ended the ability to hold human beings as property, they did not overturn the institutional foundations upon which slavery had been built or challenge the racialized ideologies that had long justified the institution in the first place. No ruling could return Black Americans to bondage, but judges in Kentucky nevertheless insisted that the state possessed the authority to deny rights to freedpeople and established that slavery, as a legal institution and a social practice, would remain actionable in and relevant to American law well after its ostensible demise. The facets of slavery that remained unresolved hampered efforts to achieve slavery's total eradication—its true abolition—and to guarantee equal citizenship for all Black Kentuckians.

Kentucky's exclusion from the Radical dictates of Reconstruction policy facilitated judicial resistance to any transformational changes that should have accompanied Black freedom and citizenship. Unlike in other loyal border states, such as Maryland and Missouri, an antislavery coalition never took control of the Kentucky statehouse.[6] Kentucky's loyalty to the Union exempted it from Presidential or Congressional Reconstruction.

It did not have to be readmitted to the Union because it had never seceded. The Reconstruction Acts of 1867, which ushered in Radical Reconstruction and military occupation in the former Confederacy, did not apply there. To the contrary, except for the presence of Freedmen's Bureau personnel, martial rule in the state *ended* in October 1865. Kentucky was not compelled to ratify the Reconstruction Amendments or to produce a new state constitution that protected Black rights, even though Black residents urged such reforms.[7] An interracial governing coalition, as appeared in states under military governorship, never emerged. Republicans (or Unconditional Unionists) were a minority in the state and did not identify with the Radical faction of their party. As Eric Foner explains, Kentucky "clung to the decaying body of slavery" throughout the Reconstruction era.[8]

Black Kentuckians imagined citizenship, traditionally defined in opposition to slavery, as offering the basic civil and political rights that their bondage had denied them: to earn a wage (i.e., self-ownership), to move freely, to own property instead of being defined as property, to serve in the military and possess a weapon, to form a legitimate (legally protected) family, and for some, to vote.[9] The Kentucky Court of Appeals, however, resisted the extension of rights to freedpeople. In an appellate suit that tested the extension of civil rights to emancipated people, for example, the Kentucky Court of Appeals upheld the state's ban on testimony by Blacks against white defendants, thus nullifying the Civil Rights Act of 1866.[10] Claiming that Congress had no authority to dictate the terms of state citizenship, the court held, "The utmost legal effort of the [Thirteenth Amendment] was to declare the colored *as free as the white race* in the United States," and, according to the court, that meant being subject to the laws of individual states, even when they were racially specific.[11]

The Court of Appeals consistently approached litigation from this narrow perspective. Recognizing freedom was unavoidable, but accepting equal rights was not. This impulse is most evident in three primary types of suits: cases related to military operations and Blacks' enlistment in the Union army, the financial consequences of emancipation, and the legitimacy of the Black family. Suits concerning Blacks' enlistment were distinctive; they emerged from Kentucky's unique wartime circumstances. The courts of other former slave states rarely, if ever, addressed the issue, but Kentucky's court heard nine such cases.[12] These suits illustrate the state's fierce resistance to emancipation and, because they were among the first cases decided during Reconstruction, set the conservative judicial trajectory that the Court of Appeals maintained throughout the period.

Other suits presented the same issues heard in the courts of all former slave states. Cases initiated by members of the fallen planter class reveal the Kentucky Court of Appeals' acceptance of the view that emancipation did nothing to alter the financial obligations related to slavery. In so ruling, the court ensured that the commerce of slavery continued well beyond slavery's actual practice. In suits related to the Black family, the court had to reconcile the long-standing "disabilities" that slavery had imposed on the domestic lives of those formerly held in bondage—especially the inability of enslaved people to contract legal marriages.[13] Black families suffered profound consequences when judges could not or would not resolve the ongoing effects of their previous illegitimacy.

In general, white litigants demanded to have the traditional prerogatives and privileges associated with slaveholding upheld. Black litigants, however, insisted on having their newly acquired rights honored and their disputes resolved accordingly. They used litigation, in other words, to affirmatively claim their citizenship. But when freedpeople approached the bench for the first time as legitimate legal subjects, they found that such suits pitted existing legal doctrine and ossified racial assumptions about racial inferiority against congressional promises of equal rights and freedpeople's own desire to have them realized. All of these legal disputes arose from conditions that arose from slavery. In Kentucky, judges consistently refused to challenge or dismantle those conditions.

No topic sparked more consternation in wartime Kentucky than Black enlistment, and it remained a fraught issue well after the war ended. Many believed that remaining loyal to the Union would (and should) protect slavery in Kentucky because the federal government had no constitutional authority to violate the personal-property rights of loyal citizens. Proslavery Kentuckians adamantly resisted any federal policy, enlistment included, that threatened the institution. The Emancipation Proclamation drew particular ire, even though it did not apply to border states or to other Union-held territory. Many in Kentucky declared it dead on arrival; they viewed it as little more than an unconstitutional overreach of federal power. State officials refused to recognize the freedom of any Black person who claimed liberty under its dictates.[14]

Although some nonslaveholders had favored Black enlistment as a means of reaching federal draft quotas without requiring white men to fight, their voices were drowned out by those staunchly opposed to a policy they saw as a direct threat to slavery. Politicians expressed their disapproval of the idea as early as 1861, when the Kentucky General Assembly adopted a resolution calling for the removal of Secretary of War Simon Cameron after he suggested that enslaved people be armed. Congressman John Crittenden of Kentucky voiced similar outrage in 1863, condemning Black enlistment as an affront to white men. The state's senators were blunter: pursuing Black enlistment could prompt the state to secede. Kentucky newspapers decried the move as either an abolitionist plot designed to "subjugate the south" or the first step toward racial equality. Both prospects were unacceptable to whites.[15]

Initially, the federal government accommodated Kentucky's demands. Union officials knew that Kentucky had more slaveholding families than any other border state, that it had a large contingency of Confederate sympathizers, and that Kentucky representatives served in both the US and Confederate Congresses and in their respective armies.[16] President Abraham Lincoln and his second secretary of war, Edwin Stanton, constantly worried about Kentucky's allegiance to the Union and even went as far as to exempt the state from some wartime policies, including the provisions of the Enrollment Act of 1863, in order to shore up its support. They did impress some enslaved Kentuckians into service but did not officially free them. Unlike refugees from Confederate states, these "slave soldiers" were not designated "contraband" of war. Instead, the Union paid loyal Kentucky slaveholders for the labor of their bondspeople, while it paid wages directly to Black people claimed by those deemed disloyal to the Union.[17] When a unit of federal troops from Kentucky heard about John C. Frémont's attempts to confiscate slaves in Missouri and "threw down their arms and disbanded," Lincoln amended Frémont's orders, noting that otherwise "the very arms we had furnished Kentucky would be turned against us." Lincoln believed that "to lose Kentucky is nearly the same as to lose the whole game."[18] He needed to recruit white soldiers in the state and to prevent the state's outright secession.

By 1864, however, the US army began actively recruiting and mustering Black Kentuckians into Union regiments. In January of that year, it established a recruitment post in Paducah specifically to attract Black enlistees. Some enraged white residents reported that Union officers seized their slaves or lured them off plantations with the promise of $300 bounties for enlisting. Motivated by his constituents' outrage, Governor Thomas E. Bramlette, a Union Democrat, managed to work out a compromise directly with President Lincoln: counties that furnished their draft quotas with white soldiers would not be subject to Black enlistment, loyal slaveholders would receive $300 compensation for each bondsman who enlisted with their owner's consent, and any Black soldiers from the state would be trained outside its borders.[19]

By the end of March 1864, though, Kentucky counties had already failed to meet their quotas with white enlistees alone. The following month, Commander of Kentucky General Stephen "Butcher" Burbridge resumed the recruitment and enlistment of enslaved men. Once he did, the superintendent of the state's Black soldiers, James S. Brisbin, did exactly what Kentucky slaveholders feared: he made liberal use of enlistment laws to destroy slavery from within. He accepted Black men of all ages and physical conditions into the ranks to emancipate them, with or without consent from their enslavers. He only intensified his efforts to enlist and free African Americans after the Kentucky Legislature refused to ratify the Thirteenth Amendment in February 1865. In April 1865, Brisbin wrote to Governor Bramlette, "Slavery is at an end and why deny it or, by withholding proper State Legislation seek to retain longer the shadow of an institution that was always worthless?"[20]

Federal officials had adjusted their policies in response to evolving circumstances on the ground. Well before Union leaders acknowledged it, bondspeople knew that the Civil War was ultimately about their freedom and that it had opened the door to self-liberation.[21] Using established communication networks (including those that had served the Underground Railroad), and gathering information from Black people on the move, enslaved people found their way to freedom. They abandoned plantations, flooded Union encampments, and crossed into free states. In so doing, they led a revolution that destroyed slavery from within and challenged the nation to live up to its founding ideals.[22]

Before the adoption of the Thirteenth Amendment, escape or military service constituted the only viable avenues to freedom for enslaved Kentuckians. Both carried significant risks. Nevertheless, many fled to free territory or to one of the state's military encampments, seeking not only liberty but also protection from Confederate incursions (which might lead to reenslavement in the deeper South) and from the guerilla "regulators" who used violence to maintain bondage and white supremacy in Kentucky.[23] The exodus intensified after news of the Preliminary Emancipation Proclamation spread. The announcement marked a shift in the federal position about slavery, amplified hopes for abolition, and held out the prospect of Black enlistment.

When that prospect became policy, Black men jumped at the opportunity to fight for universal freedom. Black military service upended the traditional dictates of slavery. It allowed Black men to possess weapons, actively resist white oppression, assert their manhood, and prove themselves worthy of citizenship in free American society.[24] At the outset of the war, only 5 percent of the nation's Black population resided in Kentucky, yet 13 percent of Black troops mustered into Union service came from the state.[25] More than twenty-three thousand free Black and enslaved Kentuckians joined up—second only to the number from Louisiana.

The Enlistment Act of 1865 further incentivized enrollment by promising liberty to the families of Black men who enlisted. An additional twenty-eight thousand enslaved people became free thanks to the law. The statute's exceptional provisions attest to its emancipatory intent. For instance, because the domestic ties of enslaved people lacked legal standing, the law provided that evidence of a marriage ceremony or cohabitation would be sufficient to establish a marital union, "whether such marriage was or was not authorized or recognized by law." It also accepted the children of such marriages as legitimate and therefore qualified for freedom, even if the original marriage had been "dissolved" prior to the enlistment. Some enslaved women encouraged their husbands to enlist specifically to liberate their children, and some Union officials performed marriages to expand the reach of the law.[26]

The enrollment of Black soldiers and the emancipation of their family members triggered litigation that continued after the end of slavery. For example, in January 1864 Marshall Ward's slaveholder, Ben Hughes, had hired him out to Harry Todd. The contract between the men stipulated that the term of hire would last until Christmas Day of the same year. By June, however, Marshall had "escaped" his enslavement and had "voluntarily enlisted as a solder in the Federal Army." Todd saw no reason to pay what he owed to Hughes since he did not receive the year's worth of labor their contract had stipulated. Hughes sued, charging that the hirer had aided Marshall's escape and that "if the negro's services were lost by any means not occasioned by" Hughes himself, then he remained bound by his contractual obligation. Todd responded to the suit by arguing that Marshall had been taken by the federal government "for public purposes, and in pursuance of a public law." For that, he could not be held responsible. (Marshall himself took no part in the court proceedings.)[27]

Similarly, the employment of Joe Wharton's wife, Milly, prompted a conflict about her status. "As a free woman, by her own voluntary consent," she found employment with Abram Corbin that paid her a wage for the first time in her life. Claiming her as his enslaved woman, however, Benedict B. Marsh sued Corbin, alleging that he "unlawfully took . . . Milly from [his] possession and has detained said slave without right." Marsh sought the return of Milly plus $500 "for the taking and detention of her and for other proper relief." Any work Milly did for Corbin needed to have been contracted with Marsh, and he, as her lawful owner, was entitled to any monies paid for her labor. For his part, Corbin claimed to be the beneficiary of federal enlistment law. Milly's husband, Joe, had brought his wife to Corbin on March 14, 1865, just days after Congress passed the law that purportedly freed her, and arranged for her to work for him. Corbin owed nothing to Marsh, he contended, because he had hired a free woman.[28]

The Kentucky Court of Appeals ruled on *Hughes v. Todd* and *Corbin v. Marsh* just days before Secretary of State William Seward certified the Thirteenth Amendment's addition to the US Constitution. Slavery was all but destroyed, even in loyal Kentucky. That did not stop Chief Justice George Robertson from condemning federal policy on both Black enlistment and emancipation. In *Hughes*, Robertson rejected the claim that Todd had abetted Marshall's escape. Instead, he granted that "the flight and enlistment seem to have been the voluntary acts of Marshall himself. He was not drafted or forcibly taken from the hirer by the Federal government." As a consequence, Hughes could not be held responsible for the loss, and Todd remained bound to pay the entirety of his debt to Hughes.

Even so, Robertson insisted that litigation did not provide adequate remedy for the injury sustained by the hirer. Instead, Todd "must look alone to the government for reparation. And, if the government has neither paid him nor will pay him, its act was unconstitutional and void as to him, and was, therefore, not a lawful eviction under title, but a wrongful abduction without title." Robertson reasoned that though the federal government had not drafted Marshall, it had enticed him to flee by allowing him to enlist in the Union army in exchange for liberty. It was therefore responsible for the financial loss of the man who had hired him. Robertson admitted that the government had a legitimate military interest in staffing its ranks, but using enslaved people to do so came with conditions. The federal government could either take enslaved people for military service and then return them to their lawful owners, or it had to pay for the property it commandeered. The government had done neither.[29]

Robertson broadened his remarks in *Corbin*. The military enlistment of slave property was bad enough, but the liberation of their family members, who served no legitimate military purpose, was inexcusable under any circumstance. Robertson wrote, "We are not prepared to acknowledge the power to emancipate the soldier slave. But a concession of that power would not extend its principle to the soldier's 'wife, children, and friends.'" Clearly, Robertson concluded, the government had more nefarious aims. "The object was, not to supply soldiers that could not be otherwise as certainly obtained, but only to cripple slavery, and inaugurate the ultimate abolition of it." In this, he correctly assessed congressional intent. But to him the problem was that the "costly and invidious burden, imposed on comparatively a few men for the benefit of all the public, was not only unnecessary, but was unconstitutional on account of its glaring inequality." While Robertson lamented the hardship of emancipation on slaveholders, the "inequality" of the enslaved never crossed his mind.[30]

The opinions in *Hughes* and *Corbin* channeled the legacy of the Kentucky Resolutions of 1798 (the origin of the compact theory of the Constitution) and reasserted the state's right to invalidate federal law it deemed unconstitutional. Robertson symbolically nullified two congressional enlistment laws even though they had no legal effect after the war. Emancipation by legislative fiat was always unconstitutional as long as slavery itself remained a legal institution, he argued. Only the Thirteenth Amendment had the power to emancipate any people still enslaved in Kentucky, and even then, Robertson believed, their owners must be compensated for their losses.

Robertson ignored the fact that during the war Lincoln had attempted compensated emancipation in Kentucky and the other loyal border states. In March 1862, Lincoln presented a plan: if the state agreed to a specific end date for slavery—as late as 1882 even—he would encourage Congress to allow a $400 payment to enslavers for each bondsperson emancipated. For those concerned about the creation of a large free Black population, he suggested colonization—the removal and resettlement of Black Americans in another country (e.g., Liberia) or territory—as an appropriate measure. Lincoln warned the congressmen of all the loyal slaveholding states that failure to take him up on the offer would almost certainly result in emancipation by "friction and abrasion—by the mere incidents of the war."[31] Kentuckians rejected the overture, anyway. They denied that the Constitution allowed for the destruction of slavery at all and believed they were fighting a war to preserve the Union created under that constitution, not to undermine the peculiar institution.[32]

Even after the war ended as Lincoln predicted it would, Kentuckians sought remuneration for their losses. Robertson used his opinions to add to the drumbeat of calls for compensated emancipation. He knew that his rulings would have limited effect; enslaved people had been liberated by constitutional amendment. But in late 1865 he believed payment for lost slave property remained constitutionally possible. The judge invoked the takings clause of the Fifth Amendment—as in the US Supreme Court decision in *Dred Scott* in 1857—to attack the actions of the national government and argue for recompense.[33] He deemed emancipation through enlistment or other means an unconstitutional "mockery" of personal-property rights. "The act of taking the slave was . . . unconstitutional and void as to its legal effects, unless the government either prepaid or assured the payment of his actual value to his owner." "If this be not so," he continued, "the boasted palladium of private property against arbitrary power is but a mockery, and the constitution itself may become a dead letter."[34] Because Kentucky had not seceded and its residents remained citizens of the United States, Robertson argued, the federal government had no legal grounds to take enslaved or any other property without due process and compensation.

Slaveholders throughout the South agitated for "reparation" for years after Lee's surrender. But Kentucky faced different circumstances than the states of the defeated Confederacy. Conquered states were not in a position to reject the Thirteenth Amendment, but the Kentucky Legislature could and did refuse to ratify the Thirteenth Amendment because, it argued, the amendment failed to provide compensation to slaveholders for their loss of enslaved property. The General Assembly originally sought $34 million from Congress, which equaled the assessed value of all Kentucky slaves in 1864, then later asked for a staggering $100 million.[35] In addition, Kentucky congressmen appealed to the wartime enlistment policy to justify arguments for remuneration. A section in the Enrollment Act of 1864 had promised the creation of a commission in loyal slave states that would pay enslavers between $100 and $300 for each enslaved person who was freed through military service.[36] The congressmen believed the provision demonstrated federal intent to compensate loyal slaveholders for their losses and demanded it be honored. Few ever saw a penny. Finally, section 4 of the Fourteenth Amendment specifically eliminated the possibility of compensation for slaves. Over strenuous objections from Kentucky's congressmen, the amendment passed both houses of Congress in 1866 and was ratified in 1868.

Justice Robertson's personal experience with emancipation almost certainly shaped his rulings. Born in Mercer County, Kentucky, Robertson rose to legal and political prominence. He was a successful lawyer, congressman, Speaker of the Kentucky House, and secretary of the State of Kentucky and served as the publicly elected chief justice of the Kentucky Court of Appeals twice (1829–1834 and 1864–1871). Like many other men of his class, he had been a slaveholder. As a fellow Whig, he had been friends with Abraham Lincoln since the 1840s, despite their differing views on slavery. Their relationship became strained in 1862 when Lincoln issued the Preliminary Emancipation Proclamation. As emancipatory policies took effect, Robertson became furious that military forces were "forcibly detaining the slaves of Union Kentuckians." His fury intensified when an enslaved man he owned—Adam—fled to the Union camp of the Twenty-Second Wisconsin Volunteers, seeking liberty. Robertson demanded that the commander return the slave, but Colonel William Utley denied the judge entrance into the camp or to release the man in question. In response, Robertson sued Utley for violating the Fugitive Slave Act of 1850 and had him indicted for "harboring a slave." When Lincoln learned of the situation, he offered Robertson $500 for the lost property, but Robertson refused to accept it. He replied that his "object in that suit . . . was solely to try the question of whether the civil or the military power is Constitutionally supreme in Kentucky."[37]

Robertson did not relent. Even after the Fugitive Slave Act had been repealed and the Thirteenth Amendment had been ratified, he continued to pursue (using the legal remedy of replevin) a civil case against Utley for seizing his private property. In 1871, Utley was convicted in federal court and was ordered to pay Robertson $934.46.[38] The US Treasury compensated Utley after Congress enacted a law to indemnify him.[39] Robertson had always believed the government owed the same compensation to other slaveholders in Kentucky, but unlike the litigants who entered his courtroom, he managed to use his personal connections and sway to actually get it.[40]

Aside from seeking reparations, Kentuckians maintained their crusade against federal incursion into state affairs by prosecuting the Union officials who governed the state after martial law was declared in 1863. For example, they insisted that Major General John M. Palmer, appointed by Lincoln in early 1865 as commander of the Department of Kentucky, illegally "invited slaves to 'crowd' Camp Nelson and other encampments of his army; and induced many of them to 'rush' to Louisville, 'claiming to be free,' and *expecting* the aid of his army in the assertion of that claim." Kentucky's attorney general and future US Supreme Court justice John Marshall Harlan prosecuted Palmer in 1866 for violating the state's law against enticing "a slave to leave his owner," including anything "purporting to liberate a slave" or "aid[ing] or assist[ing] a slave to make his escape." By issuing the order, Harlan claimed, Palmer had helped an enslaved woman named Ellen "escape from her owner" by granting her a pass to travel to the free state of Indiana. The Emancipation Proclamation "afforded no semblance of pretext for a claim to freedom by the slaves of Kentucky," state officials believed, and "Palmer knew he had no right to liberate them." Yet he nevertheless "induced them to desert their owners."[41]

Palmer's presence in the state had only affirmed what Black Kentuckians already knew: the war would soon end, and so would slavery. Their actions gave the commander the pretense to act. As Black refugees flooded Louisville, Palmer feared that disease and destitution would spread throughout the city. He issued General Order No. 32 on May 11, 1865, to encourage unemployed African Americans to move elsewhere. To facilitate the relocation effort, the order required the "conductors and managers of *all* . . . means of travel out of and from the city of Louisville" to transport all African Americans with a military-issued pass out of the area.[42]

Kentuckians had correctly assessed Palmer's emancipatory aim. The major general knew that the promise of travel passes—quickly known as "Palmer passes" and considered to be papers to freedom by those who possessed them—would do more than avert an epidemic. It would also encourage Black Kentuckians—ultimately twenty-eight thousand of them—to move into the city seeking asylum from bondage and would give Palmer the opportunity to facilitate their freedom. His self-proclaimed plan to "'drive the last nail in the coffin' of the 'institution'" worked.[43] By the end of 1865, more than 70 percent of the state's enslaved people had been liberated.[44] The Thirteenth Amendment freed the rest.

By the time the Kentucky Court of Appeals heard the case, the Thirteenth Amendment had been ratified. Moreover, Palmer's counsel argued, his actions were undertaken "officially and by authority of the President of the U.S." and could not be judged by the Commonwealth of Kentucky.[45] Although the trial court agreed, the Court of Appeals did not. At the time Palmer had issued General Order No. 23, slavery was still legal in Kentucky. Consequently, a "military commandant," Attorney General Harlan's brief read, "had no more right to aid the slaves of our people to escape than the commandant in Ohio had to take[,] seize[,] or destroy the property of a citizen of that state."[46] Justice Robertson's opinion echoed the same. The state's statute remained in effect as long as slavery itself was still lawful. Palmer's actions were therefore "voluntary" and "uncontrolled" by the War Department. He would have to face the "penal consequences of an illegal act of glaring usurpation."[47]

It is not immediately obvious why the Commonwealth prosecuted Palmer or why after it failed at the trial level, it continued to seek a conviction on appeal. The people of Kentucky had nothing to gain, at least materially, from a guilty verdict; it would not restore slavery to the state or generate any financial recompense for its loss. But Kentuckians blamed Palmer for emancipation and the degradation of state sovereignty that came with military rule. Their anger and desire for retribution, it seems, motivated the Commonwealth's ongoing action against the major general. A concurring opinion specifically identified Palmer's order as "injurious to the interest and harassing to the feelings of the people of Kentucky."[48] Invoking states' rights, the Court of Appeals insisted that martial law could not invalidate the constitutional rights of loyal Kentuckians or, "with impunity, violate the laws of this state."[49]

Palmer, for his part, believed Robertson's opinion was personal. In 1865, the two men had had a "tart" correspondence about one of Robertson's bondsmen that Palmer believed influenced the judge's opinion in his case.[50] Whatever motivated the criminal prosecution and subsequent conviction, it does not appear that Palmer was ever punished. The law he violated had been repealed, and as Robertson admitted, the Kentucky Legislature would have to determine "its operation on crimes committed before the repeal."[51] Palmer resigned from the military in 1866 and became governor of Illinois just two years later. John Marshall Harlan, appointed to the US Supreme Court by Rutherford B. Hayes, ultimately came to believe that the Reconstruction Amendments had revolutionized the Constitution and transformed American federalism. He went on to write the lone dissent in *Plessy v. Ferguson* (1896), in which he denounced racial segregation and the denial of civil rights.[52]

Close to half of the slavery-related suits heard by the Kentucky Court of Appeals after the war, including *Hughes* and *Corbin,* related to the financial disaster caused by Black freedom. This issue was not unique to the Bluegrass State; slaveholders everywhere had bought, sold, mortgaged, hired out, and bequeathed their human chattel. They had relied on enslaved people to grow their wealth, establish their social standing, and protect themselves against financial downturns. In short, as the historian Walter Johnson writes, slaveholders had "construct[ed] themselves out of slaves."[53] After emancipation, they turned to the courts in an effort to salvage what they could from the wreckage of slavery.

Still, most southerners had not owned any bondspeople at all. On the eve of the Civil War, only 28 percent of Kentucky households possessed bondspeople, and most of the households that did own slaves—about 64 percent of slaveholding families—owned fewer than five.[54] The state's landscape was not dotted by large plantations, as in the Deep South, or home to the region's largest planters. Nevertheless, slavery composed a substantial part of Kentucky's antebellum economy. Enslaved people in Kentucky tended to work alongside slaveholders "as farmers, handymen, cattlemen, and merchants," raising livestock and cultivating hemp or tobacco rather than cotton.[55] Adding to slavery's economic value, the state served as a primary node in the internal slave trade that shuttled bondspeople from the Upper South to the cotton plantations "down river." By 1860, enslaved people considered "prime" could fetch up to $2,000 each.[56] Slaveholders could also hire out their bondspeople, which generated still more revenue for them (they owned any wages earned), and offered their slaves' labor at comparably lower prices to those in need of a larger or seasonal workforce. In short, slavery had undergirded Kentucky's economy.

More broadly, the economy of the whole slaveholding region and an outsize portion of the financial value that composed it had been based on what became worthless property when slaves were emancipated. For those who managed to become a part of the slaveholding class, estates tended to be financially lopsided. Many invested more of their wealth in bondspeople than in land or other property. For elite planters especially, the economic historian Gavin Wright reminds us, "wealth and wealth accumulation meant slaves, and land was distinctly secondary."[57] Those who had the greatest financial stake in slave property suffered disproportionately from its destruction. But because slavery was interwoven so thoroughly in the economy, even those who owned few or no enslaved people at all often found themselves in dire financial straits when the institution collapsed.

During Reconstruction, members of the fallen planter class and small-holders alike attempted to recover either monies invested in enslaved people or to limit the toll that emancipation had on the value of their estates. Most litigation of this type involved contracts for the sale or hire of enslaved people. The suits typically fell into two categories. The first included litigants who refused to finish paying debts owed for bondspeople. The second involved litigants hoping to recover monies they had already paid. *Hughes,* for example, fell into the first category (the hirer refused to pay), but suits without concerns over the legality of enlistment better represent the typical issues faced by litigants in Kentucky and elsewhere. But all of these lawsuits represent what one scholar calls the "mourning process" that white southerners experienced "before finally accepting emancipation."[58]

Superficially, suits forced courts to assume the responsibility of allocating the financial losses of emancipation. Courts had to decide whether outstanding debts for enslaved people remained enforceable after emancipation, as creditors hoped, or whether the freedom guaranteed by the Thirteenth Amendment prohibited the continued exchange of monies for human chattel, as debtors demanded. A closer look reveals that those seeking shelter from the financial ruin of emancipation asked state court judges to sort out their circumstances in ways that not only served their own personal interests (as all litigants do) but also honored the prerogatives of their race and former status—to reify the advantages of their membership in the slaveholding class by enforcing their debts. Chastened by emancipation but not willing to concede defeat, they attempted to bridge the divide between the old South and the new one they hoped to construct in its image.

Those who had already paid for enslaved property in full turned to a common feature of contracts—a warranty—as the basis for financial relief. Warranties had conventionally guaranteed title, the health—or "soundness"—of an enslaved person, and that the property would be "a slave for life." Since emancipated people had not remained in bondage for the duration of their natural lives, some litigants argued that their warranty had been breached and that they were thus entitled to an abatement from sellers. George B. Howard made such a claim after the Thirteenth Amendment freed Caroline. The Kentucky court, however, ruled that the warranty guaranteed only that Caroline "was a slave for life" according to the circumstances "at the date of the sale," when slavery remained legal. The Thirteenth Amendment had changed those circumstances. Caroline had remained enslaved for the life of the *institution,* even if not for the entirety of her actual life. That was all the warranty could ever have protected unless it "expressly covenanted that the Constitution and Laws of Kentucky by which slavery was tolerated, should never be changed." The judges in *Bailey v. Howard* reminded the litigants that a risk to slavery had always existed, even if they had not perceived it. People who traded in slaves always "took them subject to any change in the laws by which such property was held that the people of the United States, or their legally constituted agents might make." Very few Kentuckians had ever accounted for such contingencies.[59]

Kentucky courts, like most southern tribunals, maintained that as long as parties had agreed to the terms of an exchange while slavery remained legal, the agreements continued to be enforceable. To do otherwise, many courts—and ultimately the US Supreme Court—ruled, would violate the Constitution's prohibition against impairing contracts. As the Kentucky court noted in one ruling in 1868, "Even if there was no value *per se* in the slaves" when a note came due, "that fact did not destroy the legal obligation of the bonds given." Contracts, mortgages, and all other debts for enslaved people remained enforceable even though the property at the heart of those agreements no longer existed as property at all.[60]

The Kentucky Court of Appeals' view on this issue generally aligned with the courts of most former slave states. There was, however, another option: because the Thirteenth Amendment banned slavery, some judges argued that courts had become constitutionally prohibited from enforcing any agreement related to it. Louisiana's Supreme Court enforced this interpretation—the only state to successfully do so.[61] Its court ruled, "The sovereign power, the paramount law, puts an end to the ownership. The effect of the act which terminates the owner's right to the slave is not limited merely to that result. It necessarily involves the entire contract, and annuls it throughout."[62] By this logic, the status of the property conveyed in any contract had to overrule any concern about contract rights. Many other states considered adopting this position and usually declined to do so only by a narrow margin. A vote of one justice often made the difference. Unlike other tribunals, though, the Kentucky court never seriously considered this possibility; it maintained an unflinching commitment to upholding agreements for slaves.

The Kentucky Court of Appeals was similarly consistent in cases related to inheritance, in which generational wealth was at stake. This type of litigation demonstrated how significantly emancipation shaped the futures of white southerners and how personal and emotionally complex the cost of Black freedom became for them. Many expected to acquire enslaved property from relatives who had purposefully bequeathed their chattel to support their children and other heirs. Emancipation annulled those legacies. For instance, Black freedom denied the heirs of Sallie Bush the value of twenty-one enslaved people. Bush's heirs sued her estate in 1873, hoping to get the monetary value of the enslaved people bequeathed to them, if not the persons themselves. The court rejected such claims; it could not conjure wealth where none existed. "The destruction of the property held in the slaves consequent upon the adoption of the thirteenth article of amendment to the Federal constitution left nothing to be divided. Hence the relief sought in the equitable action has not and can never be afforded." Judges could not change the fact of emancipation; they could only determine who would absorb the financial losses it produced.[63]

The winners and losers in these cases, however, matter far less than understanding the cases' larger significance. A large number of postemancipation cases heard in southern courts of appeal—more than 40 percent—reflected the economic demands of white litigants, *not* the needs of freedpeople. In fact, courts treated the formerly enslaved people at the heart of the squabbles as merely disputed objects, not as the legal subjects they had become. In actuality, however, such cases shaped the prospects for slavery's total eradication from life and law. By focusing on the contracts and commercial law doctrine, judges could sidestep the fact that each transaction conveyed an enslaved human being, not just another piece of property, thus affirming the very privilege white Kentuckians sought to reinstitute and validating the value that had been assigned to Black persons as property.[64]

While white families struggled to maintain financial solvency, the end of slavery meant freedpeople could secure their families for the first time. But as a consequence of their previous status as chattel property, Black

Americans entered freedom without legal pasts or legal identities. Enslaved people had no legal right to marry, own property, or retain custody of their children. Thanks to *partus sequitur ventrem*, the legal doctrine introduced in Virginia in 1662, children born to enslaved mothers shared her servile condition. Without the protection of domestic legitimacy, sale and separation regularly shattered enslaved families—especially in a state that was so integral to the internal slave trade.[65] Emphasizing the fragility of domestic bonds, an enslaved preacher from Kentucky solemnized the customary marriages of his parishioners by proclaiming "until death or *distance* do you part."[66]

The formation of free Black families was highly contingent on the laws, politics, and circumstances of Reconstruction. For one, many emancipated people had to *find* their loved ones before they could consider reconstituting any kind of family.[67] For another, not all wished to remain in their preexisting domestic arrangements. New state laws were passed to compel freedpeople into conventional families, but some wished to design and erect their households in ways that reflected their own values, beliefs, and customs rather than conform to someone else's rules—as they had been forced to do in bondage.[68] None of this is to say that African Americans, either during or after slavery, did not share some or even all of the family values accepted in white society. In 1870, for example, 71 percent of freedchildren in Louisville lived in two-parent households.[69] But it is important to stress that assuming the presence of the "Black family" or "household" ignores the fact that such a category, if it were to exist at all, had to be *reimagined, reconstructed,* and *redefined* in the aftermath of emancipation, and that part of this project happened in state courtrooms.[70] African Americans became litigants in order to engage in a process of self-making that confronted the new realities of freedom on their own terms.

Both the Kentucky General Assembly and the Freedmen's Bureau addressed these demands and the legacies of customary practices. The state's resistance to recognizing Blacks' rights, coupled with the increasing number of atrocities committed against freedpeople, had prompted the extension of the bureau into Kentucky in December 1865.[71] It was the only Union state to which the bureau was dispatched, and white Kentuckians protested it wildly. In their estimation, it was a "base usurpation" of their rights as free, sovereign citizens. Local officials refused to aid bureau agents, many of whom faced the threat of violence from enraged Kentuckians.[72] Despite the public outcry, the results of this federal intervention were dramatic. Fearing the continued presence of bureau agents, the General Assembly finally began enacting laws to aid its sizeable freed population (a little more than sixty-five thousand at war's end).[73] Passing legislation to validate the Black family was among the first matters the legislature addressed after the arrival of bureau officials.

Part of the Department of War, the Bureau of Refugees, Freedmen, and Abandoned Lands had been designed to address the immediate needs of freedpeople and destitute white southerners—to provide food, shelter, clothing, medical care, and other necessities to those who had been displaced by the Civil War.[74] Bureau agents played a crucial role in facilitating the establishment of free Black communities and families. They helped reunite loved ones, solemnized marriages, and mediated disputes between kinspeople. These efforts were both humanitarian and paternalistic in nature. Officials worked to integrate formerly enslaved people into civil society, but only according to accepted sociolegal norms. The customs developed during slavery—including bigamy and community-sanctioned "divorce"—would not be tolerated after freedom.[75] As the historian Nancy Cott describes, the bureau assumed the task of "reform[ing] the sexual practices and family patterns" of the formerly enslaved, including by performing marriages en masse and issuing a pamphlet titled *Marriage Rules* to help educate them about "the sacred obligations of the marriage state."[76] Rampant illiteracy among the formerly enslaved population almost certainly blunted the intended effect of the pamphlet, but its existence corroborates the ideology behind bureau policy: make Black society conform to established (i.e., white) standards of living. The success of the Freedmen's Bureau, however, was highly contingent on the availability of personnel, their geographic reach, and, perhaps more important, the willingness of individuals to avail themselves of the aid it offered. Lawmakers across the former slaveholding states shared the same paternalistic concerns. They worried about immoral cohabitation of unmarried freedpeople, illegitimate children, and, in particular, the dependency of formerly enslaved people (women and children especially) on the state. In response, they passed laws that recognized marriages of and children born to former bondspeople. Most states accepted continued cohabitation of man and wife after emancipation as validation of a marriage, but a few, including North Carolina and Missouri, required marriages to be certified by a state official. Kentucky adopted legislation in February 1866 that obligated freedpeople to register marriages so that county officials had records of their unions. But unlike other states, it also required a fee of fifty cents to do so—a significant sum for those who entered freedom penniless. The same law also granted legitimacy to the children born to enslaved parents who remained married after emancipation. These provisions extended domestic legitimacy to—but also state control over—newly freed persons. In particular, legally sanctioned marriage allowed the state to intervene in and regulate the personal relationships and behavior of freedpeople. Although new statutes bestowed legitimacy to the Black family for the first time, they did not necessarily reflect lawmakers' care or concern for freedpeople's well-being.[77]

Irrespective of the motivation behind the new laws, many formerly enslaved people eagerly created legal families. The ability to do so signaled both the new enjoyment of civil rights and the end of the instability that had long plagued Black communities. But blanket regulation of the freed family failed to account for the varied circumstances of Kentucky's Black residents or the way that enslavement had shaped their domestic lives. Some had no knowledge of the state's new law until they ran afoul of it; others saw no need to register unions that they already considered valid; and some could not afford to pay the fee the state required. Still more found themselves in situations the statute did not address at all: living in a plural marriage, having an as yet unlocated spouse, or caring for a child fathered by an enslaver or other uncommitted partner.

Kentucky courts heard more family law cases than any other former slave state.[78] Freedpeople initiated some, but the state prompted the litigation in other instances by charging freedpeople with criminal offenses—including bigamy, adultery and fornication, and bastardy. In all of these cases, the Kentucky courts wrestled with the same fundamental problem: how to make the customary relationships that had developed during slavery and the children born to them conform to both new statutes and longstanding legal principles of family law.[79]

Whether they knew it or not, couples who failed to register their unions according to the state's new statute continued to live without the legal protections marriage afforded. This marked an important change in Kentucky law. Prior to Reconstruction, free white or Black persons, otherwise "competent to make a binding contract," could establish a common-law marriage simply by cohabitating. As Chief Justice Robertson ruled in one case after the war, however, the new statute effectively repealed the common-law right to marriage for everyone. "Without conformity to this statutory mode" of marriage established in 1866, "there is now no law in

Kentucky to legalize cohabitation and recognition alone as marriage."[80] Freedman Joseph Rogers of Madison County discovered as much after his wife of fifteen years, Sally Ann Estill, died in April 1866. Rogers, who had enlisted in the US Army, had become free before formal emancipation. He believed that his enlistment had also freed his wife. The couple lived together until Sally Ann's death, thinking they had established a legitimate common-law marriage. After she died, however, Sally Ann's brother Harvey argued that their failure to register their marriage precluded Rogers from serving as administrator of her estate. The court agreed. After emancipation, the state determined that only marriages "solemnized in presence of an authorized person or society" would be recognized as legitimate. Neither the proof of a fifteen-year-long personal relationship between Joseph and Sally Ann that had lasted beyond emancipation nor their personal belief that they were married mattered to the court. With Black freedom came both rights and obligations, which included abiding by newly enacted statutes and increased state intervention into private lives.[81]

A lawful marriage also determined the legitimacy of offspring. Consequently, additional complications arose over the status of children born to formerly enslaved parents. The issue became especially challenging for parents who decided not to continue their relationships after emancipation. In his opinion for the Kentucky Court of Appeals, Judge Rufus Williams identified one of these problems: Could "a slave father, who [had] a slave child by a slave mother, without lawful wedlock, . . . be held responsible, after they are all freed by constitutional amendment, for the support of such child?" The answer would shape the free lives of Henry Lewis and Julia Martin. While enslaved, the couple had a child. The couple "never married according to the custom" of enslaved people, and court records do not indicate that they ever had an established relationship, either during or after the end of slavery.[82] Nevertheless, Julia and Union County officials believed Lewis had a responsibility to pay child support. Lewis claimed that because the child was born while both parents were enslaved, he could not be required to provide financial support. His counsel argued, "To sustain the judgment . . . we would not only be constrained to give the act such a broad construction but in addition would be compelled to give it a retrospective operation." The court agreed. The law could not make him the legal father of Julia Martin's child or convict him of bastardy because, the opinion stated, neither existing nor new law was ever "intended . . . to reach back into the days of slavery."[83] But that was exactly what cases such as *Lewis v. Commonwealth* required—a sorting out of the past in order to accommodate the new realities of Black freedom.

The fundamental principle that guided the court's ruling in *Lewis* may have produced the desired outcome for Henry Lewis, but it harmed fathers who wished to claim paternal rights to their children. Many freed fathers saw paternal rights as confirmation of their manhood and validation of their freedom. They could finally form legitimate families and be heads of their own households. As Republican ideology reinforced, becoming a head of household capable of supporting a family served as a rite of passage for emancipated men by allowing them to prove their suitability for and fully claim their citizenship.[84]

In 1871, the Kentucky Court of Appeals denied these rights to Charles Allen, who sought custody of his son, Henry. Henry had been born enslaved to Charles and his customary wife, Mary. Upon their emancipation, Mary and Charles did not "continue their assumed marital relations" or register their former union with the state, as postemancipation Kentucky statute required. Instead, Charles "abandoned" Mary "and married another woman." At the same time, he claimed young Henry as his legitimate son and hired him out for wages. Mary also asserted custody of the boy and sued her former partner for parental rights and the wages Henry had earned.[85]

Once again, the key factor that determined the outcome of the suit was the marriage between Charles and Mary. If the court lacked the ability—or willingness—to validate that union, then Henry could only have entered freedom as a bastard in the eyes of the law. In these particular circumstances, the otherwise pernicious label worked in favor of Mary's claim to the custody of her son. The court ruled that since the couple never enjoyed a lawful marriage, Charles, "as the putative father of Henry, was not . . . entitled to have the custody or control of him, or the benefit of his labor."[86] Suits like this one underscore the uncertainty about the guarantees of freedom, expose the ongoing legal fluidity that emancipation produced during Reconstruction, and confirm that the law could not resolve some consequences of slavery.

The notion of "retrospective operation" of marriage rights, which the court considered in *Lewis,* would have helped Charles Allen retain custody of his son. The doctrine had gained traction in the courts of many former slave states. The premise of retroactive rights and the particular doctrine of "dormant rights" first emerged in Louisiana in 1819. According to the dormant-rights theory (likely derived from the Roman slave custom *contu-bernium*), the enslaved had *always* possessed the rights of free people, but the institution of slavery had rendered those rights inactive or dormant.[87] Once formerly enslaved people were free, rights attached to the former actions they had taken. For instance, a customary union between enslaved people became legitimate once the parties became free and therefore capable of contracting marriage. The state then recognized the marriage as lawful from the moment the couple had entered into it. In other words, entering into civil society rendered the marriage retroactively legal. Children born to an enslaved couple acquired legitimacy through the same process. Judges in several states, including Alabama, Missouri, Maryland, and Tennessee, used the retroactive-rights doctrine to accomplish several goals: make families legitimate and therefore morally upstanding, reduce dependency of children, and, most important, make freedpeople equal in rights to freeborn Americans.[88] As one Alabama judge ruled in a case about freedchildren's legitimacy, they "should not be made to suffer for a wrong committed, against their mothers, their father, and themselves. This would be adding wrong to wrong, without any necessity to vindicate it, except perhaps, an old prejudice, the basis of which is now swept away forever."[89]

For the most part, the Kentucky Court of Appeals was not persuaded by this approach. In *Lewis,* the court concluded that the new law regulating freedpeople's domestic lives was "never meant to attach responsibilities to the freedman for his acts as a slave when no responsibilities attached to him as such." When the child was born, the law was clear: responsibilities had "belonged to the master, . . . so that neither the parents nor children could become a public burden." But after freedom, no accommodation had been made to address the status of the children born to enslaved parents. Because "no new statute ha[d] provided that the putative slave father shall be responsible for the support of his illegitimate slave child," judges decided to follow the laws in effect prior to emancipation rather than revive a parental obligation after the fact.[90] Henry Lewis could not be financially responsible for his child because the infant was born prior to emancipation to parents who had never married either customarily or formally. Likewise, the court deemed young Henry Allen a bastard because his parents had not continued their relationship or registered it with state officials. In the absence of either, the statute meant to bestow legitimacy to freedchildren did not apply.

The court invoked the same rule in both *Lewis* and *Allen,* but the rule produced very different outcomes for the litigants: Henry Lewis escaped criminal conviction for fathering a child he had no wish to parent, whereas Charles Allen lost any chance of being recognized as his son's legal father, despite his professed desire to exercise his newly acquired parental rights. The children in the two cases, however, suffered the same consequences. Both were deemed bastards under the law. At least in Henry Allen's case, this would not have been true if he had been born free. Kentucky, along with other former slave states, never remedied this inequity.[91]

The practical effects of the rulings meant that freedchildren could be left without legal fathers. This was out of step with antebellum legal trends. Traditionally, illegitimate children existed in a legal purgatory where they were considered outside of any established household and thus outside the boundaries of the legal protections that legitimacy provided. They could not inherit and had only the "rights" to support from poor laws and to be left in the custody of their mothers.[92] But before emancipation, many states had liberalized the law of bastardy so that children born in such circumstances could inherit from their mothers—as "the woman's legitimate children." By the 1850s, state courts commonly considered legitimizing children "a favored policy," and they often assisted fathers who wished to legally recognize their children born out of wedlock. Of course, these reforms were undertaken with white children in mind. With emancipation, the historian Michael Grossberg notes, "judicial predispositions to aid bastards" that had developed in earlier decades were "put to the test" in "disputes arising from the rubble of slavery."[93]

Kentucky's judges remained steadfast. If single mothers such as Julia Martin and Mary Allen were unable to provide for their children (which was difficult for all single mothers, irrespective of race), the state would intervene. As the court reminded the litigants in *Lewis,* Kentucky had "manifested other remedies" to address formerly enslaved people, including the apprenticeship of "all freed children where their parents are not supporting them" and the taxing of "the free colored male population of a given age" in order to "support their indigent poor and school their children." Defending the levy, the court noted that "not a dollar of" the taxes collected would go "towards supporting the State government or defraying the county expenses."[94] Rather, the tax compelled the Black community to support poor and orphaned freedchildren. The rights and privileges enslaved people acquired through emancipation and enfranchisement not only had limits but in Kentucky also came at a price.

Rulings that denied domestic legitimacy had dire financial consequences for Black families. Some parents chose to apprentice their children to persons of their own choosing. These wages often supplemented the family's income and, at least in theory, provided an education for the apprentices. (The law required guardians to provide their wards with a basic education.) It may well have been, for example, that both Mary and Charles Allen needed their child's wages to survive.[95] Coerced apprenticeship, however, quickly became a favored practice of white officials who cared little about child welfare. County courts subjected Black children to long-term labor arrangements if their parents lacked the means to care for them properly. Of course, an assessment of resources and proper care was entirely subjective. Apprenticeships of this sort, as many scholars have noted, closely—and intentionally—resembled slavery.[96] Courts regularly preferred to bind the children out to their former enslavers, and in Kentucky a law passed in 1866 required it.[97] This only added to the trauma of forced separation against which freedom was supposed to protect. The historian Leon Litwack describes some postbellum apprenticeship arrangements as "[coming] close to legalized kidnapping."[98] Although the Freedmen's Bureau managed to free some of these children or renegotiate their contracts, it, too, bound out the children of parents it deemed unfit to care for their children.[99]

Black women such as Julia Martin were easy targets for compulsory apprenticeship orders. Many white southerners believed that freedwomen were "incompetent, if not abusive, parents." Worse still, some argued that freedwomen would rather commit infanticide than work to care for and support their children. Apprenticeship offered southern whites the opportunity to reinforce the long-held social conventions of white supremacy. Black mothers might teach their children to "drop all the rituals of deference and respect they had been expected to exhibit as slaves," but white guardians of their apprenticed children could reintroduce and reinforce those rituals, reminding the young Black children of their proper place in society. For southern whites, apprenticeship not only offered the chance to recapture part of their formerly enslaved labor force but also made it possible to inculcate in Black children the race-based behavioral rules they were expected to follow.[100]

Black churches and benevolent associations provided some assistance to fatherless and orphaned children, but their aid was contingent on time, place, and ideology. It took years for private aid organizations to acquire the resources necessary to assist those in need, and even then those resources were usually meager (Black churches, especially in rural areas, regularly struggled with debt during Reconstruction). Those that managed to establish funds typically served urban populations. In addition, not everyone was eligible to receive their largesse; even charities that could help may have eschewed providing aid to an unwed mother such as Julia Martin. Ministers and aid groups practiced a paternalism of their own and often insisted that congregants and aid recipients maintain unimpeachable moral lives that would demonstrate Black Americans' industry and fitness for citizenship.[101]

As a consequence of these hurdles, many parents remained at the mercy of the courts. Judicial rulings confirmed that Kentucky law had no remedy to address all the lingering disabilities, including illegitimacy, that stemmed from previous enslavement, nor were Kentucky judges particularly eager to ease freedpeople's domestic burdens. As the Court of Appeals maintained, "The amendment to the United States Constitution abolished all interest of the owner in his slave, and with its abrogation relieved him from all responsibility to support the freed slave; but this in nowise shifted the responsibility of support on to the shoulders of the legally irresponsible putative father, nor has any of our State statutes done so."[102] Emancipation had freed people from enslavement, but it did not entirely abolish the consequences of their former bondage. Many of the harms associated with enslavement, including illegitimacy and the denial of paternal rights, remained intact.

It appeared that there would be few options in Kentucky for the emancipated children born without legitimate fathers. In 1874, however, the Court of Appeals tempered its approach to when a marriage between formerly enslaved parents could be established. In *Whitesides v. Allen,* the court considered a domestic dispute between the family members of Daniel Allen. Allen died after using his soldier's pay to acquire property in Lexington. His mother and siblings, the Whitesides, claimed it for themselves, arguing they had the right to inherit as his next of kin. His wife, Jane, sought to protect the property for their children. Since Daniel and Jane Allen (no relation to Charles or Mary Allen) had never registered their marriage according to the dictates of a statute enacted in 1866, the litigation centered on the legitimacy of the couple's marriage. Without a valid marriage, precedent dictated that Daniel's children could not be declared his lawful heirs.

A revealing legal record provides some insight into the dispute between Jane Allen and Daniel's relatives (though not in their own words). Jane's former enslaver, Hiram Barkley, testified that she and Daniel had married at his home while both were enslaved and that Daniel always claimed the children born before the war as his own. But Jane reportedly gave birth to another child, which invited charges of illegitimacy. Daniel Allen served as a soldier in the Civil War, and according to the freedwoman Martha Pendleton, another of Barkley's bondspeople, Jane had another baby "about 18 months after he left," which "couldn't have been Daniel's child." Pendleton reported that "there was a fuss about it when Daniel came home," but they "finally made it up" and resumed cohabiting as a family. Jane Allen's witnesses challenged this account, contending that all her children had been fathered by Daniel.[103]

Accounts like this one emphasize that salacious but nevertheless commonplace affairs (or alleged ones) prompted critical judicial interrogations about how domestic law applied to freedpeople. Jane Allen and her children and the Whitesides family were well represented by counsel who could help them navigate these difficult waters. But others, including Henry Lewis, found themselves enmeshed in legal proceedings they did not understand. Lewis asked for help from a white man he knew from his community because he "had always been slow and was totally ignorant of the law . . . or anything of [the] sort and could not even write" or sign his name to the bond issued by the court.[104] But this self-professed ignorance became evident only after the court jailed Lewis for failing to appear in court, which violated his bail.

In the end, one key feature determined the outcome of *Whitesides v. Allen*, differentiating it from *Lewis* and *Allen:* Daniel and Jane Allen continued their relationship into freedom. Although the couple may have been guilty of violating the state's statute requiring them to marry formally, the court ruled "that the legislature never intended to declare the children of such parents . . . *bastards.*"[105] Whether with a purpose to reduce dependency or to control Black families, Kentucky legislators wrote a law that legitimized the children born to parents who maintained their relationships into freedom. In so doing, they ensured that some freedchildren enjoyed all the rights of children born to white couples, regardless of the technical status of their parents' unions.

Opinions in cases such as *Whitesides* expose the possibilities and promise that postemancipation domestic law cases held. Because their father had amassed property, and because the court deemed them his legitimate heirs, Daniel Allen's children entered adulthood in very different circumstances than most of their peers. They had not been saddled with the disabilities of illegitimacy. Instead, they acquired the means to become self-sustaining and the chance to avoid the pernicious labor contracts and sharecropping arrangements that forced most Black Americans into a permanent state of crushing poverty. The property Daniel Allen left behind had the potential to become the germ of future wealth creation that could sustain his children and other kin for generations. Illegitimate freedchildren were legally prohibited from enjoying this right.

Postemancipation family law cases prompted a reckoning with the particularly complex effects that generations of bondage had wrought on the lives and families of freedpeople. Liberation did not obviate those effects, leaving judges with the difficult task of resolving them. During Reconstruction, courts held many Black litigants to legal standards that could have applied to them only after emancipation. For some, such as Charles Allen, former enslavement made those standards unattainable. He could not register his former marriage to Mary after marrying someone else. For her part, Julia Martin was left without financial support for her child. Many who shared her precarious position apprenticed their children because they could not afford anything else. For some freedpeople, then, disabilities of one kind were replaced by those of another, and the justices of the Kentucky Court of Appeals either believed there existed no remedy or denied that one was needed. The intractable legacies of slavery determined that outcome.

During and after the Civil War, Kentucky resisted Black freedom. Even when it became clear that the Thirteenth Amendment would end slavery everywhere, the General Assembly maintained its defiance. It did not ratify the amendment or the other Reconstruction Amendments until 1976. The General Assembly also declined to grant many civil rights to freedpeople (e.g., to testify or serve on juries) and refused to repeal the state's slave code. The state lived under the Constitution of 1850 until 1891, well after any promise of racial equality had faded away. The state did not experience a Radical phase; state officials, including judges, were never removed from their positions, as similar officials were in former Confederate states placed under military governorship. It is no wonder, then, that Kentucky became the only loyal state to which the Freedmen's Bureau was dispatched and that legal conflicts about the consequences of emancipation arose with such frequency.

The Kentucky Court of Appeals shared the perspective of the General Assembly. The decisions in suits about wartime affairs, largely unique to the state, set the tone for the court's positions on emancipation throughout Reconstruction.[106] As opinions in *Hughes* and *Corbin* reveal, Chief Justice George Robertson thoroughly—and retroactively—condemned federal laws that granted freedom, and he demanded compensation for lost slave property. Even in the suits that raised identical questions to those heard in other former slave states, Kentucky consistently maintained a more conservative course. In suits related to the financial costs of emancipation—those that raised questions about contract and other debts—Kentucky judges never considered the possibility that by prioritizing contract law, their courts were ignoring the human property being conveyed in them.[107] In states where judges raised these objections, courts had to at least contemplate a fuller eradication of slavery from law and society. No such consideration took place in Kentucky.

Though contract suits may seem entirely divorced from deliberations over the status and rights of freedpeople, the rulings in such suits underscored the judicial commitment to the slave past. By focusing on contract doctrine alone, judges ensured that the business of bondage survived slavery's practical end. Though nothing would restore the slave regime, the property interest that had been vested in the bodies of enslaved people continued to pay. As long as some white Americans could capitalize on slavery, abolition remained incomplete.[108]

Abolition was also elusive for those who struggled to establish domestic legitimacy. To be sure, cases raised by and about freedpeople held the greatest potential for reimagining Kentucky as a free state and for integrating Black people as equal citizens into its body politic. Kentucky's Court of Appeals, however, remained unwilling to fully acknowledge freedpeople's new place in American society. Rather than recognize rights retroactively, as many other states did in order to provide equity to families of the formerly enslaved, Kentucky judges largely ruled that the disabilities of enslavement—namely, the inability to marry legally and therefore to bear legitimate children—could not be overcome by newly acquired freedom and citizenship. Freedpeople would carry their slave pasts with them. In part, this interpretation resulted from the General Assembly's stringent requirements for domestic legitimacy. The ruling in

Whitesides, however, illustrates how a looser interpretation of that statute might have bestowed legal status and the benefits that flowed from it to formerly enslaved children. Young Henry Allen and the child of Julia Martin found no such relief.[109]

None of this is to say that courts and state governments in other former slave states did not revert back to as much of the status quo ante as soon as they could. When Redeemers recaptured statehouses, they did. But for a time a window of possibility opened for freedpeople—and for abolition—in these states. The Kentucky Court of Appeals refused to consider opening that window. Some judges, including George Robertson, barely acknowledged it existed. Enslavement had ended, and the state was forced to recognize the basic rights of freedom. But many Kentucky judges refused to consider a society that was not ordered by race and status, freedom and unfreedom. The court never broached the more difficult task of deconstructing slavery's legacies to ensure truly equal citizenship.

Freedpeople lived with the consequences of this failure. Without the full abolition of slavery or the enshrining of legal protections for Black citizens, vestiges of slavery lived on in law and in life. Like African Americans elsewhere, Black Kentuckians were summarily denied the rights of citizenship. In addition to the civil rights denied to Black Kentuckians during Reconstruction, the General Assembly welcomed Jim Crow to the state by enacting a separate coach law in 1892 that segregated rail cars. It went on to adopt several other discriminatory statutes in the years following the ruling in *Plessy v. Ferguson* (1896), which permitted the development of an American apartheid.[110] Racial violence was endemic in Kentucky and persisted well into the twentieth century. According to the Equal Justice Initiative, Fulton County had one of the highest rates and largest numbers of lynchings in the decades following the Civil War.[111] Just as Lincoln had feared during the Civil War, by the turn of the twentieth century Kentucky had formally cast its lot with the states of the former Confederacy.

Acknowledgments

The author thanks the volume editor as well as Amy Murrell Taylor and Chris Bovbjerg, who offered excellent insights and editorial advice on her chapter.

Notes

1. The Kentucky Court of Appeals was the highest court in the state until the Kentucky Supreme Court was established in 1975. "Slave states" permitted the lawful practice of slavery before and during the Civil War.

2. Despite their status as property without rights, some enslaved people had knowledge of the law. See, for example, Laura F. Edwards, *The People and Their Peace: Legal Culture and the Transformation of Inequality in the Post-revolutionary South* (Chapel Hill: University of North Carolina Press, 2009); Ariela J. Gross, *Double Character: Slavery and Mastery in the Antebellum Southern Courtroom* (Athens: University of Georgia Press, 2006); Loren Schweninger, *Appealing for Liberty: Freedom Suits in the South* (New York: Oxford University Press, 2018).

3. Eric Foner, *Reconstruction: America's Unfinished Revolution, 1863–1877* (New York: HarperCollins, 1988), xxiii.

4. Foner, *Reconstruction,* 603.

5. Laura F. Edwards, *A Legal History of the Civil War and Reconstruction* (New York: Cambridge University Press, 2015).

6. An antislavery movement had existed in Kentucky from statehood until the ratification of the Thirteenth Amendment, but pro-slavery forces remained in political control of the state. See, for example, Lowell Harrison, *The Antislavery Movement in Kentucky* (Lexington: University Press of Kentucky, 1978); and Harold D. Tallant, *Evil Necessity: Slavery and Political Culture in Antebellum Kentucky* (Lexington: University Press of Kentucky, 2003).

7. Darrel E. Bigham, *On Jordan's Banks: Emancipation and Its Aftermath in the Ohio River Valley* (Lexington: University Press of Kentucky, 2006), 141–42.

8. E. Merton Coulter, *The Civil War and Readjustment in Kentucky* (Chapel Hill: University of North Carolina Press, 1926), 259; Ira Berlin, Steven F. Miller, Joseph P. Reidy, and Leslie S. Rowland, eds., in *The Wartime Genesis of Free Labor: The Upper South,* vol. 2 of *Freedom: A Documentary History of Emancipation, 1861–1867* (New York: Cambridge University Press, 1993), 625; Ross A. Webb, *Kentucky in the Reconstruction Era* (Lexington: University Press of Kentucky, 1979), 9–15; Foner, *Reconstruction,* 37–38.

9. Judith N. Shklar, *American Citizenship: The Quest for Inclusion* (Cambridge, MA: Harvard University Press, 1991); Elizabeth Regosin, *Freedom's Promise: Ex-Slave Families and Citizenship in the Age of Emancipation* (Charlottesville: University Press of Virginia, 2002); Bigham, *On Jordan's Banks;* Foner, *Reconstruction;* Steven Hahn, *A Nation under Our Feet: Black Political Struggles in the Rural South from Slavery to the Great Migration* (Cambridge, MA: Belknap Press of Harvard University Press, 2005).

10. The ban remained in effect until 1872, when the state legislature adopted a new statute.

11. *Bowlin v. Commonwealth,* 65 Ky. 5 (1867), at 7–8, emphasis in original.

12. Enslaved people from Confederate states who enrolled in the military would have been considered "contraband" of war. Only loyal slaveholders from Union states could argue that enrollment constituted illegal taking of property. Maryland was the only other state to hear cases on the matter, and it decided only two.

13. The legal disabilities of slavery stemmed from slaves' status as property. They included the inability to own property, testify in court, and marry, among other things.

14. Webb, *Kentucky in the Reconstruction Era,* 7; Coulter, *The Civil War and Readjustment in Kentucky,* chap. 11; Foner, *Reconstruction,* 137.

15. Berlin et al., *Wartime Genesis of Free Labor,* 183; John David Smith, "The Recruitment of Negro Soldiers in Kentucky, 1863–1865," *Register of the Kentucky Historical Society* 72, no. 4 (October 1974): 365–69, 389; James McPherson, *Battle Cry of Freedom: The Civil War Era* (New York: Oxford University Press, 1988), 357; Amy Murrell Taylor, *Embattled Freedom: Journeys through the Civil War's Slave Refugee Camps* (Chapel Hill: University of North Carolina Press, 2018), 186.

16. Military service among Kentuckians was similarly split; 30,000 joined the Confederacy, while 64,000 enlisted with the Union (Webb, *Kentucky in the Reconstruction Era,* 9).

17. Marion B. Lucas, *A History of Blacks in Kentucky,* vol. 1: *From Slavery to Segregation, 1760–1891* (Frankfort: Kentucky Historical Society, 1992), 150.

18. Abraham Lincoln to Orville H. Browning, September 22, 1861, in Abraham Lincoln, *Collected Works of Abraham Lincoln,* 9 vols., ed. Roy P. Basler (New Brunswick, NJ: Rutgers University Press, 1953), 4:532.

19. "An Act for Enrolling and Calling Out the National Forces, and for Other Purposes," 12 Stat. 731; Smith, "Recruitment of Negro Soldiers in Kentucky," 374–76, 383–84; Taylor, *Embattled Freedom,* 186.

20. James S. Brisbin to Thomas E. Bramlette, April 14, 1865, BR5-185 to BR5-188, in *Civil War Governors of Kentucky Digital Documentary Edition,* Kentucky Department for Libraries and Archives, Frankfort, at http://discovery.civilwargovernors.org/document/KYR-0001-003-0109.

21. On self-liberation, see Ira Berlin, Barbara J. Fields, Steven F. Miller, Joseph P. Reidy, and Leslie S. Rowland, *Slaves No More: Three Essays on Emancipation and the Civil War* (New York: Cambridge University Press, 1992); Taylor, *Embattled Freedom;* W. E. B. Du Bois, *Black Reconstruction in America, 1860–1880* (New York: Free Press, 1935).

22. Berlin et al., *Slaves No More,* 33.

23. Victor B. Howard, *Black Liberation in Kentucky: Emancipation and Freedom, 1862–1884* (Lexington: University Press of Kentucky, 1983), 108. In 1862, Union military officials prohibited enslaved people from living in or near the camps. Once the Emancipation Proclamation took effect, that policy changed.

24. Berlin et al., *Slaves No More,* chap. 3. Black enlistment declined by the summer of 1864 but never stopped (Smith, "The Recruitment of Negro Soldiers in Kentucky," 385).

25. Berlin et al., *Slaves No More,* 207. Many more Black men had fled to Northern states and to Tennessee to enlist before they were allowed to do so at home (Berlin et al., *Slaves No More,* 207).

26. "A Resolution to Encourage Enlistments and to Promote the Efficiency of the Military Forces of the United States," in *U.S. Statutes at Large, Treaties, and Proclamations of the United States of America*, vol. 13 (Boston, 1866), 571; Webb, *Kentucky in the Reconstruction Era,* 36; Howard, *Black Liberation in Kentucky,* 121.

27. *Hughes v. Todd,* 63 Ky. 188 (1865), Brief for Appellees, 1, Kentucky Court of Appeals no. 135, Public Records Division, Kentucky Department for Libraries and Archives. The law to which they refer is "An Act for Enrolling and Calling Out the National Forces, and for Other Purposes," 13 Stat. 6, enacted February 24, 1864. It allowed for the enlistment of Black soldiers.

28. *Corbin v. Marsh,* 63 Ky. 193 (1865), Court of Appeals transcript, at 2–3.

29. *Hughes v. Todd,* 63 Ky. 188 (1865), at 189–90.

30. *Corbin v. Marsh,* 63 Ky. 193 (1865), at 198–99.

31. Abraham Lincoln quoted in Lowell H. Harrison, "Slavery in Kentucky: A Civil War Casualty," *Kentucky Review* 5, no. 1 (Fall 1983): 35.

32. Harrison, "Slavery in Kentucky," 33. See also Eric Foner, *The Fiery Trial: Abraham Lincoln and American Slavery* (New York: Norton, 2010), 181–84. Congress enacted the Compensated Emancipation Act in 1862, which paid slaveholders in Washington, DC, for their chattel property.

33. *Dred Scott v. Sandford,* 60 US 393 (1857).

34. *Hughes v. Todd,* 63 Ky. 188 (1865), at 190–91. On postemancipation calls for compensation, see Amanda Laury Kleintop, "Life, Liberty, and Property in Slaves: White Mississippians Seek 'Just Compensation' for Their Freed Slaves in 1865," *Slavery & Abolition* 39, no. 2 (2018): 383–404.

35. Coulter, *The Civil War and Readjustment in Kentucky,* 259; Webb, *Kentucky in the Reconstruction Era,* 9–15.

36. "An Act to Further Regulate and Provide for the Enrolling and Calling Out the National Forces," §24; Amanda Laury Kleintop, "The Balance of Free-

dom: Abolishing Property Rights in Slaves during and after the US Civil War," PhD diss., Northwestern University, 2018, 160; Smith, "The Recruitment of Negro Soldiers in Kentucky," 389.

37. Robertson quoted in Jerrica A. Giles and Allen C. Guelzo, "Colonel Utley's Emancipation—or, How Lincoln Offered to Buy a Slave," *Marquette Law Review* 93, no. 4 (2010): 1280.

38. The case presumably ended up in federal court because of a diversity claim. Utley was a citizen of Wisconsin, whereas Robertson was a citizen of Kentucky. It was heard by the US Circuit Court for the Eastern District of Wisconsin.

39. Lincoln's attorney general James Speed represented Utley in Court. Senator Timothy Howe of Wisconsin pursued the legal indemnification in Congress.

40. Giles and Guelzo, "Colonel Utley's Emancipation"; William B. Allen, *A History of Kentucky* (Louisville, KY: Bradley & Gilbert, 1872), 261–64; Sanders [*sic*], "Judge George Robertson," ExploreKYHistory, n.d., at http://explorekyhistory .ky.gov/items/show/40; Kurt X. Metzmeir, "History of the Courts of Kentucky," in *United at Last: The Judicial Article and the Struggle to Reform Kentucky's Courts* (Lexington: Kentucky Court of Justice, 2006).

41. *Palmer v. Commonwealth,* 65 Ky. 570 (1866), at 574–75, emphasis in original.

42. General Order No. 32, May 11, 1865, Headquarters Department of Kentucky, Louisville, in *Palmer v. Commonwealth,* 65 Ky. 570 (1866), at 573, emphasis in original.

43. John McAuley Palmer, *Personal Recollections of John M. Palmer* (Cincinnati: Robert Clarke, 1901), 242.

44. Harrison, "Slavery in Kentucky," 39. The calculation is based on the number of people enslaved in 1860.

45. *Palmer v. Commonwealth,* Brief for Palmer, Kentucky Court of Appeals no. 247, at 4, Public Records Division, Kentucky Department for Libraries and Archives.

46. *Palmer v. Commonwealth,* Brief for Commonwealth, Kentucky Court of Appeals no. 247, at 2–3, Public Records Division, Kentucky Department for Libraries and Archives.

47. *Palmer v. Commonwealth,* 65 Ky. 570 (1866), at 576.

48. *Palmer v. Commonwealth,* 65 Ky. 570 (1866), at 579.

49. *Palmer v. Commonwealth,* Brief for Commonwealth, at 2, opinion at 574.

50. Palmer, *Personal Recollections of John M. Palmer,* 247–48.

51. *Palmer v. Commonwealth,* 65 Ky. 570 (1866), at 577.

52. *Plessy v. Ferguson,* 163 US 537 (1896).

53. Walter Johnson, *Soul by Soul: Life inside the Antebellum Slave Market* (Cambridge, MA: Harvard University Press, 2001), 88. On slaves as insurance,

see Jonathan Levy, *Freaks of Fortune: The Emerging World of Capitalism and Risk in America* (Cambridge, MA: Harvard University Press, 2012).

54. Harrison, "Slavery in Kentucky," 32. For a compilation of slave ownership, population, and holding by state, see Jenny Bourne, "Slavery in the United States," Economic History Association, *EH.Net Encyclopedia,* March 26, 2008, at https://eh.net/encyclopedia/slavery-in-the-united-states/.

55. Lucas, *A History of Blacks in Kentucky,* 1:2–4.

56. Lucas, *A History of Blacks in Kentucky,* 1:85.

57. Gavin Wright, *Old South, New South: Revolutions in the Southern Economy since the Civil War* (Baton Rouge: Louisiana State University Press, 1997), 19–20.

58. Joseph A. Ranney, *In the Wake of Slavery: Civil War, Civil Rights, and the Reconstruction of Southern Law* (Westport, CT: Praeger, 2006), 58.

59. *Bailey v. Howard,* 2 Ky. Op. 294 (1868), at 294–95. Such a contingency was included in the contract reviewed by the court in *Noland's Executor v. Golden,* 66 Ky. 84 (1867). See also *Thomas v. Porter,* 66 Ky. 177 (1867), and *Porter v. Ralston,* 69 Ky. 665 (1869).

60. US Constitution, Art. 1, sec. 10; *White v. Hart,* 80 US 646 (1872); *Whitmer v. Nall's Executors,* 2 Ky. Op. 361 (1868), at 364.

61. Georgia also refused to enforce contracts for enslaved people, but it did so on different grounds. The court ruled that the constitutional prohibition against the impairment of contracts did not apply to states of the former Confederacy as conquered territory. In *Texas v. White,* 74 US 700 (1869), the Supreme Court of the United States ruled that no state had legally seceded.

62. *Wainwright v. Bridges,* 19 La. Ann. 234 (1867), at 239.

63. *Bush v. Groom,* 72 Ky. 675 (1873), at 678–79.

64. Diane J. Klein, "Paying Eliza: Comity, Contracts, and Critical Race Theory—19th Century Choice of Law Doctrine and the Validation of the Antebellum Contracts for the Purchase and Sale of Human Beings," *National Black Law Journal* 20, no. 1 (2006): 1–41.

65. Maryland, Louisiana, and Tennessee offered a quasi-legality to slave marriages that had the sanction of the enslaver. Although these marriages were not legally binding during slavery, rights were attached to the unions upon the couple's freedom. See *Jones v. Jones,* 36 Md. 447 (1872); *Girod v. Lewis,* 6 Mart. 559 (1819); and *Andrews v. Page,* 50 Tenn. 653 (1871).

66. Leon Litwack, *Been in the Storm so Long: The Aftermath of Slavery* (New York: Random House, 1979), 240, emphasis in original.

67. See especially Heather Andrea Williams, *Help Me to Find My People: The African American Search for Family Lost in Slavery* (Chapel Hill: University of North Carolina Press, 2012).

68. Hahn, *A Nation under Our Feet;* Thavolia Glymph, *Out of the House of Bondage: The Transformation of the Plantation Household* (Cambridge: Cambridge University Press, 2008); Dylan C. Penningroth, *The Claims of Kinfolk: African American Property and Community in the Nineteenth-Century South* (Chapel Hill: University of North Carolina Press, 2003); Deborah Gray White, *Ar'n't I a Woman? Female Slaves in the Plantation South* (New York: Norton, 1999), chap. 6; Leslie A. Schwalm, *A Hard Fight for We: Women's Transition from Slavery to Freedom in South Carolina* (Chicago: University of Illinois Press, 1997), chap. 7.

69. Bigham, *On Jordan's Banks,* 231–32.

70. For comments on the problematic use of the phrase "Black family," see Melinda Chateauvert, "Framing Sexual Citizenship: Reconsidering the Discourse on African American Families," in "Discourses on Race, Sex, and African American Citizenship," special issue of *Journal of African American History* 93, no. 2 (Spring 2008): 198–222; and Brenda E. Stevenson, "The Question of the Female Slave Community and Culture in the American South: Methodological and Ideological Approaches," *Journal of African American History* 92 (Winter 2007): 74–95.

71. Webb, *Kentucky in the Reconstruction Era,* 16, 40–41; John E. Kleber, *The Kentucky Encyclopedia* (Lexington: University Press of Kentucky, 1992), 757.

72. Bigham, *On Jordan's Banks,* 131–32; Webb, *Kentucky in the Reconstruction Era,* 43–44.

73. Foner, *Reconstruction,* 37.

74. "An Act to Establish a Bureau for the Relief of Freedmen and Refugees," 13 Stat. 507.

75. Tera W. Hunter, *Bound in Wedlock: Slave and Free Black Marriage in the Nineteenth Century* (Cambridge, MA: Harvard University Press, 2017), esp. 30–35; Laura F. Edwards, "'The Marriage Covenant Is at the Foundation of All Our Rights': The Politics of Slave Marriages in North Carolina after Emancipation," *Law and History Review* 14, no. 1 (Spring 1996): 111.

76. Nancy F. Cott, *Public Vows: A History of Marriage and the Nation* (Cambridge, MA: Harvard University Press, 2000), 85–86. See also Litwack, *Been in the Storm so Long,* 240.

77. Edwards, "'The Marriage Covenant Is at the Foundation of All Our Rights,'" 93. On dependency, see, for example, Peter W. Bardaglio, *Reconstructing the Household: Families, Sex, and the Law in the Nineteenth-Century South* (Chapel Hill: University of North Carolina Press, 1995); and Laura F. Edwards, *Gendered Strife and Confusion: The Political Culture of Reconstruction* (Champaign: University of Illinois Press, 1997).

78. It is not clear why Kentucky heard more family lawsuits than other former slave states. It may have resulted from the change in the state's policy on common law marriages, which were prohibited by the new statutes intended to regulate the Black family. Couples had to register—for a fee—any union; they could no longer simply cohabitate to establish a lawful union.

79. Bardaglio, *Reconstructing the Household;* Edwards, "'The Marriage Covenant Is at the Foundation of All Our Rights'"; Herbert G. Gutman, *The Black Family in Slavery and Freedom, 1750–1925* (New York: Vintage Books, 1976); Noralee Frankel, *Freedom's Women: Black Women and Families in Civil War Era Mississippi* (Bloomington: Indiana University Press, 1999); Schwalm, *A Hard Fight for We;* Wilma A. Dunaway, *The African-American Family in Slavery and Emancipation* (New York: Cambridge University Press, 2003); Litwack, *Been in the Storm so Long,* 241–42. As Noralee Frankel notes, pension records corroborate that many couples "were comfortable with their community-sanctioned slave marriages" and felt no need to have an official remarry them (*Freedom's Women,* 80).

80. *Stewart v. Munchandler,* 65 Ky. 278 (1867), at 280.

81. *Estill v. Rogers,* 64 Ky. 62 (1866), at 65, Kentucky Court of Appeals no. 556, Public Records Division, Kentucky Department for Libraries and Archives. Records do not disclose the contents of Sally Ann Estill's estate, but her brother Harvey became its administrator.

82. *Lewis v. Commonwealth,* 66 Ky. 539 (1868), Kentucky Court of Appeals no. 1972, Public Records Division, Kentucky Department for Libraries and Archives.

83. *Lewis v. Commonwealth,* 66 Ky. 539 (1868), at 441.

84. Cott, *Public Vows,* 82; Edwards, *Gendered Strife and Confusion,* 18; Amy Dru Stanley, *From Bondage to Contract: Wage Labor, Marriage, and the Market in the Age of Slave Emancipation* (Cambridge: Cambridge University Press, 1998), ix.

85. *Allen v. Allen,* 71 Ky. 490 (1871), at 490.

86. *Allen v. Allen,* 71 Ky. 490 (1871), at 492.

87. On the origins and relationship of dormant rights to *contubernium,* see Michael Grossberg, *Governing the Hearth: Law and the Family in Nineteenth-Century America* (Chapel Hill: University of North Carolina Press, 1985), 130–32.

88. Giuliana Perrone, "'Back into the Days of Slavery': Freedom, Citizenship, and the Black Family in the Reconstruction-Era Courtroom," *Law and History Review* 37, no. 1 (February 2019): 125–61; Adrienne D. Davis, "The Private Law of Race and Sex: An Antebellum Perspective," *Stanford Law Review* 51, no. 2 (January 1999): 221–88; *Girod v. Lewis,* 6 Mart. 559 (1819). During the antebellum period, Thomas R. R. Cobb noted the concept of dormant rights in *An*

Inquiry into the Law of Negro Slavery in the United States of America, vol. 1 (Philadelphia: T. & J. W. Johnson, 1858).

89. *Stikes v. Swanson,* 44 Ala. 633 (1870), at 637.

90. *Lewis v. Commonwealth,* 66 Ky. 539 (1868), at 542–43.

91. *Lewis v. Commonwealth,* 66 Ky. 539 (1868), at 543. Other states struggled with legitimating children born to parents whose marriages did not continue after emancipation. See, for example, *Timmins v. Lacy,* 30 Tex. 115 (1867), and *Pierre v. Fontenette,* 25 La. Ann. 617 (1873).

92. Grossberg, *Governing the Hearth,* 207.

93. Bardaglio, *Reconstructing the Household,* 91–92; Grossberg, *Governing the Hearth,* 205–7, 212, 221. Paternal preference was granted by law in both Mississippi and Texas, at least for a time. However, there was a more general move to grant custody rights to whichever parent the court deemed to be in the best interest of the child. In the civil law of Louisiana, fathers who wished to legitimize their children needed only a "notarial act" to do so.

94. *Lewis v. Commonwealth,* 66 Ky. 539 (1868), at 543–44.

95. Bigham, *On Jordan's Banks,* 137.

96. Foner, *Reconstruction,* 201; Bigham, *On Jordan's Banks,* 136. See also Karin L. Zipf, *Labor of Innocents: Forced Apprenticeship in North Carolina* (Baton Rouge: Louisiana State University Press, 2005).

97. *Journal of the House of Representatives of the Commonwealth of Kentucky* (Frankfort, KY: State Printing Office, 1865), 562, at https://uknowledge.uky.edu/ky_state_journals/43/. Other states, including North Carolina, had apprenticeship laws that gave preference to former enslavers. The statutes allowed the state to return the labor of emancipated children to their former owners.

98. Litwack, *Been in the Storm so Long,* 237.

99. Howard, *Black Liberation in Kentucky,* 126.

100. Schwalm, *A Hard Fight for We,* 251–52; White, *Ar'n't I a Woman?,* 170.

101. Bigham, *On Jordan's Banks,* 258–59, 263.

102. *Lewis v. Commonwealth,* 66 Ky. 539 (1868), at 544.

103. *Whitesides v. Allen,* 74 Ky. 23 (1874), Kentucky Court of Appeals no. 7457, Public Records Division, Kentucky Department for Libraries and Archives.

104. *Lewis v. Commonwealth,* 66 Ky. 539 (1868), Kentucky Court of Appeals no. 1972.

105. *Whitesides v. Allen,* 74 Ky. 23 (1874), at 24, emphasis in original.

106. Specifically, such cases included those related to the enlistment of enslaved men, the emancipation of their family members, and the use of substitutes in the Union army. This litigation made up 11 percent of the total number

of suits related to slavery heard by the Kentucky Court of Appeals during Reconstruction.

107. Justice Rufus Williams dissented in *Hughes* and *Corbin* on the grounds that the US government had the authority to commandeer and emancipate enslaved people during wartime. He did not otherwise challenge the recovery of debts for enslaved people.

108. Like Orlando Patterson and others, I consider emancipation as a constitutive element of slavery. See Orlando Patterson, *Slavery and Social Death: A Comparative Study* (Cambridge, MA: Harvard University Press, 1982); and Saidiya V. Hartman, *Scenes of Subjection: Terror, Slavery, and Self-Making in Nineteenth-Century America* (New York: Oxford University Press, 1997).

109. In *Hall v. United States*, 92 US 27 (1875), the US Supreme Court ruled against the use of retroactive marriage rights, but not until 1875. That ruling did not prohibit granting retroactive legitimacy to formerly enslaved children. See also Perrone, "'Back into the Days of Slavery,'" 31–33.

110. Anne E. Marshall, "Kentucky's Separate Coach Law and African American Response, 1892–1900," *Register of the Kentucky Historical Society* 98, no. 3 (Summer 2000): 241–59.

111. Equal Justice Initiative, "Lynching in America: Confronting the Legacy of Racial Terror," Montgomery, AL, 2017, at https://eji.org/wp-content/uploads/2005/11/lynching-in-america-3d-ed-052421.pdf.

6

William J. Simmons and the Kentucky Normal and Theological Institute

Erin Wiggins Gilliam

I wish the book to show to the world—to our oppressors and even our friends—that the Negro race is still alive, and must possess more intellectual vigor than any other section of the human family, or else how could they be crushed as slaves in all these years since 1620, and yet to-day stand side by side with the best blood in America, in white institutions, grappling with abstruse problems in Euclid and difficult classics, and master them? Was ever such a thing seen in another people? Whence these lawyers, doctors, authors, editors, divines, lecturers, linguists, scientists, college presidents and such, in one quarter of a century?

—William J. Simmons, *Men of Mark: Eminent, Progressive and Rising* (1887)

The African American church has been the cornerstone of African American life and culture from slavery to freedom. It is the oldest and most visibly active institution that addresses the challenges and concerns facing African Americans. The church space allowed African Americans to escape from the brutalities of a racist society. Therefore, comprehensibly, the roots of African American education in Kentucky are found in the early nineteenth-century Black churches. The pride and joy of the Kentucky African American Baptists was the Kentucky Normal and Theological Institute (its name changed to Simmons University in 1919),[1] which opened in Louisville in 1879. The opening of the institution was one of the greatest accomplishments of the General Association of Colored Baptists of Kentucky and a beacon of pride for African Americans across the Commonwealth of Kentucky and the nation. The institute reached the monumental heights of being an independent and autonomous university that trained African American teachers, ministers, lawyers, and physicians in its college, medical, and law departments. The unparalleled leadership provided by "talented-tenth" institutions such as the African American Baptist Church of Kentucky and members such as William J. Simmons and Charles Parrish Sr. laid the foundation for what would later be renamed Simmons College of Kentucky.[2]

Scholarly studies that focus on African American education after the Civil War focus their analysis primarily on former Confederate states. This article adds to this literature by focusing on the influential role of African Americans in the border state of Kentucky in the movement for racial uplift through education.

At the end of the Civil War, African Americans celebrated their freedom and immediately pursued independence from white institutions and control. In August 1865, a few short months after the conclusion of the Civil War, the Kentucky State Convention of Colored Baptists, which later merged into the General Association of Colored Baptists of Kentucky in 1869, proposed the establishment of Kentucky's first postsecondary educational institution for African Americans.[3] It was no coincidence or happenstance that the fruition of an African American institution for higher learning happened the same year as the conclusion of the Civil War. In essence, it was the Kentucky Black Baptists' declaration of independence. As with other acts of independence initiated by African Americans, the building of the Kentucky Normal and Theological Institute came with fear and apprehension. However, the Black Baptist church had little choice but to lead the education efforts of African American education. According to the historian George C. Wright, the African American church "sustained black folk during slavery and the early days of freedom and continued to provide valuable assistance during the last decades of the nineteenth century," and "several of the churches would lead the first black assault on Jim Crow."[4]

African American leaders placed significant value on the role education could play in challenging the racial system in Kentucky and other southern states. In 1869, Reverend Henry Adams was the moderator of the General Association of Colored Baptists of Kentucky, and the association's new constitution established its purpose: "The object of this Association shall be the promotion of purity of doctrine, union fellowship and cooperation in promoting Sabbath schools and missionary operations and advancing the cause of our Lord Jesus Christ, throughout the entire State by meeting annually for mutual and religious counsel."[5] The association's top priority was the establishment of an autonomous African American educational institution with the goal of educating ministers and teachers who could promote and encourage the growth of Christianity outside of the church.

The Kentucky Normal and Theological Institute was successful and inspired other African American institutions, such as Virginia Baptist Theological Seminary, Arkansas Baptist College, and even the mecca of African American institutions, Howard University. These institutions emulated the qualities and specific initiatives of the Normal Institute, especially Kentucky's African American Baptist community's ability to build and provide an independent, Christ-centered educational institution.

Six years after visiting the Kentucky Normal and Theological Institute in 1880, Phillip F. Morris and delegates of the Virginia Negro Baptist State Convention founded the Virginia Baptist Theological Seminary during the 1886 session of the Virginia Negro Baptist State Convention in Lexington, Virginia. In 1890, the school opened its doors in Lynchburg. The delegation's visit to the Kentucky Normal and Theological Institute ten years earlier had represented an opportunity to gain an understanding of how the school functioned independently and efficiently without much influence and support from white Americans. Indeed, the Kentucky school was the model institute for Virginia Baptist Theological Seminary and other institutions of higher education.[6]

Howard University is one of the most well-known historically Black colleges and universities and is undeniably a representative of one of the finer ideals of American higher education past and present.[7] However, the Kentucky Normal and Theological Institute accomplished a mountainous goal for its period, one that cannot be claimed even by Howard University, by establishing an independent and autonomous denominational institution that had the goals of racial uplift and the education of future Black ministers and teachers. In contrast, Howard University was founded in 1867 by General Oliver Howard and other white missionaries of the First Congregational Society. Prior to serving as the inaugural president of

Howard University, General Howard was the commissioner of the Freedmen's Bureau and always considered himself sympathetic to the plight of African Americans.[8] Despite the success of this prominent university for African American education and the subsequent growth that occurred in the Black community, the white founders, benefactors, and presidents influenced the policy and design at Howard University, and the same occurred at other Black colleges. They "were reluctant to entrust control of the institutions to black people. In addition, it was correctly believed the white college presidents would be far more successful in raising money for the institutions among foundations and white benefactors."[9] Thus, white leadership and benefactors controlled the curriculum and major functions of the university with the hopes that the African American graduates would return to their own Black communities to serve as ministers and teachers in their churches and schools. In a paternalistic sense, white benefactors wanted to ensure that they had "raised" productive Black citizens who would uplift the Black population at the turn of the twentieth century and not fulfill the stereotype of the listless and lazy African American.[10]

Howard University did not have its first African American president until 1926. Until that time, perhaps the Black faculty and students envied the self-sufficiency and racial pride of Simmons University and other independent African American institutions. After the Progressive Era and World War I, there was a rise in African American consciousness and confidence that propelled African American students and faculty of white-dominated institutions to demand a say in their education and institutions. For example, in 1926 the relationship between African American faculty and the white president of Howard University, Stanley Durkee, was delicate and especially tense as Black leaders called for a more active role for themselves in the development of the university. Thus, the next president, Mordecai Johnson, was the first of a continuous line of African American presidents at the premier institution since then.[11]

The early history of the Kentucky Normal and Theological Institute paints a picture of sacrifice and determination. Henry Adams, the first president of the Kentucky State Convention of Colored Baptists, was not alone in his quest for an independent institution of higher learning. Twelve other prominent pastors and ministers of Black Baptist churches in Kentucky joined him in establishing not only an institution but also a governing body for African American Baptist churches. Among them were Elisha W. Green, Richard Sneathen, Richard Dupee, Richard Adams, and Frederick Braxton—all well-established Black preachers who influenced the growth of the Black Baptist church in Kentucky.[12]

For instance, Reverend Elisha Green, a former slave, was one of the most well-known preachers in the state. In 1818, Green was born into slavery as the property of Jane Dobbins in Bourbon County, Kentucky. At the age of ten, he was separated from his family and sold to a farmer in Mason County. Being torn from his family at a young age guided and impacted many of his later decisions in life. Elisha was one of the few enslaved African Americans who purchased his freedom as well as the freedom of his wife and three children. He was never able to purchase his oldest son, John, who was sold at a slave market in Old Washington, Kentucky.[13]

Like many African American minsters of the South, Elisha Green saw his position as a pastor as a way to influence and positively change his community. In 1883, while traveling to Paris, Kentucky, to conduct church business, he was physically attacked because he refused to give up his seat on the train when a group of white female pupils, their music teacher, and the president of their college boarded the train. His attackers—the music teacher and the college president, who was a fellow minister from Millersburg, Kentucky—inflicted multiple lacerations on Elisha's head and hands. Reverend Green successfully filed suit against the men in a court of law for assault and was awarded $24 in punitive damages. The life of Elisha Green demonstrates the fortitude that Kentucky African American leaders of the Baptist church possessed and needed for creating an independent institution of higher learning during an era when slavery remained a recent memory. He is remembered as an electrifying minister (having reportedly baptized six thousand African Americans), the founder of Bethel Baptist Church of Maysville, an agent of change, an educator, and one of the founders of the Kentucky Normal and Theological Institute.[14]

Kentucky Normal and Theological Institute opened its doors in 1879 with thirty-nine students. With its opening, Kentucky's General Association of Colored Baptists proclaimed, "We thank God that those old dark days of slavery have passed away, and that we have lived to see the day that the doors of the school-houses and colleges are standing wide open for the reception of all who will come and receive classical education."[15] The institute's founding represented years of dedication and work on the part of the Black Baptist community. At the Kentucky General Association of Colored Baptists meeting in 1869, Elder A. Allensworth urged his fellow clergymen to support an institution that "connects with our churches as a fit place to send our children, and that our pastors will give it their hearty support." However, the establishment of a Christ-centered institution for higher learning in the nation and the Commonwealth of Kentucky was not without trial and error. Prior to the opening of the Kentucky Normal and Theological Institute in 1879, the General Association of Colored Baptists had made at least two other attempts to support schools or properties.[16]

Originally, this Kentucky Baptist institution of higher education was to be located in Frankfort, Kentucky. In 1866, under the leadership of Reverend Henry Adams, the newly organized State Convention of the Colored Baptists of Kentucky purchased property in the capital city. Members of the white First Baptist Church of Frankfort sold a fifty-acre property to the Colored Baptists of Kentucky for $2,000. The convention referred to it as the "Hill property." Pastors belonging to the State Convention were asked to request each member of their congregation to donate five cents to the school building fund, and each church was obligated to pay a maximum of $100 depending on the size of its congregation. Because of the collective organizing power of Black Baptists, the Hill property debt was quickly eliminated within two years, and the State Convention of Colored Baptists of Kentucky immediately began to focus on establishing educational buildings on the Hill property.[17]

From 1866 to 1869, the State Convention made plans to establish a brick-and-mortar school on the Hill property in Frankfort. However, in 1869 the new merger of organizations—the State Convention of Colored Baptists and the General Association of Colored Baptists of Kentucky— voted twenty-five to twenty-four to locate the Kentucky Normal and Theological Institute in Louisville. The General Association of Colored Baptists voted to make repairs to the Hill Street property with hopes of renting out the small house and use any profit to help finance the building of the new school in Louisville. The maintenance and the leasing of the Hill property, however, became an arduous task that distracted the General Association from focusing its educational finances and energy on establishing the Normal and Theological Institute. In May 1879, the General Association sold the Hill property for $2,000, allowing the association to concentrate its efforts on establishing a campus in Louisville.[18]

On November 24, 1874, in McCracken County, Mount Olivet Baptist Church School opened its doors as the first institution supported by the Kentucky General Association of Colored Baptists. Unfortunately, after only five months the Olivet Baptist Church School closed its doors because of poor attendance and lack of support from African American Baptist constituents throughout the region. The humble Mount Olivet school had to compete with Wilberforce University of Ohio, an institution established by the joint effort of the Methodist Episcopal Church and the African Methodist Episcopal Church. By 1863, Wilberforce University was solely owned and operated by the African Methodist Episcopal Church and home to the first African American president of an institution of higher learning, Daniel A. Payne. Ohio was considered a safer place for African Americans to reside and gain an education because it was not considered a southern state with racial tensions tied to violence and Jim Crow laws like its conjoining state to the south, Kentucky. The obstacle of segregation made it difficult for the Kentucky General Association of Colored Baptists institution to compete with Wilberforce University and other northern schools of higher education that admitted African Americans. Therefore, Wilberforce University and other schools for African Americans such as the Nashville Institute had a "head start" in prestige and finances.[19]

The Kentucky Normal and Theological Institute eventually gained prestige because of the foundation provided by its first president and manager, Reverend Elijah P. Marrs. He was born a slave to a free father and an enslaved mother on a small plantation in Shelbyville, Kentucky. In contrast to many enslaved African Americans, he was taught to read by his Christian master, who felt it was a sin if a believer could not read the scriptures for himself. While serving in the Civil War, Marrs was quickly promoted to sergeant of Company L of the Twelfth United States Heavy Artillery unit of Louisville because he could read and write. Both white and Black soldiers asked Marrs to write letters home on their behalf.

> I had in camp some reputation as a writer, though I had little confidence in myself, coming as I did just out of the bondage of slavery. I appeared, however, to be above the average of those in our quarters, and many former friends who had joined the army before me employed me to do their writing. Soon the officers learned that there was a little fellow from Shelby County that was skilled in the use of the pen, and they sought to find me. They found me surrounded by a number of the men, each waiting his turn to have a letter written home. The officers soon

made known their wishes, which was to find a man who was a penman who they wished as a Duty Sergeant.[20]

At the conclusion of the Civil War, Elijah P. Marrs briefly attended the Nashville Institute.[21] Eventually, at the encouragement of his friends and family, he began a career as a teacher. Marrs taught primary school throughout Kentucky. His greatest educational legacy was his service as the inaugural president of the Kentucky Normal and Theological Institute in 1879–1880.[22]

On November 29, 1879, under the leadership of President Marrs, the Kentucky Normal and Theological Institute opened its doors for the first time. The institute was on a two-and-a-half-acre lot at the southwest corner of Seventh and Kentucky Streets in the heart of downtown Louisville. The minutes of the meeting of the General Association of Colored Baptists of Kentucky in 1879 described the land as "a handsome piece of property lying high and dry. And well shaded and ornamented with a very fine selection of fruit and shade trees that would provide places for innocent amusement." This picturesque plot had been purchased for $1,783.85. The General Association opened its 1880 meeting with gratitude for the institution's initial year and Marrs's leadership. "We Thank God that those old dark days of slavery have passed away and that we have lived to see the day that the doors of the school-houses and college are standing wide open for the reception of all who will come and receive a classical education." They also asked pastors to encourage their local parishioners to "drop the axe and drawers of water" and seek a higher education.[23]

The figures of the church and the pastor were at the center of power and influence of the African American community. A pastor of a Black church had to engage his members while being able to appeal to and effectively communicate with white leaders in their communities. Hence, it was necessary to have some tenets of classical or liberal studies education. African American ministers were known for their oratorical skills, but they also needed to be able to read biblical scriptures and have the intellectual prowess to analyze and interpret their readings. Consequently, many of the first attendants of the Kentucky Normal and Theological Institute were Kentucky pastors. The first class at the institute had thirty-nine students, and it encompassed seven pastors from Kentucky churches. President Marrs remained at the institute for one session only before leaving to serve as the pastor of Beargrass Baptist Church in Louisville. Perhaps throughout his brief tenure as president, Marrs wrestled with what he perceived as his inadequacies from never gaining a formal education. However, he served the institution and the church at its inception and provided a foundation for Black Baptist education in the Commonwealth.[24]

In 1880, President Marrs invited one of the most influential and well-educated African American educators of the time, William J. Simmons, to serve as the inaugural commencement speaker at the Kentucky Normal and Theological Institute. At the time, Simmons was a young pastor at the first Black Baptist church west of the Allegheny Mountains, First African Baptist Church of Lexington. In *Black Higher Education in Kentucky 1879–1930: The History of Simmons University*, Lawrence Williams contends that it was Simmons's provocative and powerful graduation speech that garnered the attention of William Steward and other leaders of the General Association of Colored Baptists of Kentucky. "[William] Simmons inspired the people by giving the history of many great universities and concluded that what was possible with them was also possible with their school, though born in weakness and poverty."[25]

The General Association of Colored Baptists and President Marrs directly faced their shortcomings as educators and higher-education administrators and invited a more educated person to facilitate the progress of the Kentucky Normal and Theological Institute. In 1880, which marked the school's second session, the General Association appointed William J. Simmons as president of the institution that would eventually bear his name.[26]

William Simmons was born a slave in Charleston, South Carolina, on June 29, 1849. His mother, Esther Simmons, reached a point where she could no longer tolerate the brutalities of slavery and was determined not to allow her three children, William, Anna, and Emeline, to live as enslaved African Americans. Therefore, she and her young children escaped to freedom in the northern city of Philadelphia, Pennsylvania. His mother's tenacity and perseverance instilled in him a desire to fight back against an oppressive system that was designed to hinder and prevent African Americans' progress. Life in Philadelphia was not easy as the Simmons family faced extreme hardships. Simmons writes, "Without the protection of a husband and father, [they began] a long siege with poverty." The family moved throughout Pennsylvania to different hiding places because of the constant fear of the slave traders who daily sought the capture of runaway slaves. Simmons credits much of the family's survival to his uncle

Dr. William J. Simmons was born a slave in Charleston, South Carolina, and ended up president of the Kentucky Normal and Theological Institute, which is now known as Simmons College. Image of drawing from Alpha Stock / Alamy Stock Photo.

Alexander Tardiff, a shoemaker who later became a seaman to help support the Simmons family.[27]

As a fugitive slave, William could not have a formal primary education. Fortunately, his uncle Tardiff could read, write, and perform basic arithmetic; therefore, he taught the Simmons children the fundamental basics. Simmons credits the teachings of his uncle with providing the early underpinning for a love of education and "laying a foundation so broad and exact, that in after years college studies . . . were comparatively easy."[28]

Initially, William J. Simmons did not have any intention of pursuing a formal education because he had a successful apprenticeship with a prominent white dentist, Dr. Leo H. DeLange of Bordentown, New Jersey. In 1863, Dr. DeLange was elected the first mayor of Bordentown, which took him away from his duties as a dentist. However, he was confident in Simmons's abilities and periodically left him in charge of the dental practice. Simmons performed dental work on some of the most successful white families in Bordentown and regularly offered his services to Black families who did not have access to dentists. Wishing to remain in the field where he had amassed experience, Simmons applied to dental school before the Civil War but was rejected, presumably because of the color of his skin. On September 18, 1864, he enlisted in the Forty-First United States Colored Infantry. He was present for the infamous siege of Petersburg and the unconditional surrender of Confederate general Robert E. Lee in northern Virginia on April 9, 1865.[29]

In the fall of 1867, Simmons returned to Philadelphia, where he briefly apprenticed for an African American dentist, Dr. William Longfellow. However, he returned to work for Dr. DeLange because Dr. DeLange was able to offer better wages owing to his white clientele and their greater ability to pay for dental services than their newly emancipated counterparts. During this time, Simmons joined the white congregation of First Baptist of Bordentown. He felt welcomed as a member of the church and received support when he announced his call to preach and be a leader within the Baptist denomination. Recognizing his potential, the all-white congregation financially supported his education at Madison University of New York. For undocumented reasons, in 1868 Simmons transferred to Rochester University of New York, where he paid for his tuition by performing odd jobs at a local white Baptist church. In Rochester, he also became heavily involved in missionary work and in the African American Baptist community.

It was not unusual that local white leaders and missionaries helped to pay Simmons's tuition. White church missionaries drew on the tradition of humanism or a system of values and beliefs that were centered on the ideas that people (African Americans) are inherently good and that the best way to address the "Negro Problem" and issues plaguing the African American community was with religion, education, and a paternalistic-like uplift.[30]

Simmons matriculated through two institutions in upstate New York; however, it was not until he attended the historical Black college Howard

University that he completed his bachelor of arts degree in 1873. Throughout his early life, Simmons consistently struggled with poverty. In his autobiography, he recalls eating only cheese and crackers for weeks at a time and having to miss school because his only shirt was not dry enough to walk the seven miles there. His humble experiences as both a fugitive enslaved African and a struggling student did not deter him from being successful, though, and he graduated salutatorian of his class. His experiences were beneficial because they gave him the ability to mentor students such as Charles Parrish and others who also came from humble beginnings.[31]

Simmons's success as a student in higher education encouraged him to dedicate his life to Black education. Since his Christian conversion in 1867, Simmons had been interested in missionary work and evangelism. He felt that he had the moral obligation to uplift and improve African Americans through education and to spread the Christian message to as many prospective believers as possible. Paul Tillich, a Christian philosopher and theologian, contends that the Christian Church has three primary functions: education, missions, and evangelism. As teacher, minster of God's word, and later president of a growing institution, Simmons was able to accomplish these tasks simultaneously.[32]

Simmons began his teaching career at a grade school in Bunker Hill, Washington, DC, where because of his aptitude and conscientious nature he was quickly promoted to principal. On August 25, 1874, he married Josephine Silence, and their marriage produced seven children. Presumably not wanting his children to experience the hardships he had endured in his childhood, poverty and hunger, Simmons briefly left teaching in an attempt to earn more money as a citrus farmer in Ocala, Florida. While living in Florida, he became a deacon at a small Baptist church and was licensed to preach. Husband, father, farmer, and church officer were the many roles of William Simmons, yet he also still managed to be involved in local and national politics of the late nineteenth century. He served as the chairman of the Marion County Republican campaign committee and was a member of the district congressional committee. During the presidential election of 1876, pitting the Republican Rutherford B. Hayes against the Democrat Samuel Tilden, Simmons diligently worked to help register African Americans in northern Florida to vote. Despite white Democrats' attempts to intimidate Republicans to prevent them from voting, Simmons helped Marion County raise the number of registered Republican voters from 525 to 986. The compromise of 1877 confirmed Hayes's victory, but the consequences of the compromise deeply impacted the lives of African Americans, causing a reversal of racial, political, and economic progress by returning southern leadership to former slaveholders and Confederate soldiers, whose first task was to ensure the disenfranchisement of African Americans and an end to all the promises of Reconstruction. Most African Americans such as Simmons and other members of the talented tenth lost their newly gained rights. However, the leadership experience Simmons gained during Reconstruction was beneficial to him because he worked across racial lines to strengthen Republican politics. These learned skills and life lessons of navigating racial, social, and ideological differences proved valuable when he was asked to improve the Kentucky Normal and Theological Institute as president of the struggling school. Indeed, Lawrence Williams describes Simmons as a "Savior who reinvigorated and transformed the school into a college that would later receive some recognition from white and Black denominational and educational agencies."[33]

Prior to accepting the leadership role at the Kentucky Normal and Theological Institute, Simmons was asked to pastor First African Baptist Church of Lexington in 1879. As pastor, he left his mark on the historic church by eliminating all of its debt, and it is believed that he donated his salary to balance the church budget. First African Baptist Church prospered under Simmons's leadership. In return, he gained valuable experience with fund-raising and budget management that proved to be an asset in his work as an administrator in higher education.[34]

In 1881, when William J. Simmons was elected president of the Kentucky Normal and Theological Institute, it had only thirteen students and two teachers and was in a dire financial situation. In his personal memoir, Simmons stated that the treasury was empty, and the campus was dirty and sparse of furniture. Reverend Eugene Evans of Warren County, Kentucky, also indicated the dismal state of the institution in an editorial piece for the *Bowling Green Watchmen* in July 1881: "Few Men of Professor Simmons' ability and standing would have been willing to risk their future in an enterprise like the Normal and Theological Institute; an enterprise without capital and but a few friends."[35] In 1880, the year before Simmons arrived at the institute, there were a reported 157 students and 139 staff members.[36] The significant drop the following year indicates that there were issues that discouraged enrollment. Perhaps the main issue was financial, and prospective attendees were skeptical about the institution's longevity.

President William J. Simmons first sought to create a uniform and professional-looking curriculum and sent it out to African American churches in the region. Upon receiving this guide, prospective students and parents were awed by the transformation of the institution and felt that it was taking a new direction by offering an improved quality education.[37] The 1882 catalog boasted the institution's ability to prepare all students regardless of their educational levels and offered class levels ranging from grammar school to professional training. Students were taught the traditional basics—writing, reading, arithmetic, American history, and spelling. In keeping with a middle-class value system and in attempts toward racial uplift, the board of trustees and President Simmons ensured that there were mandatory etiquette, hygiene, and cooking classes. The cooking classes and similar classes in bookkeeping, household cleaning, and home economics were taught not to prepare female students to be servants in white homes or "cooks for hire" but to ensure that young women were successfully prepared to be homemakers in caring for their children and husbands. These principles espoused middle-class ideals of womanhood and women's responsibility as moral influences in the community and in their homes because they were considered the backbone and the bearers of change.[38]

The Kentucky Normal and Theological Institute's program and purpose aligned with the Du Boisian liberal arts curriculum; however, to appeal to a broader selection of potential students, the school also offered industrial courses. Students who gained a vocational education often worked in shoe making, sewing, farming, maintenance, and other industrial-related fields. The academic department or the honors program was steeped in the classics: Plato, Caesar, Cicero, and other Greek and Roman intellectuals. The scholars were also taught biblical history and the New Testament, rhetoric, and logic. Most graduates of the honors department went on to pursue teaching careers or other professional careers that were the underpinnings of the African American middle class.

Simmons ultimately wanted to gain national recognition for the Kentucky Normal and Theological Institute. Thus, in the late 1880s the institute established an affiliation with the Louisville National Medical College and the Central Law School. The institute offered a successful recruitment pool for these newly minted professional training schools. During the late nineteenth century, it was rare for African American institutions to house both a medical school and a law school. Howard University, Shaw University of Raleigh, North Carolina, and Meharry Medical College of Nashville, Tennessee, were the exceptions. However, in contrast to the Kentucky Normal and Theological Institute, these respective institutions were controlled and financed by white administrators.

African American teachers and students took great pride in their institutions and utilized their resources to the best of their abilities. In 1910, the Carnegie Foundation published a report that called for stricter admission, graduation standards, and a uniform required course of study for medical schools. The racial overtones of the period and of the report were detrimental to the Louisville Medical College and other African American institutions such as Shaw University. When Louisville Medical College closed in 1910, it left a void in affordable medical school education for African Americans in the region. Unfortunately, twenty years later the Central Law School experienced a similar fate and matriculated its last graduate in 1940 because of accreditation requirements and new standards enacted by the National Bar Association. Even though the Medical and Law Departments at the Normal Institute were forced to close, their short existence was phenomenal because they were part of a Black-owned and controlled institution of higher learning. They also speak to the academic and organizational foundation laid by William J. Simmons.

Not surprisingly, the largest department of the institute was the Theological Department, whose purpose was "to prepare students to teach the word of God acceptably." Understandably, a school started by African American Baptists had an extensive course of study in theology, and the department's success was the top priority of the General Association of Colored Baptists of Kentucky.[39]

Most historical Black colleges and universities, including the Kentucky Normal and Theological Institute, believed it was their responsibility to teach students the rudimentary basics of education but also viewed moral education as a part of their mission: "To build, fashion, and develop young men and women intellectually and morally for the higher vocation and duties of life—and particularly to secure an educated ministry and competent teachers. This is no place for the lazy and indifferent. Each student is expected to reflect honor on the Institute. . . . [A]ll who are willing to live up to these aims are welcome, regardless of religious belief and denominational convictions."[40]

Regardless of students' courses of study, they all were required to attend church and Sunday school every week unless excused by the president. Students could be dismissed from the institute for continuously being late to church services or classes. And in keeping with the values of a religious-based institution, profanity, gambling, weapons, use of tobacco and alcohol, and attendance in an "unholy" place such as a dance club or a place with live secular music were strictly forbidden in the schools' rules and policies. The moral and social demands of the Kentucky Normal and Theological Institute were consistent with Christian social norms of the late nineteenth century.[41]

William J. Simmons was one of the most influential presidents of the Kentucky Normal and Theological Institute. He died prematurely of a heart attack at the age of forty-one on October 30, 1890. However, his ideas and legacy continued to flourish not only through the work of his protégé Charles Parrish Sr. but also through the mark he left on several organizations associated with the institution and on Black Baptists throughout the Commonwealth of Kentucky and the nation. The Kentucky Normal and Theological Institute and other African American Baptist agencies are indebted to the work and dedication of William J. Simmons.

The *American Baptist* newspaper reached the height of its readership under his helm. It was the second-longest-running African American newspaper published in the United States. Only the African Methodist Episcopalian denomination had an older periodical, the *Christian Recorder,* which began publication in 1846. In 1879, Simmons and William Steward established the *Baptist Herald* and were its associate editors. Steward, chairman of the board of trustees for the Kentucky Normal and Theological Institute, changed the name of the paper to the *American Baptist* and added in-depth coverage of the Black Baptist churches across the state, of the institute, and of developments in African American education. Simmons was named the president and lead editor of the newspaper in 1882.

Simmons used the *American Baptist* as a vehicle to recruit students to the small Baptist institution of the Bluegrass. He and his staff urged its readership to fulfill their Christian duty in supporting the school. Most issues were focused on the institute and were very specific in ways that it could benefit from donated funds.[42]

For this independent Baptist college to survive, it was necessary to have the financial and enrollment support of the African American community. Their voice was the most powerful recruitment tool for the institution. In 1889, Simmons focused his interest on one part of this community and began the national Baptist publication *Our Women and Children,* the first African American women's magazine. The women's magazine's non-denominational goal was the advancement of women and children because women were viewed as the moral influence in the home and community. The magazine educated women and children in science, poetry, kitchen skills, true religion, and other valuable subjects with the intent and purpose of uplifting the African American community with the Black respectability values of morality and education. On the magazine's front cover, Simmons asserted, "We shall defend woman from wrongs and demand for her Justice."[43] He knew that at the heart of the community and its influence was the African American woman.

As made evident by the creation of the National Baptist Convention in 1880, the late nineteenth century was a time of growth and productivity for African American Baptists across the nation. Kentucky was no exception. At the summer meeting in 1882, the General Association of Colored Baptists of Kentucky made the conscious decision to change the name of the Kentucky Normal and Theological Institute to "State University." The name reflected anticipated growth while also being a recruitment tool for both students and white philanthropic funds. Members of the General Association felt that a name that contained the word *university* invoked a spirit of prestige and placed the struggling Black Baptist school on par with white universities.[44]

Perhaps the name change was the reason why the American Home Mission Society pledged up to $3,000 a year for the salaries of two teachers and scholarships for "several deserving young women" at State University for at least three years. President Simmons also secured donations from the once supervisory organization of many Kentucky Black Baptist churches, the white Kentucky Baptist Association. In *Black Higher Education in Kentucky,* Lawrence Williams argues that white philanthropic organizations such as John D. Rockefeller's General Education Board and the American Baptist Home Mission Society were hesitant to fully support independent institutions such as the Kentucky Normal and Theological Institute because many benefactors felt that African American leadership was inadequate and financially incompetent. Thus, most of the financial burden was placed on the African American Baptist churches of Kentucky. In 1886, the General Association of Colored Baptists of Kentucky collected $578.08 from Black Baptist churches throughout the Commonwealth—more than Rockefeller's $500 donation in 1884.[45]

The Rockefeller donation was used to make internal improvements to the deficient facilities of the newly minted State University. The trustees' report presented to the General Association of Colored Baptists of Kentucky in 1881 described the state of the grounds as "entirely inadequate for the accommodation of the students attending" and highlighted the need for improvement to accommodate current and future students. William Simmons, his wife, Josephine, and their seven children (Josephine, William, Maud, Amanda, Mary, John, and Gussie) uncomfortably lived in two rooms on the campus grounds, and there was no formal place for President Simmons to entertain guests of the university.[46]

Simmons and other influential leaders among the Black Baptist educational movement in Kentucky continuously looked for ways to improve the institute. One of the most important organizations of fund-raising for the institute was the Baptist Women's Educational Convention of Kentucky, created by Simmons on September 19, 1883. The first session was held at the second-oldest African American Baptist church in Kentucky, the Fifth Street Baptist Church of Louisville. Black Baptist women in Kentucky constantly struggled for voice and place in the church's male-dominated hierarchical system. The power and influence of Black women in the Baptist church was limited because, as in other organizations of the period, their leadership was discouraged. Yet President Simmons recognized the influence and collective power that African American women wielded in the Black church and community. He wanted women to have full autonomy within their new organization because they had constantly struggled with patriarchy and chauvinism. Therefore, in his first action for the Baptist Women's Educational Convention, he nominated Amanda Redd of Georgetown, Kentucky, as the chairperson to oversee the inaugural election of the convention's president. It was not a coincidence that the first president of the organization, Amanda Nelson, was a former parishioner of William J. Simmons at the First African Baptist Church of Lexington and a former student. She was also a classmate of Charles Parrish Sr., who was one of Simmons's first students at the institute. As a grade-school teacher in Jefferson County, Kentucky, President Nelson was invested in education.[47]

Article 2 of the constitution for the Baptist Women's Educational Convention of Kentucky stated that "the object of the convention shall be to encourage attendance of students in the Kentucky Normal and Theological Institute for Christian Education, to contribute to funds for operation of the Kentucky Normal and Theological Institute and to develop in its members a greater missionary spirit."[48] On September 20, 1883, the second day of the inaugural convention, the new members of the Women's Convention, accompanied by William J. Simmons and William H. Steward, spent the morning touring the institute and taking notes on its needs. Their report stated, "The work seems in a state of progression and as education is one of the main hinges of our future prosperity, it behooves us to push to the front." At that inaugural meeting, the Women's Convention collected more than $700.[49]

The Women's Convention continuously demonstrated its fund-raising abilities and persuasion tactics. One of its greatest sources of fund-raising was the corporation dinner, held at the end of each spring term in May on the campus. The first dinner served 450 clergymen and Baptist supporters as well as celebrated the graduates of the class of 1885. The inaugural corporation dinner collected $26 after expenses were paid. The Women's Convention was by far the largest financial contributor to Simmons College. In 1887, it collected $1,207.70, almost double the $800 collected from the Black Baptist churches that same year. From 1883 to 1914, the convention raised almost $35,000 dollars for the institute.[50]

In 1908, all of the convention's hard work and fund-raising came to tangible fruition with the building of a girls' dormitory. The dormitory also served as the domestic-science building and contained the modern luxuries of coal-powered heat, electricity, and indoor plumbing. The construction of the girls' dormitory cost the General Association of Colored Baptists $20,000. Fortunately, the American Baptist Home Mission Society donated $5,000. However, it was the fund-raising and organizing efforts of the Women's Convention that successfully eliminated any debt associated with the girls' dormitory in less than a year.[51]

The building of the girls' dormitory happened under the leadership of Mamie Steward, who was the longest-serving president of the Women's Convention, from 1900 to 1930. She was the wife of William Henry Steward, chairman of the board of trustees for the institute and its music teacher for more than thirty years. Mamie Steward demonstrated her belief in the mission and purpose of the Women's Convention. On March 5, 1898, at the twenty-fifth anniversary celebration of the granting of the Kentucky Normal and Theological Institute's charter, she gave a rousing speech titled "The Women's Convention as an Adjunct in the Educational Work." She argued that women were the backbone of the Baptist church and demanded respect for their efforts. "It is safe to say that nine-tenths of the teachers in our Sunday schools are women. The Sunday school, being a part of the church work, makes the woman an important factor, not only in engaging in the work of the church as it is commonly understood, but also places her where she can even make the future church what she desires it to be."[52] Due in part to Mamie Steward's conviction, the Women's Convention collected almost $200 at the celebration.[53]

The Baptist Women's Educational Convention of Kentucky served as an example to other women's conventions across the nation. Reverend Edward Brawley, president of Alabama Baptist Normal and Theological School (Selma University), was a contributing writer and editor for the *American Baptist* who traveled throughout the South observing and reporting on African American Baptist churches and institutions. Upon returning to Alabama, Brawley encouraged the women of his state to form their own educational convention. On January 27, 1886, the Baptist Women's Educational Convention of Alabama was launched, modeled on the Kentucky plan.[54]

William J. Simmons was a life member of the Baptist Women's Educational Convention of Kentucky. The Women's Convention was perhaps his greatest legacy outside of the Kentucky Normal and Theological Institute. However, the Women's Convention was not the first time that he and other members of the General Association of Colored Baptists of Kentucky attempted to create an organization with the sole purpose of fund-raising and encouraging attendance at the Kentucky Normal and Theological Institute.

Simmons's influence was embedded in every entity that served African American Baptist education in Kentucky. In 1890, to everyone's surprise, Simmons left the institute to establish an industrial school in Cane Springs, Kentucky, the Eckstein Norton Institute. His departure was worrisome for the African American Baptist educational system in Kentucky. The institute's board of trustees was reluctant to lose his guidance, so he was asked to join the board.[55]

The effects of Simmons's departure were further exacerbated when his protégé and most able successor, Charles Parrish Sr., followed him to Eckstein Norton Institute. With Parrish gone, the board of trustees was forced to look at applicants outside of the Kentucky African American Baptist network. The Kentucky Normal and Theological Institute named former Arkansas Baptist College president James Garnett as the new president.

Unfortunately, William J. Simmons did not live long enough to see the continued growth of his namesake institution or of Eckstein Norton Institute because of his death in 1890.

Other African American institutions of higher education, such as Eckstein Norton Institute and Kentucky State University, flourished more than Kentucky Normal and Theological Institute (Simmons College). Both institutions benefited from white benefactors and supporters. However, the Kentucky Normal and Theological Institute was the cornerstone of African American control and autonomy in higher education. Charles Parrish Jr. argued in an interview in 1977 that the institute "qualified as a senior college" prior to Kentucky State University or Eckstein Norton Institute. He further commented that "there was some rivalry between Simmons and the Kentucky State College."[56]

The influence and philosophy of the "Father of Negro Baptist Education of Kentucky," William J. Simmons, underpinned the Kentucky Baptist educational movement and the growth of an independent Black Baptist college that was a leading example for African American colleges throughout the United States. As a member of the Kentucky talented tenth and the influential Baptist community, Simmons believed that the solution to the "Negro problem" in Kentucky was found at the intersections of education, civic duty, and Christian morality. His greatest work, the Kentucky Normal and Theological Institute, his namesake, lived on because of his hard work and dedication.[57]

Notes

1. For the name change, see Lawrence H. Williams, *The Charles H. Parrishes, Pioneers in African-American Religion and Education, 1880–1989* (Lewiston, NY: Edwin Mellen Press, 2003), 11–13, 20.

2. W. E. B. Du Bois, "The Talented Tenth," in *The Negro Problem,* ed. Booker T. Washington (New York: James Pott, 1903,) 31–76. The core of Du Bois's argument in "The Talented Tenth" was that an elite class of African Americans would uplift the race through education and Black respectability, therefore demonstrating their fitness for citizenship to white America. The "talented tenth" concept is perhaps one of Du Bois's most well-known arguments, but he did not create the phrase. Henry Lyman Morehouse, a white Baptist minister and corresponding secretary for the Baptist Home Mission Society, coined the term and concept in an article almost a decade earlier. He argued, "The tenth man, with

superior natural endowments, symmetrically trained and highly developed, may become a mightier influence, a greater inspiration to others than all the other nine, or nine times nine like them" (*Independent* magazine, April 1896).

3. George C. Wright, *Life behind a Veil: Blacks in Louisville, Kentucky 1865–1930* (Baton Rouge: Louisiana State University, 1985) 20.

4. Wright, *Life behind a Veil*, 37, 126.

5. Minutes of the First General Association of Colored Baptists of Kentucky, 1869, box 2, folder 8, Simmons University Papers, Archives and Special Collections, University of Louisville, Louisville, KY.

6. Evelyn Brooks Higginbotham, *Righteous Discontent: The Women's Movement in the Black Baptist Church, 1880–1920* (Cambridge, MA: Harvard University Press, 1993), 44, 58.

7. Jacqueline Fleming, *Blacks in College: A Comparative Study of Student Success in Black and White Institutions* (San Francisco: Jossey-Bass, 1984).

8. Walter Dyson, *The Founding of Howard University* (Washington, DC: Howard University Press, 1921).

9. "The Tradition of White Presidents at Black Colleges," *Journal of Blacks in Higher Education,* no. 16 (1997): 93.

10. Joel Williamson, *A Rage for Order: Black/White Relations in the American South since Emancipation* (Oxford: Oxford University Press, 1986).

11. Rayford W. Logan, *Howard University: The First Hundred Years* (New York: New York University Press, 1968), 16–20; Cora Lee Upshur-Ransome, *A Comparison of the African American Presence in an Earlier and Later American History Textbook* (New York: University Press of America, 2000), 10–12.

12. William H. Steward, "History of the General Association of Colored Baptists in Kentucky," in *The Golden Jubilee of the Colored Baptists in Kentucky: The Story of 50 Years' Work from 1865–1915,* ed. Charles Parrish (Louisville, KY: American Baptist, 1915), 90–95.

13. Elisha Green, *Life of the Reverend Elisha Green: Written by Himself* (Louisville, KY: Bradley and Gilbert, 1895). For more on Green, see also Randolph Paul Runyon, *The Assault on Elisha Green: Race and Religion in a Kentucky Community* (Lexington: University Press of Kentucky, 2021).

14. Green, *Life of the Reverend Elisha Green.*

15. Minutes of the First General Association of Colored Baptists of Kentucky, 1886–1887, box 2, folder 14, Simmons University Papers.

16. Minutes of the First General Association of Colored Baptists of Kentucky, 1869, box 2, folder 8, Simmons University Papers.

17. Steward, "History of the General Association of Colored Baptists in Kentucky," 89–92; Green, *The Life of Reverend Elisha Green,* 25–27.

18. Minutes of the First General Association of Colored Baptists of Kentucky, 1870, 1879, box 2, folders 6 (1870) and 12 (1879), Simmons University Papers.

19. Frederick McGinnis, *A History and an Interpretation of Wilberforce University* (Blanchester, OH: Brown, 1941).

20. Elijah P. Marrs, *Life and History of the Reverend Elijah P. Marrs: First Pastor of Beargrass Baptist Church* (Louisville, KY: Bradley and Gilbert, 1885), 23.

21. Ronald Roach, "American Baptist College Designated as a Historically Black Institution," *Diverse Issues in Higher Education,* April 24, 2013, 1–4.

22. Marrs, *Life and History of the Reverend Elijah P. Marrs,* 119–24; Marion B. Lucas, *A History of Blacks in Kentucky,* vol. 1: *From Slavery to Segregation, 1760–1891* (Frankfort: Kentucky Historical Society, 1992).

23. Minutes of the First General Association of Colored Baptists of Kentucky, 1880, box 2, folder 12, Simmons University Papers.

24. Lawrence N. Jones, "Urban Black Churches: Conservators of Value and Sustainers for Community," *Journal of Religious Thought* 39, no. 2 (1982): 41–51; Marrs, *Life and History of the Reverend Elijah P. Marrs,* 120.

25. Lawrence H. Williams, *Black Higher Education in Kentucky 1879–1930: The History of Simmons University* (Lewiston, NY: Edwin Mellen Press, 1987), 71–77; Marrs, *Life and History of the Reverend Elijah P. Marrs,* 119–24.

26. William J. Simmons, *Men of Mark: Eminent, Progressive and Rising* (Cleveland, OH: Geo M. Revell, 1887), 4.

27. Simmons, *Men of Mark,* 1–6. The historian Lawrence H. Williams describes Simmons as "the most prominent African-American Baptist clergy during the final decades of the nineteenth century and one of the truly outstanding African-Americans of the period" (Williams, *The Charles H. Parrishes,* 9).

28. *Diamond Jubilee of the General Association of Colored Baptists in Kentucky: The Story of Seventy-Five Years of the Association and Four Years of Convention Activities* (Louisville, KY: American Baptist, 1943), 49–52; Howard D. Gregg, *History of the African Methodist Episcopal Church* (Nashville: African Methodist Episcopal Church, 1980), 210 (quotation).

29. Arlene S. Brice, *Bordentown,* Images of America (Charleston, SC: Arcadia, 2002), 33.

30. William H. Watkins, *The White Architects of Black Education: Ideology and Power in America, 1865–1954* (New York: Teachers College Press, 2001), 14–15.

31. Simmons, *Men of Mark,* 40–43.

32. Paul Tillich, *Love, Power, and Justice: Ontological Analyses and Ethical Applications* (New York: Oxford University Press, 1954), 9–10.

33. Williams, *Black Higher Education in Kentucky,* 78.

34. Laurie F. Maffly-Kipp, "Denominationalism and the Black Church," in *Reimagining Denominationalism: Interpretive Essays,* ed. Russell Richey and R. Bruce Mullin (Oxford: Oxford University Press, 1994), 58–73; Simmons, *Men of Mark,* 46; L. H. McIntyre, *One Grain of Salt: The First African Baptist Church West of the Allegheny Mountains* (Lexington, KY: self-published, 1986), 43–44.

35. Reverend Eugene Evans, "Wm. Simmons and the School," *Bowling Green Watchmen,* July 1881.

36. Minutes of the First General Association of Colored Baptists of Kentucky, 1879, Simmons Bible College Records, box 2, folder 13, Archives and Special Collections, University of Louisville.

37. Fifth Street Baptist Church Minutes, 1883, box 1, Fifth Street Baptist Church Papers, Archives and Special Collections, University of Louisville.

38. *Simmons University Course Catalogue,* box 3 of 9, Simmons Bible College Records, 1869–1971, Archives and Special Collections, University of Louisville; Cheryl Townsend Gilkes, *"If It Wasn't for the Women . . . ": Black Women's Experience and Womanist Culture in Church and Community* (Maryknoll, NY: Orbis Books Press, 2001), 15–17.

39. *Simmons University Course Catalogue,* box 1 of 9, Simmons Bible College Records, 1869–1971; Williams, *Black Higher Education in Kentucky,* 36–37.

40. *Simmons University Course Catalogue 1881–1882,* box 1 of 9, Simmons Bible College Records, 1869–1971.

41. Charles Henry Parrish Jr., interviewed by Dwayne Cox and William Morrison, tape 210, February 21, 1977, African American Community Interviews, Oral History Center, University of Louisville.

42. "How to Help the School," *American Baptist,* August 21, 1900, 3.

43. *"Our Women and Children* Advertisement," Minutes of the Baptist Women's Educational Convention for the Years 1883, 1884, 1885, and 1886, American Baptist Historical Society Special Collections and Manuscripts, Mercer University, Atlanta, GA.

44. Steward, "History of the General Association of Colored Baptists in Kentucky," 106–7.

45. Watkins, *The White Architects of Black Education,* 118–29; Williams, *Black Higher Education in Kentucky,* 82–84.

46. Minutes of the Eighteenth Annual Session of the General Association of Colored Baptists of Kentucky, 1881, box 2 of 9, folder 4, Simmons Bible College Records, 1869–1971; Simmons, *Men of Mark,* 44–46, "State and Rockefeller," *American Baptist,* April 2, 1886, 4.

47. Minutes of the Baptist Women's Educational Convention of Kentucky, 1883–1884, American Baptist Historical Society Special Collections and Manuscripts.

48. *The Kentucky Baptist Women's State Educational Convention Centennial Memoirs, 1883–1983,* Simmons Bible College Records, box 3, folder 5, Archives and Special Collections, University of Louisville.

49. Minutes of the Baptist Women's Educational Convention of Kentucky, 1883–1884, session 1, American Baptist Historical Society Special Collections and Manuscripts.

50. Mamie Steward, "The Women's Convention as an Adjunct in the Educational Work," Baptist Women's Educational Convention of Kentucky, in *The Golden Jubilee,* ed. Parrish, 138–48.

51. Mamie Steward, "Woman in the Church," *National Baptist Magazine* 6 (August–October 1898): 145–46; Williams, *Black Higher Education in Kentucky,* 55–61.

52. Steward, "The Women's Convention as an Adjunct in the Educational Work," 142.

53. *State University Quarto-Centennial Bulletin,* box 3, folder 5, Simmons Bible College Records.

54. Minutes of the Sixth Annual Session of the Baptist State Women's Convention, June 25–28, 1891, Special Collections, Second Baptist Church, Eufaula, AL.

55. Williams, *The Charles H. Parrishes,* 18–19; *Diamond Jubilee of the General Association of Colored Baptists in Kentucky,* 45–51; Minutes of the General Association of Colored Baptists of Kentucky, 1890, box 2, folder 12, Simmons University Papers.

56. Parrish Jr., interviewed by Cox and Morison, tape 210, February 21, 1977.

57. Dr. Kevin Cosby was named the thirteenth president of Simmons College of Kentucky in 2005. The institution is now recognized as a member of the Historically Black Colleges and Universities.

7

"Very Strong Colored Women"

Black Women's Uplift, Activism, and Contributions to the Rosenwald Rural School-Building Program in Kentucky

Le Datta Denise Grimes

When Mollie E. Poston was hired as one of Kentucky's first Black industrial supervisors, she was described as "very *black*," a woman "in close touch with her people in South Western Kentucky."[1] In this context, the term *black* did not simply denote skin color, nor did it really pertain to her appearance at all. Instead, her Blackness was politicized. It was an assessment of her ideas, how she approached life, the pride she had in her people, and the work she did to uplift them. In short, Poston was a "race woman," a woman deeply invested in racial consciousness and solidarity as well as the overthrow of white supremacy.[2] Born on October 1, 1872, and educated at Roger Williams University in Nashville, Poston was a wife, a mother of seven, a club woman, and a teacher. She taught in Kentucky schools from 1886 to 1912 before becoming an industrial supervisor in 1913, working with Black communities in Christian County to build better schools, learn new skills, and improve their lives.[3]

In the early twentieth century, women like Poston represented a class of professional Black women who established identities for themselves outside the home and beyond motherhood and marriage. These Black women did not, however, disparage or resent their domesticity. Instead, they esteemed it, built social activist platforms around it, and helped shape ideas about Black womanhood, responsibility, uplift, racial equity, and first-class citizenship both inside and outside the home sphere.[4] Their work embraced an ethos of "socially responsible individualism" that involved commitment to their own personal growth, education, and advancement as well as to the uplift of their communities. This idea was in direct contrast to the larger society's ideals of *rugged individualism*, and within this context "Black women emerged as leaders."[5]

Driven by ideas of self-determination, racial pride, and growing access to higher education, Black women in Kentucky created a platform for themselves at the intersection of educational debate, philanthropic interventions, and community building. They wielded multiple stratagems to achieve racial uplift and equity while simultaneously creating spaces of empowerment for themselves within the Jim Crow commonwealth. Because of their grit and dedication to both self-improvement and community uplift, Poston and Kentucky women like her played a key role in what the historian James D. Anderson has called the "second crusade for black common schools in the rural South."[6] This crusade was also known as the "Rosenwald rural school-building program" (Rrsbp).[7] Conceived in 1912, the social construction of the Rrsbp set it apart in varying ways from other agencies working to shape Black southern education during the Progressive Era. First, it was the brainchild of Booker T. Washington, a southern Black man interested in the uplift of the Black South. Though Washington's intentions—whether he sought Black uplift or his own self-aggrandizement—have long been questioned, there is no evidence of him betraying Black southerners. Second, the program was initially run by Black men and women at Tuskegee—not by outside reformers—who orchestrated a symbiotic partnership with Black communities like those in Kentucky and aided them in building more than 158 schools and teacher cottages. Washington's insistence on Black agency as well as southern Black communities' activist inclinations to build and support local schools are what made the Rrsbp's local impact so distinctive. Whereas most philanthropies took a paternalist tone and told Black communities what they would do for them, the Rrsbp involved them in the work and empowered them at the local and state levels. Beyond this, it afforded Black southerners a world-renowned, highly respected leader and ally in their fight to build schools. Last, the Rrsbp included specific roles for Black women as Jeanes teachers and industrial supervisors that provided them both professional growth and a springboard into county and state government. Partially funded by the Anna T. Jeanes Foundation, one of many northern philanthropies working to shape Black education, this group of women worked at the county level teaching industrial and homemaking skills. Because of their skill and professionalism, they were often known as unofficial county superintendents.

Black women in Kentucky—much like those across the South—embraced the Rrsbp because it aligned itself with the goals they had set for themselves and the work they had been doing to uplift their communities. Women such as Poston boasted a long and sustained history of educational activism in the late nineteenth and early twentieth centuries. In the aftermath of slavery, Black women helped establish schools such as Ladies' Hall in Lexington, Kentucky, in 1866 and petitioned local governments for schools even as they worked with local churches to create their own.[8] In September 1883, Black Baptist women formed the Baptist Women's Educational Convention of Kentucky to raise funds for State University in Louisville, formerly the Kentucky Normal and Theological Institute and later Simmons University. This group, which engaged women from across the state, began with the threefold purpose of encouraging attendance at Simmons, paying off the school's debt and building a new dormitory for women, and promoting missionary work. Ultimately, it raised more than $12,000 to build a women's dorm on campus and pay off the school's debt.[9] In 1877, both Black women and men formed the State Association of Colored Teachers, which later became the Kentucky Negro Educational Association. Outside the classroom, Black women were just as active and just as vocal. As early as 1886, Black women in Kentucky demanded the right to vote. And in 1892 they decried their unfair treatment on state railroads before the Kentucky General Assembly.[10] Then in December 1911, the State Federation of Colored Women's Clubs declared "rural schools their especial work" at the annual State Association of Colored Teachers' meeting and began planning, organizing, and recruiting women to its cause. Less than a year later, the group had established fourteen new Parents' Clubs to aid rural schools in their work.[11] During this same period, in what was hailed as a "great move for the education of the colored race in Kentucky," Black communities in Louisville and surrounding counties banded together to create the Kentucky Rural School Improvement League. Though R. D. Roman, a man, was named president of the league, Black women—Ms. Laura Chase of LaGrange (first vice president), Miss E. D. Alexander of Louisville (second vice president), Mrs.

Anna C. Ingram of Louisville (secretary), Mrs. Olivia Morton (assistant secretary), and Mrs. A. Estes of Eminence (treasurer)—made up the overwhelming majority of the leadership.[12]

This grassroots activism formed the bedrock of the Rosenwald rural school-building program. Across the state, Black women led Rosenwald school-building campaigns, taught in the schools, donated land, raised money, and led local parent–teacher associations. Despite these contributions, in historical accounts they have largely been overshadowed by their Black male counterparts, but they weren't overlooked in the early twentieth century. Because of their civic engagement and education, Black women's activism in Kentucky often drew the praise of Francis Christopher (F. C.) Button, one of the state's supervisors of rural schools. In fact, when the Rrsbp arrived in Kentucky in 1917, Button readily thought of a Black woman for the job. He wrote in April 1918, "We have a few very strong colored women in this State, about whom I have been thinking along this line."[13] Though Button did not explain what he meant by "very strong Colored women," his words demonstrated both his respect and confidence in the training, education, and leadership ability of Black women in Kentucky. Although the job ultimately went to Francis Marion Wood, a prominent Black male leader in Black Kentucky education, Button's suggestion that a Black woman be appointed to a state office highlights both the quality and the impact of Black women's activism in early twentieth-century Black education. It also hints at the importance of their work to the Rrsbp.

Black Middle-Class Club Work

Black women's club work sprang from the Black church. Though denied leadership roles in the pulpit, Black women were often the heads of various missionary societies and ministries within the church. This experience afforded them multiple skillsets, such as organizational development, strategizing, and fund-raising, which proved beneficial outside the church walls and in the larger community. In the aftermath of slavery, Black women used club work and missionary societies to meet the needs of their communities and to respond to racial, gendered, and cultural oppression. They believed it to be their Christian duty to alleviate Black suffering due to systemic injustice, racism, and prejudice through collective work and social engagement.[14] In the early twentieth century, greater access to higher education created a growing class of Black women whose education and training carried them beyond manual field labor and domestic service. These women attended schools such as Howard and Fisk Universities and were employed as teachers, nurses, and librarians in their communities. They were also wives and mothers, and care for themselves and their families meant care for their larger world. For these women, private life and public life were deeply intertwined. Their duties as professionals, wives, and mothers overlapped with their commitment to the larger society, and "their desire to nurture their own kin expanded out of the private realm and into public activities that advanced the interests of black people as a group."[15] In short, self-care meant community care, and protecting and providing for their families by combating white racist ideologies that oppressed, demeaned, and belittled Black women, their families, and Black communities. Black women's club work was a radical form of self-care and self-help. During this period, club work served as the very center of Black female intellectual life. Club meetings and work created safe spaces for them to express their ideas and "throw up highways" over the gendered, racist, and negatively sexualized barriers they faced. Such spaces provided a means of developing self-confidence and agency that allowed them to break through social barriers to become leaders and advocates in Black communities across the nation.[16]

In the early twentieth century, Black middle-class clubwomen positioned themselves as the true leaders of the race, and they defined themselves over and against Black men and white women. Because of disenfranchisement, Black clubwomen deemed themselves equal to Black men and just as capable of tackling the race problem. Like Black men, Black women could not vote, and they were equally susceptible to poverty, lynching, Jim Crow laws, and white supremacy. In addition, some Black women had lost faith in Black men's ability to uplift the race, and they asserted that they were better able to address the nation's race problem. They argued that women "were more nurturing, moral, and altruistic" than men, who were "belligerent, aggressive, and selfish."[17] Separated from traditional ideas of femininity and precluded by racism from fully participating in the larger women's movement in the United States, Black women organized through their club work to orchestrate personal, professional, and political gains. This necessarily differentiated their work from that of white women's clubs, which focused primarily on gender equality. Black women were not afforded the luxury of such a specific focus because "the race was under assault from all sides." Chief among their attackers were white women, who, Black clubwomen argued, should instead be playing a larger role in African Americans' fight for equality. Part of Black women's club work and liberation efforts meant forcing white women to see them as equals and garnering their support as they fought against lynching, peonage, disenfranchisement, race riots, and white supremacy. White women, however, continued to align themselves with white men, asserting both gender and racial superiority to Black women.[18]

Black women in Kentucky formed the Kentucky Association of Colored Women's Clubs in 1903 to create a centralized and united front against the varying forces of oppression they faced, including poverty, disenfranchisement, school inequality, and economic insecurity. It consisted of thirteen women's clubs—the Improvement Club; King's Daughters, led by the famed Kentucky educator Mary V. Parrish; the Women's Industrial Club, led by the state and national activist Nannie Helen Burroughs; the YMCA Auxiliary; the Economical Club; the Ladies Sewing Circle; the Sunshine Club; the Music and Literary Club; the Music and Literary Club No. 2; the Normal Hill Reading Circle; the Baptist Women's Educational Convention Board of Managers; the Ladies Domestic and Economical; and Children's Friend—and was established to "secure harmony of action and co-operation among all women in raising to the highest plane: Home, Moral and Religious, and Civic life." This was done by "securing the interest and support of the best women of the community, encouraging club work throughout the state where there was none, and educating Black women on the varying ways club work could impact their communities." Education was a primary focus of the state-wide movement, and one of the association's first projects was the Scholarship Loan Department, established in 1913 to aid Black youths in getting an education.[19]

When the need for a new school arose in Mayslick, Kentucky, Black women embraced the cause as their "duty" and created a Health and Welfare League. With $500 promised from the Rosenwald Fund, Julius Rosenwald's philanthropic agency that funded the Rrsbp as well as other programs, the group sought to relieve overcrowding in the Mayslick Black community's school and create a space where domestic science and manual training could be taught. Led by Mrs. W. A. Taylor, president, and Mrs. Mary E. Foley, secretary, the league implored the community to attend a rally in March 1919 to raise funds for a new school. According to newspaper accounts, the goal was to raise $1,000 in a single day. The program began with a 2:00 p.m. sermon by Reverend Robert Jackson of

Bethel Baptist Church in Maysville, and music was provided by Professor William H. Robinson. A short solicitation speech was given by Mr. Will Pointer, and Mr. J. H. Hicks and Mr. W. A. Taylor served as soliciting captains. Each family was asked to give at least $20, and those who could do more were asked to give up to $100. As an incentive, donors' names were to be published in both local and state newspapers "so that every-body will know just who is aiding in this great movement."[20]

The group raised more than $500 during the event and planned another rally for May 4 "to go over the top."[21] They implored readers of a local newspaper to do their part in supporting the school. They wrote, "We are asking those who have already given to do more if you can, and those who have never given to, to help your own children." A year later, Black men in the community—James Hicks, W. A. Taylor, Eli Bolden, J. W. Story, and Vernon Holtz—filed articles of incorporation for the Mayslick Health and Welfare Company to "construct school buildings, store houses, dwellings and other edifices, and to hold real estate."[22] Com-bined, the fund-raising efforts in this period raised more than $10,000, and for $17,650 the community built a four-teacher building that sat on two-and-a-half acres of land.[23]

When the Rosenwald Fund began offering new schools, libraries, industrial shops, and bus transportation in urban areas, Elizabeth "Lizzie" Beatrice Cooke Fouse of Lexington threw her support behind the program and invited the state's Rosenwald agent to her home to meet with local women.[24] Born on May 14, 1875, Fouse attended both Eckstein Norton Institute and State University, which later became Simmons University, before embarking on a career in education and a lifetime of community uplift and activism. Fouse taught school in Lexington before marrying William Henry Fouse in 1898 and joining him to teach in Indiana. In 1904, she quit teaching to turn her attention to club work and community engagement. She was a charter member of the Kentucky Association of Colored Women and was serving as president of the organization by 1913. She also held various positions in the National Association of Colored Women's Clubs, and she worked across racial lines in other organizations, such as the United Council of Church Women, the Southern Regional Council, and the Kentucky Commission on Negro Affairs.[25]

Such associations and power made Fouse an important leader in Black education in Kentucky, and her support for the Rosenwald School move-ment helped build both a school and a workshop in Lexington.[26] In 1929,

Elizabeth Beatrice Cooke Fouse. Photograph from Fouse Family Photographs, 1860–1951 (PA53M58), Special Collections Research Center, University of Kentucky, Lexington.

the Douglass School opened at the corner of Price Road and Chiles Avenue. Named for the famed abolitionist Frederick Douglass, the school cost $30,000 and was insured for $18,000 under a new Rosenwald mandate. The eight-teacher school had both a $120 elementary library and a $120 high school library. Grades one through twelve were taught at the school, and two hundred pupils were initially enrolled there. A few years later, a $2,000 two-room workshop for industrial sciences was also built on the grounds. Beyond being the only Rosenwald School in Lexington, the Douglass School and its shop were unique accomplishments for another reason. In both instances, Blacks donated very little financially to their construction. Rosenwald records indicate that Blacks contributed only $140 to the total cost of both the school and the shop over a four-year period. This low amount was likely due to financial blight caused by the Great Depression, which affected Blacks, who had very little to begin with, more severely throughout the nation.[27]

Jeanes Supervisors and Industrial Teachers in Kentucky

Booker T. Washington readily understood the importance of Black women's contributions to Black uplift. Just as he created a role for Black men as state Rosenwald agents, he strategically positioned Black women to be an integral part of the Rrsbp. This was accomplished by tying the work of the Rrsbp to the Anna T. Jeanes Foundation and by mandating that all communities receiving Rosenwald aid engage the aid of a Jeanes supervisor or teacher.[28] The Anna T. Jeanes Foundation—the Negro Rural School Fund or Jeanes Fund, as it was also known—was one of the many northern philanthropic agencies working to shape Black southern education during the Progressive Era. In 1907, the Philadelphia Quaker Anna T. Jeanes established a $1 million fund to be devoted "solely to the assistance of Rural, Community, or Country Schools for *Southern* Negroes and not for the benefit or use of large institutions, *but the purpose of rudimentary education* and to encourage moral influence and social refinement which shall promote peace in the land, and good will among men."[29] More specifically, the foundation, which was the only white philanthropy to allow Blacks on its board, worked to foster industrial education and homemaking skills. It aligned neatly with Booker T. Washington's platform of self-help and uplift for the Black southern masses. Over time, the Anna T. Jeanes Foundation clarified and defined its contribution to Black education by employing a cadre of Black female educators to promote industrial education in schools across the South. These women were appointed by county superintendents and worked alongside both rural Black teachers and students to improve their lives through education. This work was expansive and knew few boundaries: it depended simply on the needs of each specific community. Nevertheless, it had some basic duties, such as teaching classes, conducting workshops on sewing and cooking, strengthening lesson plans, encouraging students to stay in school or further their education, and creating various clubs. Such work lay at the very heart of the Rrsbp pedagogy, making Jeanes supervisors critical to the program.[30] Together, "the Jeanes teachers provided the necessary leadership to fulfill the Rosenwald contract stipulations, profoundly shaping the establishment and maintenance of the African-American educational system in the South," and "the success of the Rosenwald program was largely the result of their work."[31]

Virginia Estelle Randolph served as the first Jeanes supervisor in the South. She was hired in 1908, and the program was patterned after her work at the Old Mountain Road School in Henrico County, Virginia.[32] Her belief in hands-on education, school beautification, parent involvement, educational rigor on par with white schools, teacher training, and schools' ability to shape and mold the whole child served as guidelines for the hundreds of Black women across the South who followed her in working as Jeanes supervisors. In this role, Black women traveled from school to school, crafting ideas and curricula that met Black communities' needs for education. Some women managed whole counties, while others had several districts under their jurisdiction. They interacted with both white school authorities and Black communities, and they were free "to do anything they deemed fit for the educational benefit of the community and the school."[33] Such power was typically not a feature of Black women's lives in the early twentieth century, making the Jeanes Foundation an important component of Black female empowerment and enrichment in the South during this period.

In Kentucky, F. C. Button secured funding for the first Jeanes supervisors in 1912, but the program was put on hold for nearly a year as Kentucky state school officials sparred over how the program should work. The main issue was oversight. Though Superintendent of Public Instruction Barksdale Hamlett "was very anxious to have these workers" and gave Button "cordial support," he "insisted that these supervisors come under the State [Public Education] Dept."[34] This requirement was problematic because both the Rrsbp and Jeanes supervisors were designed to work at the county level. Button resolved this issue by writing to both Wallace Buttrick of the General Education Board (a Rockefeller philanthropic organization) and James Dillard of the Jeanes Fund in both an official and an unofficial capacity.[35] In formal typewritten statements, Button wrote of his trouble hiring the new Jeanes supervisors. He asked for clarity, guidance, and direction in the matter and assumed an objective, professional posture. In handwritten letters, however, he laid bare state officials' varying motives and agendas and asked the head of these agencies for help. Button's ploy demonstrated the influence and power of national philanthropic agencies to sway state leaders and legislation. Kentucky, like most southern states, relied heavily on outside sources for educational funding and could not easily resist such agencies' requests. His approach also revealed the duplicitous nature of state officials in Kentucky, where in one breath they were "very anxious" to have the work begin but in another were covertly working to receive funds for use in programs for white Kentuckians and not the education of Blacks. Knowing this, Button used this combined official/unofficial method repeatedly to win gains for Black education in Kentucky. When Hamlett sought to "hold up the appointment of colored supervisors in Ky," in February 1913 Button secretly approached Buttrick to force Hamlett's hand. He wrote, "Can you not write me demanding at once a list of the supervisors and the counties in which they are to work, together with the dates when they are to begin. You may make this demand as abrupt and mandatory as you think necessary."[36] One month later, the first supervisors were named and hired, with Button proclaiming to Buttrick, "Your letters did the work."[37] The victory, however, came too late to secure much funding for that year. The Jeanes Fund allotted only $360 for one Jeanes worker, which went to Clark County. The General Education Board funded the remaining industrial supervisors, resulting in two separate groups of Black women—Jeanes supervisors and state industrial supervisors—working to shape Black rural life in Kentucky. These women worked year-round, with only four to six weeks of vacation, and though the two groups were funded separately and administered differently—one at the county level and the other at the state level—they functioned in largely the same manner.[38]

Florence G. Anderson Muir served as the first Jeanes supervisor in Kentucky and later became the state's first Black state supervisor of colored rural schools. Born in 1891, Muir was a member of Louisville's burgeoning Black middle class. Her father was Dr. Charles W. Anderson Sr., and her brother was Charles W. Anderson Jr., Kentucky's first Black legislator. Muir attended Louisville Central High School and later both Lincoln University and the Hampton Institute (now Hampton University). She then taught domestic science at the Denton Institute in Maryland, where she was "the only teacher in [the] institute in her teens," as well as at the Tuskegee Institute before returning to Hopkinsville, Kentucky, in 1912 to teach.[39] One year later, Muir was appointed as Jeanes supervisor in Clark County. Though no records have been found detailing Muir's efforts as a Jeanes worker, a letter she wrote earlier in her career reveals her thoughts on Black education. While attending a summer institute for teachers in Hopkinsville, Muir drew a direct "correlation between home and school life." Practicality was a major theme in her work. Education that bore immediate and palpable results demonstrated the importance of education and bolstered communities' support for it. "Our aim and purpose," she wrote "was to teach such things in rural schools that could be taken home, and there help beautify the homes, improve the farms, so as to obtain the best results; to construct such things from wood and lumber that not only added to the homes, but improved the sanitary conditions on the farm and around the grounds."[40]

In 1915 at age twenty-four, Muir became the first Black state supervisor of colored rural schools in Kentucky.[41] In this role, she worked out of Frankfort but traveled throughout the state, organizing "county institutes for colored teachers," and she had "supervision in a general way over the women doing homemaker club work."[42] Muir's work, however, extended well beyond these duties. On a three-day visit to Earlington, Kentucky, in 1915, Muir worked in various capacities in the Black community. She visited the school, attended a teachers' meeting, and spoke at the local Baptist church.[43] In 1916, she married James Muir, an educator, but her new role as wife did not stop her work or travel. That same year, Muir attended Montgomery County's inaugural industrial exhibition, where she was a featured guest alongside Lizzie Fouse, an esteemed educator in Kentucky and leader in the Black club women's movement in the state. The event, which was held at the local school and attended by both Blacks and whites, was hailed as an event "second to none of its kind in the state."[44] Beyond this, Muir was a member of the Hospital Club in Winchester and the Church Aid Club in Frankfort.[45]

Unlike Muir, most Jeanes teachers and industrial supervisors were not middle-class women. They were afforded this status, however, by virtue of their position and the power it provided them. In reality, most had attended industrial-base schools that were not very far removed from rural lives. Because of this rural background, these supervisors better understood the communities they served and did not try "to impose their views and values on an oppressed group."[46] Instead, they worked to improve the everyday lives of the Black rural communities. Though outsiders in many of the communities served by the Rrsbp, Black female supervisors quickly ingrained themselves in the daily lives of Black rural families. Whereas white county supervisors showed little interest in the educational needs of poor rural Blacks and often blamed them for their conditions, Black female supervisors worked diligently to understand the specific needs and challenges of the communities they served, and their duties extended well outside the educational realm. Black female industrial workers visited the sick, spoke at local churches, attended Sunday schools, and sought to do the "next needed thing," whether it was working across the color line to secure funding for a much-needed school or writing letters for community residents and mailing them. Assimilating poor, rural Blacks to white standards was not the goal. The Jeanes teachers and supervisors instead shared their education and skills and sought to create agency among distressed rural populations.[47] This meant teaching rural Blacks varying skills and techniques to improve rural living rather than imposing the teachers' own standards and goals upon them.

Mayme L. Copeland used education and her position as an industrial supervisor to achieve middle-class status. Born in Paducah in 1884, Copeland was the daughter of a brick mason and thus not very far removed from rural life. She married Reverend Dr. Thomas H. Copeland, a Black Methodist Episcopal minister, and began a family before completing her education and embarking on a lifelong career as an educator, journalist, clubwoman, political activist, and church organizer. In 1914, Copeland moved to Hopkinsville when her husband became pastor of the Freeman Chapel. In Christian County, where there were seven Rosenwald Schools—the Blue Spring, Crofton, Dyer's Chapel, Garrottsburg, Hensleytown, Lafayette, and West Union schools—Copeland served as the supervisor of music and head of the commercial department at Attucks High School for fifteen years. Later, she studied at Kentucky State Industrial College, where she received a bachelor's degree in 1933. She then earned a master's degree from Columbia University in 1937 and later received an honorary doctorate degree from Mississippi Industrial College in 1955.[48]

Mayme L. Copeland, Class of 1933 (*fourth picture in the fourth row*), Kentucky State Industrial College. Photograph courtesy of Special Collections and Archives, Kentucky State University, Frankfort.

For Copeland, such opportunities for education and social advancement meant double occupation, that of home life plus community activism and uplift. Like many women of her time, Copeland was socialized to believe that "not to contribute to the public good was to waste their lives. Not to assume or create community work options for themselves, whether paid or not, would have been to deny their missions and the important roles as community leaders for which they had prepared. And the more skills, training, or preparation they had, the truer this was. Not to use their advantages for the advancement of the race was deemed selfish and even traitorous."[49]

After completing her education, Copeland embarked on a life of service. The scope of her work reached across local, state, and national boundaries and demonstrated the various ways Black women used their time, energy, and resources to create opportunities for themselves and their community. This did not mean that they were endowed with superhuman strength and that their public and private lives were not sometimes in conflict.[50] Rather, their private and public work demonstrated a belief, obligation, and undying faith in Black ability and promise that compelled them forward. Embracing the ethos of "socially responsible individualism," Copeland forged a career for herself and simultaneously worked to uplift the Black community.[51] Regarded as "an educational worker whose contribution during the last generation or more has been incalculable," Copeland worked in Christian County schools for several years while also serving as the head of the Kentucky Negro Educational Association's Rural Department. She additionally served as the head of the Rural Department of the American Teachers Association. In 1937, she was appointed state supervisor of rural schools, making her "the first colored person working out of the Kentucky State Department of Education for more than 20 years." In this role, she worked to improve rural Black education and taught part-time at Kentucky State Industrial College. Beyond these jobs, Copeland led a meaningful civic and social life. One of her most notable roles was leading the Colored Women's Division of the Kentucky Republican Party in the 1920s. In 1935, she worked alongside the city councilman and mortician Edward W. Glass to raise funds for the Hopkinsville Red Cross. Serving as the dean of pledges, Copeland was also a member of Iota Phi Lambda, a business sorority begun in 1929 to "encourage young women to enter the Business Field by means of business training." Last, Copeland, like many women of her era, was heavily engaged in church work. Married for nearly fifty years to a leader in the Colored Methodist Episcopal Church, she was voted president of its missionary board in 1920. Upon retirement, she turned her attention to rural church work.[52]

Organization and "building community" were key themes in the work of E. Birdie Taylor. Born on March 10, 1880, Taylor was one of four Black female industrial supervisors hired by the State of Kentucky in 1913 "to help the colored people live better." These women—who also included Julia Ferguson of Charlottesville, Virginia, Lula Coleman of Franklin County, and Mollie Cox Poston of Christian County—were lauded as "high class and experienced colored women," and they worked at the county level to teach industrial arts and foment grassroots community development.[53] In the schools, industrial supervisors taught basic skills such as sewing, gardening, cooking, and canning. They also instructed teachers on the latest pedagogies, helped improve attendance, and promoted interest in higher education. For the home, they continued their industrial arts training, but they also promoted good health, sanitation, hygiene, and cleanliness. The bulk of their work, however, consisted of rural Black women's club work. Taylor and Kentucky's Black female industrial supervisors sought to unify the rural communities they served by creating communal activities that benefited both personal and public interests. In 1915, E. Birdie Taylor over-saw more than twenty clubs: nine senior leagues, fifteen junior leagues, girls' canning and homemaking clubs, boys' corn clubs, church improvement clubs, as well as a moral uplift club.[54]

Long before the Rrsbp's arrival in Kentucky, senior school-improvement leagues were working "towards the improvement of the school buildings, and towards buying some of the necessary equipments [sic] of the school, not furnished by the school board." Each league met monthly to discuss "topics of vital interest to the school and community" and to raise funds to meet a school's needs, which varied from location to location. In Fayette County, two leagues built kitchens for their schools, painted them, and then supplied cabinets and tables. One league painted its school, and others built porches, fences, and stables for their schools. Another league focused its attention on buying a two-acre lot on which to build a new school. To accomplish all this work, fund-raising was a must in each school-improvement league. Members paid five cents in dues but raised "most of their money by giving entertainments and soliciting." Beyond the focus on serving schools' physical needs, Taylor used the senior school-improvement leagues to inspire interest in the schools and to establish themselves as stakeholders in both the school and the community. She wrote, "The objects [sic] in having them to meet at the schools are to make the schools the social center and to bring about a better cooperation between the teachers and the patrons." Like senior improvement leagues, junior improvement clubs focused on the needs of each local school. These clubs were made up of students, and their central focus was the "tidiness, cleanliness and beauty of the school building and grounds." Youth groups met twice a month to plant shrubs, flowers, and trees. They also swept, laundered curtains, dusted, washed windows, and cleaned outbuildings. In the neighborhoods, they whitewashed buildings and held clean-up days throughout the community. To raise funds, some schools offered a "potato, onion, apple and egg day." On these days, students brought one of each to school, learned to cook them, and then served them as penny lunches. In addition, youths formed a "morals and manners" committee to "see after the conduct of the pupils on the grounds and in this way they [were] taught government."[55]

Homemaking Clubs were another important form of uplift and engagement, and in 1914 the General Education Board allotted $1,500 for this work in Kentucky. That year, Taylor traveled 2,864 miles across Kentucky and established 122 clubs in Christian, Todd, Daviess, Clark, and Fayette Counties. These clubs served nearly a thousand rural Black mothers and daughters and taught skills such as gardening, sanitation, hygiene, cooking, sewing, and food preservation. Though Taylor noted that in the first year the Homemaking Clubs "did not do so well," she also wrote that Black women and their daughters were "very anxious to make a success of the work." And there were some successes. In her report to the state, Taylor wrote that "many homes were made more beautiful and home-like by the efforts of the clubs," and she highlighted three young women who raised gardens and made enough money to pay their first month's rent in boarding school, "where they went after finishing the county schools."[56] Beyond beautifying homes, the goal of Black Home-making Clubs was to establish relationships between industrial supervisors and rural Black women in the community. This was necessary because Black women influenced and controlled Black homes and were responsible for what Black children learned and practiced in the home. Without the cooperation and approval of Black mothers, supervisors lacked the support they needed to be successful, and there was pushback at times against supervisors who sought to change how Black mothers conducted things in their homes. Beyond this, Home Making Clubs allowed supervisors insight into students' home life, where they could assess issues such as hygiene, health, and sanitation, which had a direct impact on school life and atten-dance. Children who received proper medical care, were well fed, and dressed appropriately were more likely to attend school regularly. The clubs also provided supervisors with opportunities to encourage parents to keep their children in school. Beyond these things, there was an economic com-ponent to the clubs. Communities canned and sold a large portion of their goods to raise money to build and maintain their local schools.[57] A second economic component benefited Black mothers themselves. In Kentucky, where Black women's career opportunities were limited, domestic training and work often aided families that fell on hard times. The "domestic skills they developed at home and in school allowed them to earn a living and helped avert economic disaster" if their families needed additional income.

Such skills as washing, ironing, and sewing allowed Black women the opportunity to stay home, be mothers, maintain their own households, and provide for their families when their husbands' income could not.[58]

In early 1916, Taylor wrote to Button about the importance of this work and its impact on Black communities: "I find that organization in the communities is necessary for the success of the school. In the communities that have good School Improvement Leagues, and where the people come together often in Literary societies, socials and other gatherings such as lectures pertaining to the welfare of the community, healthfully, morally, and industrially, I have observed that the school in every particular is much better and is more easily managed. The people manifest a greater interest and school life is more pleasant and effective, and the home training is better." Unsuccessful schools, however, were a direct result of division. Taylor observed that communities that were separated or "never [came] together in a social or business-like way" had poor schools that "seemingly accomplished nothing."[59]

Because of their positions as industrial supervisors, women in these roles, such as E. Birdie Taylor, became community leaders and were highly esteemed by both county superintendents and the Black communities they served. Nannie G. Faulconer, superintendent of Fayette County schools, praised the work of E. Birdie Taylor. She wrote that Taylor "has proven herself capable of handling this work judiciously and well. She has aroused great enthusiasm among the colored people in this county in regard to domestic science and manual training."[60] In Muhlenberg County, Superintendent Amy M. Longest reported that the county paid its industrial supervisor's travel expenses, but the Black community provided for her other needs. Rural Black teachers donated $1.50 each to buy materials for industrial education. Students and their parents provided room and board for teachers as well as travel to and from the train station. School patrons also donated a stove and cooking utensils for the school's use. When funds for additional supplies ran low to furnish the school's kitchen, the school principal bought wood for $10 and trained the boys in carpentry. Such work, Longest wrote, made industrial work one of the "best things we have in our colored schools."[61]

In Mercer County, at least one principal credited the county's rural supervisor with building two new Rosenwald Schools. Ananias Lorenzo "A. L." Garvin served as principal of the Black school in Mercer County from 1903 to 1920 as well as the state's first African American extension

agent. When he arrived in Harrodsburg in 1903, there was no school building for Black youths, and the rural community owed $400 in back rent for
two cottages where classes were once taught. By 1920, however, the Black
community had paid the debt owed for the cottages, bought four acres of
land, and "made appropriations for two Rosenwall [sic] schools." The first
Rosenwald School in Mercer County was the Harrodsburg School, a six-
teacher school built under the aegis of the Tuskegee Institute for $6,000.
Blacks raised $750 to build and equip the school, and the Rrsbp donated
$900. According to Garvin, the school was "fully equipped with black-
boards, desks, [a] domestic science department and a manual training
department." The second school was the Mayo School, a two-teacher facility
that cost $3,000, of which Blacks contributed $100 and Rosenwald $400.
Writing about the schools' history some years later, Garvin wrote that
"much of this, if not all, was brought about by the efforts" of Effie Williams
Garvin, his wife, who was the rural county supervisor for Mercer County.[62]

The early success of Kentucky's Jeanes and industrial supervisors both
laid the foundation for and sustained the Rosenwald School movement in
the Bluegrass. Their intense fund-raising campaigns, club work, and organizing efforts were critical to local campaigns to build the schools and garner
favor for them. Because of this work, a state education report in 1925 argued
that "numerous modern Rosenwald school buildings are monuments to the
public spirit and industry of these Jeanes teachers."[63] As industrial supervisors, Black women worked across racial lines to create goodwill for Black education in much the same way F. M. Wood did as a Rosenwald building agent.
Wood, however, worked at the state level, traveling the Bluegrass and spend-
ing a minimal amount of time in each community. Black industrial supervisors, in contrast, served their counties and districts daily, forming intimate
bonds and relationships with both Black and white men and women. Their
work with the Homemaker Clubs provided much needed funding for the
new schools in each community, and their grassroots efforts both amplified
and improved upon the work already being done in such communities. Over
time, as white county supervisors realized the value of Kentucky's Jeanes and
industrial supervisors, they gave them more administrative duties and oversight of Black schools. Because of this greater power, the Kentucky Black
chemist, civil rights activist, and educator Atwood S. Wilson noted in 1933
that "Jeanes teachers are teachers who are in reality assistant county superintendents."[64] Such statements evidence the importance of Kentucky's industrial supervisors to their counties, their schools, and the Rrsbp.

Traditional Teachers

Black education in the early twentieth century served as "one of the most important political battlegrounds in the South," and "black teachers were at the center of this battlefield." In the aftermath of slavery, widespread illiteracy in Black communities "made teachers a vital source of political leadership." Black male teachers entered the political realm and rose through the ranks of the Republican Party. After disenfranchisement, Black teachers continued to view education and politics as "inextricably woven." They formed state organizations, lobbied state legislatures across the South, and remained vocal on various issues affecting Black communities. Such actions won Black teachers considerable influence in southern Black life, and during this period schools stood second only to the Black church in importance and influence in Black communities, which revered Black teachers in the same manner they revered Black preachers. Both inspired hope, and both served as community leaders. While preachers offered salvation for the Black soul, Black teachers offered a more secular deliverance. They "personified the belief that education meant liberation," and in the minds of the Black southern masses Black teachers were the very key to a life free from illiteracy, poverty, discrimination, and second-class citizenship. Beyond this, the profession was esteemed because it attracted the ablest and most intelligent among the race. In 1910, more than half of Black college graduates became teachers, whereas only one-sixth became preachers. By 1940, there were more than sixty-three thousand Black teachers in the United States.[65]

In the classroom, the presence of Black teachers in Kentucky—as across the South—was politicized. In the early twentieth century, Black parents demanded Black teachers as an expression of "racial pride, cultural difference and group solidarity." They understood that "even the best-intentioned whites found it difficult to accept blacks as equals," and they sought to shelter their children from such racist ideas. Black teachers embraced the challenge of advancing the race. They sought to prove that Black youths were as capable and as intelligent as white youths and just as deserving of a proper education. One way in which Black teachers demonstrated the ability of Black youths was through prominent commencement services. Black graduations were public events for both local Blacks and whites and often served as the biggest social gatherings of the year. They were not only celebrations of students' accomplishments and acknowledgement of the matriculation but also demonstrations of respectability. At

Black commencement services, or "School Closings," as they were also known, "Black celebrants found a public voice for making moral and political claims on the rest of society." Beyond this, Black closing ceremonies garnered the support of local Blacks for the schools, which further solidified the bonds between teachers and their communities.[66]

Despite the magnitude of the work performed by Black teachers, the earliest historiographies of southern Black education centered their attention on negative issues of inequality, such as substandard housing, inadequate funding, overcrowding, lack of transportation, and shortened school terms. More recent studies, however, highlight the power and agency of all-Black education. Studies by Vanessa Siddle Walker, Carter J. Savage, and David Cecelski examine the positive outcomes of an all-Black education and contend that segregated Black schools fostered academic pride and excellence, encouraged higher education, instilled self-discipline and confidence, offered social support through home visits, and taught Black students to "deflect the negative messages aimed at African Americans coming from white-dominated society."[67] Understanding and fearing the power that Black teachers wielded and their ability to politicize the Black masses, northern philanthropists in the early twentieth century refused to fund liberal arts colleges for Blacks. They instead funneled their investments into schools such as Tuskegee and Hampton, which promoted industrial-based education, in this way hoping to control Blacks' ambition and secure their status as second-class citizens.[68] Regardless of this lack of support, Black teachers emerged as community leaders and gatekeepers in the fight for social, economic, and political equality.

Before Alice Dunnigan became a renowned journalist, she both attended and taught at a Rosenwald School. Her story demonstrates the role that Black teachers played in rural Kentucky communities as well as the challenges they faced from both Blacks and whites. Born on April 27, 1906, near Russellville, Kentucky, Dunnigan won national acclaim as the first Black woman to cover the White House Press Corps and the Supreme Court and to travel with a US president (Harry S. Truman), but her defiance of racial southern norms began during her youth and continued into her teaching years. Dunnigan grew up rural and poor and attended Knob City High School, a Rosenwald School in Logan County, which offered grades one through eight, plus two years of high school.[69] Inequality was a regular part of her life, and it was during her youth that she "began to feel the sting of racial discrimination." In her autobiography, *Alone atop the Hill* (2015), Dunnigan writes that racism

Alice Dunnigan, 1982. From *Women of Courage: An Exhibition of Photographs by Judith Sedwick Based on the Black Women Oral History Project*, sponsored by the Arthur and Elizabeth Schlesinger Library on the History of Women in America, Radcliffe College, Cambridge, MA.

became real to her when she discovered as a child that there were no public restrooms for Black women in Russellville. Although Black men could "easily step into an alley, partially conceal himself behind a wagon or parked car," Black women were forced to find the home of a Black friend because the only public restroom "was clearly marked White Ladies." Despite Jim Crow laws, Dunnigan defiantly used the "White Ladies" restroom and vowed early in life to "break down discrimination wherever [she] found it."[70]

Dunnigan's defiance continued after she became a teacher, and her time in Kentucky's rural schools demonstrated the dire circumstances rural students faced as well as the work teachers did to overcome these conditions. After graduation from Knob Hill, Dunnigan attended both Kentucky Normal and Industrial Institute in Frankfort and the Western Kentucky Industrial College in Paducah. She later taught in several rural schools, and she noted distinct differences between the typical rural schools she taught at and the Rosenwald School in New Hope. Dunnigan's first teaching assignment was at "a drab, ramshackle frame building with rough, weather-beaten sides, a rusty tin roof, and . . . several broken windowpanes . . . covered with squares of yellowing cardboard" in Mount Pisgah.

Dunnigan later taught at the New Hope school in Logan County, a distinct contrast to the poorly cared for school at Mount Pisgah. She described it as a "a modern Rosenwald School . . . with one large classroom, two cloakrooms, and a kitchen, as well as a large front porch where the children could play games during recess on rainy days." Despite the new school building, there were still challenges. During a mandatory meeting of county teachers at the opening of the school year, Black teachers and white teachers sat separately. Dunnigan bristled at the idea and asked other Black teachers to join her in sitting among whites. They refused initially, saying there was no need to "create confusion." Ultimately, she and another teacher desegregated the room by sitting among whites without disturbance.[71]

Dunnigan's account demonstrates that rural Black teachers fought for equality in numerous ways. They worked both inside and outside the classroom to uplift the race in a wide range of duties that were both expected of them and fulfilled in numerous ways. Like Dunnigan, Carrie B. Laine was a longtime educator. Born November 28, 1882, she contributed $10 to the Berea College Industrial School fund in 1908. A year later, she was one of eight people in Winchester to pass the civil service exam to become a postal carrier, though she did not get the job.[72] In addition, Laine bought a two-acre parcel of land for $850 on Forest Grove–Becknerville Pike (now Waterworks Road) to build the Howard's Creek Rosenwald School in Clark County, where she also taught. The school, which was built in 1929, was a two-teacher facility that cost $5,000.[73]

Parent–Teacher Associations and Community Days

The Rrsbp's success was rooted in collective engagement and cooperation. The program relied on Blacks' financial support, personal investment, and ongoing interest in and upkeep of the schools. One of the key ways local

Black women supported their schools was through the Parent–Teacher Association, most prominently known as the PTA. Although the meetings and activities of school-improvement leagues, tomato clubs, and Home-making Clubs could be held in the home in support of the schools, PTA meetings were community events that brought parents—primarily mothers because of their role as caregivers in the home—teachers, students, and the community to the schoolhouse for both business and social engagement. During these meetings, principals and teachers informed parents about their children, their academic progress, and the life of the school. They often spoke about their schools' needs and shared why certain equipment, books, and improvements were necessary. This was not, however, a one-way street. In a nonthreatening, easygoing environment, Black parents actively engaged school personnel, questioning them and expressing their own concerns about the school or their children. These exchanges then became the basis for "collaborative plans of action that were formed to address the needs in question."[74] Beyond these exchanges, PTA meetings served as major social events where women served homemade refreshments and oftentimes watched their children perform in plays, musicals, or recitals.

Of all these things, fund-raising was one of the most important functions of the PTA. When white county superintendents refused to distribute funds for Black schools appropriately, PTA dues and fund-raisers filled this void, as was demonstrated in a Henderson County community. In 1925, the Henderson PTA purchased a new high school for Blacks. The unique way they did so showcased the organizing skills of Black women and the contributions they made to local schools through the organization. After raising $2,000 for a new school, Blacks in Henderson turned to their PTA to secure the remaining $1,000 needed to buy a new building. Under the leadership of PTA president Mrs. O. K. Glass and Supervising Principal F. A. Taylor, Blacks were organized military style. Five majors, two captains, and ten lieutenants led the masses in canvassing the city for donations, and in just three days the PTA raised $1,200 with the aid of local citizens, businesses, lodges, and clubs. "With such an organization working with this superior system it was an easy matter to go over the top," wrote the *Louisville Leader* in praise of the Henderson PTA's efforts.[75] A few years later, this same community would pool its resources to build its own Rosenwald School. In 1931–1932, a ten-room facility was built for $47,000 and insured for $15,000.[76]

Like the PTA in Henderson, most clubs were run by Black women, and in many schools the county's Jeanes supervisor took the lead in organizing the PTA. In fact, this task was often written into the supervisors' job description. In 1932, Adair County's superintendent of schools requested $315 in aid from the Jeanes Fund to hire Miss Emma J. Alexander. In addition to the overall well-being of the schools, such as the "promotion of health and attendance and industrial training," she was also tasked with "P. T. A. and community work." That same year, Mrs. Blanche G. Elliott of Muhlenburg County was charged with similar duties.[77] In 1936, Fayette County applied for $247.50 to hire Ethel Baker Peyton as a Jeanes supervisor. In addition to teaching first grade half a day and having charge of the county's nine Black schools, Peyton "assist[ed] the regular teachers in organizing P. T. A. and mother clubs and in preparing for community entertainment." Within a few years, however, Peyton's work had gone from working to organize the clubs to working "through the County Teachers' Association; the P. T. A. groups; and with individuals to bring about a closer co-operative effort between the home and the school."[78]

In Kentucky, Black women's activism foregrounded and undergirded the work of the Rrsbp. Despite the racial and gendered limitations placed on them, Black women became leaders in their communities through church auxiliaries and their club work. Through their activism and community engagement, they identified rural education as a problem and were working to improve it long before the Rrsbp became available in Kentucky. When the Rrsbp finally arrived in 1917, Black women in Kentucky pushed the movement forward through a shared consciousness and belief in education as a tool for uplift and activism. In it, they found a paid platform that supported their own goals of personal growth and development as well as their desire to uplift and improve their communities. As Jeanes teachers, Black women served as unofficial school superintendents, doing the equivalent work of white male school officials without benefit of the dignity, respect, resources, or salaries these men received. They did so, however, out of a sense of duty and pride in themselves and their communities, believing that uplifting the race was an inseparable component of uplifting themselves.

In the classroom, Black women won respect as teachers and led the fight against illiteracy and subjugation. Though the Rrsbp was rooted in industrial education, Black teachers and principals determined what was best for their communities and what was taught in the classroom. Whereas northern philanthropists sought to use industrial training and the Black teaching force to handicap rural southern Blacks by confining them to manual labor, Black women used the Rrsbp to combat the illiteracy that kept Blacks socially and economically oppressed. In addition, some women such as Muir and Copeland used the program to catapult themselves into the highest ranks of state government, which was unheard of for a woman, especially a Black woman, in this period. As teachers and Jeanes workers, Black women functioned as double agents with roles in both the larger white society and their own segregated Black communities. Interacting with communities across the Bluegrass—in their homes, in their schools, in their churches, at their rallies—Black women set the tone and agenda for Rosenwald Schools and Black segregated schools throughout the South.

Notes

1. F. C. Button to Dr. Wallace C. Buttrick, August 13, 1919, series 1.1, box 79, folder 692, General Education Board Papers, Rockefeller Archives Center (GEB-RAC), Sleepy Hollow, NY, emphasis in original. Mollie E. Poston is referred to as "Mrs. E. Poston" in this letter and as "Mollie Cox Poston" in other documents.

2. Hazel V. Carby, *Race Men* (Cambridge, MA: Harvard University Press, 1998) 4.

3. "Mollie Poston," in *Who's Who of the Colored Race: A General Biographical Dictionary of Men and Women of African Descent,* vol. 1: *1915,* ed. Frank Lincoln Mather (Chicago: Memento, 1915), 221–22.

4. Jacqueline Anne Rouse, "Out of the Shadow of Tuskegee: Margaret Murray Washington, Social Activism, and Race Vindication," *Journal of Negro History* 81, nos. 1–4 (1996): 32–33, at http: //www.jstor.org.ezproxy.uky.edu /stable/2717606.

5. Stephanie J. Shaw, *What a Woman Ought to Be and to Do: Black Professional Women Workers during the Jim Crow Era* (Chicago: University of Chicago Press, 1996), 218.

6. James D. Anderson, *The Education of Blacks in the South, 1860–1935* (Chapel Hill: University of North Carolina Press, 1988), 52.

7. Anderson, *Education of Blacks in the South,* 52. In using the abbreviation "Rrsbp" rather than RRSBP, I follow Mary S. Hoffschwelle, *The Rosenwald Schools of the American South* (Gainesville: University Press of Florida, 2006).

8. Marion B. Lucas, *A History of Blacks in Kentucky,* vol. 1: *From Slavery to Segregation, 1760–1891* (Frankfort: Kentucky Historical Society, 1992), 239–40.

9. Evelyn Brooks Higginbotham, *Righteous Discontent: The Women's Movement in the Black Baptist Church, 1880–1920* (Cambridge, MA: Harvard University Press, 1994), 59–61.

10. Karen Cotton McDaniel, "Local Women: The Public Lives of Black Middle Class Women in Kentucky before the 'Modern Civil Rights Movement,'" PhD diss., University of Kentucky, 2013, 16.

11. F. C. Button to Dr. Wallace Buttrick, January 18, 1912, box 80, folder 697, GEB-RAC.

12. F. C. Button to Hon. Barksdale Hamlett, September 30, 1912, box 80, folder 697, GEB-RAC.

13. F. C. Button to Prof. C. J. Calloway, April 15, 1918, Clinton J. Calloway Collection, Tuskegee University Archives, Tuskegee, AL.

14. McDaniel, "Local Women," 3, 79.

15. Jacqueline Jones, *Labor of Love, Labor of Sorrow: Black Women, Work, and the Family, from Slavery to the Present* (New York: Basic, 1985), 3.

16. Shaw, *What a Woman Ought to Be and to Do,* 1.

17. Deborah Gray White, *Too Heavy a Load: Black Women in Defense of Themselves, 1894–1994* (New York: Norton, 1999), 37–40.

18. White, *Too Heavy a Load,* 347–40.

19. Charles H. Wesley, *The History of the National Association of Colored Women's Clubs, Inc.: A Legacy of Service* (Washington, DC: National Association of Colored Women's Clubs, 1984), 422–24.

20. "Mayslick Rally for New Colored School on Sunday," *Public Ledger* (Maysville, KY), March 21, 1919.

21. "Our Colored Citizens," *Public Ledger,* April 22, 1919.

22. "Mayslick Colored People Organize Corporation," *Public Ledger,* November 18, 1920.

23. Rosenwald School, Mayslick, KY, Rosenwald Database, at http://Rosenwald.fisk.edu/.

24. Untitled notes, February 14, 1932, box 3, folder 1, Fouse Family Papers, Special Collections, University of Kentucky, Lexington.

25. Karen Cotton McDaniel, "Fouse, Elizabeth Beatrice Cook, 'Lizzie,'" in *The Kentucky African American Encyclopedia,* ed. Gerald L. Smith, Karen Cotton McDaniel, and John A. Hardin (Lexington: University of Kentucky Press, 2015), 185–86.

26. All other Rosenwald Schools in the county were built in rural settings, such as Avon, Cadentown, Coletown, Ft. Springs, and Uttingertown.

27. "Douglass High School," n.d., at http://lexhistory.org/wikilex/douglas-high-school; Rosenwald School, Lexington, KY, Rosenwald Database, at http//Rosenwald.fisk.edu.

28. "Plan for the Distribution of Rosenwald Aid in the Erection of Rural Schoolhouses," September 20, 1917, box 11, folder 90, Calloway Collection.

29. Lance G. E. Jones, *The Jeanes Teacher in the United States, 1908–1933: An Account of Twenty-Five Years' Experience in the Supervision of Negro Rural Schools* (Chapel Hill: University of North Carolina Press, 1937), 17–19, emphasis in original.

30. Linda B. Pincham, "A League of Willing Workers: The Impact of Northern Philanthropy, Virginia Estelle Randolph and the Jeanes Teachers in Early Twentieth-Century Virginia," *Journal of Negro Education* 74, no. 2 (2005): 115–18.

31. Valinda W. Littlefield, "'I Am Only One, but I Am One': Southern African American Women School Teachers, 1884–1954," PhD diss., University of Illinois at Urbana-Champaign, 2003, 15, 39–40.

32. Jones, *The Jeanes Teacher*, 22–38.

33. Pincham, "A League of Willing Workers," 118.

34. F. C. Button to Wallace Buttrick, July 9, 1912, box 79, folder 692, GEB-RAC.

35. Button made monthly reports of his work to Wallace Buttrick at the General Education Board. He also wrote letters throughout the month concerning various issues. These letters were typewritten. Whenever he had problems with state officials, he wrote private letters by hand or scribbled notes in the corners of typewritten letters.

36. F. C. Button to Wallace Buttrick, February 25, 1913, box 79, folder 692, GEB-RAC.

37. F. C. Button to Wallace Buttrick, March 11, 1913, box 79, folder 692, GEB-RAC.

38. F. C. Button to Dr. Wallace Buttrick, March 17, 1913, box 79, folder 692, GEB-RAC.

39. "Muir, Florence G. Anderson," Notable Kentucky African Americans Database, n.d., at http://nkaa.uky.edu/nkaa/items/show/2630; "Graduates and Ex-students," in *The Southern Workman* (Hampton, VA: Press of the Hampton Normal and Agricultural Institute, 1915), 414, at https://hdl.handle.net/2027/mdp.39015018059967?urlappend=%3Bseq=458; "At Kentucky's Capital," *Freeman,* September 23, 1911, 8, at https://infoweb-newsbank-com.ezproxy.uky.edu/apps/readex/doc?p=EANX&docref=image/v2%3A12B28495A8DAB1C8%40EANX-12CC9D3939D96708%402419303-12CC2FB359A52B98%407-12E052CAB1E066F0%40At%2BKentucky%2527s%2BCapital.%2BProf.%2B

George%2BW.%2BHays%2BElected%2Bto%2BFaculty%2Bof%2Bthe%
2BNormal%2BInstitute—Federation.

40. Florence Anderson to F. C. Button, "The History of Our Summer School," n.d., GEB-RAC.

41. "Graduates and Ex-students," 414.

42. E. Birdie Taylor, "Report of Colored Supervision—Fayette County," Barksdale Hamlett, LL.D., comp., *Biennial Report of the Superintendent of Public Instruction of Kentucky for the Two Years, Ending June 30, 1915* (Frankfort, KY: State Journal Company, 1915), 117.

43. "Industrial Exhibition," *Mount Sterling Advocate,* April 18, 1916, 10.

44. "Industrial Exhibition."

45. It is unclear how long Muir remained state supervisor of rural colored schools. By 1921, however, she taught in Mt. Sterling at the local Black school, where her husband served as principal. She died in 1932.

46. Valinda Littlefield, "'To Do the Next Needed Thing': Jeanes Teachers in the Southern United States 1908–34," in *Telling Women's Lives: Narrative Inquiries in the History of Women's Education,* ed. Kathleen Weiler and Sue Middleton (Philadelphia: Open University Press, 1999), 141.

47. Littlefield, "'To Do the Next Needed Thing,'" 141.

48. "Copeland, Mayme L.," Notable Kentucky African Americans Database, n.d., at http://nkaa.uky.edu/nkaa/items/show/378; "Kentucky Woman Made Supervisor of Rural Schools," *Pittsburgh Courier,* September 11, 1937, 7; "Educator Is Dead at 78," *Louisville Courier-Journal,* November 27, 1962, 15; "Churchwoman Gets Doctorate," *New York Age,* June 11, 1955, 5.

49. Shaw, *What a Woman Ought to Be and to Do,* 119.

50. Shaw, *What a Woman Ought to Be and to Do,* 112.

51. Shaw, *What a Woman Ought to Be and to Do,* 7.

52. "Kentuckian Gets High Post," *Capitol Plaindealer* (Topeka, KS), September 11, 1937, n.p.; "Prominent Kentucky School Teacher Will Retire July 1," *Capitol Plaindealer,* June 20, 1947, n.p.; Joshua D. Farrington, "Mayme L. Brooks, Copeland," in *The Kentucky African American Encyclopedia,* ed. Smith, McDaniel, and Hardin, 122; "History," Iota Phi Lambda Sorority, n.d., at https://iota-deltaphi.org/history; "Dr. Weber Speaks to Negro Workers at M. E. Meeting," *Paducah (KY) Sun-Democrat,* October 28, 1920, 3.

53. "Origin of the Bureau of Supervision," in Barksdale Hamlett, comp., *Biennial Report of the Superintendent of Public Instruction of Kentucky for the Two Years, Ending 1911–1913* (Frankfort, KY: State Journal Company, 1913), 288–99.

54. Taylor, "Report of Colored Supervision," in Hamlett, *Biennial Report of the Superintendent of Public Instruction, June 30, 1915,* 117.

55. E. Birdie Taylor, "Senior School Improvement Leagues" and "Junior Improvement Leagues," in Hamlett, *Biennial Report of the Superintendent of Public Instruction, June 30, 1915,* 118–19.

56. Taylor, "Report of Colored Supervision," in Hamlett, *Biennial Report of the Superintendent of Public Instruction, June 30, 1915,* 120.

57. Littlefield, "'To Do the Next Needed Thing,'" 138–39.

58. Shaw, *What a Woman Ought to Be and to Do,* 116.

59. E. Birdie Taylor to Dr. F. C. Button, February 14, 1916, box 79, folder 694, GEB-RAC.

· 60. Nannie G. Faulconer, report, in Hamlett, *Biennial Report of the Superintendent of Public Instruction of Kentucky for the Two Years, Ending June 30, 1913* (Frankfort, KY: State Journal Company, 1913), 293–94.

61. Amy M. Longest to F. C. Button, April 29, 1916, box 79, folder 694, GEB-RAC.

62. William McKinley Wesley, "The History of Education in Mercer County, Kentucky," master's thesis, University of Kentucky, 1929, 188–89.

63. "The Jeanes Fund," in McHenry Rhoads, comp., *Biennial Report of the Superintendent of Public Instruction of the State of Kentucky for the Two Years Ending June 30, 1925* (Frankfort, KY: State Journal Company, 1925), 37.

64. Atwood S. Wilson, "Research Abstracts on Negro Education," *Kentucky Negro Educational Association Journal* 3, no. 2 (January–February 1933): 18, at http://kdl.kyvl.org/catalog/xt72v698690418?.

65. Adam Fairclough, *Teaching Equality: Black Schools in the Jim Crow South* (Athens: University of Georgia Press, 2016), 1–2, 4–5, 9.

66. Fairclough, *Teaching Equality,* 6–8.

67. Donna Jordan-Taylor, "African American Educators Misconstrued," *Journal of African American History* 95, no. 1 (2010): 92. For more on Black educators, segregated education, and the role of Black women, see Vanessa Siddle Walker, *Their Highest Potential: An African American School Community in the Segregated South* (Chapel Hill: University of North Carolina Press, 1996); David S. Cecelski, *Along Freedom Road: Hyde County, North Carolina, and the Fate of Black Schools in the South* (Chapel Hill University of North Carolina Press, 1994); and Carter J. Savage, "Cultural Capital and African American Agency: The Economic Struggle for Effective Education for African Americans in Franklin, Tennessee, 1890–1967," *Journal of African American History* 87 (2002): 206–35.

68. Anderson, *Education of Blacks in the South,* 114–15.

69. The seven-teacher Rosenwald School in Logan County was built prior to 1920 under the Tuskegee Institute and cost $11,550. Of this total, Russellville Blacks paid $500, while local whites donated $150, and Rosenwald paid $1,200.

See Rosenwald School, Russellville, KY, Rosenwald Database, at http://Rosenwald.fisk.edu/.

70. Alice Dunnigan, *Alone atop the Hill: The Autobiography of Alice Dunnigan, Pioneer of the National Black Press* (Athens: University of Georgia Press, 2015), xi, 34–35.

71. Dunnigan, *Alone atop the Hill,* 79–81.

72. "Contributions for the Colored League," *Winchester (KY) News,* December 18, 1908, 3; "Mr. John W. Compton Gets Appointment," *Winchester News,* March 11, 1909, 6.

73. Jerry Cecil, *Handout of Early Clark County Colored Schools 1869–1930,* pamphlet, p. 115, Clark County Deed Book 107, Clark County Court House, Winchester, KY; Rosenwald School, Winchester, KY, Rosenwald Database, at http://Rosenwald.fisk.edu/.

74. Vanessa Siddle Walker, *Their Highest Potential: An African American School Community in the Segregated South* (Chapel Hill: University of North Carolina Press, 1996), 71.

75. "P. T. A. Raises $1,000 in Three Days," *Louisville Leader,* April 11, 1925, *Louisville Leader* Collection, 1917–1950, Archives and Special Collections, University of Louisville, Louisville, KY, at https://digital.library.louisville.edu/cdm/ref/collection/leader/id/3128.

76. Rosenwald School, Henderson, KY, Rosenwald Database, at http://Rosenwald.fisk.edu/.

77. "Application for Jeanes Fund Aid," Adair County, KY, 1932, box 23, folder 3, Southern Education Foundation Archives, Robert W. Woodruff Library, Atlanta University Center, Atlanta, GA; application for Jeanes Fund Aid, Muhlenberg County, 1932, box 23, folder 3, Southern Education Foundation Archives.

78. Application for Jeanes Fund Aid, Fayette County, KY, 1936, box 25, folder 3, Southern Education Foundation Archives; application for Jeanes Fund Aid, Fayette County, KY, 1939, box 113, folder 13, Southern Education Foundation Archives.

8

"Home Ain't Always Where the Heart Is"

African American Women, Confinement, and Domestic Violence in the Gilded Age Bluegrass

Charlene J. Fletcher

Each May, horse racing fans gather in Louisville for the Kentucky Derby. The festivities are dotted with bourbon-filled mint juleps, fancy hats, and rousing renditions of Stephen Foster's ballad "My Old Kentucky Home" from 1853. For some Derby goers, Foster, a Pennsylvania native, conjured visions of a nurturing, humble environment—a place they really could call home. However, all whiskey is not bourbon, the home is not a monolithic space, and for many Kentuckians home was anything but nurturing. Foster's original ballad spoke of Kentucky's enslaved African American population as "darkies" and sang of the end of confinement by being "sold down river" to meet death on sugar plantations.[1] These stanzas are unfamiliar to today's Derby revelers, but they speak directly to the central Kentucky "home" of Fannie Keys Harvey and Lila White. A home of enslavement and, even after emancipation, a home of confinement. These women navigated homes filled with family violence and the limitations of social and economic mobility. This essay argues that for many Black women, including Fannie and Lila, the home served as a site of confinement with two distinct, restrictive forces: domestic labor and domestic violence. I further argue that freedom wasn't the main objective in the midst of the struggles in the home but rather a temporary respite or relief provided by the transition to other—state-sanctioned forms—of confinement.

Rural Bourbon County is approximately twenty-two miles from Lexington's urban center and was the birthplace and first home of Fannie Keys Harvey. Fannie was presumably born free in December 1865 to George and Hannah Kees in a small Bourbon County town called Centerville, and by 1870 the Kees family, along with Fannie's younger sister, Mattie, lived with several other families in a boardinghouse.[2] Centerville sits at the junction of the Paris–Georgetown and Lexington–Cynthiana Roads. The town became a frequent stop for farmers taking produce and livestock to market; as a result, Centerville's population increased, and so 1,167 people—668 white and 499 African Americans—made the town their home by 1870. Centerville maintained several shops, taverns, and a blacksmith, and it was a stop on the railroad.[3] The town was also known for its large African American population. Black Centerville residents came to enjoy a Baptist church, a school, two general stores, two blacksmiths, a post office, and a physician's office.[4]

In Lexington, Fayette County's bustling metropolis, lived Lila B. White, a young domestic laborer and a member of the city's Black middle-class community. The Whites were one of Lexington's most respected Black families. Lila was the youngest of five children born to Peter and Jemima White on March 11, 1875.[5] She was quite young when her mother died, and in 1882 Peter married his second wife, Eliza Johnson.[6] The couple were members of the First African Baptist Church, the oldest Black congregation west of the Allegheny Mountains. Peter worked as a driver for W. J. Treacy and R. E. Wilson, proprietors of Horseman's Headquarters, one of the leading businesses that served Lexington's horse-farming and racing industries.[7]

Yet despite differences in family structures, rural and urban landscapes, and conditions of employment, Fannie and Lila shared similar experiences of confinement in the home. For many Black women like Fannie and Lila, the home served as a site of confinement, where they lived in the shadow of domestic labor and domestic violence.

Domestic Labor

By 1880, fifteen-year-old Fannie worked as a live-in domestic in the home of Elizabeth Rank, a white widow. Fannie shared this living space with

Rank's adult children, Isaac, Nellie, and Maggie, and a seventeen-year-old Black farmhand named James Robertson. Fannie's closest relative was her grandmother, for whom she was named and who worked on the nearby Cantrell farm. Census records do not reveal where Fannie's parents or younger sister, Mattie, lived in 1880, but apparently the small family had left both Fannie and Bourbon County behind.[8]

After the Civil War, employment in Kentucky's urban centers was scarce, and newly arriving migrants faced not only significant competition from long-standing residents seeking work but also high unemployment rates. Economic opportunities in rural areas were just as bleak as Black agricultural laborers faced pressure to find employment under Kentucky's new vagrancy laws. Vagrancy had originated as a criminal statute of England's poor laws. Designed to target the poor and working class, the law encompassed offenses such as drunkenness, prostitution, disorderly conduct, panhandling, and trespassing.[9] After the Civil War, southern states passed similar statutes as a way to control the movements of recently freed African Americans. Kentucky's vagrancy laws, passed in 1869, permitted the sale at auction of people charged with unemployment and/or homelessness for indefinite periods of time.[10] Scarce employment opportunities made it easy for law enforcement to arrest and confine newly emancipated people throughout the Commonwealth. Many rural Black laborers thus turned to sharecropping, domestic work, and other labor contracts with white farmers and in white households to avoid what was essentially a return to slavery. The contracts usually resulted in conflicts between Blacks and whites, however. White employers consistently accused Black laborers of being lazy or of stealing or of terminating their employment at will. In 1866, the Kentucky Legislature passed a law that in order to be considered valid, a contract had to be "fulfilled in its entirety" and witnessed by a white person. These stipulations proved to be painful reminders of slavery as Black laborers were typically forced to forfeit all the wages they had earned when white employers deliberately terminated contracts prematurely to try and avoid paying their laborers.[11]

Other forms of labor agreements common in postemancipation Kentucky included apprenticeships, which were typically used to employ Black children, "whether orphaned, abandoned, or poverty stricken,"[12] and contracts for Kentucky's domestic workers, who, regardless of location, earned between only $25 and $125 per year. Contracted domestic workers not only complained about their low wages but also spoke of "eight-day weeks" and abusive treatment from their employers.[13] Fifteen-year-old Fannie's employment was likely dictated by one of these domestic-labor contracts. The agreement would have included the length of service, wages, and the conditions of boarding. Although the US census of 1880 reveals that Fannie was employed in Elizabeth Rank's home, when she began working there is unknown. It is possible that she was orphaned or abandoned and had entered into an apprenticeship in the Rank household. These contracts were the standard method of employing children and/or placing them in trades.[14]

Although Lila was not orphaned, she also may have been employed via an apprenticeship, but her family's socioeconomic status enabled her to work for a member of Lexington's elite. Her experience was in stark contrast to Fannie's rural toils in domestic work. Lila began working as a live-out domestic at age eleven, and by fifteen she worked in the Mill Street home of the Fayette County comptroller, Frank Bissicks. The details of Lila's contract with the Bissicks family are unknown, but the archive reveals that she consistently endured physical punishment at her own home for staying "away too much nights." During those nights "away," she could be found in the Bissicks house, learning to read and write, finding refuge in her employer's home from the abuse that she suffered at 55 Dewees Street at the hands of both her father and her stepmother.[15]

Contracts applied to all domestic workers, but those who worked as live-in domestics experienced a greater loss of freedom than those who lived out. The employer's home stood as a site of confinement because a working woman's diet, living quarters, and movement were dictated by those who paid her salary. Some Black domestics shared the same meals as their employer, albeit in the kitchen or another segregated area, but others were compelled to eat separate meals with cheaper ingredients. The work week was also a source of contention: domestics were supposed to have Sunday as a day of rest but were often given additional tasks to complete that day.[16] Restricted living quarters also limited a domestic worker's ability to entertain guests, which interfered with her ability to foster relationships, and it also increased the likelihood of sexual abuse by white employers. Black women always had the threat of sexual abuse hanging over them, but that threat increased for those who lived in white households.[17]

Although both Lila and Fannie ultimately resorted to crime, each first negotiated her confinement in the home through truancy. Stephanie M. H. Camp defines truancy as "temporary escapes from the oppressive regimes that compelled [enslaved people] to work as drudges for most of their lives and that intended to limit the time for and meanings of independent activity." Antebellum truants would periodically run to nearby plantations, swamps, or woods for brief periods of time—overnight and up to several weeks—only to return to the plantation. Gender ideals and family dynamics—in particular the prevalence of female-headed households, the stigma placed on women who abandoned their children, and the importance placed on familial duty in relationship to Black womanhood—meant that more women committed truancy rather than becoming permanent runaways.[18] Although Camp's discussion of truancy is rooted in slavery in the antebellum South, it certainly applies to Gilded Age Kentucky of the late nineteenth century.

Fannie appears to have entered into a sexual relationship with William Shropshire, a white bachelor who owned a neighboring farm. The Shropshires were a prominent white planter family in central Kentucky and were very active in Bourbon County politics. Young William was a single farmer who lived with his sister and widowed mother across the road from the Rank farm. In 1882, Fannie became pregnant by Shropshire and delivered a healthy baby boy named George in June 1883. It may have been a struggle for Fannie to reveal her relationship with William Shropshire and his paternity of her child. The archive doesn't tell us if Fannie's relationship with Shropshire was consensual. However, revealing the relationship and pregnancy may have terminated her employment contract in the Rank household, subsequently creating more significant financial obstacles to caring for her young son.[19] Perhaps Fannie used the relationship to avoid sexual abuse by her employer's son, Isaac Rank. This strategy would not have offered Fannie complete liberation from the sexual advances of white men, in particular those of her employer, but it may have given her the ability to negotiate her safety and the terms of her sexuality while confined in her employer's home.

Fannie could have engaged in a relationship with her coworker, James Robertson, or another person of color, but a relationship with the prominent William Shropshire may have offered her more protection. The idea of having a consensual relationship with one white man in order to stave off the advances of an employer or slave owner correlates with the experiences of the slave Harriet Jacobs, who in her narrative speaks of a similar strategy to block the abuses of her owner, Dr. Flint.[20] The act of using one's sexuality to negotiate the home as a confined space supports Tera

Hunter's argument that Black women often viewed freedom as meaningless without "ownership and control over one's body."[21] Fannie's relationship with William Shropshire could also be considered an act of truancy because it offered Fannie a temporary escape from the working and living conditions in the Rank household.

Her relationship with the eligible Shropshire likely caused quite the controversy in Bourbon County. For some unknown reason, Fannie lost her job working for the Rank family. She may have been fired for breach of contract for getting pregnant. Other white families in the area could have viewed Fannie's pregnancy as grounds for premature termination of her contract as a domestic worker. Elizabeth Rank may have refused to increase Fannie's wages, making it impossible for the girl to provide for her infant. In addition, the pregnancy might have been what ultimately encouraged Fannie to move to Lexington in search of improved economic prospects. Regardless of the reason, Fannie Keys Harvey was only one of the many Black Centerville natives who made the move to Lexington during the 1880s. Despite its economic and community successes, Centerville's population dwindled in the 1880s as more and more Black residents made their way to nearby urban centers for the cities' perceived "better" economic opportunities.[22]

Black Life in the Postbellum Bluegrass

Postemancipation Black populations in Lexington, Louisville, and Covington boomed as newly freed Blacks sought out new lives and new opportunities, hoping to create new homes, escape racial violence, and cut ties to their former owners.[23] Between 1860 and 1870, Lexington blossomed into a bustling metropolis. The city's white population grew at a rate of 20 percent, while the Black population boomed more than 130 percent within the city limits and surrounding counties. The area held the largest concentration of Blacks in the state.[24] However, these new Black communities struggled with rampant disease, inadequate housing, and minimal economic opportunities.[25] The growing postbellum Black population was clustered inside the city limits near stockyards, bridges, and railroads, particularly along Town Branch, a large tributary of the Kentucky River that flowed through the city. Black Lexingtonians created neighborhoods such as Goodloetown, Kinkeadtown, Lee's Row, Taylortown, and Brucetown, often named for the estate or developer responsible for the land. Residents lived in "shotgun"-style, single-family homes, typically one room wide and three to five rooms deep, while alleyways and narrow streets provided access to these communities from larger city blocks.[26] Older, antebellum Black settlements in downtown Lexington remained, but as the urban sprawl continued in the 1880s, Town Branch became polluted and filled in to accommodate new construction.[27]

Lila White and her family were residents of Lexington's East End, occupying homes on Short, Wilson, and Dewees Streets at various times. The East End neighborhood was interracial yet segregated; Black families filled in particular areas of the neighborhood such as Dewees Street, while whites occupied homes on East Third Street. The neighborhood was home to several African American businesses, including a pharmacy, and German immigrants owned and operated grocery and butcher shops in the area. In the 1940s, the East End became home to the Lyric Theatre, an African American entertainment hub and Lexington's answer to Harlem's Apollo Theater.[28]

Once Fannie Keys Harvey was in Lexington, she lived only a few blocks from Lila but in a very different section of downtown Lexington, known as Branch Alley. Branch Alley was located on East Water Street (now East Vine) between Ayres Alley and South Mulberry Street (now South Limestone) in the heart of the city's central business district. By 1890, Branch Alley was the only section of town that still had access to Town Branch, but the creek offered nothing but polluted, stagnant water that Branch Alley residents often used for washing. In 1888, local newspapers described Branch Alley as "a stream of almost living filth," and because the alley was situated at the foot of Hill Street, it was prone to flooding during storms. In addition, unlike African American residents in other downtown Lexington alleyway communities, most Branch Alley residents rented rooms from white absentee landlords.[29] The area was known for numbers running, violence, and prostitution and was described as "a hotbed of sin and wretchedness[,] an abode of filth and misery."[30]

Wage-labor disputes between Black workers and white landowners were a common cause of racial violence in the state, and Black women suffered the greatest injustices in any industry. In 1911, Governor Augustus E. Willson ordered a state commission to investigate women's working conditions. The report consistently noted that the state's segregated workforce ensured that Black women had access only to the lowest wages and worst working conditions and that they were typically restricted to piece-rate employment—compensation based on the number of units completed, not on the number of hours worked—while their white counterparts were paid a weekly salary.[31]

Despite their paltry wages, Black people managed to establish churches, benevolent societies, and other social organizations that helped to create places of respite from the constrictions of Progressive Era race, class, and gender ideologies. In 1903, the Kentucky Association of Colored Women's Clubs was established and immediately began working to address public-health concerns facing the Black community. The organization, comprising mainly middle- and upper-class Black women, worked alongside Black churches and used Black uplift ideologies to demonstrate to whites that Blacks were worthy of citizenship.[32] Black uplift ideologies focused on respectability and material and moral improvement among African Americans to combat white racism.

Lexington went through a technological revolution in the 1880s. Electricity replaced gas streetlamps and residential lighting, and the city made improvements to the waterworks, streetcar system, and railroad service.[33] As Lexington grew, people from surrounding rural areas came to start new lives in the metropolis, and African Americans were among the new groups of migrants entering the city. These changes led to an economic boom, increasing employment opportunities and encouraging the development of new businesses. Black bakeries, groceries, furniture stores, and barbershops prospered, and Black men found work in cigar shops and as handymen and gardeners, carriage men in the horse industry, and laborers in hemp and tobacco factories.[34]

Kali Gross argues that southern Black women at this time began to move north, with their sights on economic opportunity, personal autonomy, citizenship, and "a reclamation and reconfiguration of womanhood."[35] Upon their arrival in northern cities, however, Black women were once again confined to domestic-service positions, while white women often filled the available factory jobs. Like their sisters in other cities, Black women in Lexington often worked as laundresses or were hired to wait on tables as the city's hospitality industry grew, but the vast majority of the city's working Black women found employment only as domestic servants.[36] Domestic labor controlled Black women's quality of life and housing options. Low wages confined working Black women to the most dilapidated areas in any given city, limiting the spaces where they could create their homes. Whereas Lila resided in a middle-class neighborhood with her father and stepmother, wages earned by domestic labor confined Fannie and her son, George, to Branch Alley, one of Lexington's hotbeds of vice and other illegal activity.[37]

Low wages and the confines of domestic labor encouraged many women to find economic opportunities beyond housework in places such as Branch Alley. The informal economy provided those opportunities, and Black women challenged the restrictions on their labor by engaging in better-paying, "unsavory professions" such as gambling and sex work. Stephanie Camp, LaShawn Harris, and Cheryl Hicks rightfully argue that parties, saloons, dance halls, and brothels were sites of pleasure,[38] but these places also served as respites from the constraints of respectability politics and Victorian ethics. Fannie's employment in the informal economy enabled her to eventually withdraw from legal or "respectable" work in domestic service. The growth of the illicit economy prompted religious and temperance reformers to be more vigilant in their quest for morality and social order in the African American community. The Black church led the charge in these reform movements. While white women's clubs and societies worked on morality and respectability, Black women utilized the politics of that respectability with the intention to help the African American community. Black reformers viewed educational attainment, Victorian morals, and the maintenance of stable homes and families as paramount to acquiring the rights of citizenship, and they used religious spaces as the platform to deliver their message.

Evelyn Brooks Higginbotham argues that the Black church was the only accessible space for the African American community, thus becoming the center of racial and gender uplift. Respectability politics has been central to uplift in the Black community, and Higginbotham defines it as adhering to standards that would acquire "a measure of esteem from white America" by means of "the Black lower class's psychological allegiance to temperance, industriousness, thrift, refined manners, and Victorian sexual morals."[39] The National Association of Colored Women's motto, "Lifting as We Climb," put uplift ideology simply: if Black people are respectable, white people will give them equal treatment and citizenship, and in turn Black respectable people would promote these ideals among the poor and working class to advance the entire race.[40]

Kentucky's Baptist churches fully embraced and promoted racial uplift strategies. Issues of civil and voting rights were initially at the forefront of church activism, but as ideals of respectability took hold, industry, temperance, and morality became the championed causes. Black men served as the face of church leadership, but Black women were very present in the movement for respectability. In 1880, Louisville church women began publishing *Our Women and Children,* a nationally acclaimed magazine that promoted juvenile literature and articles on racial uplift and morality for adults. The magazine won such fame that it attracted prominent contributors, such as Ida B. Wells. Lexington's church women were just as active. Women church leaders served as schoolteachers and held classes at Ladies' Hall, a building located in downtown Lexington on Church Street, purchased by a collective of Black women after just one year of fund-raising. The Ladies' Hall schools served as a repository of academic knowledge and a training ground for respectability and racial uplift in the Bluegrass.[41]

In the quest for a "measure of esteem from white America," class divisions were established and solidified in communities of color, even within congregations. Indeed, even those who followed the tenets of respectability could experience issues regarding respectability. The First African Baptist Church was established in 1790 by Peter "Captain" Durrett, an enslaved man born in Caroline County, Virginia. This Black congregation is the oldest in the Commonwealth of Kentucky and the third oldest in the United States. In the 1810s, Durrett copastored the congregation with London Ferrell, a biracial enslaved man who also held membership in the First Baptist Church (white) in Lexington as well as in the Elkhorn Baptist Church Association. Both Durrett and Ferrell sought the association's recognition for their congregation. Ferrell remained at the First African Baptist Church as pastor after Durrett's death, and the congregation continued to grow and purchase property to accommodate services and a religious school. Tensions then began to grow between Ferrell and one of the church's original deacons, Henry Quills, and Quills's supporters. Those issues came to a head in 1822, when Ferrell and his supporters were accused of immorality by Quills and his supporters. This resulted in a split between the factions, with Quills and his supporters establishing the Pleasant Green Baptist Church near the Patterson Stone Quarry. The congregation continues to meet on that land today. The ill will from the secession ran rampant through both churches and persisted through the nineteenth and twentieth centuries. The hostilities were known to impact familial relationships among members, including the family of Lila White. Terse discussions of the origins of the secession still take place today.[42]

Standard-bearers of respectability reinforced negative stereotypes of those who did not conform to the system's behavioral politics. Assimilation trumped self-representation, and Black culture was sanctioned by condemning certain styles of dress and music and by stifling the creativity and culture of working-class members of the community. Although respectability politics and racial uplift strategies were designed to be a moral compass for all African Americans and their capacity for citizenship, much of this burden fell on the shoulders of Black women as the mothers and nurturers of the family. Thus, Black women bore enormous responsibility for the success or failure of the race.[43]

It wasn't uncommon for Black women to engage in the underground economy in the late nineteenth century, and Kentucky didn't prove to be much different from other southern locales. In Louisville, Black businesses increased in the postbellum period, but scores of Black women continued to toil in domestic positions as laundresses, cooks, and seamstresses. In addition to being confined to manual labor, the city's Black population regularly contended with meager wages and periods of unemployment. A significant portion of the city's common laborers found lodging in filth-ridden alleyways. Some Louisville women accepted boarders; in fact, divorced and widowed women comprised one-third of those accepting boarders in their homes. Not all women took in boarders to make ends meet; many others saw economic viability in the streets.[44] Black women entered the illicit market as sex workers, numbers runners, saloon workers, peddlers, drug dealers, and thieves. LaShawn Harris argues that Black women often waived notions of "uplift" and respectability in favor of the informal economy because illicit work better allowed for "individual empowerment, self-sufficiency, and fiscal stability." Harris also notes that the "monetary earnings from informal work allowed many to sustain themselves and their families; financially assist relatives living in the South and Caribbean; [and] take care of their unemployed and lethargic husbands and male companions."[45]

In Lexington, the horse-racing industry delivered the right mix of vice to increase such economic opportunity, and this was certainly the case for Fannie. Her income provided for her son, George, as well as for her common-law husband, James Harvey, known on the streets as "Bouncer White." Bouncer, originally from Nashville, was a common laborer, hustle man, and alcoholic numbers runner with a host of violent tendencies. Young Fannie had likely met him on her daily walks while living and navigating Branch Alley. This was life for Fannie and her young son as she moved from the confines of her employer's home in rural Bourbon County to the confines of a rented home situated in poverty and filth and steeped in criminal activity in Lexington's urban alleyways. There is no evidence that Fannie turned to prostitution to make ends meet, but her arrest record shows that she was certainly exposed to and engaged in Lexington's informal economy.[46]

Domestic Violence

While domestic labor confined Black women's bodies in the homes of their white employers, domestic violence—the pattern of behaviors employed by an individual to maintain power and control over a partner in a domestic relationship—served as their captor within their own homes. The term *domestic violence* conjures up thoughts of sexual or physical violence, but it can also include psychological and emotional abuse, economic deprivation, and physical and sexual threats and intimidation, and these dynamics can be found in any type of relationship.[47]

Antebellum temperance reformers were the first to draw attention to domestic violence, focusing solely on eliminating access to alcohol to control male violence, but these advocates failed to devote any real attention to the victims. Women's rights activism developed out of this crusade in the 1840s and 1850s, pushing for divorce rights for women and providing a legal apparatus for domestic-violence victims to flee their marriages. Antebellum feminists "placed the emancipation of women ahead of the preservation of the family," stating that it was "preferable for a mother and her children to live alone rather than to remain bound to the inebriate husband."[48]

Temperance advocates identified a causal relationship between alcohol and domestic violence, and that direct correlation lingered into the twentieth century. In the eighteenth century, the family was not subject to community surveillance, and by the nineteenth century the family was completely isolated from the public eye. Popular culture also reinforced the notion of the home as the woman's sphere. Confining women to the home, publications such as *Ladies' Magazine* and *Godey's Lady's Book* presented women as defenders and enforcers of piety and modesty, while men governed economics both in and out of the home.[49]

Victorian sexual attitudes presented quite a contrast to this assumed domestic power for women. Nineteenth-century women were presumed to be chaste, lacking any passion or sexual desire, while men were considered to be "brutish," incapable of controlling their sexual urges, particularly when intoxicated. These double standards became the topic of public discourse in postbellum America as magazines and newspapers featured sensational stories of divorce, crimes of passion, and details of courtroom dramas between husbands and wives as well as between domestic partners.[50]

Fannie and her son, George, were no strangers to domestic violence. Her marriage to Bouncer White limited her finances as well as her own and her son's physical and psychological safety. It is impossible to discern when the violence began in the Keys-Harvey household, but it escalated in September 1890 when Bouncer was arrested for cutting and wounding Fannie.[51] She was arrested for the same charge, likely returning Bouncer's violence with her own. By 1891, Fannie had a long history of arrests for robbery, public intoxication, vagrancy, and improper language. Bouncer White first appears in Fayette County police court records in 1888 for a murder charge, which was dismissed in Circuit Court. He did not limit his violent behaviors to Lexington's citizens; he also regularly abused Fannie. While she was being treated at St. Joseph's Infirmary in July 1892, Bouncer was arrested for trespassing on the hospital grounds. Later that year, in September, Lexington police arrested Bouncer again for cutting and wounding Fannie. He was confined to the workhouse for the assault and was rearrested later that month for escaping from said workhouse.[52]

Domestic violence was not taken seriously during the last quarter of the nineteenth century. Lawmakers were more concerned with controlling the lower classes than with protecting victims' rights. In Lexington, no distinct city ordinances addressed domestic violence as late as 1903, with the exception of insulting language "used by a man to a woman," in which case "the highest penalty shall be imposed." The ordinance goes on to read, "The truth of the charges made may be proven in defense," thus defending Victorian standards of womanhood and patriarchy while simultaneously placing the character of the woman and the validity of her testimony in question.[53]

By the 1920s, reform efforts had failed, and family-violence cases were handled separately—spouse and child—seeking to preserve the family relationship without imposing a significant punishment on the abuser.[54]

Lila White's father, Peter, likely desired this right to privacy to govern his household as he saw fit. Peter White had been enslaved in urban Lexington and had a very different experience than most bondsmen in

Kentucky. He was born near Veracruz, Mexico, sometime between 1830 and 1840.[55] During the Mexican-American War, he worked as a body servant for an American army officer, presumably General Leslie Combs, and returned to Kentucky with Combs.[56] White was required to care for and jockey Combs's thoroughbreds, riding Boston and Lexington at the Georgetown Pike racetrack in the 1850s.[57] He was one of several enslaved men to work in the horse industry. A slave in the United States, Peter White was consistently described as "Negro" or "Colored" by census enumerators, and although he could have been Afro-Mexican, his exact heritage is unknown. He immersed himself in Lexington's African American community, however. He married Lila's mother, Jemima White, a Black laborer owned by the prominent Payne family of neighboring Scott County, and Lila was born free in Lexington in 1875.[58]

By 1890, Peter, his second wife, Eliza, and sixteen-year-old Lila lived at 55 Dewees Street and shared their home with Eliza's brother, Daniel Frazier, and his wife, Eliza, both of Louisville. The White home was described as "being furnished with more than the ordinary provision for comfort."[59] The material wealth provided very little "comfort" for Lila, though, as the Dewees Street home served as an early site of confinement. If Peter adhered to the "family ideal," Lila did too, at first. She endured regular beatings from her father, and he authorized his wife, Eliza White, to participate in those beatings. Eliza also engaged in psychological abuse, perhaps unbeknownst to Peter, by stealing Lila's clothes from her wardrobe. All the while, Lila remained quiet, perhaps from fear of the shame it would bring to the family or the worry of even greater punishment in retaliation. It does not appear that she reported the abuse to any person of authority, not even to her employer, Mrs. Frank Bissicks. Lila instead worked long hours, learned how to read, and sought comfort in alternative yet respectable social circles. Peter and Eliza claimed that Lila was "difficult to manage" and frequently beat Lila as punishment for the company she kept. That "company" was made up of members of Pleasant Green Baptist Church, the bitter rival congregation of First African Baptist Church, where Peter and Eliza held membership.[60] Although Peter deemed her behavior to be rebellious, Lila was clearly willing to challenge the confines of her home and tried to negotiate the parameters of her own freedom.

On Sunday, January 18, 1891, Lila set out for morning worship at Pleasant Green, openly defying her father's order to attend First African Baptist. Upon her return home, Peter and Eliza administered their last brutal beating for Lila's attendance at the rival church. Lila arose the next morning, still tattered and bruised from the previous evening's beating. She prepared for work, and as she left the home, she emptied a four-ounce vial of arsenic into the family's coffeepot.[61] After the remaining members of the White household—Peter, Eliza White, and Daniel and Eliza Frazier—sat down to enjoy breakfast, Peter began complaining of stomach illness and retreated to the yard, violently vomiting. As the two women began to complain of similar issues, Daniel Frazier retreated, seeking the help of one of Lexington's Black physicians, P. D. Robinson. Daniel thought he had avoided the poisoning, but upon returning to 55 Dewees Street, he, too, fell ill. Dr. Robinson administered milk, albumen, and lard, standard antidotes for arsenic poisoning, but within forty minutes of Dr. Robinson's arrival Daniel Frazier was dead.[62] Eliza White was the only member of the household well enough to lead police and Dr. Robinson to connect Lila to the arsenic in the coffee grounds. As Dr. Robinson conducted and confirmed the ingestion of arsenic using the Marsh Test, Lexington police officers Reagan and Hale made their way to the Bissicks home to arrest sixteen-year-old Lila White.[63] Although the two women on which this chapter focuses, Fannie and Lila, came from two very distinct walks of life—rural and urban, working and middle class, illicit and respectable economies—their confining homes placed them on similar trajectories, and these pathways similarly came to a tragic destination in February 1891, when they met, presumably for the first time, as confined women in the Fayette County Jail.

Confinement in the Fayette County Jail

The desperate resort of a desperate girl to rid herself of parental control—she awakens to find herself a murderess.
—*Lexington Press,* January 20, 1891

Word of the White family poisoning spread like wildfire. After several hours at the police station, Lila supposedly admitted to receiving a bottle of arsenic from another teenage domestic, Lizzie Hawkins, in whom she had confided the abuse. Further investigation concluded that Lizzie Hawkins knew of the abuse Lila endured but that she was not involved in the poisoning. The press alleged that Lila implicated Lizzie after a disagreement, likely to depict Lila as manipulative and callous. Lila then confessed to receiving the poison from another teenage girl, Julia Miller, and to pouring the powder from a small bottle bearing a skull and cross-bones into the coffee pot, stating defensively that she only sought to make her stepmother ill.[64]

Local papers enthralled Lexington residents with the tale, and much of the Bluegrass region considered Lila's behavior to be "unbelievable" or "amazing," considering that she had been raised by "respectable colored parents." Respectability provided Lila no relief, however, as the press deemed her to be "nothing more than a callous wench." Journalists also critiqued her demeanor with headlines that read she "bears her imprison-ment well," although she "says she's getting tired of it."[65]

In the first few days of her incarceration at the county jail, Lila was visited by prominent members of Bluegrass society, including John Payne, the Fayette County fiscal judge. Payne's family had at one time enslaved Lila's mother, Jemima, and her grandmother, Mishea Thomas, who remained in the Paynes' Scott County home as a domestic worker. Payne reportedly came to offer Lila love and greetings from her grandmother, who was not well enough to make the trip to Lexington, and Lila tearfully confessed to Judge Payne, saying, "I bet I never do such a crazy thing again."[66] The coroner's jury returned two indictments against Lila for the murders of Daniel and Eliza Frazier on February 2, 1891, and she was remanded to the Fayette County Jail, where on February 14 she met Fan-nie Keys Harvey.[67]

Fannie had been arrested and indicted for robbing Thomas Howard, a white man, of $3.75 on December 8, 1890, in Lexington. She was held over on a $200 bond and remained in jail. While she was incarcerated, her son, young George, experienced his first arrest for petit larceny on Sep-tember 2, 1891. He was but nine years old at the time of the arrest, and this was likely the first time he saw or was even remotely close to his mother since her arrest.[68] The archive does not indicate where George resided during Fannie's incarceration. There is no record of his enrollment at the Lexington Colored Orphan Industrial Home, and it is possible that he lived with his aunt Mattie until Fannie's release.

Fayette County Circuit Court, May Term, 1891

The May term of the Fayette County Circuit Court was a busy one. Judge Jeremiah Morton began the term by admonishing the all-male jury to "look after the morals" of society and "into the general welfare of your neighbor."[69] The fifteen white men, twelve jurors and three alternates, employed as farmers and local merchants, were sworn in and prepared to tackle those charged with a crime in the Commonwealth's docket. Fannie and Lila were among the lot.[70] Lila's attorneys, James R. Jewell and George C. Webb, demanded the two murder indictments be thrown out, claiming Lila was illegally forced to appear before the grand jury, which would have been questionable considering a defendant was not required by law to appear before a grand jury, particularly if her counsel was not notified of the prosecution's request.[71] The tactic failed. Lila and Fannie entered the courtroom on May 26, 1891. Fannie's case was disposed of that morning, and she was quickly convicted of robbing Thomas Howard and sentenced to a year in the county jail. Local newspapers commonly listed Circuit Court adjudications, and the *Lexington Press* mocked Fannie's conviction, saying she had been ordered to "stay with Uncle Billy Wilkerson," the county jailer, "but she will have an opportunity to inspect the inside of the new city jail."[72]

Lila's trial began at 3:00 that afternoon. Despite sensationalized reporting by the press, the case failed to draw a crowd. The seventeen-year-old Lila appeared before Judge Morton, the white male jury, and prosecutors C. J. Bronston and John R. Allen.[73] Peter White, Lila's father, was the first to testify against his daughter. He recounted the events of the day of the poisoning, the weeks of suffering and healing he and his wife, Eliza White, experienced, and appeared woeful to the jury and journalists, hoping to "shield his daughter, and if possible, save her from a judicial death." Peter's testimony touted his care and concern for Lila, although he claimed she was "inclined to be a trifle wild child," and the jury appeared sympathetic toward him, even though he was a "Negro." Eliza White, the stepmother who had physically and psychologically abused Lila, was the only other witness who testified that day and offered her account of the poisoning. The defense tried to cast doubt on Lila's guilt by demonstrating that other parties would have rejoiced at the death of Daniel and Eliza Frazier, but by the end of the first day of testimony the journalists observing the trial reported that the jury didn't buy the defense.[74]

The second day of Lila's trial drew a much larger crowd. C. J. Bronston opened the trial with testimony from Julia Miller, the fourteen-year-old acquaintance who had supplied Lila with the arsenic. Julia told the court that Lila had asked her to go to the drugstore to purchase five cents' worth

Ad for Rough on Rats, c. 1870–1900. Courtesy of the Boston Public Library Digital Commonwealth.

of "Rough on Rats." The pharmacist told Julia he could not sell such a powerful substance in such small quantities, but he could sell her a small vile of pure arsenic. When Julia reported back to Lila, Lila told her to return to the druggist to make the purchase, instructing Julia to say it would serve a "special purpose."[75] In response, the defense tried to argue that the confessions made at the time of Lila's arrest were inadmissible as wild utterances, but the court deemed that Lila's admissions stood. Lila then took the stand in her own defense and recounted the mistreatment she had endured from her stepmother, in particular the regular beatings and the theft of her clothes. Lila was composed on the stand, so much so that the press criticized her as lacking "any emotion," and she answered "all the questions clearly and distinctly." She testified that she knew nothing of the poisoning until the officers arrived at the Bissicks home and that it was the officers who urged her to confess with the promise of release. After she provided her account of the poisoning, the defense called a number of character witnesses—unnamed in the court record and newspaper accounts—who defended Lila's impeccable reputation. The second day of testimony concluded with these words weighing on the minds of the jurors.[76]

Bronston and Jewell gave closing arguments on the third day, and the jury left to deliberate that afternoon. The jurors were deadlocked into the wee hours of the morning, and public opinion was that the jury would fail to reach a verdict. At noon on May 29, 1891, the civil servants returned to the courtroom. It was a hung jury—two members of the jury believed Lila was innocent. She had dodged a death sentence, at least for now, but Bronston was prepared to move forward with a second trial in the Circuit Court's November term.[77]

Fayette County Circuit Court, November Term, 1891

The November term began with Lila and Fannie in the Fayette County Jail and Fannie's husband, Bouncer White, appearing in court again for a new charge of malicious cutting and wounding of a Black woman named Laura Peyton. During a Saturday night of drinking in November 1891, Bouncer was at Peyton's home when "other parties" arrived. Bouncer got angry, and when he threw beer in Peyton's face, she ordered him out of the house. Bouncer then broke a beer glass and cut Peyton's thigh, leaving her bedridden for twelve days. Bouncer was convicted of "cutting in sudden heat and passion" and remanded to the county jail until a fine of $200 could be paid to the court.[78] Bouncer thus joined Fannie and Lila behind bars.

Lila's second trial began on November 30, 1891. C. J. Bronston returned for the Commonwealth and placed Lila on the stand first to recount her story yet again. Lila revealed that she had begun working as a domestic at the age of eleven and had generally remained home on Sundays. She openly declared that she had never held any ill will toward Eliza's brother, Daniel Frazier, or his wife but reiterated the conflict she had with her stepmother. Lila corroborated her father's previous testimony about being beaten for attending Pleasant Green Baptist Church. She and her stepmother, Eliza, had not been on speaking terms for two weeks prior to the poisoning because Eliza was in the habit of stealing her clothes. When Lila had confronted Eliza about it, the woman told Lila that if she did not like it, she "had better keep the wardrobe locked." The night of the final beating, Lila had left the wardrobe unlocked. The defense took this opportunity to create reasonable doubt by inferring that this meant someone else could have placed the vial of arsenic in Lila's wardrobe without her knowledge.[79]

In addition to Lila's testimony, the jury heard from the arresting officers. Officer Hale recounted the excited utterances of both Lila and Peter. When he had arrived on the scene at the White house, Hale had asked Peter who poisoned him, to which Peter replied, "Nobody but my poor little daughter." Hale had used that response in an effort to appeal to Lila's emotions. Hale had spoken to her, saying, "Lila, you have laid your uncle and aunt out on the cooling board, and your poor old father will soon be dead." "Oh, let me go to see my papa before he dies," Lila had responded. "Papa whipped me and made me mad, and I threw the pisin [sic] in the coffee pot before I left." Hale's recollection of his conversation with Lila seemed to be particularly damning, so the defense followed it with another round of character witnesses, including Judge Payne, Mrs. Bissicks, and her daughters. The day concluded with closing arguments and jury instructions, and the deliberations on Lila's fate began yet again. After another three-day trial, the jury returned for a second time without a unanimous verdict. This time, only one juror held out for acquittal. Bronston would not relinquish his pursuit of Lila, however. She returned to the county jail to await trial number three.[80]

Fayette County Circuity Court, May Term, 1892

Lila's two previous trials had resulted in a hung jury, a jury that fails to reach a verdict within the required voting margin, which in this case had to be unanimous. Hung juries typically lead to a retrial of the case because no verdict has been rendered, and double-jeopardy protections are not guaranteed. It is not clear why Bronston and Allen were so persistent in pursuing this case.[81] Lila was scheduled to appear for her third trial during the March 1892 term, but before the court could reconvene, she made the news yet again. In January 1892, word of a massive jailbreak scheme circulated throughout the Bluegrass and as far north as Cincinnati. Three trustees, Bouncer White, Hamp Hathaway, and Bob Branch had concocted an escape plan, stealing the jailer's keys and unlocking a manhole cover in the pavement adjacent to the jail door. The press called it a "most cunning" escape plot, "made feasible by the new jail's peculiar construction." Twenty incarcerated people were planning to escape, among them Lila White and most likely Bouncer's wife, Fannie Keys Harvey. The whole thing failed when another inmate alerted the jailer's staff about the plot. Bouncer, Hathaway, and Branch were placed in thumb stalls until they confessed the details to Jailer Wilkerson.[82] The failed jailbreak orchestrated by Hathaway and Bouncer, although daring, would have likely been short-lived. If and when law enforcement apprehended the motley crew, they would have faced additional charges, or the escape may have been considered a mitigating circumstance to increase their sentences at the time of conviction. Lila became the focus of the headlines as one of the inmates who was planning to break out of the jail, especially since rumors were already brewing that a rescue attempt was being planned on her behalf by members of the local Black community.[83] Newspaper accounts never made it exactly clear just who these rogue members of the community supposedly were.

Additional rumors now began to surface about Lila and her supposed "condition," and in March 1892 a meeting was called at Ladies' Hall by prominent, respectable Black men in the community to investigate if Lila were pregnant. Word of the meeting spread as far north as Louisville, but minutes of the meeting—if any were taken—cannot be located.[84] A grand jury also investigated rumors of Lila's pregnancy, but news reports stated that no evidence was found to substantiate the claim. Lila, however, was indeed pregnant, and the *Cincinnati Enquirer* named "Allen Hathaway," the jailbreak mastermind, as the father of her child.[85] It is likely that the paper was referring to the incarcerated man Hamilton "Hamp" Hathaway, son of Reverend Allen Hathaway, a respected Lexington minister, and printed the name incorrectly. According to his death record, Allen Hathaway was born in 1839 and served as a private in the United States Colored Troops during the Civil War. His son Hamp was born in 1869, the second of three children, and is listed as the father on the death certificate of Lila's daughter, Miami Saunders. Census records use the names "Hampton" and "Hamilton" interchangeably, and city directories reveal that three men, Allen and his sons, Hamp and Robert, maintained residences at 445 Mill Street and 737 Mill Street over a period of three decades. The US census of 1900 serves as an example of the interchanging of names, with the father, Allen, listed as "Robert," sharing the home with both sons.[86]

The *Enquirer* was the only newspaper to run any story related to the jailbreak or to Lila's pregnancy. According to the *Lexington Morning Transcript,* the *Enquirer* correspondent was a friend of Lila's attorneys and likely had an interest in pushing another angle of such a sensationalized case, but the *Transcript,* one of Lexington's major local newspapers, refused to publish the story, despite rumors of the jailbreak and the pregnancy, due to the "feeling of delicacy and a disinclination to do possible injury to the officials responsible for the young woman's safekeeping."[87]

Lila had lived with the confining force of domestic violence in the home, and her "truancy" had manifested in late nights spent learning to read and write in her employer's home. Her attendance at Pleasant Green Baptist Church had been another form of temporary escape from the confinement she experienced at home, providing brief opportunities to worship and commune in a space of her own choosing, independent of her abusers and the definitions of respectability enforced by her parents. While incarcerated in the county jail, Lila's sexual relationship with Hamp Hathaway possibly allowed her control over her own body and of her carceral space and served as a mental and physical escape from the regulations of imprisonment, or it may have been another instance in which Lila experienced abuse. Lila could not have known for certain she would get pregnant; no couple trying to conceive ever knows for sure when pregnancy will occur. What is clear is that she had sex with Hamp Hathaway, although it is not known if their relationship developed as a respite of momentary pleasure while incarcerated or from calculated need or by force. The resulting pregnancy may or may not have been desired, but it did serve as another form of resistance against the expectations of her father and of a community that embraced racial uplift ideologies. Further, the sexual relationship and her resulting pregnancy ultimately served as Lila's permanent escape from the gallows and a life sentence in prison. Lila's and Fannie's truancy thus allowed both women to negotiate the terms of their confinement and served as a form of resistance against their abusers. It is important to note that these acts of resistance also preceded the inevitable measures of violence each woman used to protest the restrictions she experienced in her home.

The May 1892 term and Lila's third trial approached. Lila, now eighteen years old, was visibly pregnant and confessed that Hamp Hathaway—one of the jailbreak leaders—was the father of her child. Lila had initially been indicted on two counts of murder, so she entered the third trial facing the death penalty or life in prison if convicted. Journalists with the *Lexington Morning Transcript* argued that Lila did not "expect or fear such a result."[88] Knowing public sentiment in the Commonwealth would not sanction the execution of a pregnant woman, Lila accepted a plea of one count of voluntary manslaughter with a term of fifteen years in the Kentucky State Penitentiary at Frankfort.

Conclusion

Warsan Shire's poem "The House" uses the home as a metaphor for a woman's body. Each body contains rooms of lust, grief, and apathy that a woman has allowed a man to enter and at times damage while occupying it. Shire notes, "Sometimes the men—they come with keys / and sometimes, the men—they come with hammers." Keys can unlock spaces in pursuit of freedom or lock doors for confinement.[89] For Lila, her father, Peter, certainly came with keys. Lila loved her father, as evidenced by the way she wept for him in her jail cell and by the way he spoke of her in his testimony, but as Peter's reputation grew, his adherence to the tenets of respectability solidified. His keys to Lila's physical and emotional bodies began locking her doors and confining her to the family ideal and a reinforcement of patriarchy through Victorian morals and racial uplift ideologies. For Fannie, William Shropshire may have freed her from the advances of her employer, but he also placed her in the confines of motherhood and lack of opportunity. And while Bouncer White may have initially appeared as a loving companion, his hammers of domestic violence locked Fannie and her son, George, in a revolving door of confinement from home to hospital to prison.

Fannie was released from the county jail in June 1892 and reunited with George. Although freed from a carceral space, she returned to a confining home with Bouncer White. The small family relocated to Covington, Kentucky, shortly after Bouncer's release from jail. Lila was admitted to the Kentucky State Penitentiary on June 28, 1892, and in October she suffered a miscarriage. These transitions meant that Lila and Fannie temporarily parted ways, but their responses to confinement would reunite them once again at the Frankfort Penitentiary in 1895.

Home should be a warm space, one that provides a respite from long laboring days, comfort from the world's troubles, and safety from the dangers you meet on life's journey. But the lives of Fannie Keys Harvey and Lila B. White demonstrate how the home could also be a site of confinement through the toils of domestic labor and the pains of domestic violence. The 1890s witnessed significant activism among women for temperance and suffrage, but whereas the right to vote was imperative to the women's movement during the Gilded Age, the ability to challenge gendered confinement seemed impossible. Everything has a history, and Fannie and Lila's stories are much older than the advancements made in the domestic-violence movement. Fannie and Lila's voices are significant— significant in revealing how survivors established agency—and encourage historians to reconsider concepts such as gender, kinship, violence, and resistance. They did not have access to the resources available today, and recent changes to domestic-violence-related legislation hinder others from accessing those resources even in the twenty-first century. These stories give historians new perspectives in identifying and examining survivors' stories in the archive and must encourage us to take a critical look at how we define family violence and how we work to eradicate it in our communities. So while we celebrate the warrior women who championed suffrage, let us also remember the unknown women who negotiated for freedom in their own homes.

Notes

1. Stephen Collins Foster, "My Old Kentucky Home" (Pond, Firth, 1853), Notated Music, Library of Congress, at https://www.loc.gov/item/ihas.200187239/.

2. US Bureau of the Census, Ninth Census of the United States, 1870, Centerville, Bourbon County, KY, roll M593_447, p. 2783A, image 31, Ancestry.com. The family appears on enumeration records spelling their surname "Kees." Subsequent court, prison, and vital records document Fannie's surname as "Keys" or "Keyes." For simplification, the spelling "Keys" is used in this essay.

3. D. G. Beers, *Atlas of Bourbon, Clark, Fayette, Jessamine, and Woodford Counties, KY: From Actual Surveys and Official Records* (Philadelphia: J. H. Toudy, 1877), 4.

4. *Bourbon County Towns,* exhibition, Hopewell Museum, Paris, KY. For more on Bourbon County history, see H. E. Everman, *The History of Bourbon County, 1785–1865* (Bourbon County, KY: Bourbon Press, 1977).

5. US Bureau of the Census, Tenth Census of the United States, 1880, Lexington, Fayette County, KY, roll 412, p. 273B, Enumeration District 065, image 0739, Ancestry.com; "Lila White (col), Certificate of Death," file 32670, Bureau of Vital Statistics, Kentucky Department for Libraries and Archives (KDLA), Frankfort.

6. "White, Peter, and Johnson, Liza," Record of Colored Marriages, 1882, p. 179, Fayette County Clerk's Office, Lexington, KY.

7. Pleasant Green Baptist Church and the First African Baptist Church engaged in a long-standing feud regarding land ownership and naming rights in the early nineteenth century. The hostilities were known to impact familial relationships among members, including the family of Lila White. See "By Poison," *Lexington Press,* January 20, 1891, 1; and L. H. McIntyre, *One Grain of the Salt: The First African Baptist Church West of the Allegheny Mountains* (Lexington, KY: n.p., 1986), 1.

8. It is also possible George and Hannah Keyes died prior to 1880. The 1880 US census lists several people with the same name in Lexington, and the 1900

census lists a couple of people with the same names and similar ages living in western Kentucky. However, there is not enough concrete evidence to prove any relationship to Fannie and her sister. See US Bureau of the Census, Tenth Census of the United States, 1880, Centerville, Bourbon County, KY, roll 403, p. 148B, Enumeration District 065, image 024, Ancestry.com.

9. William O. Douglas, "Vagrancy and Arrest on Suspicion," *Yale Law Journal* 70, no. 1 (1960): 5–6. For more on vagrancy in English common law, see Sir James Fitzjames Stephen, *A History of the Criminal Law of England,* 3 vols. (London: Macmillan, 1883).

10. "Kentucky Vagrancy Law [Ben Burton]," Notable Kentucky African Americans Database, n.d., at https://nkaa.uky.edu/nkaa/items/show/2004.

11. Marion B. Lucas, *A History of Blacks in Kentucky,* vol. 1: *From Slavery to Segregation, 1760–1891,* 2nd ed. (Frankfort: Kentucky Historical Society, 1992), 270.

12. Lucas, *History of Blacks in Kentucky,* 1:272.

13. "Eight-day weeks" is a phrase used to describe the long working hours expected of Black Kentuckians working as domestic laborers after the Civil War (Lucas, *History of Blacks in Kentucky,* 1:268–69, 272, and esp. 277).

14. Lucas, *History of Blacks in Kentucky,* 1:272; US Bureau of the Census, Tenth Census of the United States, 1880, Centerville, Bourbon County, KY, roll 403, p. 148B, Enumeration District 065, image 024, Ancestry.com.

15. "The Commonwealth," *Richmond (KY) Climax,* January 2, 1891, 1.

16. Elizabeth A. Perkins, "The Forgotten Victorians: Louisville's Domestic Servants, 1880–1920," *Register of the Kentucky Historical Society* 85, no. 2 (1987): 125–26.

17. Perkins, "Forgotten Victorians," 126.

18. Stephanie M. H. Camp, *Closer to Freedom: Enslaved Women and Everyday Resistance in the Plantation South* (Chapel Hill: University of North Carolina Press, 2004), 36–37.

19. Fannie's son, George, died in 1915 due to complications with tuberculosis. His death certificate is the only archival evidence of William Shropshire's paternity, and Fannie is named as the informant. See "Certificate of Death, Geo. Shropshire," file no. 19241, Bureau of Vital Statistics, Commonwealth of Kentucky, Frankfort.

20. Harriet Jacobs, *Incidents in the Life of a Slave Girl* (1861) (New York: Penguin, 2000), 44–66.

21. Tera Hunter, *To 'Joy My Freedom: Southern Black Women's Lives and Labors after the Civil War* (Cambridge, MA: Harvard University Press, 1997), 27–29.

22. *Bourbon County Towns,* Permanent Exhibition, Hopewell Museum, Paris, KY.

23. The focus of this study is central Kentucky, with an emphasis on Lexington and Frankfort. For more on African American life in Louisville, see George C. Wright, *Life behind a Veil: Blacks in Louisville, Kentucky, 1865–1930* (Baton Rouge: Louisiana State University Press, 1985).

24. Lowell H. Harrison and James C. Klotter, *A New History of Kentucky* (Lexington: University Press of Kentucky, 1997) 236.

25. Lucas, *History of Blacks in Kentucky*, 1:196–200; George C. Wright, *A History of Blacks in Kentucky*, vol. 2: *In Pursuit of Equality, 1890–1980* (Frankfort: Kentucky Historical Society, 1992), 2.

26. John D. Wright Jr., *Lexington: Heart of the Bluegrass* (Lexington, KY: Lexington-Fayette County Historical Commission, 1982), 98.

27. Douglas Appler, *Interpreting Downtown Lexington's Town Branch History* (Lexington: University of Kentucky, 2016), 23.

28. US Bureau of the Census, Eighteenth Census of the United States, 1880, Lexington, Fayette County, KY, roll 412, p. 273B, Enumeration District 065, image 0739, Ancestry.com.

29. Appler, *Interpreting Downtown Lexington's Town Branch History*, 26–28.

30. "The Fire," *Lexington Daily Press*, May 16, 1876 (quotation); Maryjean Wall, *Madam Belle: Sex, Money, and Influence in a Southern Brothel* (Lexington: University Press of Kentucky, 2014), 36.

31. Wright, *A History of Blacks in Kentucky*, 2:15; Alex G. Barret and Ruth Sapinsky, *Report of the Commission to Investigate the Conditions of Working Women in Kentucky* (Louisville, KY: Allied Printing Trades Council, 1911), 1–55, reel 828, no. 6689, Indiana University Library, Bloomington.

32. Wright, *A History of Blacks in Kentucky*, 2:34, 36.

33. Wright, *Lexington*, 107.

34. Lucas, *History of Blacks in Kentucky*, 1:278–79.

35. Kali N. Gross, *Colored Amazons: Crime, Violence, and Black Women in the City of Brotherly Love, 1880–1910* (Durham, NC: Duke University Press, 2006), 68.

36. Gross, *Colored Amazons*, 68; Lucas, *History of Blacks in Kentucky*, 1:278.

37. US Bureau of the Census, Tenth Census of the United States, 1880, Lexington, Fayette County, KY, roll 412, p. 273B, Enumeration District 065, image 0739, Ancestry.com; Appler, *Interpreting Downtown Lexington's Town Branch History*, 23.

38. Camp, *Closer to Freedom*; LaShawn Harris, *Sex Workers, Psychics, and Numbers Runners: Black Women in New York City's Underground Economy* (Urbana: University of Illinois Press, 2016); Cheryl D. Hicks, *Talk with You Like a Woman: African American Women, Justice, and Reform in New York, 1890–1935* (Durham: University of North Carolina Press, 2010).

39. Evelyn Brooks Higginbotham, *Righteous Discontent: The Women's Movement in the Black Baptist Church, 1880–1920* (Cambridge, MA: Harvard University Press, 2006), 7, 14.

40. Deborah G. White, *Too Heavy a Load: Black Women in Defense of Themselves, 1894–1994* (New York: Norton, 1999), 54–55.

41. "Howard School / Normal Institute / Chandler Normal School / Webster Hall (Lexington, KY)," Notable Kentucky African Americans Database, n.d., at http://nkaa.uky.edu/nkaa/items/show/2153; "Our Women and Children," Notable Kentucky African Americans Database, n.d., at http://nkaa.uky.edu/nkaa/items/show/710.

42. See T. H. Peoples, *Essence of a Saga: A Complete History of the Oldest Black Baptist Congregation West of the Allegheny Mountains, Historic Pleasant Green Missionary Baptist Church (Formerly African Baptist Church)* (Lexington, KY: n.p., 1990); and McIntyre, *One Grain of the Salt*.

43. Victoria W. Wolcott, *Remaking Respectability: African American Women in Interwar Detroit* (Chapel Hill: University of North Carolina Press, 2001), 34–39, 168–69.

44. Dean T. Ferguson, "Living by Means Unknown to Their Neighbors: The Informal Economy of Louisville's Blacks, 1865–1880," *Filson Club History Quarterly*, no. 4 (1998): 357–78, esp. 365–69.

45. Harris, *Sex Workers, Psychics, and Numbers Runners*, Kindle ed., loc. 126, 569.

46. "Fannie Keyes," Arrest Record Book, 1890–1892, Fayette County Recorder's (Police) Court, Department of Finance, KDLA.

47. The women's rights movement of the 1970s drew attention to domestic violence as a threat to women and children, mobilizing grassroots organizations to establish the first "battered women's shelter" in 1974. In the 1980s, Congress recognized violence against women and children as a systemic issue and authorized the Family Violence Prevention and Services Act, creating funding for domestic-violence prevention programs. Despite these twentieth-century efforts, America's history of family violence is much older than this and runs much deeper than many people may realize. As early as 1640, the Puritans enacted laws to curb occurrences of domestic abuse among spouses and between parents and children. Elizabeth Pleck's examination of familial violence in early America argues that colonial ideologies likened family tyranny to America's colonial relationship with Britain—identifying the country as an overbearing mother and the king as a tyrannical father. Antebellum cities such as Baltimore employed peace warrants as a common solution to family violence. These warrants functioned as a predecessor to modern-day restraining orders, enforcing fines if violence in the

home persisted. Women, in particular women of color, did not regularly obtain these warrants for fear of bringing shame upon the home. See Charlene Fletcher-Brown, "Early Stories of Domestic Violence Raise Awareness, Foster Healing," *Kentucky Historical Society News,* November 6, 2016, at https://history.ky .gov/2016/11/04/early-stories-of-domestic-violence-raise-awareness-foster-healing/; Randolph A. Roth, "Spousal Murder in Northern New England, 1776–1865," in *Over the Threshold: Intimate Violence in Early America,* ed. Christine Daniels and Michael V. Kennedy (New York: Routledge, 1999), 65–93; and Elizabeth Hafkin Pleck, *Domestic Tyranny: The Making of American Social Policy against Family Violence from Colonial Times to the Present* (New York: Routledge, 1999), 65.

48. Pleck, *Domestic Tyranny,* 49.

49. Pleck, *Domestic Tyranny,* 52–53.

50. Pleck, *Domestic Tyranny,* 49–53.

51. "Bouncer White," Arrest Record Book, 1890–1892, p. 352, Fayette County Recorder (Police) Court, Department of Finance, KDLA.

52. "Bouncer White," Arrest Record Book, 1890–1892, pp. 352, 390.

53. "Whoever shall in the City of Lexington, in the presence of another person or persons, use any abusive or insulting language, intending thereby to insult such other person or persons, or with the intention to provoke an assault, shall be fined not less than twenty nor more than fifty dollars, and any person who shall print or publish any abusive or insulting language reflecting on the integrity or moral character of any person or persons, or with the intention of provoking an assault, he shall be fined not less than twenty-five nor more than one hundred dollars, or shall be confined in the City Jail not less than one nor more than twelve months, or both so fined and imprisoned, at the discretion of the court. When such abusive language is used by a man to a woman the highest penalty shall be imposed. The truth of the charges made may be proven in defense" (§296 of *Revised Ordinances of the City of Lexington, Kentucky* [Louisville, KY: Courier-Journal Job Printing, 1903], 46–47).

54. Pleck, *Domestic Tyranny,* 136–37.

55. US Bureau of the Census, Tenth Census of the United States, 1880, Lexington, Fayette County, KY, roll 412, p. 273B, Enumeration District 065, image 0739, Ancestry.com; "Peter White Says He Is Aged 103," *Lexington Leader,* April 9, 1916, 8.

56. General Leslie Combs (1793–1881) was a lawyer, member of the Kentucky House of Representatives, and celebrated militia officer in the War of 1812. In 1836, he raised a volunteer militia to aid in tensions with Mexico, but President Andrew Jackson disbanded the regiment. Combs raised another regiment in

1846 to deploy in the Mexican-American War but was not selected as the commanding officer and subsequently resigned from military service. In an interview in the *Lexington Ledger* in 1912, Peter White stated he was a body servant in Mexico for Combs. Combs owned Peter White, but White does not appear on any muster roll for service in the Mexican-American War. It is not clear if Combs resigned from the militia while he was still in Mexico or when he was back on his Lexington estate. It is more likely that White became a body servant for another Kentucky militia officer during the war, who sold him to Combs upon returning to Lexington. In addition to his political and military exploits, Combs served as president of the Lexington and Danville Railroad and the Kentucky Association Track (a horse-racing organization). Combs is also my sixth great-granduncle. For more on General Combs, see "Combs, Leslie," in *The Kentucky Encyclopedia,* ed. John E. Kleber (Lexington: University Press of Kentucky, 1992), 219; and General Leslie Combs, *Narrative of the Life of General Leslie Combs: Embracing Incidents in the Early History of the Northwestern Territory* (Washington, DC: J. T. and Lem Towers, 1855).

57. "Peter White Says He Is Aged 103."

58. US Bureau of the Census, Ninth Census of the United States, 1870, Lexington, Ward 2, Fayette County, KY, roll 412, p. 38, image 326805, Ancestry.com; Lucas, *History of Blacks in Kentucky,* 1:280–81.

59. "Can Not Agree," *Lexington Press,* December 3, 1891, 1.

60. See note 7 and the earlier discussion in the text about the feud between the Pleasant Green and First African Baptist Churches.

61. "Can Not Agree."

62. "By Poison"; James C. Whorton, *The Arsenic Century: How Victorian Britain Was Poisoned at Home, Work, and Play* (Oxford: Oxford University Press, 2010), 126.

63. Prior to the 1830s, arsenic was a common method of poisoning because it was difficult to trace. In 1836, the British chemist James Marsh developed the highly effective Marsh Test, which revealed the presence of arsenic. The test required food or body tissue to be combined with zinc and acid in a glass vessel. The combination would produce arsine gas and hydrogen if arsenic were present. This was the first test successfully used to prove arsenic poisoning in a jury trial. See Whorton, *Arsenic Century,* 126.

64. "Totally Depraved," *Cincinnati Enquirer,* January 21, 1891, 1.

65. Quotations from "By Poison." It's important to note that *wench* was an early English term used to describe young, unmarried, generally lower-class women who were seen as sexually promiscuous, in contrast to *wives,* or married women, who upheld the social order. During the colonial period, womanhood

began to be defined by race, reinforcing ideas of ladyhood and sexual purity regardless of economic status. Although "wenches" were initially seen to be lower-class white women who challenged the social order and patriarchy, by the eighteenth century the term was exclusively reserved for Black women as the ideological and legal foundations of racial slavery. By calling Lila White a "wench," the papers were thus already judging her as a promiscuous Jezebel in how they chose to label her. In an examination of the development of political and power structures in early America, it is beneficial to approach the inquiry with a gendered lens. Kathleen Brown's work takes this approach, arguing that the entangled categories of race and gender redefined and supported patriarchal power and the planter class in colonial Virginia. Her thesis extends the work of the historian Joan Scott, who in her article "Gender: A Useful Category of Historical Analysis" defines gender as a "constitutive element of social relationships based on perceived differences between the sexes, and . . . a primary way of signifying relationships of power." Brown's investigation begins in Elizabethan England, noting that male authority rested on the ability to command an orderly home and a "good wife." The English believed this hierarchal relationship to be divinely ordained and utilized the concept to legitimize English concepts of domination and social order. Women who challenged the conventional social order or who belonged to the lower classes were deemed "nasty wenches" and considered unnatural disruptions to English patriarchy. Despite the negative connotations placed on lower classes of women, Brown notes that legalizing sexual access to women was a defining feature of class divisions in colonial Virginia, reinforcing Scott's definition of gendered influences on power. Although gender is a determining feature of power relationships, Scott argues that changes in these relationships result in changes in representations of power. Brown illustrates this through the concept of "gender frontiers," or the "meeting of two or more culturally specific systems of knowledge about gender and nature." Encounters with Native Americans and Africans challenged English notions of gender and superiority, which inevitably led to the use of gender in the creation of racial slavery and social order. See Kathleen M. Brown, *Good Wives, Nasty Wenches, and Anxious Patriarchs: Gender, Race, and Power in Colonial Virginia* (Chapel Hill: University of North Carolina Press, 1996) 3, 9, 33; and Joan W. Scott, "Gender: A Useful Category of Historical Analysis," *American Historical Review* 91 (1986): 1053–75 (quote on 1067). See also Deborah Gray White, *Ar'n't I a Woman? Female Slaves in the Plantation South* (New York: Norton, 1999), 29, 47; and Martha S. Jones, *All Bound Up Together: The Woman Question in African American Public Culture, 1830–1900* (Chapel Hill: University of North Carolina Press, 2009), 32–33, 141.

66. The details of Judge Payne's visit to Lila are given in "By Poison."

67. The indictment against Lila states that a grand jury investigated and returned two true bills against her for the murder of Daniel and Eliza Frazier; however, the *Cincinnati Enquirer* reported that Lila's case was investigated by a coroner's jury—a group of six citizens selected by the county coroner to investigate potential homicides. The Fayette County coroner inquest records no longer exist, so it can't be determined with certainty which pretrial mechanism was used to bring forward the two indictments, but the makeup of the jury was detailed in the *Enquirer* article "Totally Depraved." See "Commonwealth of Kentucky vs. Lilly White, Indictment for Murder," drawer 124–26, box 14, Department of Finance, KDLA; and "Totally Depraved."

68. "George Keyes," Arrest Record Book, 1890–1892, p. 193, Fayette County Recorder's (Police) Court, Department of Finance, KDLA.

69. Judge Morton quoted in "Judge Morton's Charge," *Lexington Press*, May 19, 1891, 1. Jeremiah Rogers Morton (b. 1842) was born in Clark County, Kentucky, and studied with Alexander Campbell, president of Bethany College. Morton taught elementary school before enlisting in the Confederate army under the command of General John Hunt Morgan. After the war, he completed his law degree at Kentucky University and served as city and county attorney in Lexington until his election as Circuit Court judge in 1886. He went into private practice in 1893 (H. Levin, *The Lawyers and Lawmakers of Kentucky: Arranged and Edited under the Supervision of H. Levin, of the Illinois Bar* [Chicago: Lewis Publishing, 1897], 609–10).

70. The twelve white male jurors and three alternates, all of Fayette County, were C. F. Brower, J. H. Wilson, D. C. Logan, T. A. Hornsey, W. H. Graham, A. L. Carithers, H. A. Nichols, Jacob Smedley, Oscar Featherstone, J. C. Curd, Samuel Haggin, B. F. Williams, J. A. Curry, J. B. Wallace, and C. F. Featherstone. Nineteenth-century Kentucky juries were composed solely of white men. Black activists challenged the Commonwealth's judiciary, yet the Kentucky Court of Appeals ruled that "the absence of Blacks from a jury did not mean discrimination had taken place." That decision was overturned in 1938 when Joe Hale, a Black man from Paducah, was convicted by an all-white jury for the murder of a white man and sentenced to death by hanging. The NAACP appealed the verdict. The Court of Appeals upheld the ruling, but the US Supreme Court overturned the conviction and determined Hale's civil rights had been violated due to the explicit exclusion of African Americans from the jury. See "Judge Morton's Charge"; Wright, *A History of Blacks in Kentucky*, 2:89–90, 187; and *Hale v. Kentucky*, 303 US 613 (1938).

71. Lila's attorneys, Webb and Jewell, were not listed among the lawmakers in Levin's volume, *Lawyers and Lawmakers of Kentucky*, but the *Lexington City*

Directory for 1902 indicates that Webb served as master commissioner of the Circuit Court and for 1923 lists him as an attorney with Morton, Webb, & Wilson, a private firm. James R. Jewell was elected to serve as Lexington's Police Court judge. In the 1880 census and prior to the start of his legal career, Jewell listed his profession as a "dealer in whiskey and wine." See "Lillie White's Case," *Lexington Press,* May 22, 1891, 1; *The Lexington City Directory and Rural Postal Delivery Routes for 1902–1903,* vol. 1 (Columbus, OH: R. L. Polk, 1903), 560; *Lexington City Directory, 1923* (Maryville, TN: Baldwin-Franklin Directory Company, 1923), 790; and US Bureau of the Census, Tenth Census of the United States, 1880, Lexington, Fayette County, KY, roll 413, p. 329C, Enumeration District 066, Ancestry.com.

72. "Circuit Court," *Lexington Press,* May 26, 1891, 5.

73. Charles Jacob (C. J.) Bronston (1848–1909) was a Kentucky native and graduate of the Kentucky University at Lexington. He earned a law degree from the University of Virginia and went into private practice with James B. McCreary, Kentucky's twenty-seventh governor, while teaching as a law professor at the Central Kentucky University (now Centre College). Bronston served as the Commonwealth's attorney for the Tenth Judicial District (Madison, Fayette, Clark, Scott, Woodford, Jessamine, and Bourbon Counties) between 1879 and 1895. He also served as a member of the Kentucky Constitutional Convention of the State (1890–1891), a delegate to the National Convention of the Democratic Party for the Seventh District, and a Kentucky state senator (1896–1900). As a senator, Bronston led the charge on a prison-reform bill in 1898 that was widely shaped by the events of a prison investigation that involved Fannie Keys Harvey and Lila White. John R. Allen (b. 1857) attended the Kentucky Military Institute, the Virginia Military Institute, Southwestern University, and the Kentucky University School of Law. He served as city attorney, master commissioner of the Circuit Court, county attorney, and the Commonwealth's attorney after C. J. Bronston's resignation from the post in 1896. Allen served in the Kentucky Militia and was a lawyer in private practice with Bronston beginning in 1890 (Levin, *Lawyers and Lawmakers of Kentucky,* 589–93).

74. "Her Life or Liberty," *Lexington Press,* May 27, 1891, 5.

75. "Totally Depraved"; "Her Life or Liberty."

76. "Totally Depraved."

77. "The Jury Disagreed," *Lexington Press,* May 30, 1891, 5.

78. "Commonwealth of Kentucky vs. Bouncer White, Indictment for Malicious Cutting and Wounding," drawers 121–23, box 13, Department of Finance, KDLA.

79. Details of this second trial come from "Can Not Agree."

80. "Can Not Agree."

81. For more on hung juries, see Janet E. Findlater, "Retrial after a Hung Jury: The Double Jeopardy Problem," *University of Pennsylvania Law Review* 129 (1981): 701–37; *United States v. Perez,* 22 US 579 (1824); and *Koon v. United States,* 518 US 81 (1996).

82. The thumb stall was a glovelike device that was usually used for protecting an injured thumb but was also used to suspend incarcerated people in the air by their thumbs. See "Very Near It," *Cincinnati Enquirer,* January 11, 1892, 2.

83. "Lily White Owns Up," *Lexington Leader,* May 22, 1892, 3.

84. "They Will Investigate," *Louisville Courier-Journal,* March 23, 1892, 2.

85. "Very Near It."

86. "Colored Notes," *Lexington Leader,* November 14, 1913, 6; US Bureau of the Census, Tenth Census of the United States, 1880, Lexington, Fayette County, KY, roll 413, p. 386C, Enumeration District 068, Ancestry.com; US Bureau of the Census, Eleventh Census of the United States, 1900, Lexington, Ward 2, Fayette County, KY, p. 15, Enumeration District 0016, microfilm 1240519, Family History Library, Salt Lake City, Utah, Ancestry.com; "Allen Hathaway," Interment Control Forms, 1928–1962, A1 2110-B, *Records of the Office of the Quartermaster General, 1774–1985,* Record Group 92, National Archives and Records Administration, Washington, DC; *The Lexington City Directory 1904–1905,* vol. 2 (Columbus, OH: R. L. Polk, 1905), 336; "Certificate of Death, Miami Saunders," December 1, 1935, file no. 29005, Bureau of Vital Statistics, Commonwealth of Kentucky, Frankfort.

87. "A Sensation," *Lexington Morning Transcript,* May 24, 1892, 1.

88. "A Sensation."

89. Warsan Shire, "The House," Poetry Foundation, October 31, 2017, at https://www.poetryfoundation.org/poems/90733/the-house-57daba5625f32.

9

The "Live Issue" of Black Women Voters in Kentucky

Melanie Beals Goan

The year 2020 marked the centennial anniversary of the Nineteenth Amendment to the US Constitution, which ended sex discrimination in voting, and the milestone prompted a much-needed reassessment of the woman suffrage movement's impact. Americans have long heralded 1920 as the year when their democracy corrected one of its most obvious injustices and made all women voters. New scholarship, however, emphasizes what this milestone, although important, left undone: Jim Crow restrictions meant too many women, in particular women of color in the South, remained disenfranchised until the Voting Rights Act of 1965 offered additional protections.[1]

When considering the impact of woman suffrage across the "great divide" of 1920, contemporary observers and scholars alike roundly conclude that it failed to transform the nation in meaningful ways, whether because women did not vote as a bloc as expected or because racism and other prejudices interfered. "The suffrage amendment—highly anticipated and hotly debated—landed like a thud," the historian Liette Gidlow explains. Too few women voted, hardly any ran for office, and Progressive causes lost momentum in the decade that followed.[2]

It was a thud that some women anticipated, including Mary Church Terrell, the first president of the National Association of Colored Women (NACW).[3] After traveling to the Northeast to register voters in October 1920, stinging from harassment she experienced on the trip, she predicted,

"The colored women of the South will be shamefully treated, and will not be alowed [*sic*] to vote, I am sure. I hope the Republicans will do something toward enforcing the Fifteenth Amendment. We are so helpless without the right of citizenship in that section of the country where we need it most."[4]

The miscarriage of justice Terrell forecast unfortunately played out as if according to script in many communities across the United States, in particular those in the Deep South, but it did not happen everywhere. In Kentucky, Black women were an anomaly, voting in significant numbers in 1920 and in the years that followed. Although they had prioritized other concerns over gaining the ballot before 1920, Black women, like Black men, bravely and enthusiastically leveraged its power when given the chance. Their enthusiastic turnout influenced contests, both directly by adding votes to the Republican Party's tally and indirectly by spurring white women's participation. Historically, Kentucky had posted unusually high voter turnouts in national contests, and in 1920, as a new day dawned, its women continued that tradition.[5]

A leading Democratic Party newspaper, the *New York World,* deemed Black Kentucky women a "live issue" in the fall of 1920. Kentucky was one of several states where the Black vote would likely be the "deciding factor," it stressed, giving Black Americans the power to determine the next president and Senate control.[6] What this publication failed to acknowledge, however, was that Black women did not just suddenly spring to action in 1920. Rather, they had been a significant force for at least four decades, working for change through schools and churches and within organizations such as the Kentucky Association of Colored Women's Clubs. The vote, however, represented a new weapon in their arsenal that fall, and they enthusiastically lined up to use it, recognizing its power to roll back segregation, combat racism, and build healthier and more prosperous families and communities.

The history of the American woman suffrage movement dates back to the 1840s, when it developed as an offshoot of abolition. Women decried the evil of human bondage, and as they did, they could not help but notice that they were similarly limited by sex. What started with calls for property rights and expanded educational opportunities led to even bolder demands for the franchise.[7]

Suffragists began with lofty goals of winning universal voting rights, eager to fulfill the Constitution's bold promises of liberty and justice for all. White suffragists' egalitarian priorities, however, soon wore thin, especially when the Fifteenth Amendment, which partly corrected race but not sex restrictions in voting, demanded a response. The American Woman Suffrage Association and the National Woman Suffrage Association parted ways in the 1870s, and race was the key dividing point.[8]

During that same decade, Kentucky became the first southern state to establish a viable suffrage movement. Bold calls for women's equality in a border state that had been deeply divided during the Civil War highlighted the many obstacles that stood in the way of equality. The Kentucky movement's aims were always fairly limited, influenced by white leaders' deep and abiding racism, their desire to protect their privileged positions, and a halting sense of pragmatism. By the time the Kentucky Equal Rights Association (KERA) formed in the 1880s, national suffragists' inclusive rhetoric had softened, and Kentucky leaders, most notably Laura Clay, helped swing the National American Woman Suffrage Association (NAWSA, formed by the merger of the American Woman Suffrage Association and the National Woman Suffrage Association in 1890) farther in that direction. Expediency won out as national white suffragists sought to recruit southern women to a cause often painted as radical, unwomanly, and threatening to the entire social order. One important way Clay and her colleagues made suffrage appear less threatening was by keeping KERA a whites-only organization. It welcomed only white women throughout its four-decade history, viewing Black women as a threat rather than as possible allies.[9]

It is anyone's guess what might have happened if white Kentucky suffragists had been more willing to cooperate across the color line. Black women in the state had a natural interest in the vote and in at least one case demonstrated a bold willingness to demand it publicly. Mary Ellen Britton, Berea College graduate, Black schoolteacher, famous national writer, and self-proclaimed "agitator," delivered the first recorded speech in Kentucky arguing for women's voting rights at a Colored State Teachers' Association meeting held in Danville in July 1887. Citing examples of strong biblical women, Britton critiqued a culture that silenced women. Enfranchising "creation's gentle half" would purify society, pushing out the "bad men" who wasted public money on cigars and whiskey, Britton argued. Five other Black women participated in a public forum with Britton that day, outlining the ways the vote could advance their reform goals.[10]

Colored Orphan Industrial Home Board of Managers, Lexington, Kentucky, c. 1900. *Seated left to right:* Mrs. Whitney, Mrs. E. Belle Jackson, Mrs. C. V. Robinson, Mrs. Mary Fletcher, and Mrs. Angus Ware. *Standing left to right:* Mrs. Mary A. Gillis, Charlotte Pogue, Mrs. Moses Mason, Katie Ryan, Ella Henderson, Fannie Wilhite, Alice Clay, and Mrs. Fannie Chiles. Photograph courtesy of the Robert H. Williams Cultural Center, Lexington, KY.

The teachers' call for the franchise, however, did not lead to further direct action. Black women in many parts of the country, including neighboring Indiana, specifically mobilized to win the vote, but in Kentucky they focused on different issues. "Dramatic protest," the historian Evelyn Brooks Higginbotham stresses, often took a backseat to "everyday forms of resistance" for educated, reform-minded women of color. Black literacy rates rose from 5 percent in 1860 to 70 percent in 1910 nationally, an important prerequisite for organized activism. Darlene Clark Hine credits Black club women for "making community" and for creating the essential structures that allowed Black people to survive the indignities of Jim Crow. They denounced lynching, promoted temperance, and fought to expand educational opportunities. White Kentuckians liked to claim that race relations were good in their state and that both races were content with the established order, but Black women looked at the violence, poverty, degradation, and humiliation that their families faced every day and vowed to force change.[11]

Churches were the primary site that drew reform-minded Black women together. They were "literally the backbone of the community," Karen Cotton McDaniel explains in her study of Black Kentucky club women. Churches were more than a place to worship. They were a place to talk politics, to learn to read and write, to borrow books, to play a team sport, and to hear music concerts. Many denominations ran their own publishing houses. The Black church emphasized self-help, but it was equally focused on liberation. Black women capitalized on this perspective and developed a "feminist theology" that offered an important rationale for expanding their public roles. They focused on the Bible—the most trusted source of authority—and used it to upend proscriptions that limited women's place in society.[12]

Male Black church leaders did not always endorse women's increased visibility and sometimes tried to mute them, but Black women pushed back, emphasizing their essential contributions, particularly their relentless fund-raising efforts. Black men were the recognized leaders of the church, but Black women were its muscle. For instance, in 1883 Baptist women formed the independent Baptist Women's Educational Convention of Kentucky to support Louisville's State University (known earlier as Kentucky Normal and Theological Institute and later as Simmons College). Between 1883 and 1914, the Baptist Women's Convention raised almost $35,000 for Simmons, with part of that amount financing construction of a dormitory for female students.[13]

The church was an outwardly male world, steeped in patriarchy. By contrast, schools provided natural positions of influence for women, highlighting their roles as caregivers and nurturers. The Kentucky State Association of Colored Teachers formed in 1877, and Black women actively participated in its yearly conferences and frequently served as officers. Annual meetings were long affairs, typically stretching five days, and covered a broad range of issues, many only tangentially related to education, but all related to improvement of the race. At the meeting in 1886, the year before Britton gave her suffrage speech, Lucy Wilmot Smith read a paper on new employment opportunities for girls. She encouraged girls to be entrepreneurial and to "trust their own brains." Do not settle for washing and cleaning houses, she urged. Consider beekeeping, run a dairy, or grow fruit instead. Above all, "despise mediocrity."[14]

School and church work led to women's first forays into politics. In the 1870s, for example, Black educators, male and female, lobbied for a redistribution of Kentucky school tax revenues. The per capita sums allocated for white children were four times that for Black children, they emphasized, resulting in low teacher salaries and few opportunities for students beyond the elementary level. The State Association of Colored Teachers won a significant victory in 1882 when the federal circuit court ruled in *Kentucky v. Jesse Ellis* that separate school funds were unconstitutional.[15]

The following decade, women active in Black church and school organizations assumed an even more visible role in a political fight concerning African Americans' access to public transportation. Gaining and protecting the right to ride freely had long been a priority for Black Kentuckians, as their successful efforts to desegregate Louisville streetcars in 1870 demonstrated. When legislatures in states across the South, including Kentucky, began to consider separate coach laws in the 1890s, which promised to relegate African American rail passengers to inferior accommodations, African Americans fought back.[16]

Black women especially resented separate coach laws and the threat they posed to women's dignity. The laws were an "unchristian humiliation," Nannie Helen Burroughs, head of the National Training School for Women and Girls in Washington, DC, and a one-time Louisville resident, insisted. It was an insult "to be ushered from clean homes, with an atmosphere saturated with pure ozone," only to be stuffed into dirty smoking cars. Lavinia B. Sneed, a State Normal School professor, joined a group of female teachers who addressed the Kentucky legislature in 1892 in protest. She later remembered how shocked she felt as "one of the weakest of God's creatures, and a Negro" to be speaking to such a powerful group on such an important issue. When the women's efforts failed to stop the measure from passing, women worked for its repeal. They published newspaper protests, raised money, and tested the law directly, allowing themselves to be forcefully thrown off the trains so that they could sue for damages.[17]

They also turned to white suffragists for help, pointing to their shared vulnerability and their mutual commitment to defending morality. Mrs. Lottie Wilson Jackson, a delegate from Michigan, raised the issue of separate coach laws at the NAWSA convention in 1899, but she found little sympathy from the white women present. Jackson, described in the convention minutes as "so light-compexioned [*sic*] that most people would not have supposed that she had any tincture of colored blood," proposed a resolution: "That colored women ought not to be compelled to ride in smoking cars, and that suitable accommodations should be provided for them." Jackson described what it was like to travel by train throughout the South, where "the filthy state of the cars" made it almost impossible for her to maintain her respectability.[18]

Kentucky's Laura Clay, however, objected vigorously to Mrs. Jackson's resolution, personally wounded, it seemed, by the accusations leveled against the South. It was not fair to southern delegates who had traveled all the way to Grand Rapids to attend a suffrage convention to have a measure that was completely off topic sprung on them, Clay snipped. She first defended separate coach laws and then stoutly denied that the conditions Mrs. Jackson described existed, certainly not in Kentucky and likely nowhere in the region. Other white delegates backed Clay, agreeing that they never had seen Black women suffer the way Jackson described. Eventually, a sympathetic white delegate proposed removing the word *colored* from the resolution, noting she herself had been "saturated with tobacco smoke" on the train, but Mrs. Jackson held fast—the resolution should be passed or defeated as worded. Susan B. Anthony finally intervened, reminding listeners that she had long proven herself a "true friend to the colored race." She concluded that it was best to drop the matter. As members of a "helpless, disfranchised class," women were in no position to pass resolutions against railroad companies or anyone else.[19]

As the lines of segregation hardened across the nation at the turn of the century, reinforced by court rulings such as *Plessy v. Ferguson* (163 US 537 [1896]), racism permeated every facet of American life, including the activities of women's organizations. Like NAWSA, the General Federation of Women's Clubs (GFWC) refused to include Black clubwomen as affiliates or even to consider their concerns. In 1902, the GFWC bowed to the demands of disgruntled white southerners, including women from Kentucky, and officially declared itself an all-white organization, a move that sharply contradicted its motto: "Unity in Diversity."[20]

Black women had already formed the separate National Association of Colored Women six years earlier under the leadership of Mary Church Terrell. Members created a number of departments that reflected the broad range of their concerns, including education, employment, and temperance, but the NACW's main goal was racial uplift and self-help, as reflected in its motto, "Lifting as We Climb." They also formed a suffrage department, aware of the vote's power to make other goals possible. Though few women could yet cast ballots, the NACW's constitution of 1904 in an aspirational move stipulated that each member was free to choose her own political affiliation.[21]

Black women of Kentucky subsequently formed the Kentucky Association of Colored Women's Clubs (KACWC) in 1903. Thirteen local clubs affiliated, led by Miss Georgia A. Nugent, president. Through the KACWC, Black Kentucky women continued to perform the same uplift work they did before its creation, but the new federation gave them a more structured vehicle for doing this work, Karen Cotton McDaniel emphasizes.[22]

Unlike the NACW, which prioritized suffrage work, the KACWC pursued other goals. The group's top objective, McDaniel explains, was "to move the masses into a new way of life through their programs." For example, Mrs. Elizabeth "Lizzie" Fouse, president of the organization in 1912–1913, focused on "educational attainment, the adoption of Victorian ethics and behavior, and the maintenance of stable homes and families." Beyond her work on the state level, Fouse was active nationally, chairing the NACW's Mother, Home, and Child Department and taking on other leadership roles as needed. KACWC's emphasis on domesticity led it to focus on national food-conservation efforts during World War I. KACWC president Martha E. Williams encouraged members to fight the war with a knife and fork.[23]

References to suffrage show up infrequently in KACWC records, although the effort to accomplish other goals is occasionally framed in terms of their potential to advance voting rights. In her presidential address to the group in 1914, printed in full in the *Lexington Leader,* Mrs. Eliza Belle Jackson encouraged colleagues across the state to support Cora Wilson Stewart's Moonlight Schools and literacy projects. She urged members to go door to door, especially in rural areas, to ferret out every person of color who could not read and write. Jackson viewed literacy as a route to the ballot box for Black women. Women should throw their "heart and soul" into literacy now, for, she predicted, "the time is not far distant when women will have the right to vote on all the questions of the day."[24]

Black Kentucky women rarely referenced suffrage publicly or specifically organized to win the vote, but they clearly intended to use the right, if offered, just as Black men had done since 1870. Following the Civil War, formerly enslaved persons identified the ballot as the preeminent symbol of their newly won freedom. At gatherings held annually across the state to mark Emancipation Day and American Independence, they demanded the vote. Speakers enthusiastically supported universal suffrage, a right, they argued, that thirty thousand Black soldiers had purchased with their blood.[25]

Although men would likely be the only ones to cast ballots, women joined them side by side at these lively political rallies. For example, when a Colored Convention met in Lexington in March 1866, it included a "large concourse of ladies and gentlemen." Women offered musical entertainment, sat on the fund-raising committee, and readily chimed in with their own petitions. They met in Ladies' Hall, a school building funded by women, which gave their demands added weight. The historian Elsa Barkley Brown emphasizes that family and community were the "unifying thread" in the postslavery world, and thus Black women's political participation seemed entirely natural. "The fact that only men had been granted the vote did not mean that only men should exercise that vote," she notes. Women's opinions mattered as plans were made for freedom, and the practice of taking votes by voice or by rising meant that everyone in attendance had a say.[26]

The Reconstruction Act of 1867 gave freedmen in states that had left the Union the ballot, but Black men in Kentucky had to wait for the Fifteenth Amendment to be added to the US Constitution three years later. By the time the amendment was ratified by a needed majority of states in February 1870 (Kentucky didn't ratify it until 1976), Kentucky Blacks had already organized a statewide Republican committee and local societies in nearly every county and town. Black leaders convened in Frankfort that January, promising to use their votes "judiciously and with becoming dignity." At a meeting in Lebanon later that spring, the gathered delegates promised to vote as a bloc, standing as "one man for the party that freed them." At a Fifteenth Amendment celebration in Mount Sterling, an older man in the "evening" of his life communicated the significance of the milestone. "His time was short," he acknowledged, and slavery had worn him out, but he would vote if he had to crawl to the polls.[27]

Violence and intimidation, which, considering the state's record on lynching, were constant worries, and other unofficial methods of disenfranchisement—insufficient polling stations and harassing questions, for instance—were all too common. Some Democrats organized militias and began drilling in a hostile attempt to intimidate Black would-be voters. Others threatened to fire employees or evict tenants who had the audacity to go to the polls. In an unusual move, Bourbon County Democrats entrapped and arrested Black would-be voters in an illegal game of craps in 1900 to keep them from voting.[28]

Undeterred, Black men demonstrated high rates of participation, with the vast majority of them voting Republican. Over the next sixty years, they occasionally wavered in their loyalty to the Party of Lincoln, fed up with its empty promises and its failure to nominate Black candidates for office, but their votes helped to elect three Republican Kentucky governors between 1895 and 1920.

As one of the few states with a significant Black population whose votes were not systematically erased in the decades following the Fifteenth Amendment's ratification, Kentucky consistently registered some of the highest African American turnouts in the nation. Andrew B. Humphrey, a Berea College graduate and correspondent to the NAACP's newsletter *The Crisis,* projected that the "Negro vote" in the presidential election of 1912 would total six hundred thousand, with seventy-five thousand of those votes coming from Kentucky. Kentucky was home to only 2.6 percent of the nation's Black population, according to the US census of 1910, but it was likely to yield 12.5 percent of the Black votes cast if Humphrey's predictions held.[29]

Like their fathers, husbands, and sons, Black Kentucky women also enthusiastically stood up to vote when the chance came. Prior to the Nineteenth Amendment, many Kentucky women could vote in only one type of election: school contests. In fact, Kentucky women were among the first in the nation to become voters, in 1838, when the legislature inserted a provision to a common-schools bill allowing them to vote on tax levies and to elect school trustees. At first, only widows and single women from a few select communities who paid school taxes could participate. In 1894, however, KERA finally persuaded the legislature to give all women in Kentucky's second-class cities the school vote.[30]

White suffragists celebrated their victory and pledged to make sure every woman—white and Black—exercised their new right. During the summer of 1895, KERA members from Lexington, Covington, and Newport jumped into gear to prepare for the fall contest. The addition of women voters complicated election preparations. Officials had to create special polling sites separate from the saloons and stables where men traditionally voted, and they had to print new sex-differentiated ballots.[31]

Women also needed to be instructed and encouraged to register in advance, a reality that led the exclusively white KERA to cross race lines for the first time and one of the only times in its history. Its corresponding secretary Eugenia Farmer understood that high turnout would prove wrong those men who claimed women really did not want the vote, thus invalidating their favorite argument against woman suffrage. Hoping for robust participation, Farmer encouraged Black women from her northern Kentucky community not only to vote but also to establish the first and only Black suffrage "local" in the state. The Covington Colored Organization appears to have lasted only a few months, but it sent a report to KERA's annual convention in 1895, which Mrs. Farmer read aloud. White suffragists in Fayette County did not go as far as Farmer, but they also made overtures to Black women. They stopped short of going door-to-door in Black neighborhoods, as they did in white areas to boost registration, but they met with Black school leaders, who promised to encourage participation.[32]

Black women pledged to vote, and they swore they would use their ballots with the utmost care. When an Independent School Board ticket consisting of four white Fayette County women asked for their votes, Eliza Belle Jackson first demanded to know if a rumor going around that the female candidates planned to fire all the Black teachers and replace them with white instructors was true. Jackson and her associates agreed to back the ticket only after the candidates denied the rumors and affirmed that Black students learned best with Black teachers.[33]

Black women helped to elect the women's ticket in Lexington that November. "It was the first time in the history of Kentucky politics that the ladies had figured conspicuously in politics," the *Kentucky Leader* (Lexington) announced. They "marched boldly up," with slightly more Black women than white casting ballots, according to reports. Although female candidates did not win in Campbell or Kenton Counties, they made respectable showings there also.[34]

KERA leaders were elated. The school vote represented an important intermediate step to winning full suffrage, and they focused on extending it to all Kentucky women in the next legislative session. When attempts to enfranchise women in Kentucky's first-, third-, and fourth-class cities failed in 1896, suffragists vowed to try again. Instead of making progress, however, they soon found themselves in a battle just to maintain ground already won. In 1902, the Democratic state lawmaker Billy Klair filed a bill to rescind school suffrage. The reason: too many Black women voted.[35]

Black women in Lexington likely would have chosen to vote regardless of the circumstances, but in 1900 they had an extra incentive to go to the polls: they were dissatisfied with the leadership of their children's schools. They were upset that Supervisor of Schools Green Pinckney Russell cavalierly used schools for political ends, and they disagreed with his decision to focus the curriculum of Black schools on manual training. Black mothers who wanted more for their kids vowed to see Russell, a Democrat, defeated, and so with the support of mobilized Black mothers, Republicans decisively won the school board election in Fayette County that year.[36]

In 1901, the pattern repeated. Far more Black than white women registered to vote, prompting Billy Klair, Lexington's entrenched machine politician, to raise the warning flag: "Colored women," he warned, "practically controlled the results of the elections." Revoking the school vote for women was necessary to keep Kentucky safe from Black rule, he concluded. Kentucky women responded vigorously when Klair proposed a bill to rescind school suffrage, but even white suffragists' suggestion that a literacy requirement be added, which would have disenfranchised many Black women, failed to stop rescission. The Klair bill passed the House and Senate by a straight party vote. A decade would pass before Kentucky women would recover their right to vote in school elections, and then only those who could read and write would get it back.[37]

Black women's enthusiastic voting records reinforced white suffragists' commitment to fight for only limited suffrage and seemingly validated Laura Clay's argument that white suffragists had to tread lightly around the issue of race. In the 1890s, NAWSA made expanding the suffrage movement in the South a key goal. It launched a speaking tour through major southern cities in 1895 and worked to form state organizations throughout the heart of Dixie. It also elected its first southerner, Laura Clay, to its executive board the following year. In this push through the South, though, the organization firmly committed to respecting state sovereignty and to empowering each local branch to follow the customs of its own region. State organizations could keep their memberships all white, advocate for suffrage as a protection for white supremacy, and focus their work exclusively on state rather than federal means of winning the vote. This commitment was a clear step away from the egalitarianism of the early suffrage movement, but one that Clay applauded as necessary.[38]

NAWSA remained committed to this state-by-state approach to winning the vote, preferred by southerners, until 1916, when its president, Carrie Chapman Catt, announced her "Winning Plan." That year, at a very contentious emergency meeting, the organization pledged to make a federal amendment its primary goal, a move that southerners protested. Clay argued to no avail that it would crucify them "on a Federal cross with the same nails used by our Republican conquerors after a bloody war."

Making matters worse, NAWSA went further, instructing states to shelve their own plans for state suffrage amendments in order to pursue the national plan.[39]

Laura Clay and other leading southern suffragists denounced NAW-SA's dictate, sure that a federal amendment would undercut the South's ability to define its electorate. Clay pledged to uphold "states' rights suffrage" as the only way to win the vote. This unshakable commitment led her to do the unthinkable when the amendment finally passed the US Senate in 1919 after forty-one long years of consideration in Congress: she severed ties with the movement to which she had devoted four decades of her life. She resigned from NAWSA and KERA, established a rival suffrage organization, the Citizens Committee for a State Suffrage Amendment, and notoriously began working for the Nineteenth Amendment's defeat.[40]

In spite of Laura Clay's best efforts to turn Kentucky suffragists and politicians against a federal amendment, however, Madeline McDowell Breckinridge, KERA's president, directed a masterful fight to win over lawmakers. She skillfully guided the campaign to victory, achieving an historic first-day passage on January 6, 1920. Kentucky became one of only four southern states to ratify. It is likely no coincidence, one commentator has noted, that three of those states—Kentucky, Texas, and Tennessee—could argue that enfranchising women would guarantee the political supremacy of the white race because they had more white women than Black men and women combined. As extra insurance in case the additional necessary twelve states failed to ratify the amendment in time, Kentucky lawmakers also granted women presidential suffrage.[41]

Women across Kentucky, knowing they would vote in November regardless of ratification's outcome, began to flex their new political muscles. Many white suffragists converted their KERA memberships to enrollment in the League of Women Voters, which fashioned itself a force to "humanize" government and to equip "USEFUL CITIZENS." "It is not a Woman's Party. It is not a club. It does not limit membership to certain groups," promotional materials emphasized. Its claim that it was "INCLUSIVE not exclusive," however, referenced partisan affiliation, not race. The league did not welcome Black women. As Carolyn Jefferson-Jenkins explains, it "made a strategic choice to shrewdly discourage the inclusion of women of color."[42]

Black women instead would mobilize separately. In May 1920, W. E. B. Du Bois called on them to "Get Ready—Woman suffrage is coming."

They must make plans, he emphasized; "the white South is." He warned that white southerners were forming secret societies and colluding with each other after their Black servants left for the night. They were relying on·Black apathy and empty promises to maintain their control, but they must not be allowed to disenfranchise Black women as they had Black men. "Set your faces like flint," he enjoined, and "let no threat of poverty, riot or murder turn you from a determination to cast your vote according to the law."[43]

During the spring and summer of 1920, reflecting World War I's push for 100 percent Americanism, citizenship classes became extremely popular, held in communities large and small across Kentucky but always segregated by race. The NAACP and the NACW offered courses meant to prepare new voters. Topics included "the use of the ballot—how to qualify—how and when to register—how to mark a ballot—and how to examine the past records of aspirants for office for whom votes are to be cast." Stressing that "the ballot without intelligence back of it is a menace instead of a blessing," Kentuckian Georgia Nugent oversaw NACW efforts to prepare women for the "reverent responsibility" of voting. Even the Kentucky Negro Educational Association devoted its meetings in 1920 to "Good Citizenship Drives."[44]

The KACWC's annual report for 1920 noted that "club women are awake in politics." Besides training citizens, the women also organized Republican clubs throughout the state. Among the first, in late May 150 Richmond women gathered at the First Baptist church to organize the Colored Women's Republican Club. In Lexington, Black women of "Republican tendencies" met at the Booker T. Washington School in September 1920 to discuss plans for a "Women's Campaign Division." The Lexington Colored Women's Republican Club formed soon after, with Mrs. Eliza Belle Jackson serving as chairman.[45]

Republican and Democratic organizers alike moved quickly to woo new voters, tripping over themselves to prove their parties valued women's involvement. "Hardly was the amendment ratified," the *Woman Citizen* reported, "when the political leaders began showering marked attention upon the suffragists in the hope of lining them up." Republicans and Democrats invited women to their state and national conventions, and nearly every district sent at least one female delegate to the state meetings in March. Mrs. Annie Simms Banks, a noted "race worker," teacher, and wife of a well-known publisher, made history by becoming the first Black woman to serve at the Kentucky Republican State Convention, representing the Seventh

District. Other Black women watched the proceedings closely, *New York Age* reported.[46]

It was anyone's guess how a potential 20 million new female voters would change the rules of the political game that fall, but few doubted they would have a significant impact. In a memo addressed to "Fellow Voter," John Junior Howe, the Commonwealth's attorney from the Fifteenth Judicial District, stressed, "'The hand that rocks the cradle' will certainly '*rock the boat.*'" Both Republican and Democratic campaigns leaned on white female speakers to agitate for their candidates, sure that the message would be best heard by women voters if delivered by a member of the same sex. State Democrats chose Mrs. Samuel Wilson to run its female speakers' bureau, while Republicans chose Mrs. John Langley, the wife of a US representative from eastern Kentucky, to lead their effort.[47]

In Kentucky, questions swirled not just about the effect women in general would have on election outcomes but specifically about how *Black women's votes* would change the calculus. Even though the state's African American population was small in comparison to the Black populations in its Deep South neighbors—by 1920, it represented just 9.8 percent of the state's total population—Black Kentucky voters mattered. The legislature considered but failed to pass disenfranchisement measures, and that failure, combined with Black men's loyalty to the Republican Party, meant that Kentucky remained a viable two-party state. It was a "pivotal" place where African Americans held the balance of voting power, according to *The Crisis.* Concerned observers automatically assumed that Black women would vote and that their voting decisions would match those of Black men, thus granting the race an outsize impact.[48]

Unsurprisingly, Democrats paid little mind to Black women as potential allies. On occasion, they suggested that party representatives might campaign in Black neighborhoods, but they emphasized that such representatives would *not* enter the homes of "Negro" women voters. A leading Democratic organizer bluntly rejected the idea of courting Black women voters. It would be wasted effort, serving only to double the Republican vote, she concluded.[49]

The Republican Party, by contrast, strategized ways to reach Black women, but its efforts were half-hearted and reflected the pervasive racism of the period. Party operatives assumed that they would struggle to find Black female speakers to "preach republicanism" to Black women in Kentucky, but they were surprised to find a wealth of talent. Republicans made tepid overtures to Black women, but they were always balanced by the party's competing desire to secure white women's loyalty and to prove that the party was "lily white."[50]

When soliciting new white women voters, the Democratic Party highlighted the danger that Black women represented and the "great and righteous cause" that lay before all white women in the state. If Republicans won, Wilson warned, apathetic white women would be to blame. The "vote evader" was little better than the "draft dodger," one Democratic Party mass letter stressed, leveraging war patriotism. White women must put aside their squeamishness and register in order to protect white supremacy. The *Elizabethtown News* warned that eighty thousand Black female voters were prepared to come out "en masse" and vote Republican. Republican operatives would be walking to the polls "arm in arm with the colored cooks, washerwomen and other dusky belles," the *Kentucky Irish American* predicted. An especially shrill piece of fearmongering in the *Owensboro Messenger* stressed that white women must vote as a matter of "self-preservation."[51]

Democrats pressed election officials to make the registration and voting process as safe, respectable, and comfortable as possible to accommodate hesitant ladies. The *Danville Advocate-Messenger*'s editor urged leaders to avoid the "ancient custom of picking the nearest barber shop or shoe-shine parlor." Schools, "the cradle of good citizenship," would make good voting sites instead. Owensboro promised that each precinct would have women on hand to monitor and facilitate registration. Fear of mixing with "vile characters and colored women" should not stop white women from doing their duty to improve the nation, a writer from Slade urged in the *Clay City Times*. "We live in the same world with this class of people, we ride the same trains, we sit in the same pews (not with colored people)." Thus, white women should commit to voting, the correspondent reasoned.[52]

Communities anxiously awaited registration results because registration numbers generally paralleled election-day returns. Women in rural areas by law did not have to register, but those in first-, second-, third-, fourth-, and fifth-class cities had to secure a registration certificate on the first Tuesday of October. In most cases, voters were trusted to keep their registration papers safe and bring them to the polls on election day, but in Danville Black voters' forms were placed in a box for safekeeping, a paternalistic gesture that sparked protest.[53]

Across the South, Black women boldly presented themselves to registrars, but far too many left disappointed. The NAACP reported that election officials in many states administered exceedingly difficult literacy tests to new Black voters, including one woman in New Bern, North Carolina, who had to read and write the state's entire constitution. Undeterred, she accepted the challenge, but the registrar swiped the paper away, stating that even "if she was the President of Yale and colored she could not register." Only about one thousand Black aspiring female voters managed to register statewide in North Carolina. In Americus, Georgia, an election official hid to avoid registering Black women; one of his peers in Muskogee, Oklahoma, resigned rather than fulfill his duty. The fear of violent or economic retribution kept many more Black voters from exercising their new rights.[54]

In Kentucky, however, Black women successfully registered in significant numbers. The *Danville Advocate-Messenger* reported that at least 100 men and women were waiting at each Black precinct by 8:00 a.m. on registration day, leaving many white families to cook their own breakfasts. They were "out in full force" in Louisville, according to the *Louisville Courier-Journal,* where 12,417 "colored women" registered compared to 12,276 "colored men." In addition, 16,962 white men and 13,347 white women registered Republican, and 24,945 white men and 21,214 white women registered Democrat. The failure to specify Black voters' party designations implied that the Republican Party had received the entirety of their support. Mount Sterling and Frankfort were the only cities to register a single Democratic Black woman, according to news reports. In Lexington, nearly 100 percent of those eligible registered, and an estimated 95 percent did so in Paris.[55]

Even though Democrats recorded gains statewide, the final tally showed Republicans with a little more than a thousand-vote advantage going into election day, prompting Democrats to cry foul. They accused Black voters of registering more than once, among other forms of fraud, but their concerns centered mainly on Republican Party officials, who, they claimed, had unscrupulously injected race into the election. One way they had supposedly done so was by highlighting the Democratic Party's failure to denounce lynching and to support civil rights measures. "We wonder what 'rights' they [African Americans] desire that they do not enjoy now," an editorialist mused in the *Danville Advocate-Messenger.* "The Negro is given his education mostly at the expense of the white people. They are free and equal, when it comes to business opportunities—they can go about their business in their own way and, if they are law abiding citizens, are not molested in any way. What other rights do they want or expect?"[56]

Repeating claims that spread widely following registration day, the former Louisville chief of police J. H. Haager accused Republicans of making false promises to Black voters, such as equal privileges at parks, theaters, and other public spaces. Women organizing on behalf of the Republican Party, he charged, told Black women that if they voted Republican, their children would be able to go to school with white children, and the separate coach law would be repealed. In addition, according to the rumors, white women had used their cars to transport Black women to registration sites, prompting the *Owensboro Messenger* to ask in complete seriousness, "What next? Will the black women be inviting the white women to their bridge parties?" Political equality was dangerous enough, but its potential to encourage social equality appeared even more threatening.[57]

H. E. C. Bryant, a correspondent for the *Suffragist,* similarly declared the situation in Kentucky "most interesting" and noted that Louisville was shaping up to be a "storm center" because the race issue had "bobbed up." In a subsequent issue of the publication, a New York antilynching activist took Bryant to task, challenging his cavalier characterization of Kentucky's situation and underscoring what lay at stake: "Has H. E. C. Bryant ever been present when the race issue 'bobbed up'? It is more than 'interesting,' and something not easily forgotten in one's dreams."[58]

Kentucky Democrats warned that the election of 1920 had the potential to unravel segregation and to undermine American democracy. White women alone held the power to prevent "negro domination." No matter if they had opposed suffrage or felt uncomfortable voting, they must protect white supremacy at all costs. In addition to addressing barriers that might discourage white women from voting, such as unsavory polling sites, Democratic Party representatives also lured them to the polls by emphasizing the issues that mattered most to them. In particular, they leveraged the League of Nations, billed as key to avoiding future wars and keeping their sons safe, as a way to get out the vote. Democratic leaders started out lukewarm on the issue, but after learning that their mothers and sisters supported it so vigorously, they began elevating its importance in campaign materials.[59]

More than issues, however, Democrats relied on racist threats to carry the day. If Black women were allowed to dominate, Kentucky would become a place where the servants were the masters and where "Negro" postmistresses became common. Former police chief Haager went further, ominously suggesting that white women's safety was at stake. Who knew what "indignities" they would suffer at the hands of "negro rowdies" if they failed to heed the call? Ralph Gilbert, a Democratic candidate for US Congress, closed a campaign speech in Lawrenceburg by urging women to vote the Democratic ticket: "It means a vote for national prosperity, for peace on earth, and good will to men; IT MEANS A VOTE FOR WHITE SUPREMACY in the land of the free and the home of the brave."[60]

On November 2, 1920, an estimated 10 million women in the United States, including some 678,000 from Kentucky, went to the polls and cast their first votes for president. Women in Owensboro followed advice and voted early, even before they cleaned up the breakfast dishes. News reports concurred that it was a remarkably quiet day across the state, a result in no small part due to the civilizing influence of female voters and poll workers. Voters demonstrated "courtesy and restraint." They did not gather as usual outside of polling sites, and the "necessary accompanying evils of election day"—drinking and gambling—were absent. As the sun set, those anxious to find out the tallies gathered to hear them announced by megaphone and recorded on a chalkboard. It had been "the quietest election ever held in Daviess County," the *Owensboro Messenger* declared.[61]

America elected the Republican Warren G. Harding as the twenty-ninth president of the United States, but Kentucky gave its electoral votes to his Democrat opponent, Governor James M. Cox of Ohio. Kentucky Republicans at least could celebrate that their votes sent Richard P. Ernst to the US Senate, helping their party maintain control of the chamber. Ernst, a women's suffrage supporter, ran against J. C. W. Beckham, who had opposed votes for women.[62]

It is impossible to determine just how many Kentucky women voted that day. Indiana was the only state that recorded women's votes separately from men's votes, and public-opinion polls that pundits rely on today to measure election participation demographics did not exist until the 1930s. By comparing the vote count in 1920 to the numbers polled in the gubernatorial election of 1919, the *Hartford (KY) Republican* estimated that 4,075 of Ohio County women voted, and it even went so far as to speculate that 54 percent preferred Harding. The *Louisville Courier-Journal* reported that Kentucky's presidential vote tally increased from 511,884 in 1916 to 906,353 in 1920, the surplus coming from new women voters. The *Danville Advocate-Messenger* gave women credit in passing a $100,000 water-bond referendum. The measure had previously failed twice, but now with women's enthusiastic support it carried by more than three to one.[63]

Using sophisticated statistical methods, the political scientists Kevin Corder and Christina Wolbrecht have estimated women's voting rates in ten states, including Kentucky, in 1920. Their findings support the conventional wisdom that women across the nation did not turn out in numbers equivalent to men and would not do so until the 1960s. They find, however, that Kentucky women were among the most enthusiastic new voters in the nation, with an extraordinary 57 percent turnout. By comparison, a little less than 40 percent of Illinois women and only 6 percent of Virginia women voted.[64]

Corder and Wolbrecht offer several explanations for Kentucky's unusually high rates. Importantly, it was a competitive state with a healthy two-party system, meaning elections mattered there, unlike in Deep South states, where the results were a foregone conclusion. It also had few voting restrictions in place. In states with little competition and many barriers to voting, women, whom the authors classify as "peripheral" (sometimes) rather than "core" (always) voters, tended not to participate; Kentucky was a state with much competition and few barriers. Corder and Wolbrecht also speculate that Kentucky women's participation drove men's unusually high turnout numbers, which topped 85 percent that year, compared to 68 percent nationally.[65]

Based on registration numbers and the state's high turnout rates, it is evident that Black women voted in significant numbers in 1920. Furthermore, newspaper evidence shows that they remained politically active throughout the decade. The Lexington Colored Women's Republican Club began as a temporary measure, but its organizers soon made it permanent and affiliated with the National League of Republican Colored Women. Under the direction of Eliza Belle Jackson and Emma Clay, it became an active force every fall, sometimes meeting at Republican headquarters and sometimes at Mrs. Jackson's funeral parlor. Club members divided the city into precincts, each led by a female captain. They also registered women, hosted "speakings," and encouraged ministers to instruct female congregants on the importance of voting. In Louisville, Black women formed two National League affiliates, on the city's west and east ends. Members played a key role in passing a $5 million municipal bond issue in 1925, $1 million of which went to the University of Louisville to expand education for African Americans.[66]

Rather than seeing the Nineteenth Amendment as a story of pure triumph or the final culmination of a "Century of Struggle," historians who have reconsidered woman suffrage at its centennial show that too many women in the United States, particularly women of color, continued to be denied the rights the amended Constitution promised. African Americans hailed the suffrage victory, seeing it as their best chance to vote since 1890 and as presenting a "crack in the edifice of white supremacy," but in southern state after southern state existing Jim Crow disenfranchisement methods along with new tactics, such as the all-white primary, prevented them from voting.[67]

Although Kentucky is rarely held up as a model of democracy, considering its history of enslavement, violence against Blacks, and policies that made voting more difficult throughout the twentieth century, such as felon restrictions, its record of allowing many Black men to vote after 1870 and Black women to vote after 1920 deserves careful reexamination. The state did not follow the example set by its southern neighbors. It considered but did not pass disenfranchisement measures following Reconstruction, which meant that Black women were a "live issue" when women's voting rights were won. For years, they had worked through church, civic, and educational organizations to improve their communities, and now they lined up enthusiastically to vote in 1920.

Notes

1. Martha S. Jones, *Vanguard: How Black Women Broke Barriers, Won the Vote, and Insisted on Equality for All* (New York: Basic, 2020); Cathleen D. Cahill, *Recasting the Vote: How Women of Color Transformed the Suffrage Movement* (Chapel Hill: University of North Carolina Press, 2020).

2. See, for example, J. Stanley Lemons, *The Woman Citizen: Social Feminism in the 1920s* (Urbana: University of Illinois Press, 1973); and Kristi Andersen, *After Suffrage: Women in Partisan and Electoral Politics before the New Deal* (Chicago: University of Chicago Press, 1996). For a new appraisal, see Liette Gidlow's introduction to a special suffrage issue of the *Journal of Women's History* 32, no. 1 (Spring 2020): 11–13, quote on 12.

3. The organization changed names in 1904, becoming the National Association of Colored Women's Clubs. I have chosen to use National Association of

Colored Women because that was its name when Terrell was president from 1896 to 1901.

4. Mary Church Terrell to Moorfield Storey [Morefield Story], October 27, 1920, Mary Church Terrell Papers, Manuscript Division, Library of Congress, Washington, DC.

5. Kentucky registered 81.7 percent voter turnout in 1916, compared to 61.8 percent for the United States as a whole and just 31.7 percent in the South. See Malcolm E. Jewell and Everett W. Cunningham, *Kentucky Politics* (Lexington: University of Kentucky Press, 1968), 8.

6. "Race Issue Looms Large as Negroes Present Demands," *Owensboro (KY) Messenger,* October 24, 1920, 13, reprinted from the *New York World.*

7. Ellen Carol DuBois, *Woman Suffrage and Women's Rights* (New York: New York University Press, 1998).

. 8. Faye E. Dudden, *Fighting Chance: The Struggle over Woman Suffrage and Black Suffrage in Reconstruction America* (Oxford: Oxford University Press, 2011).

9. Allan J. Lichtman, *The Embattled Vote in America: From the Founding to the Present* (Cambridge, MA: Harvard University Press, 2018). The Kentucky Woman Suffrage Association formed in 1881 and was later renamed the Kentucky Equal Rights Association in 1888. For a full history of the Kentucky movement, see Melanie Beals Goan, *A Simple Justice: Kentucky Women Fight for the Vote* (Lexington: University Press of Kentucky, 2020). The National Woman Suffrage Association and the American Woman Suffrage Association merged in 1890 to form the National American Woman Suffrage Association. For a discussion of racism's role in the national movement, see Lorraine Gates Schuyler, *The Weight of Their Votes: Southern Women and Political Leverage in the 1920s* (Chapel Hill: University of North Carolina Press, 2006), 5.

10. Mary E. Britton, "Woman's Suffrage: A Potent Agency in Public Reforms," *American Catholic Tribune,* July 22, 1887, 1; *Danville Kentucky Advocate,* July 8, 1887, 5. Britton calls herself an "agitator" in "'MEB' Talks to the Point," *Cleveland Gazette,* October 1, 1887, 4. For biographical information, see "Miss Mary E. Britton (MEB)," in *The Afro-American Press and Its Editors,* ed. Irvine Garland Penn (Springfield, MA: Willey, 1891), 415–19.

11. For more information on Indiana's Black suffragists, see Anita J. Morgan, *We Must Be Fearless: The Woman Suffrage Movement in Indiana* (Indianapolis: Indiana Historical Society, 2020). To understand Black women's reform goals, see Evelyn Brooks Higginbotham, *Righteous Discontent: The Women's Movement in the Black Baptist Church, 1880–1920* (Cambridge, MA: Harvard University Press, 1993), quotes on 2, 11; and Darlene Clark Hine, *Hine Sight: Black Women and the Re-construction of American History* (Bloomington: Indiana

University Press, 1994), xxii. For a discussion of race relations in Louisville and the ways "polite racism" functioned, see George C. Wright, *Life behind a Veil: Blacks in Louisville, Kentucky, 1865–1930* (Baton Rouge: Louisiana State University Press, 1985).

12. Karen Cotton McDaniel, "Local Women: The Public Lives of Black Middle Class Women in Kentucky before the 'Modern Civil Rights Movement,'" PhD diss., University of Kentucky, 2013, 72–80; Higginbotham, *Righteous Discontent*, 2, 120.

13. Higginbotham, *Righteous Discontent*, 3; Carol Mattingly, "African American Women and Suffrage in Louisville," African American Women and Suffrage in Louisville (AAWSL) project, n.d., at https://storymaps.arcgis.com /stories/0b16aa6c036846d096cff8c22474a7e0; Erin Wiggins Gilliam, "'A Beacon of Hope': The African American Baptist Church and the Origins of Black Higher Learning Institutions in Kentucky," PhD diss., University of Kentucky, 2018, 133. The AAWSL project, researched and written by Carol Mattingly, includes dozens of biographical sketches of active Black women. The sum of $35,000 at the turn of the twentieth century is equivalent to approximately $1 million dollars today according to http://westegg.com.

14. "Kentucky Negro Educational Association," Notable Kentucky African Americans Database, n.d., at https://nkaa.uky.edu/nkaa/items/show/410 (the Kentucky State Association of Colored Teachers changed its name to Kentucky Negro Educational Association in 1913); "State Teachers' Association, Colored," *Richmond (KY) Climax*, July 11, 1888, 3; "Colored State Teachers," *Louisville Courier-Journal*, July 7, 1886, 3. For biographical details on Lucy Wilmot Smith, see Carol Mattingly, "Lucy Wilmot Smith (1861–1889): Suffragist, Journalist," AAWSL project, at https://louisville.app.box.com/s/hzdwqng3bpai8aijke9k4lnkd3lfpb9q.

15. "News and Notes," *Woman's Journal*, September 20, 1879, 301, at https://iiif.lib.harvard.edu/manifests/view/drs:48874698$307i; Randolph Hollingsworth, "African-American Women Voters in Lexington's School Suffrage Times, 1895–1902: Race Matters in the History of the Kentucky Woman Suffrage Movement," *Ohio Valley History* 20, no. 1 (Spring 2020): 37.

16. Wright, *Life behind a Veil*, 52–55; George C. Wright, *A History of Blacks in Kentucky*, vol. 2: *In Pursuit of Equality, 1890–1980* (Frankfort: Kentucky Historical Society, 1992), 70–71.

17. N. H. Burroughs, "An Appeal to the Christian White Women of the Southland," in *The United Negro: His Problems and His Progress*, ed. I. Garland Penn and J. W. E. Bowen (Atlanta: D. E. Luther, 1902), 522; "Delegation of Ladies before House of Representatives," in *History of the Anti–Separate Coach Movement in Kentucky*, ed. S. E. Smith (Evansville, IN: n.p., n.d. [c. 1895]), 35;

"Furninst [*sic*] the Separate Coach Law," *Stanford Interior Journal,* June 14, 1892, 1. For a description of some of the lawsuits women launched, see Wright, *History of Blacks in Kentucky,* 2:72–75; and Goan, *A Simple Justice,* 66–69. For biographical details on Sneed, see Carol Mattingly, "Lavinia B. Elliot Sneed (circa 1867–1932): Teacher, Speaker, Community Activist," AAWSL project, at https://louisville.app.box.com/s/bh5h9wpxfr2714bg9cfd98w8103lnjca.

18. "Public Meeting, 9:30 A.M., May 2, 1899," in *Proceedings of the Thirty-First Annual Convention of the National American Woman Suffrage Association at the St. Cecilia Club House, Grand Rapids, Mich., April 27, 28, 29, 30, and May 1, 2, 3, 1899* (Warren, OH: Press of Perry, n.d.), 56–61, quotes on 58, 59, at https://babel.hathitrust.org/cgi/pt?id=wu.89073162059.

19. "Public Meeting, 9:30 A.M., May 2, 1899," 59–61.

20. Mary Jane Smith, "The Fight to Protect Race and Regional Identity within the General Federation of Women's Clubs, 1895–1902," *Georgia Historical Quarterly* 94, no. 4 (Winter 2010): 479–513. Kentucky clubwomen's position is documented in "Kentucky Club Women to Act on the Race Question," *Louisville Courier-Journal,* June 4, 1901, 5; "Women," *Louisville Courier-Journal,* June 6, 1901, 2; and "Barred Out," *Louisville Courier-Journal,* June 7, 1901, 2.

21. Higginbotham, *Righteous Discontent,* 152; Alison M. Parker, *Unceasing Militant: The Life of Mary Church Terrell* (Chapel Hill: University of North Carolina Press, 2020); Constitution of the National Association of Colored Women, box 3, folder 1, Fouse Family Papers, 1854–1952, University of Kentucky Special Collections Research Center (UKSCRC), Lexington; Rosalyn Terborg-Penn, *African American Women in the Struggle for the Vote, 1850–1920* (Bloomington: Indiana University Press, 1998), 82–85; Sara Hunter Graham, *Woman Suffrage and the New Democracy* (New Haven, CT: Yale University Press, 1996), 23.

22. "Federation of Women's Clubs," *American Baptist,* January 8, 1904, 1; McDaniel, "Local Women," 16. For biographical details on Georgia Nugent, see Carol Mattingly, "The Nugent Sisters: Georgia (circa 1872), Alice (1875), Ida (1880), and Mollie (1867)," AAWSL project, n.d., at https://louisville.app.box.com/s/imw0ligmb2x3uhmucuqefiluev0kun85.

23. Karen Cotton McDaniel, "Elizabeth 'Lizzie' Fouse (1875–1952): Challenging Stereotypes and Building Community," in *Kentucky Women: Their Lives and Times,* ed. Melissa A. McEuen and Thomas H. Appleton (Athens: University of Georgia Press, 2015), 280; Lucy Harth Smith, *Pictorial Directory of the Kentucky Association of Colored Women* (Lexington: Kentucky Association of Colored Women, 1946); Nikki Brown, *Private Politics and Public Voices: Black Women's Activism from World War I to the New Deal* (Bloomington: Indiana University Press, 2006), 9–10.

24. "State Federation of Women's Clubs," *Lexington Leader,* November 29, 1914, 16. For biographical information on Eliza Belle Jackson, see the entries "Jackson, Eliza" and "Women," in *The Kentucky African American Encyclopedia,* ed. Gerald L. Smith, Karen Cotton McDaniel, and John A. Hardin (Lexington: University Press of Kentucky, 2015), 269, 539.

25. Victor B. Howard, *Black Liberation in Kentucky: Emancipation and Freedom, 1862–1884* (Lexington: University Press of Kentucky, 1983), 147–48.

26. *Proceedings of the First Convention of Colored Men of Kentucky, Held in Lexington, March 22d, 23d, 24th, and 26th, 1866,* Colored Conventions Project, at http://omeka.coloredconventions.org; "Howard School / Normal Institute / Chandler Normal School / Webster Hall (Lexington, KY)," Notable Kentucky African Americans Database, n.d., at https://nkaa.uky.edu/nkaa/items/show/2153; Elsa Barkley Brown, "To Catch the Vision of Freedom: Reconstructing Southern Black Women's Political History, 1865–1880," in *African American Women and the Vote, 1837–1965,* ed. Ann D. Gordon (Amherst: University of Massachusetts Press, 1997), 67, 82.

27. Wright, *History of Blacks in Kentucky,* 2:90–96. For "judiciously and with becoming dignity" and "party that freed them," see Howard, *Black Liberation in Kentucky,* 154. For "time was short," see Marion B. Lucas, *A History of Blacks in Kentucky,* vol. 1: *From Slavery to Segregation, 1760–1891* (Frankfort: Kentucky Historical Society, 1992), 301.

28. Ross A. Webb, "Kentucky: 'Pariah among the Elect,'" in *Radicalism, Racism, and Party Realignment: The Border States during Reconstruction,* ed. Richard O. Curry (Baltimore: Johns Hopkins University Press, 1969), 129; Howard, *Black Liberation in Kentucky,* 157; Lucas, *A History of Blacks in Kentucky,* 1:305–7; Tessa Bishop Hoggard, *In the Courthouse's Shadow: The Lynching of George Carter in Paris, Kentucky* (N.p.: Murky Press, 2021), 25.

29. "Political," *The Crisis* 5, no. 4 (September 1912): 215; US Bureau of the Census, *Thirteenth Census of the United States: 1910,* vol. 1: *Population* (Washington, DC: US Department of Commerce, 1911), chap. 2, at https://www2.census.gov/library/publications/decennial/1910/volume-1/volume-1-p4.pdf, with Black population of Kentucky calculated from national and state numbers on pages 126 and 141. For details on Humphrey, use the finding aid to the Andrew B. Humphrey Collection, Berea College Special Collections and Archives, Berea, KY, at https://berea.libraryhost.com/index.php?=collections/findingaid&id=183&q=&rootcontentid=132977.

30. Goan, *A Simple Justice,* 13–14, 50. The Kentucky Constitution of 1891 created six classes of cities based on population. This section was repealed in 1994.

31. Goan, *A Simple Justice,* 72–73.

32. "Editorial Notes," *Woman's Journal*, December 1, 1894, 377, at https://iiif.lib.harvard.edu/manifests/view/drs:49673169$100i; Kentucky Equal Rights Association (KERA), *Minutes of the Eighth Annual Convention of the Kentucky Equal Rights Association, December 10th, 11th, and 12th, 1895, Court-House of Richmond, KY* (N.p.: n.p., 1895), 6, 10, 22, UKSCRC; Hollingsworth, "African-American Women Voters," 37.

33. "The Women," *Kentucky Leader* (Lexington), October 8, 1895, 1; E. B. Jackson, "Colored Women Declare Themselves for the Women's Ticket," *Kentucky Leader*, October 18, 1895, 4.

34. "The Women," *Kentucky Leader*, November 6, 1895, 7; Hollingsworth, "African-American Women Voters," 37.

35. KERA, *Minutes of the Eighth Annual Convention of the Kentucky Equal Rights Association*, 14; *Journals of the Ninth Annual Convention* [*of the Kentucky Equal Rights Association*], *Held at Guild Hall, Trinity Church, Covington, KY, October 14 and 15, 1897, and the Tenth Annual Convention, Held at Court House, Richmond, KY, December 1, 1898* (London, KY: Mountain Echo, [1899]), 41, UKSCRC; Goan, *A Simple Justice*, 97.

36. Hollingsworth, "African-American Women Voters," 35.

37. "A Hot One for Klair," *Lexington Leader*, January 22, 1902, 4; "Voice from the Other Side," *Lexington Leader*, January 27, 1902, 3; James Duane Bolin, *Bossism and Reform in a Southern City: Lexington, Kentucky, 1880–1940* (Lexington: University Press of Kentucky, 2000), 55–56.

38. Elna C. Green, *Southern Strategies: Southern Women and the Woman Suffrage Question* (Chapel Hill: University of North Carolina Press, 1997), 8–10, 89; Graham, *Woman Suffrage and the New Democracy*, 22; Marjorie Spruill Wheeler, *New Women of the New South: The Leaders of the Woman Suffrage Movement in the Southern States* (New York: Oxford University Press, 1993), xxi, 21. Wheeler argues that NAWSA did not just bow to southerners' racist demands but also exploited those demands for its own gains.

39. Graham, *Woman Suffrage and the New Democracy*, 149–50; "A Federal cross," quoted in Elaine Weiss, *The Woman's Hour: The Great Fight to Win the Vote* (New York: Viking, 2018), 126.

40. Southern States Woman Suffrage Conference pamphlet, appended to Alice Lloyd to Dunster Foster, April 25, 1920, box 64, folder 4, Pettit, Duncan, Gibson Family Papers, 1730–2008, UKSCRC. For a full rendering of Laura Clay's break from her suffrage colleagues and her work to defeat the Nineteenth Amendment, see Goan, *A Simple Justice*.

41. "Suffrage Measure Passed by Senate with 30 to 3 Vote," *Lexington Herald*, March 16, 1920, 1; Rose Young, "The Governor Did Sign," *Woman Voter 7*,

no. 2 (February 1917): 16, at https://babel.hathitrust.org/cgi/pt?id=chi.21171404&view=1up&seq=384&q1=kentucky. On Breckinridge's essential role, see Melba Porter Hay, *Madeline McDowell Breckinridge and the Battle for a New South* (Lexington: University Press of Kentucky, 2009). Arkansas was the other southern state that ratified.

42. "Why Join the Kentucky League of Women Voters?," box 6, folder 3, Anna Dudley McGinn Lilly Papers, 1895–1985, UKSCRC; Carolyn Jefferson-Jenkins, *The Untold Story of Women of Color in the League of Women Voters* (Santa Barbara, CA: Praeger, 2020), 7.

43. "Opinion of W. E. B. DuBois," *The Crisis* 20, no. 1 (May 1920): 5–6.

44. Goan, *A Simple Justice*, 211; "The New Citizen and Her Vote," *The Crisis* 20, no. 6 (October 1920): 279; "Guide to the Microfilm Edition of the Records of the National Association of Colored Women's Clubs, 1895–1992," at http://www.lexisnexis.com/documents/academic/upa_cis/1555_recsnatlassoccolwmsclubpt1.pdf; "I See in *The Courier-Journal*," April 3, 1920, 4.

45. Elizabeth Lindsay Davis, "History of the State Federation of Kentucky," in *Lifting as They Climb* (Washington, DC: National Association of Colored Women, 1933), 406; "Colored Column," *Richmond (KY) Daily Register,* May 22, 1920, 4; "Colored Women Meet Monday Night," *Lexington Leader,* September 19, 1920, 2; "Colored Notes," *Lexington Leader,* October 21, 1920, 2.

46. "Organization News," *Woman Citizen,* January 24, 1920, 764, at https://babel.hathitrust.org/cgi/pt?id=inu.30000098651064;view=1up;seq=692; "Negro Women Take Part in Kentucky G. O. P. Convention," *St. Louis Post-Dispatch,* March 3, 1920, 3; "Autobiography," appended to "Negro Woman Sits as Delegate in Kentucky Republican Convention," n.d., Women's Suffrage in Tennessee Digital Collection, Tennessee Virtual Archive, at https://cdm15138.contentdm.oclc.org/digital/collection/p15138c01127/id/557/rec/1; "Negro Woman Sits as Delegate in Ky. Republican Convention," *New York Age,* March 13, 1920, 1.

47. John J. Howe to Fellow Voter, n.d., box: September–December 1920, Samuel M. Wilson and Mary Shelby Wilson Democratic Party Papers, 1896–1952, 1920–1930 (bulk dates), UKSCRC, emphasis in original; "1920 Suffrage Victory Year," *Louisville Courier-Journal,* December 26, 1920, 25.

48. US Bureau of the Census, *Fourteenth Census of the United States: 1920, Bulletin: Population: Kentucky,* 1920, at https://www2.census.gov/library/publications/decennial/1920/bulletins/demographics/population-ky-composition-and-characteristics.pdf; "The New Citizen and Her Vote," 279. Kentucky had unsuccessfully considered disfranchisement measures similar to those adopted in the Deep South. The Heflin bill would have instituted both a literacy requirement and a grandfather clause, but it died in committee in 1904. Kentucky did

adopt the Australian Ballot, often identified as a disenfranchisement tactic, but its tradition of emblazing ballots with party symbols (log cabin for Republicans, rooster for Democrats) allowed illiterate voters to cast a straight party vote. Kentucky sanctioned poll taxes, another favorite southern voter-suppression measure, but voters had to pay the tax to vote only in some municipal, not state and national, elections. See "'Grandfather' Bill Killed," *Lexington Leader,* February 2, 1904, 1; Jill Lepore, *These Truths: A History of the United States* (New York: Norton, 2018), 344; J. Kevin Corder and Christina Wolbrecht, *Counting Women's Ballots: Female Voters from Suffrage through the New Deal* (New York: Cambridge University Press, 2016), 100.

49. "Women in Fayette Are Enthusiastic," *Lexington Herald,* September 18, 1920, 1; Mrs. Samuel M. Wilson to Miss Elizabeth Loughridge, October 2, 1920, box: September–December 1920, Wilson Democratic Party Papers.

50. Liette Gidlow, "Resistance after Ratification: The Nineteenth Amendment, African American Women, and the Problem of Female Disfranchisement after 1920," in *Women and Social Movements in the U.S., 1600–2000* (Alexandria, VA: Alexander Street, 2017), 18; "Colored Women Will Campaign for G. O. P.," *Gadsden (AL) Times,* August 18, 1920, 4, quoting Miller.

51. Mrs. Samuel M. Wilson to Miss Rebecca Patton, September 14, 1920, and Chairman Woman's Department to Madam, September 1920, box: September–December 1920, Wilson Democratic Party Papers; "Suggested Form of Letter to County Chairmen," September 25, 1920, box: 1912–1920, Wilson Democratic Party Papers; "Democratic Women Should Votes [*sic*]," *Adair County (KY) News,* May 12, 1920, 4; *Elizabethtown News,* quoted in "Negro Women's Vote," *Owensboro Messenger,* August 26, 1920, 4; "Beckham," *Kentucky Irish American* (Louisville), August 21, 1920, 1; "The Balance of Power," *Owensboro Messenger,* September 22, 1920, 6.

52. "Voting Places for Women," *Danville (KY) Advocate-Messenger,* September 23, 1920, 4; "Registration on Tuesday to Break All Local Records," *Owensboro Messenger,* October 3, 1920, 10; "Slade," *Clay City (KY) Times,* October 14, 1920, 2.

53. Emma Guy Cromwell, *Citizenship: A Manual for Voters* (N.p.: self-published, 1920), 40, UKSCRC; "Democrats Gain," *Danville Kentucky Advocate,* October 6, 1920, 1.

54. "The Negro Vote," in NAACP, *Eleventh Annual Report* (Baltimore: NAACP, January 1921), 25, at https://babel.hathitrust.org/cgi/pt?id=uc1.b34786 05&view=1up&seq=1&q1=10uisville; Nancy F. Cott, "Across the Great Divide: Women in Politics before and after 1920," in *Women, Politics, and Change,* ed. Louise A. Tilly and Patricia Gurin (New York: Russell Sage, 1990), 53; Liette

Gidlow, "The Sequel: The Fifteenth Amendment, the Nineteenth Amendment, and Southern Black Women's Struggle to Vote," *Journal of the Gilded Age and Progressive Era* 17, no. 3 (2018): 443.

55. "Registration in Danville Is Heavy," *Danville Advocate-Messenger,* October 5, 1920, 1; H. E. C. Bryant, "Southern Women Vote," *Suffragist,* November 1920, 286, at https://babel.hathitrust.org/cgi/pt?id=uiug.30112002750062;view=1up;seq=318; "Suffragists Lag in Going to the Polls," *Louisville Courier-Journal,* October 6, 1920, 1; "Women Swell the Democratic Vote in the State," *Danville Advocate-Messenger,* October 6, 1920, 1; "The Registration in Lexington," *Lexington Herald*, October 7, 1920, 4; "City Registration Puts Crimp in Republicans," *Bourbon (KY) News,* October 8, 1920, 1.

56. "Women Swell the Democratic Vote in the State"; "The Negro in Politics," *Danville Advocate-Messenger,* October 5, 1920, 2.

57. "Haager Talks on Negro Question," *Owensboro Messenger,* October 19, 1920, 3; "Gov. Morrow," *Danville Kentucky Advocate,* October 15, 1920, 1; *Owensboro Messenger,* October 6, 1920, 6.

58. Bryant, "Southern Women Vote"; Ella Rush Murray, letter to the editor, *Suffragist,* January–February 1921, 364, at https://babel.hathitrust.org/cgi/pt?id=uiug.30112002750062;view=1up;seq=394.

59. For references to "negro domination," see the correspondence in the September–December 1920 box, Wilson Democratic Party Papers, in particular Mrs. Anna Featheraton to Mrs. Samuel M. Wilson, October 19, 1920. See also "Democrats Look to Women to Give Kentucky Victory," *Owensboro Messenger,* October 21, 1920, 3.

60. "Will the Women Vote?" and "'Keep Kentucky White' the Democratic Slogan," *Bourbon News,* October 1, 1920, 4, 8; "Haager Talks on Negro Question"; "Ralph Gilbert Opens Campaign at Lawrenceburg," *Danville Advocate-Messenger,* October 21, 1920, 2, 4, capitalization in the original.

61. The number of women voters was calculated using 1920 census data and estimates of turnout from Corder and Wolbrecht, *Counting Women's Ballots,* 138; see also "Quietest Election in History of Daviess County," *Owensboro Messenger,* November 3, 1920, 3.

62. James C. Klotter, *Kentucky: Portrait in Paradox, 1900–1950* (Frankfort: Kentucky Historical Society, 1996), 268.

63. Corder and Wolbrecht, *Counting Women's Ballots;* "Ohio County Rolls Up Good Majority," *Hartford (KY) Republican,* November 5, 1920, 1; "State's Full Vote for Cox," *Louisville Courier-Journal,* November 21, 1920, 51; "Women Help Vote Water Bond Issue," *Danville Advocate-Messenger,* November 6, 1920, 2.

64. Corder and Wolbrecht, *Counting Women's Ballots,* 136–38.

65. Corder and Wolbrecht, *Counting Women's Ballots,* 141–44.

66. "Colored Notes," *Lexington Leader,* November 18, 1920, 2; Andersen, *After Suffrage,* 84; "Colored Notes," *Lexington Leader,* October 11, 1928, September 30, 1921, as well as September 30, October 21, and November 9, 1923; "Women Organize," *Lexington Leader,* September 23, 1923, 14; Carol Mattingly, "Political Activity," AAWSL project, n.d., at https://storymaps.arcgis.com/stories /0b16aa6c036846d096cff8c22474a7e0; "Relying on Vote," *Louisville Courier-Journal,* October 20, 1925, 10.

67. Gidlow, "Resistance after Ratification," 5.

10

"Give '*Us*' Something to Yell For!"

Athletics and the Black Campus Movement at the University of Kentucky, 1965–1969

Gerald L. Smith

"The word is definitely out. No University of Kentucky coach will play a Negro, because the University of Kentucky is a member of the Southeastern Conference," wrote Herschel Weil. His statement appeared in a letter to the editor of the *Lexington Herald Leader* dated December 10, 1961. Weil was disturbed that Kentucky African Americans could play on collegiate teams in the North but were not being recruited by the University of Kentucky (UK) because of an apparent "unwritten understanding" among institutions of higher learning in the Deep South. As a 1922 graduate of the university, he encouraged UK officials to recruit eligible Black players. "And if that puts us out of the Southeastern Conference it puts us out. Our prediction is that other Universities in the Southeastern Conference would follow our example."[1] The Big Eight, Big Ten, and Missouri Valley Conference had lifted their bans on Black players soon after World War II.

In May 1963, the UK Athletic Association adopted a policy to integrate the athletic program.[2] Less than three years later, Nate Northington signed a football scholarship with UK, becoming the first African American to receive a grant-in-aid in the Southeastern Conference's (SEC) history. For four years, a copy of Weil's letter to the editor remained in the UK presidential files. On December 28, 1965, President John W. Oswald wrote Weil a letter noting that he was "pleased that we have been successful in signing our first Negro athlete and look forward to many others now that the ice has been broken."[3]

The UK Athletic Association's bold policy to integrate its teams and the eventual signing of Nate Northington was not enough, however, to ensure African American students that the university was committed to integration in athletics or the classroom. Although the "ice ha[d] been broken," the water was still very cold. The university had been forced to open its doors to Black graduate students following a successful lawsuit filed by Lyman T. Johnson, a Black schoolteacher from Louisville. Black graduate students first enrolled for classes during the summer of 1949. Mary A. Adams began working on her graduate degree in September 1949 and recalled that UK was "not very well-liked in the Black community. Most of the students and faculty pretty much ignored you." The Supreme Court decision in *Brown v. Board of Education of Topeka* in 1954 further pressed southern schools to address segregation in education.[4]

Frank R. Cannon Jr. was among the first African American students to attend UK in the 1950s. He lived off campus and had little contact with white students outside the classroom. Cannon recalled he "never had any run-ins with anyone and was not prevented from attending athletic events." He simply "had no desire to go."[5] S. T. Roach, the Black head basketball coach at Lexington's Dunbar High School, remembered acquiring two lower-arena basketball seats to watch UK play against Temple in the late 1950s. Temple had two African American star players on the team. Once Roach and Dunbar's principal, Paul Guthrie, were in their seats, they were asked to move despite presenting their tickets. As public-school employees, they decided not to protest. "The only move we were going to make was out of there," recalled Roach.[6]

As Black students enrolled in previously all-white schools, southern white players' chances of having to play against Black players increased. By the mid-1960s, SEC football teams gradually began competing against integrated teams at home and away in order to establish and maintain a national ranking. But white coaches and administrators remained reluctant to recruit Black players to their own southern teams. "Thus, the protected white space of the football field and the basketball court continued to remain relatively safe from the intrusion of African Americans for up to a decade after the initial desegregation of southern universities," writes the historian Charles Martin.[7]

In the 1960s, Black students faced a cold environment on UK's campus and questioned Coach Adolph Rupp's weak and disingenuous efforts to desegregate the basketball program. In the spring of 1967, they formed a social and political organization to unite Black students that they called "Orgena," which was "a Negro" spelled backward. That fall they protested against UK's all-white team at basketball games. Bill Turner, described as an "energetic leader" of the group, submitted a letter to the editor of the *Louisville Defender* outlining the organization's goals, which included recruitment of Black athletes. He wrote: "We consider basketball the preoccupation at this school and therefore would define our situation as closer to resolution if we had a black man on the team. We're interested in integration, whatever that means, throughout the school, not in isolated areas. We are currently demonstrating at home games as a pressuring agent on those in whose hands the recruitment lies."[8]

Black students met with the university's president, director of athletics, and basketball coach (Rupp) about their concerns. They had cheered for African American members of the football team and the one African American on the track team, but they also wanted a reason to "yell" for the UK basketball team in Memorial Coliseum. As a member of the Black Student Union (BSU), Jim Embry believed recruiting Black basketball players would "change this attitude around the state that UK is just [a] racist institution because of Rupp."[9] The recruitment of Black athletes was a signature issue for UK Black students. They strategically used it to bring attention to the myriad concerns they faced on and off campus, which included harassment and racial discrimination in housing and the classroom.

Scholars have expanded the themes, topics, and periodization of the Black freedom struggle beyond the traditional time frame, 1954–1965. The Black Campus Movement (BCM) played a key role in events shaping the academic, cultural, and political environment at both historically Black and white colleges and universities during the late 1960s and early 1970s. Black students formed their own organizations to pressure historically white institutions to recruit Black students, hire African American faculty and administrators, establish Black studies courses and departments, and create an inclusive and safe learning environment. They listed their demands, occupied buildings, and held public demonstrations. Many of these students had participated in the sit-in demonstrations, marches, and voter-registration drives in the South.[10] Martha Biondi writes: "The Black student movement was part of the Black Power movement, whose rhetoric, political analysis, and tactics broke from the civil rights movement, but whose goals of Black representation and inclusion were shared with civil rights activists."[11]

This essay explores the recruitment of Black athletes to UK as well as the challenges Black students faced in addressing the lack of racial diversity on the basketball team. Jim Embry, president of the UK BSU in the late 1960s, believed having a star Black athlete on campus would give Black students leverage as they pressed the administration to support their goals and interests. "You might say that a star athlete means more to UK than the average student. They [athletes] could do things to help themselves and other[s] concerned."[12] This perspective was central to the BCM at UK between 1965 and 1969. While other BSUs pressured administrations to increase the numbers of Black coaches, athletes, professors, and students on campus, UK's BSU recognized the school's national profile in basketball and sought to use this as an opportunity to improve African Americans' plight on campus.[13] Becoming the first SEC school to desegregate its football program was indeed a milestone for UK, but the continued existence of an all-white basketball program hindered African Americans' efforts to break down other barriers on campus. The BSU was committed to addressing Adolph Rupp's resistance to integration. They believed the addition of a Black player on the basketball team would be a "symbol" of racial progress.

As early as the 1950s, other higher-learning institutions in Kentucky eliminated the color line in their athletic programs. President Adron Doran at Morehead State University noted: "Our coaches formed a good connection in Birmingham, for example, and we just went down there and recruited all of the good athletes in football, basketball, and track that we could find. The appearance of good Black athletes assisted the movement toward integration as people became more accepting of Blacks every time a Black crossed the goal line in football or made a field goal in basketball." In 1954, University of Louisville football coach Frank Camp added Lenny Lyles and three other Black players to the team. Allan Wade Houston Sr., Sam Smith, and Eddie Whitehead were the first to play varsity basketball for the University of Louisville in 1964. Coach E. A. Diddle signed Western Kentucky University's first Black players, Clem Haskins and Dwight Smith, in 1963. By 1961, Eastern Kentucky University had two African Americans on the track team.[14]

The recruitment of Black players to UK was slow. The institution's affiliation with the SEC and Rupp's unwillingness to promote desegregation only partly explains the scene at UK. African American athletes and their families had to decide if they wanted to be the "first" to break the color barrier in the SEC. White resistance was real both outside and inside the state. For instance, W. H. Grady, a former UK athlete and later board member wrote an angry letter to President Frank G. Dickey in 1963. "Why this sudden urge and great rush to integrate U. K. athletics? How come and what for? I have the feeling that you may have been influenced by the constant and repeated agitation in our Louisville paper—The great minder of other people's business." Grady continued: "I am unalterably opposed to this repulsive thing, and respectfully request that you make this known to the Board of Trustees when or if this subject comes up before them."[15] R. C. Kash, a graduate of 1925, wrote to President Dickey in April 1963 that UK "should remain an all-white member of the SEC, and that the matter should be pressed no further. We endorse without reservation the 'tough' attitude and policies of Coach Rupp and Coach [Charlie] Bradshaw because the University of Kentucky is no place for weaklings."[16]

Yet in the early 1960s others wrote letters to the UK president and board of trustees expressing their support of a pro-integration policy toward athletics. The Lexington Board of the National Conference of Christians and Jews submitted a resolution offering "wholehearted support." A graduate of 1951 wrote: "I am proud that the University is taking the lead in integrating athletics in the Southeastern Conference." The noted Kentucky historian and member of the Athletics Association, Tom Clark, was pleased with the vote to integrate athletics. In a letter to Dickey dated May 1963, Clark described the university board's decision that year as "social history for the country as a whole." He added that it was important to establish a "due date" for the active recruitment of Black players. "I would not want to see us drag our feet, and I am sure this is not the intention of anybody."[17]

The governor of the state, Edward (Ned) T. Breathitt, played a key role in the recruitment of the first Black player on a UK team in 1965. According to Breathitt, who was also chairman of the UK board of trustees, Coach Bradshaw (football) and Coach Rupp (basketball) did not want to be the first to sign Black players in the SEC. "So [UK president John] Oswald and I said we are just going to do it." Breathitt invited Nate Northington, an outstanding student and athlete from Thomas Jefferson

Nate Northington signs letter of intent with the University of Kentucky. He is surrounded by (*left to right*) Governor Ned Breathitt, UK football coach Charlie Bradshaw, high school coach Jim Gray, and UK president John Oswald. Photograph courtesy of the University of Kentucky Athletic Department, Lexington.

High School in Louisville, along with his family, to the governor's mansion for Sunday dinner. In his autobiography, Northington described what happened following dinner. The governor "made a convincing presentation to me about going to UK" and expressed how he and the president and board wanted to integrate the athletic program. "He was a good salesman, really good," recalled Northington. The opportunity to be the first Black to sign in the SEC was significant in shaping Northington's final decision. "After [the governor] spoke of the tremendous significance of this event and the everlasting impact it would have, not only on me but on other African American athletes throughout the South, he pulled a scholarship offer from his coat pocket and asked if I would agree to accept and play football for my home state. At that point I was not only convinced, but I felt it was the right thing to do."[18]

It appeared that the signing of Northington was settled, but William and Flossie Northington, his parents, still had reservations. Mrs. Northington wrote the governor letters soon after her son's signing, expressing her concerns about his decision and for his safety in playing in the SEC. In the first letter, she noted how she and her husband did not "like the way things were handled. We should have been there when he signed. We feel like he was pushed into it by you, and [by] a lot of promises which was maybe not intended to be kept in the first place or to make a political name. I feel you are more interested in this state than in my son." In a second letter dated December 24, 1965, she wrote: "It is my impression that Nat was over-awed by your advocacy of a signing with U. Of K. This, I think, is not good. . . . [W]e are not willing to allow him to be coerced into going any-place." She further wrote: "I am apprehensive as to Nat's safety as the first Negro to play in the Southeastern Conference. I realize the importance of integration of the Southeastern Conference and as a Negro I am an advo-cate of it. But this does not mean that I would like to have my son break the race barrier, especially not before I receive guarantee of his safety." Mrs. Northington requested a meeting with the administration and coaches and noted she was not comfortable with Nate playing for UK.[19] Apparently a meeting was scheduled, and concerns were addressed because Northington matriculated at UK in the fall of 1966. There is also a photo in Northington's autobiography of his mother with Governor Breathitt, a UK football coach, and his former high school coach in what appears to be another staged signing with UK.[20]

Mrs. Edwin I. Baer, a white friend of the Northington family, also wrote to Governor Breathitt with concerns for Nate's safety: "In persuading Nat to go to U. of K. you have placed this fine American in a position that I hope you, and the U. of K. and the students of that school are going to find one of great responsibility. I truly feel that the responsibility of his safety depends on you, the school and all connected with the school who have been lucky enough to get this fine young boy to stay home." Breathitt responded by assuring Mrs. Baer that he felt "a heavy responsibility" for Northington's safety at UK and elsewhere. According to Northington, it would be more than twenty-five years before he would meet the governor again.[21]

In addition to Northington, the university offered a scholarship to Greg Page, an all-state defensive end from Middlesboro High School,[22] and track coach Bob Johnson offered long-distance runner Skip Rankin from Somerset a scholarship in 1966. This trio of Black athletes arrived on campus in the midst of the Black freedom struggle. Direct-action protests, riots, voter-registration drives, and racial violence permeated much of the nation during the 1960s.

Theodore Berry began attending classes at UK in 1965. He recalled an "atmosphere of prejudice across the campus whether you lived on campus or whether you didn't live on the campus." P. G. Peeples Sr. came in 1966 and remembered hearing racial slurs and finding out about fraternities with mascot dogs that they would sometimes sic on Black students. Peeples also recalled seeing an African American player hurt during a football game and a fan commenting, "Give him a piece of watermelon and drag him off the field."[23] It was this kind of environment that motivated Black students to pressure the administration into addressing racial problems on campus.

In April 1967, the *Kentucky Kernel,* UK's student newspaper, published a special section titled "The Negro at UK." The paper reported the myriad challenges Black students faced: "All realize that discrimination and prejudice exists, but many find it hard to pinpoint." Several Black students did share their personal experiences. For example, one student said she moved out of the dorm room because her white roommates thought she should be the one to clean the room. Another student recalled studying in a dorm room and hearing students yell "nigger" and "Ku Klux Klan." Sue Lauderdale, a Black freshman from Louisville, noted that she wanted to be on the *Kernel* staff but was "treated coldly." The *Kernel* found that Black students felt "isolated" in the dorms and that some believed their professors discriminated against them. They had no desire to join white fraternities or sororities, which they also believed were discriminatory, but they at least wanted the assurance that they could join if they wished to do so. The climate led some students to leave the university. As of spring 1966, there were only sixty-six full-time Black students on campus, down from two hundred. The track star Skip Rankin was among the students who left.[24]

Meanwhile, Page and Northington received playing time on the freshman football team and were expected to be solid contributors to the varsity squad. But this expectation changed on August 22, 1967. Page suffered what doctors described as "a probable bruise of the spinal cord" during a practice session. He was paralyzed, and a tracheotomy had to be performed to help reduce his breathing complications.

Nearly six weeks after the injury, Page died at the UK hospital. The football team had a scheduled home game against Ole Miss the next day. Page's parents insisted the school not cancel the game. On September 30, 1967, Nate Northington broke the color barrier in SEC football. He played three minutes and seventeen seconds as a safety during the first quarter. He had to leave the game because of a lingering shoulder injury. "I wish I could have played the whole game. But I was just happy to be in there."[25] Given the university's history and lack of success in recruiting Black players, rumors about Page's death swirled: "They killed Greg." By the time of his death, Wilbur Hackett Jr. from Louisville was among the three African American freshmen on the football team. His friends told him: "Man, you next."[26] This tragedy did not bode well for the university's image. Nevertheless, the school made a sincere effort to show compassion, sensitivity, and respect toward the Page family.

The death of Page hit the small number of African Americans on campus hard. They were in an ongoing struggle for support and inclusion. Inspired by the Black Power movement and social protests around the country, Black UK students were increasingly anxious to address the issues on their own campus. The Campus Committee on Human Rights, the YWCA–YMCA, and Alpha Phi Alpha, an African American fraternity, served as the main organizations to welcome them. Orgena sought to bring unity to African American students. It was the voice for Black students meeting with UK officials and provided "a social and cultural outlet for the Negro who finds such activities lacking" at UK.[27]

Northington decided to leave the school because he felt he grieved alone.[28] Remaining at UK became an increasing challenge for Black students. The *Kernel* reported that Kentucky high school guidance counselors were not encouraging Black students to attend UK because of the campus environment. Louisville school counselors disagreed and argued that students should make the decision where they wanted to attend college. The assistant principal at predominately Black Central High School said he was not sure why Black students at the school had so little interest in UK. "It'll just take some time. I think it'll take time in the SEC for them to get use to Negro ball players. Western is bringing those Negro fellows on the basketball team—it's going to help a lot. That's one of the big drawing cards. I think they feel more or less like the school is a little more liberal or open minded when they see them having any number of Negroes on athletic teams. I think athletics gives them a big impression."[29]

In the spring of 1967, the US Office of Education sought to further examine SEC schools to make sure they were in line with Title VI of the Civil Rights Act of 1964. Although UK had desegregated its football team, and Skip Rankin and Jim Green had signed with the track team, the other athletic programs—basketball, baseball, tennis, swimming, and golf—had not desegregated. The overwhelming concern was Coach Rupp's minimal effort to recruit Black players to the basketball team. His response: "We have a policy about recruiting. We're going to get basketball players. Period. Regardless of their color, we're going to get those boys who can meet our academic requirements. You can't go through a mock session in this recruiting business. You either want the boy or you don't. He can either play here or he can't. He will make his grades or he'll flunk out. We're not going to integrate just for the sake of it." Rupp often referenced the resistance of schools in the Deep South to play against Black players as his reason (excuse) for not recruiting Black players. "Have you ever been in some of those places on our schedule? A guy would have every right to be afraid," said Rupp.[30]

On April 26, 1967, Rupp appeared before a standing-room crowd in the Student Center Theater, along with athletic director Bernie Shively and Coach Bradshaw. When asked why he sought after only Black star athletes, Rupp's response was: "I have never recruited a white boy that I thought couldn't make the team. . . . [W]e go after the best." Shively was asked whether the "anti-Negro attitude" on campus affected the recruitment of Black athletes. "I don't think we have an anti-Negro feeling on this campus," he said. Audience members both applauded and booed when questions were raised about the lack of Black players on the basketball team.[31]

True enough, UK had tried to recruit Black players. Wes Unseld, an outstanding basketball player from Seneca High School in Louisville, was recruited after leading his school to state championship victories in 1963 and 1964. He was Kentucky's Mr. Basketball but received death threats and a letter from a group in Lexington discouraging him from signing with Kentucky. Larry Conley, a UK player, made a personal visit to Louisville to try and persuade Unseld to come to UK. President Oswald and assistant basketball coach Harry Lancaster visited the star player as well. Oswald's son, John, commented that his "dad felt Rupp had sort of undermined his efforts with Unseld. . . . It was almost as if Rupp were sending a message by his absence. He [Oswald] had put his prestige and commitment on the line and Rupp sent his assistant." Unseld signed with the University of Louisville and became an all-American.[32]

In 1965, UK recruited Alfred "Butch" Beard from Breckinridge County. Beard had led his high school basketball team to the state championship that year. He was a two-time All-State selection and named

Mr. Basketball. Like Unseld, though, Beard signed with Louisville. Rupp did meet with Beard and his mother, but the recruitment visit did not go well. Beard recalled how Rupp shared his harrowing experiences playing against southern teams and how he was not really convincing in his effort to recruit Black players. "We decided that Rupp was under pressure to recruit a Black player, but he didn't really want one." Pressed in an interview to explain how he knew Rupp was not serious about Black players, Beard replied: "Believe me, you know."[33]

Perry Wallace from Nashville, Tennessee, was another Black player Kentucky recruited. Wallace said he spoke to Unseld and Beard about Kentucky. "They were measured. . . . They didn't talk down Kentucky, but they didn't have a lot of good stuff to say, either. What they did say was that just in general, you'd want to be careful going in there integrating, being a guinea pig." Assistant Coaches Lancaster and Joe Hall had recruited Wallace, but Wallace had not met Rupp. "It wasn't that I wanted special treatment, it was that this was a special situation," remembered Wallace. "Anybody that wouldn't lend that personal touch, I couldn't go there. I liked Coach Lancaster and Coach Hall. If Coach Rupp had shown a little bit of that, I might have gone to Kentucky. But to have the top guy say nary a word, that was a very important consideration."[34]

Rupp was hugely successful with his all-white teams, coaching four National Collegiate Athletic Association (NCAA) championship squads and building a legendary career. Known as the "Baron of the Bluegrass," Rupp was labeled as "arrogant, egocentric, sometimes just plain rude because of his focus on winning." According to one of Rupp's former players, Bill Spivey, "He wanted everyone to hate him and he succeeded." Because his teams still remained all-white three years after UK had voted to desegregate its athletic program, there were doubts about his willingness to sign Black players. Although the governor, president, and student body had favored breaking the color barrier, Rupp's answers to his critics for not having any Black players were shallow and did little for his reputation in the Black community. Coach Roach summarized that African Americans in the state held ill feelings toward UK during the Rupp years. "With his stature, he could have made all the difference in the world," said Roach.[35]

Black student activist Bill Turner met with Rupp about recruiting Black players. According to Turner, Rupp said: "I don't need any of them. And I have never had any of them. And I don't want any of them." In

1967, Jim Embry arrived at UK as an African American freshman. He noted that there was "some awareness he [Rupp] didn't like Black folk." After Embry became president of the BSU, he, too, had a meeting with Rupp at his office in Memorial Coliseum. Rupp invited Embry to step outside his office onto the basketball court, "and he pointed and said, 'You see those banners up there? I have won these many NCAA championships, these many SEC titles and so forth,' and what he said to me was . . . 'I don't need no colored boys to win, no NCAA crown.' He was not belligerent, he wasn't hostile, but those were his words."[36]

By the mid-1960s, white coaches at predominately white schools were still sparingly playing their Black players in games. The quota was based on home and away games. "Two Blacks at home. Three on the road. And four when behind." Historically, racism had framed Black athletes as lacking the discipline, smarts, and team skills that were assumed among white players. Black players had "natural" talent but were supposedly not able to function intelligently in game-time situations.[37]

On March 19, 1966, at the Cole Field House on the campus of the University of Maryland, Rupp's Kentucky team faced the Texas Western Miners from El Paso, coached by Don Haskins. For the first time ever in college basketball, five Black players started against five white players in a national championship collegiate game. "What a piece of history," recalled Nolan Richardson, one of Haskins's first Black players at Texas Western. "If basketball ever took a turn, that was it."[38] Not much was written publicly about the racial dynamics surrounding the game, but African Americans and white fans clearly understood the social implications of this matchup. The Kentucky band played "Dixie" and paraded the Confederate flag. From the perspective of one observer on the significance of the game, "Collectively, the state they represented, the school they represented, the state of mind they represented for white America was clearly that they were carrying the banner for white America."[39]

When Texas Western guard Bobby Joe Hill stole the ball on two consecutive plays from Kentucky's players to score a layup, African American fans cheered loudly. Chester Grundy was among the UK Black students who gathered in Haggin Hall to cheer for Texas Western, placing a towel beneath the door to conceal their jubilation. "We identified with them," said P. G. Peeples. "African Americans all across Kentucky identified with Texas Western." Surprisingly, the Miners won the game 72–65. The victory was "a clear message to elite southern teams," wrote Charles Martin, "that continued segregation on the basketball court endangered their ability to compete successfully for national championships."[40]

On March 29, 1966, Robert L. Johnson, vice president for student affairs, claimed in a letter to Athletic Director Shively that President Oswald had told him that Rupp had said he "was actively recruiting two Negro athletes from Harrison County and one from Nashville, Tennessee." But, Johnson cautioned, "[I have] already had several individuals make it a point to tell me that Coach Rupp will never have a Negro basketball player and that the University is being hypocritical when it says that it is trying to recruit such young men." Johnson asked Shively to follow the process to confirm that the "University is fulfilling in spirit the public statement it has made."[41] But when the 1966–1967 season began, Kentucky's basketball roster was once again all white.

Rupp continued to defend what he considered his effort to recruit Black players. "Beard wanted to come here in the worst way and then ended up in Louisville. Unseld wouldn't even talk to us." Rupp added: "Why do people always want to point to this recruiting stuff with the Negro? It happens with a lot of boys . . . Negro and white. But to say we are not trying to recruit them is wrong. We are and will continue to until we get them on our conditions or they go elsewhere."[42]

For African American students at UK, integrating athletics was less about winning championships and more about equal opportunity. They saw the connection between athletics and the issues they were seeking to address on campus. Recruiting Black players was more about the Black students' future and the students coming after them than about the legacy of Coach Rupp. Orgena hosted a picnic for Jim McDaniels, a Black player recognized as Kentucky's Mr. Basketball in 1967. Bill Turner was president of the Campus Committee on Human Rights and traveled with Coach Hall and another person to Scottsville, Kentucky, to help recruit McDaniels. Turner does not remember many details except "being in a big state car, it looked like a state police car." Hall did most of the talking, while Turner as a young college student felt "like a potted plant." Turner did recall telling McDaniels how much his coming to UK would mean to Black students. In a *Kernel* article published in April 1967, Turner said: "Basketball is king here. If a Negro gets on the basketball team, it will be the beginning of a major breakthrough. This would be a good starting point."[43]

Don Pratt, a white student and member of the Christian Fellowship organization on the campus, claimed that a member of the Student Nonviolent Coordinating Committee told him that UK was blacklisted for not recruiting Black players. In April 1967, Phil Patton, a representative in UK's student government, introduced a resolution that was read before that government requesting an investigation of the basketball team's attempts at recruiting Black players. Although the request was tabled and given to the Human Rights Committee, there was concern that only "superstar" players (apparently nonexistent) were being sought by the coaching staff.[44]

It appeared the university would sign Felix Thurston, a six-foot-six all-state player from Owensboro as its first Black basketball player during the summer of 1967. Rupp wrote Shively to tell him that he and Lancaster had visited with Thurston and that Thurston had visited UK and met with students. Rupp said he met with Thurston's mother and assured her that her son would be fine traveling farther South. President Oswald wrote to Thurston's mother informing her "there is no reason for concern on our part relative to danger to him should he decide to participate in SEC basketball." On July 12, 1967, Thurston and his mother signed an "Inter-conference Letter of Intent" with UK. However, it turned out that Thurston had previously signed with another school, Trinity College in San Antonio, Texas, before his interest in UK, which complicated the process. Shively informed Oswald: "I feel that we have a fifty–fifty chance that the boy will enroll here in September." Thurston did not come. UK would begin another basketball season with an all-white team.[45]

By the fall of 1967, the Black Campus Movement was gathering significant momentum on the national level. There was growing interest for a "Negro History" course at UK. The Campus Committee on Human Rights organized a second "Bitch-In" to serve as a forum to discuss social issues. The first Bitch-In had been a three-hour gathering on the student center patio that attracted the interest of more than two thousand people, where the discussion ranged from whether ROTC students should receive course credit to the integration of athletics. The second Bitch-In was titled "Social Change and the Negro at UK." Bernie Shively was present to answer questions about the integration of athletics. According to Shively, UK was not able to sign McDaniels because of his poor grades. McDaniels had expressed serious interest in UK but would subsequently sign with Western Kentucky University. Years later, he recalled how Rupp did not seriously recruit him and that he had spent less than twenty minutes with Rupp during a six-day visit to Lexington. "I never felt that warm and fuzzy feeling up there and I did not want to be the first African American to go up there."[46]

On November 1, 1967, Shively and Robert Johnson met with Black leaders to discuss "the big 164-dollar question . . . How can the University attract more Negro athletes?" Orgena and the Human Rights Committee were willing to help recruit players by promoting the university. However, Dr. Zirl Palmer, a Black Lexington pharmacist, stated: "The University and its officials have placed a bad image before the people of this country and the world." The discrimination that Black UK faculty, students, and athletes had experienced made it difficult to attract Blacks' interest in the school. The idea of establishing a Booster Club to attract students and athletes to the university was discussed at the meeting. Some African Americans thought the meeting was a "sham" set up merely to minimize negative publicity of UK.[47]

Meanwhile, conditions for Black students did not improve. One student, Elaine Adams, said being a Black student on campus was "like being on the moon." Finding housing and dealing with faculty prejudice were ongoing issues. Ellis Bullock, another president of Orgena, noted how the Black students sat together at football games and had to endure racial taunts. "They yell things sometimes, Glory, Glory Segregation. . . . [T]hey hit hard on the word 'darkies' when they sing 'My Old Kentucky Home.'"[48] Embry recalled that when the band played "Dixie" and "My Old Kentucky Home," Black students "would sit down, we wouldn't stand up. . . . We were doing silent protesting, but we were there also to support the Black athletes at the game, being there cheering them on, you know, yelling."[49]

An internal struggle was shaping up among Black students at UK in the fall of 1967, according to Jim Embry. Some believed Orgena should take a "different posture." Changing the name was in discussion, and Embry believed Orgena was focused on establishing African American history courses and recruiting students. Younger Black students wanted to change the name and questioned why it was spelled backward. Looking back to the time when Orgena was first formed, Embry realized that the Black students who had started the organization "were trying to figure out how to survive and thought back then the best formation would be something that maybe nobody could read and know what it means, but then it wouldn't be in your face." African American students did not seek to address their concerns in isolation. They sought "counsel from the elders in the community."[50]

On Saturday evening, December 9, 1967, the all-white UK basketball team played a home game against Pennsylvania at Memorial Coliseum.

Black students protesting in front of Memorial Coliseum during a University of Kentucky basketball game in December 1967. Brenda Lee Garner stands at center. Photo from *Kentuckian 68* (yearbook), courtesy of Explore UK, at http://www.exploreuk.uky.edu.

Nearly forty Blacks students representing the group Orgena participated in a second demonstration at a UK game. They wanted their protest to "be a way to kind of galvanize Black students." Members of the local branch of the Congress of Racial Equality joined them. It was "inspiring and thrilling," remembered Embry. Fans attending the game jeered at them for "challenging Coach Rupp."[51] The protest was a bold expression of objection and self-determination. The group intentionally comprised Blacks only. They wanted to be identified as Black, not Negro, students. The protest also represented the gradual rise of the Black Student Union— younger Black students who likewise had been inspired by the rise of BSUs around the country.

Theodore Berry, president-elect of Orgena, said they wanted "to show that Black students are concerned about doing something about conditions here, and they want to do it for themselves. We just want to better our social lives as individuals." In Berry's opinion, more Black athletes would attract more Black students. "That would mean more power for UK Negroes." Berry maintained that the protests would continue until Blacks were recruited on the team. Bill Turner remembered picketing the games. It disturbed him that his father worked in the coal mines in Kentucky, "but his sons couldn't play basketball at Kentucky. We wanted full citizenship rights," he said. The demonstrations did not seem to faze Coach Rupp, who stood by his lackluster efforts to recruit Black players. "They couldn't get in school," he said of what he considered Black players' missing academic qualifications to attend college. "If those guys [the demonstrators] were as serious in their work as I am in mine, they would go back and start studying." But Turner saw the protest as "a way of pressuring the Athletic Department into getting some Negroes on the team. Although we're paying our taxes there are still no Negros on the team."[52]

On the same night of the protest, Bernie Shively aided a spectator at the game who had a heart attack. He missed most of the second half while assisting this fan. The next day Shively himself had a heart attack and died. He was sixty-four years old. He had served as the director of athletics since 1938. For the previous fourteen years, he had been the president of the SEC Coaches and Athletic Directors Association and had led the SEC Basketball Committee. In response to Shively's death, Rupp said: "This comes as a shock. I guess we've been closer than any other two men in the last 15 years."[53]

An editorial in the *Kernel* titled "Put Up or Shut Up" stressed that BSU itself should recruit Black athletes. Theodore Berry responded that Black students were helping. "We are putting out considerable effort in this area but we expect the University to do an equal amount of work." Berry added: "It is not our duty, it is something we want to do." To further prove they were doing their part in the process, members of BSU planned a catered reception for Curtis Price, a star player from West Virginia.[54] Despite this effort, like other Black players who had been half-heartedly recruited before him, Price chose to enroll at another school.

By 1968, African American students at UK were mounting even more pressure on the athletic program to desegregate. In January, members of Orgena voted to change their organization's name to the Black Student Union. That same month, George C. Hill, a postdoctoral fellow in the Biochemistry Department of the UK Medical Center, penned an editorial for the *Kernel* in which he challenged the notion that no African American "high school basketball player has ever had the intellectual ability to enter the University." He questioned why "all" Black athletes were turning down opportunities to play for a "world-renowned" coach such as Rupp. Hill continued by elaborating on the case for recruiting Black basketball players to UK. He noted UK's reputation for having a winning basketball program. "But to Black students in high schools across the country, it represents a club 'for whites only.' Whether intentional or not, it suggests that only white students may participate." Hill argued that it was important for the university to prove that all students were welcome to attend the school. In so doing, other Black students would be willing to come to UK. Hill wrote that he was not seeking "tokenism" but rather "for equal recruitment policies and efforts to encourage Negroes to enter UK and participate." Howard University assistant professor Bill Banks took a different position on the recruitment of Black athletes. He believed "the athletes would be 'used' to perpetuate the myth of UK's liberalism." He pointed out that the "athletes would experience the same lonely and alienated feelings that are the fate of all tokens."[55] The perspective on this issue varied according to institutions. Students at Grambling State University, a historically Black college in Louisiana, wanted their school to put less emphasis on athletics. At the University of Texas at Austin, Black students pressed for more Black athletes.[56]

In April 1968, protests erupted throughout the country following the assassination of Martin Luther King Jr. Four days after King's death, Bill Turner spoke on campus for a Focus '68 program. Drawing from his experience as a UK senior, Turner said: "White America, white Kentucky, white Lexington, and alas, white UK, the day of high fallootting [*sic*] rhetoric is past: the day of academic, philosophical and moral speculation is past; certainly the day of passive resistance is past. It shall be largely your task, white America[,] to resolve the black Frankenstein that you have created." A few weeks later, BSU cosponsored a phone-in with national civil rights leaders to discuss what could be done about the race problem in America. The crowd listened to speakers and President Oswald, who said that he had been working with BSU to recruit Black athletes and professors. He assured the crowd that the lack of success was not due to a lack of effort.[57] Although President Oswald did not say so at the time, he did not believe Rupp was doing all he could to integrate his teams. In an interview in 1987, Oswald recalled a meeting with the coach and observed that "it

The 1968 UK yearbook included a photo of Kentucky fans waving the Confederate flag in what appears to be a game at Memorial Coliseum. Photograph from *Kentuckian 68*, courtesy of Explore UK, at http://www.exploreuk.uky.edu.

was clear . . . that if he wasn't a bigot, he sounded like one. . . . [H]e used the word *nigger* all the time . . . and he used other . . . other names to refer to them."[58] Harry Lancaster was Rupp's assistant coach for twenty-six years before becoming UK's athletic director in 1968. In his book *Adolph Rupp as I Knew Him,* Lancaster wrote about Rupp's meetings with Oswald. "He would come back from those meetings and say to me, 'Harry that son of a bitch is ordering me to get some niggers in here. What am I going to do? He's the boss.'" Lancaster added: "I didn't see where we had much choice but Adolph had never been around Blacks and I think he worried about the unknown." Said Jim Embry: "People say he [Rupp] wasn't prejudiced . . . but [he] was ultimately 'forced' to integrate."[59]

Rupp failed to acknowledge issues that plagued Black students and potential recruits. The UK environment did not help. The playing of the song "Dixie" and the waving of the Confederate flag at games celebrated disparaging and mythical images of slavery and social norms of the Old South. "It was offensive," remembered Brenda Skillman, who was among the African American freshmen who entered UK in the fall of 1968. At the time, most white UK students favored the tradition of playing the song

"Dixie" at ball games. Turner recalled attending only one UK basketball game as a student, between UK and Ole Miss. "I had never seen so many Confederate flags. They sang 'Dixie' as though it was the national anthem." Embry said Black athletes on the football team did not want to hear the song and asked students "to consider their feelings." In October 1968, after a tense debate the student government voted against a bill that supported the UK band playing "Dixie." On the surface, the vote was a victory for BSU, but some white students ignored the vote and brought bugles and kazoos to the next football game and continued to play the song.[60]

Acting UK president A. D. Kirwan objected to the song. He met with the BSU and shared some of the progress on campus toward addressing African Americans' concerns. He noted that an Afro-American history course was being considered in the History Department. This course would be part of the department's curriculum rather than just an interdepartmental course, as it had been previously. He also told the group that the new athletic director, Harry Lancaster, was aware of their "unhappiness" regarding the failed recruitment of Black basketball players. "I think he will begin concentrated efforts to do something on the matter." Kirwan even criticized the basketball recruiting process, describing it as "ill conceived" because of the focus on recruiting only one superstar Black player.[61]

Meanwhile, Rupp continued to speak out. He maintained there was "no discrimination" at UK and that he tried to recruit Black players, including Ron King from Louisville Central, who had recently signed with Florida State. He explained that the team would remain all-white "until we convince the Black student they [*sic*] will be treated the same as a white student and that he will have the same opportunity to play basketball here as any other student will have."[62]

A few weeks after Rupp made these comments, he signed Tom Payne out of Shawnee High School in Louisville. On June 10, 1969, Payne became the first Black awarded a basketball scholarship at UK. At seven feet, Payne had averaged 25.8 points and 29 rebounds a game at Shawnee. He signed with UK because of its "educational program" and his belief that he could develop as a player under Rupp's coaching. Rupp had often claimed he would recruit only those Black players who had the academic qualifications to sign with UK, but, ironically, the first Black player he signed was not eligible to play his first year because of his low ACT scores and had to play with an Amateur Athletic Union team. Payne recalled years later that when he did qualify to join the team for the 1970–1971 season as a sophomore, the coaches had made it possible by having individuals take correspondence courses in his name.[63]

Payne's experiences both on and off the court were difficult. "He came to UK with an open attitude," recalled Embry. "He came believing he would be treated fairly and openly and not suffer." Payne and his wife lived in Shawnee town on campus and were neighbors of Embry and his wife. Embry attended UK games and had discussions with Payne about his experiences at UK. "Tom Payne being on the team gave me for the first time I guess in almost three years reasons to yell and cheer on the basketball team," said Embry. Yet he also witnessed racist comments from fans who became disgruntled when Payne played poorly. Fans cursed and threw pennies on the floor and called Payne "nigger" and "monkey."[64]

Payne experienced racism off the court as well. A *Louisville Courier-Journal* article reported that "threatening phone calls, broken car windows and eggs smashed on his front door became routine. He feared for the safety of his wife—whom he married right after high school—and their infant daughter." With an average of 16.9 pts per game and 10.1 rebounds, Payne entered the NBA draft after his sophomore year, joining the Atlanta Hawks with a $750,000 contract.[65] Kentucky did not sign a Black player in 1970 or the next year. Despite having a storied program, UK had still signed only one Black player to its varsity team in its history.

Payne was the first Black to receive a UK basketball scholarship, but Assistant Coach Joe B. Hall also invited Darryl Bishop, a football signee from Louisville Seneca High School, to join the freshman basketball team. During the 1969–1970 season, Bishop became the first Black player to wear a Kentucky basketball jersey for a ballgame at Memorial Coliseum. Beginning with the 1971 basketball season, several SEC schools recruited Black players. Alabama, Vanderbilt, and Florida had more than three Black members on each of their teams.[66]

Because of university governing regulations, Rupp was forced to retire at age seventy, effective July 1, 1972. Rupp's legacy and UK's recruitment of Black players have been debated. Former players, coaches, and sports writers have come to Rupp's defense. According to the writer Billy Reed, "He has been likened to Eugene 'Bull' Connor, the bigoted public-safety director of Birmingham who laughingly ordered fire hoses and attack dogs to be used against civil rights protesters in 1963. Bull and the Baron. Two of a kind, right? Absolutely not. But who in the media wants to let the truth stand in the way of a good storyline?"[67]

The role of the BCM in recruiting Black athletes to UK is not simply "a good storyline," however. The BSU was significantly involved in the process. Its members' conversations with administrators and coaches are very much a part of the shaping of Rupp's legacy at UK. They did more than complain about all-white teams. They picketed basketball games, entertained recruits, met with the coaching staff, and organized forums to discuss the issue. In February 1969, UK's BSU was in line with the BCM around the country. Its new chairperson, Marshall Jones, said, "We are trying to de-emphasize the sports thing—we realize that this is an educational institution, and we will mainly encourage enrollment of Black students of academic merit." Jones further added: "We need funds. We can't get anything done without funds." The organization wanted office space and support to attend Black conferences.[68]

On February 13, 1969, "black campus activists forced the racial reconstitution of higher education," writes Ibram H. Rogers. "Black students disrupted higher education in almost every area of the nation. . . . It was a day that emitted the anger, determination, and agency of a generation that stood on the cutting edge of educational progression." Students "protested for a relevant learning experience."[69] UK Black students did not organize massive demonstrations against the administration, but they did make their voices heard. They recognized the role that African American athletes would have in drawing attention to larger issues facing all Black students. In March 1969, representatives of UK's BSU supported the University of Louisville's BSU in its demands to increase the numbers of Black faculty and students on campus. They carried signs that read: "U of Ky Next!!! Do Your Thing, brothers. UK BSU."[70]

By the end of the 1960s, the UK administration began to conservatively address the recruitment and interests of Black students on campus. A Martin Luther King Committee comprising faculty and friends was organized to raise money for scholarships for Black students. Alvin Morris, special assistant to President Otis Singletary, spoke to a Human Rights Commission seminar held on campus. He told the group that the president was concerned about "human rights and disadvantaged Black students." Singletary had set aside $15,000 for a Black Arts Festival and support for recruitment and a tutorial program.[71]

Although the BCM at UK was not as large and nationally visible as it was on other campuses, it was equally engaged and determined to shape the university's commitment toward addressing issues of race. Orgena was committed to creating "a more pleasurable and rewarding situation for the black student." These same goals were seamlessly transferred into the founding of the BSU in 1968. Black students clearly recognized the importance of Black athletes to white institutions before white coaches, players, and fans did. Reflecting on the late 1960s at UK, Jim Embry observed: "So there's a statue of four football athletes, Black athletes, over at the [Commonwealth Stadium]. That's well deserved. But in my view, the Black Student Union did as much."[72]

Acknowledgments

The author thanks David Turpie and anonymous readers for their comments on early drafts of this chapter.

Notes

Regarding the terminology in this chapter's subtitle: Ibram H. Rogers distinguishes the Black Campus Movement (BCM) from Black student participation in civil rights demonstrations, the Black Power Movement (BPM), and the Long Black Student Movement (LBSM). He writes: "In sum, the BCM was at the same time a part of and apart from three larger social movements: the transhistorical LBSM, beginning after World War I; the transracial student movement of the Long Sixties; and the transobjective contemporary BPM of the late 1960s and early 1970s" (Ibram H. Rogers, *The Black Campus Movement: Black Students and the Racial Reconstitution of Higher Education, 1965–1972* [New York: Palgrave MacMillan, 2012], 3).

1. Herschel Weil, "UK and Negro Athletes," *Lexington Herald Leader,* December 10, 1961; Herschel Weil to Frank G. Dickey, August 5, 1956, box 33, Frank Dickey Papers, University of Kentucky Special Collections, Lexington.

2. For a more detailed account of this process, see S. Zebulon Baker, "'On the Opposite Side of the Fence': The University of Kentucky and the Racial Desegregation of the Southeastern Conference," *Register of the Kentucky Historical Society* 115, no. 4 (Autumn 2017): 584–93. See also Charles H. Martin, *Benching Jim Crow: The Rise and Fall of the Color Line in Southern College Sport, 1890–1980* (Urbana: University of Illinois Press, 2010), 27–54, 234.

3. President John W. Oswald to Herschel Weil, December 28, 1965, box 16, folder "Athletic Association General 65–66," John W. Oswald Collection,

University of Kentucky Special Collections; *Kentucky Kernel* (University of Kentucky, Lexington), April 2, 1968. Frank G. Dickey was president when the UK Athletic Association adopted the policy to integrate athletics. He served from 1956 to 1963. Alongside the margins of the newspaper clipping attached to Oswald's letter was the jotted phrase "4 years 9 days." President John W. Oswald served from 1963 to 1968.

4. Gerald L. Smith, *A Black Educator in the Segregated South: Kentucky's Rufus B. Atwood* (Lexington: University Press of Kentucky, 1994), 140–44; Mary A. Adams, interviewed by Erica N. Johnson, June 30, 2006, University of Kentucky, African American Experience Oral History Project, Louie B. Nunn Center for Oral History, University of Kentucky Libraries, Lexington.

5. Frank R. Cannon Jr., interviewed by Sharon Childs, April 7, 1997, African American Experience Oral History Project, Nunn Center.

6. S. T. Roach's story is told in Russell Rice, *Adolph Rupp: Kentucky's Basketball Baron* (Champaign: University of Illinois Press, 1994), 153–54.

7. Martin, *Benching Jim Crow*, xviii.

8. *Louisville Defender,* December 27, 1967; see also "The Negro at UK," *Kentucky Kernel,* April 17, 1967.

9. Jim Embry, interviewed by Gerald L. Smith, January 22, 2021, African American Experience Oral History Project, Nunn Center.

10. Joy Ann Williamson, *Black Power on Campus: The University of Illinois, 1965–75* (Urbana: University of Illinois Press, 2013), 24–25.

11. Martha Biondi, *The Black Revolution on Campus* (Berkeley: University of California Press, 2012), 4, 5.

12. Jim Embry quoted in *Kentucky Kernel,* August 30, 1968.

13. Ibram Rogers, "Celebrating 40 Years of Activism," *Diverse Issues in Higher Education,* June 27, 2006, at https://www.diverseeducation.com/students/article/15082219/celebrating-40-years-of-activism.

14. Donald F. Flatt, "Winning through to Fame and Glory: African-Americans and MSU," Office of Multicultural Student Services at Morehead State University, February 1999, reprinted in November 1999, 19–20 (quote from Adron Doran); Kevin Hogg, "Everett Leonard Lyles," in *The Kentucky African American Encyclopedia,* ed. Gerald L. Smith, Karen Cotton McDaniel, and John A. Hardin (Lexington: University Press of Kentucky, 2015), 341; Sallie Powell, "Wade Allan Houston, Sr.," in *Kentucky African American Encyclopedia,* ed. Smith, McDaniel, and Hardin, 254–55; Martin, *Benching Jim Crow,* 238; Pete Thamel, "Recalling Forward Thinking at Western Kentucky," *New York Times,* March 27, 2008. The University of Louisville dedicated a statue in honor of Lyles in October 2000.

15. W. H. Grady to Dr. Frank Dickey, April 29, 1963, box 34, folder "Athletics General June 1962–April 1963," Dickey Papers.

16. See R. C. Kash to Frank G. Dickey, April 16, 1963, box 34, folder "Athletics General June 1962–April 1963," Dickey Papers.

17. Shirley Rosenberg to Frank Dickey, May 17, 1963, resolution enclosed, box 34, Dickey Papers; George M. Weller to Board of Trustees, April 13, 1963, box 34, folder "Athletics General June 1962–April 1963," Dickey Papers; Charles F. Morton to Board of Trustees, April 1, 1963, box 22, Dickey Papers ("I believe the citizens of Kentucky desire the best athletic teams available"); Thomas D. Clark to Frank Dickey, May 7, 1963, box 34, folder "Athletics General June 1962–April 1963," Dickey Papers.

18. Nathaniel Northington, *Still Running: The Autobiography of Kentucky's Nate Northington, the First African American Football Player in the Southeastern Conference* (Bloomington: Indiana University Press, 2013), 7–9, 12. See also Edward Breathitt, interviewed by Betsy Brinson, February 24, 2000, transcript, Civil Rights in Kentucky Oral History Project, Kentucky Oral History Commission, Kentucky Historical Society, Frankfort.

19. Mrs. William E. Northington to Honorable Edward T. Breathitt, n.d., and Mrs. William E. Northington to Edward T. Breathitt, December 24, 1965, box 16, folder "Northington File Confidential," John W. Oswald Papers, University of Kentucky Special Collections.

20. Northington, *Still Running*, 95.

21. Mrs. Edwin I. Baer to Edward T. Breathitt, December 1965, box 16, folder 438, Oswald Papers; Edward T. Breathitt to Mrs. Edwin I. Baer, December 22, 1965, box 16, folder 438, Oswald Papers; Northington, *Still Running*, 12.

22. Gerald L. Smith, "Gregory Dewayne Page," in *Kentucky African American Encyclopedia,* ed. Smith, McDaniel, and Hardin, 391; "Only Token Integration Appears Evident in SEC," *Kentucky Kernel,* April 17, 1967.

23. Theodore Berry, interviewed by Doris Weathers, July 2, 1987, African American Experience Oral History Project, Nunn Center; P. G. Peeples Sr., interviewed by Erica Berry, July 13, 2006, African American Experience Oral History Project, Nunn Center.

24. "UK's Negroes Want Improved Race Relations" and "Negro Affiliation Remains Low," *Kentucky Kernel,* April 17, 1967.

25. *Lexington Herald Leader,* September 30, 1967; *Kentucky Kernel,* October 3, 1967.

26. Wilbur Hackett Jr., interviewed by Will James, April 1, 2005, Oral History Collection, Nunn Center. In an interview, Breathitt referenced the recruitment of Northington and said: "We told him we would get him another African-American. And we recruited one, and to our distress he was killed in

practice" (Edward Breathitt, interviewed by Betsy Brinson, February 24, 2000, Civil Rights in Kentucky Oral History Project, Kentucky Oral History Commission, Kentucky Historical Society, Frankfort).

27. "Negro Affiliation Remains Low"; *Kentucky Kernel,* September 14, 1967; *Louisville Defender,* May 4, 1967.

28. Northington, *Still Running,* 169–75; *Kentucky Kernel,* October 24, 1967; "Only Token Integration Appears Evident in SEC," *Kentucky Kernel,* April 17, 1967.

29. *Kentucky Kernel,* April 17, 1967.

30. Adolph Rupp quoted in *Kentucky Kernel,* April 17, 1967.

31. *Kentucky Kernel,* April 27, 1967.

32. Frank Fitzpatrick, *And the Walls Came Tumbling Down: The Basketball Game That Changed American Sports* (Lincoln: University of Nebraska Press, 1999), 145 (quoting Oswald's son), 189; Andrew Maraniss, *Strong Inside: Perry Wallace and the Collision of Race and Sports in the South* (Nashville: University of Tennessee Press, 2014), 90.

33. "Alfred 'Butch' Beard," *New York Times,* December 21, 1994.

34. Perry Wallace quoted in Maraniss, *Strong Inside,* 90–91.

35. Russell Rice, *Adolph Rupp: Kentucky's Basketball Baron* (Lexington: University Press of Kentucky, 2019), 1, 154; S. T. Roach quoted in Fitzpatrick, *And the Walls Came Tumbling Down,* 1.

36. William H. Turner, interviewed by Gerald L. Smith, "Racial Justice and Equality" radio segment, WEKU-FM (public radio for central and eastern Kentucky), September 24, 2020; Embry, interviewed by Smith, January 22, 2021.

37. Fitzpatrick, *And the Walls Came Tumbling Down,* 24–25; Martin, *Benching Jim Crow,* 113.

38. Nolan Richardson quoted in Fitzpatrick, *And the Walls Came Tumbling Down,* 19.

39. Bob Ryan, interviewed for *Glory in Black and White,* documentary, CBS, April 2002.

40. *Lexington Herald Leader,* March 14, 2016 (quoting P. G. Peeples); *Lexington Herald,* March 20, 1966; Bert Nelli and Steve Nelli, *The Winning Tradition: A History of Wildcat Basketball* (Lexington: University Press of Kentucky, 1998), 33; Martin, *Benching Jim Crow,* 90–92.

41. Robert L. Johnson to Bernie Shively, March 29, 1966; Joe B. Hall to Adolph Rupp, April 7, 1966; and Bernie Shively to Robert Johnson, April 19, 1966: all in box 16, folder 437, Oswald Papers.

42. Adolph Rupp quoted in *Kentucky Kernel,* April 30, 1967.

43. Bill Turner, telephone interview by Gerald L. Smith, May 13, 2016, archived at the Nunn Center; *Louisville Defender,* May 4, 1967; "Mr. & Miss Kentucky Basketball Awards Ceremony, Tuesday March 15, 2016," at https://

mrandmisskybasketball.com/mr-kentucky-basketball-history/; Bill Turner, "All-White Rupp Bourbon Bottle Jars Memories," *Lexington Herald Leader,* April 19, 2005; *Kentucky Kernel,* April 17 and September 14, 1967.

44. *Kentucky Kernel,* April 23, 1967.

45. Adolph Rupp to Bernie Shively, July 14, 1967; John Oswald to Mrs. Felix Thurston, July 6, 1967; Bernie Shively to John Oswald, July 14, 1967; Felix Thurston, "Inter-conference Letter of Intent": all in box 7, folder "242 Athletics General 1967–68," Oswald Papers.

46. *Kentucky Kernel,* March 28, April 13, and September 14, 1967; Pete Thamel, "Recalling Forward Thinking at Western," *New York Times,* March 27, 2008; Elliott Pratt, "Standing Alone: WKU's 1971 Final Four Team Remains in a League of Its Own," *Western Kentucky University Herald,* April 2, 2014, at http://wkuherald.com/sports/standing-alone-wku-s-final-four-team-remains-in-a/article_81bea07a-baaa-11e3-8f3a-001a4bcf6878.html; "Jim McDaniels: Basketball Player," Spokeo, n.d., at http://www.spokeo.com/Jim+Mcdaniels+1.

47. *Louisville Defender,* November 9, 1967.

48. Ellis Bullock quoted in *Kentucky Kernel,* November 17, 1967.

49. Embry, interviewed by Smith, January 22, 2021.

50. Embry, interviewed by Smith, January 22, 2021.

51. Embry, interviewed by Smith, January 22, 2021.

52. Theodore Berry quoted in *Kentucky Kernel,* December 11, 1967; Turner, telephone interview by Smith, May 13, 2016.

53. *Kentucky Kernel,* December 11, 1967.

54. *Kentucky Kernel,* February 1 and 22, 1968.

55. George C. Hill, editorial, *Kentucky Kernel,* January 15, 1968; Bill Banks, quoted in *Kentucky Kernel,* January 15, 1968. George Hill would become the sponsor for UK's BSU. He would also write several editorials pressing UK to desegregate the basketball program.

56. Ibram H. Rogers, *The Black Campus Movement: Black Students and the Racial Reconstitution of Higher Education, 1965–1972* (New York: Palgrave MacMillan, 2012), 117.

57. *Kentucky Kernel,* April 8 (quote from Turner) and May 1, 1968.

58. John W. Oswald, interviewed by Terry L. Birdwhistell, August 11, 1987, University of Kentucky Presidents' Journal: John W. Oswald Oral History Project, Nunn Center.

59. Harry Lancaster, *Adolph Rupp as I Knew Him* (Lexington, KY: Lexington Productions, 1979), 88; James Embry, interviewed by Eric N. Johnson, June 19, 2006, African American Experience Oral History Project, Nunn Center.

60. *Kentucky Kernel,* October 4, October 7, and November 4, 1968; Brenda Skillman, interviewed by Erica N. Johnson, July 7, 2006, African American

Experience Oral History Project, Nunn Center; Turner, telephone interview by Smith, May 13, 2016; Embry, quoted in *Kentucky Kernel*, October 4, 1968.

61. *Kentucky Kernel*, September 11, 1968.

62. Adolph Rupp quoted in *Lexington Leader*, June 2, 1969.

63. James Duane Bolin, *Adolph Rupp and the Rise of Kentucky Basketball* (Lexington: University Press of Kentucky, 2019), 322; *Kentucky Kernel*, June 19, 1969.

64. Embry, interviewed by Smith, January 22, 2021.

65. Bolin, *Adolph Rupp and the Rise of Kentucky Basketball*, 322–23.

66. *Kentucky Kernel*, February 19, 1970; *Louisville Courier-Journal*, May 25, 1971.

67. Bolin, *Adolph Rupp and the Rise of Kentucky Basketball*, 270–71 (quoting Billy Reed), 324, 330, 336–37.

68. Marshall Jones quoted in *Kentucky Kernel*, February 19, 1969.

69. Rogers, *The Black Campus Movement*, 2.

70. *Kentucky Kernel*, March 10, 1969

71. *Kentucky Kernel*, October 23, 1969.

72. *Louisville Defender*, December 21, 1967; Embry, interviewed by Smith, January 22, 2021.

11

Archer Alexander and Freedom's Memorial

Alicestyne Turley

As compared with the long line of his predecessors, many of whom were merely the . . . servile instruments of the Slave Power, Abraham Lincoln, while unsurpassed in his devotion to the welfare of the white race, was also in a sense hitherto without example, emphatically, the black man's President; the first to show any respect to their rights as men.
—Frederick Douglass, "Speech of Abraham Lincoln," June 1865

In 2020, controversies surrounding the police killing of George Floyd in Minneapolis, Breonna Taylor in Louisville, and countless other African Americans in cities around the United States swept the nation, as did the public outcry for removal of Confederate Civil War monuments. In Kentucky alone, a border state that had remained loyal to the Union, there are only nine monuments to the Union cause but more than thirty-seven state monuments to the Confederacy, a count that does not include commemoration of Confederate roads, historic sites, and other Kentucky namesakes. Moreover, the fate of not just Confederate monuments is in the balance. The Emancipation Memorial, featuring Abraham Lincoln and a freed slave, has also been targeted for removal from Lincoln Park in Washington, DC. Although today we may feel uncomfortable with how the monument impacts us visually, emotionally, and psychologically, those who sacrificed to bring the memorial into existence deserve our respect. Sentiment against maintaining the monument in its prominent Washington location rose to a fever pitch during the summer of 2020, when District of Columbia Police felt the need to protect the monument from enthusiastic citizens intent upon its removal.[1] A voice that joined the call for the monument's removal was that of legislator Eleanor Holmes Norton. On June 23, 2020, Norton introduced legislation to the Senate calling for immediate removal because "the statue failed to note how enslaved African Americans pushed for their own emancipation." In Norton's view, it was time for the memorial to surrender its valuable Washington real estate in favor of placement in a museum.[2]

The Emancipation Memorial—also known as "Freedom's Memorial," "Freedman's Memorial," and from 1876 to 1922 the "Lincoln Memorial"— is considered America's first national monument to Abraham Lincoln. Erection of the memorial was controversial from its beginning; only the reasons calling for the monument's removal have changed. Ironically, efforts to remove the Emancipation Memorial are led by African Americans and Senate Republicans, the same voices that lobbied for its installation on April 14, 1876. Unveiling ceremonies for the monument were presided over by the first dean of Howard University Law School and former Ohio Underground Railroad operative John Mercer Langston. Frederick Douglass delivered the keynote address, and those in attendance included President Ulysses Grant, members of his cabinet, and Supreme Court justices. The memorial was paid for by the wages of newly freed slaves and members of the United States Colored Troops (USCT). The monument faced the US Capitol until 1974, when it was rotated on its base to face the Mary McLeod Bethune Monument.[3] Dedication ceremonies for the monument occurred eleven years following the close of the Civil War and as soon as African Americans' fund-raising efforts would allow. The monument was cast, installed, and dedicated during a time when pro-Confederate forces were demanding an end to American Reconstruction policies meant to empower Black voters.

Formerly enslaved African Americans raised more than $28,242 for installation of the monument in Lincoln Square—a successful community accomplishment even by today's standards. The monument portrays the image of a powerful Black man rising to his feet, eyes fixed on the Emancipation Proclamation, poised like a runner in the starting block of a race. His figure contrasts with the distant and restrained raised hand of Lincoln, which hovers over his body as if offering a vague and uncertain blessing. The image of the slave symbolized the last slave captured under the Fugitive Slave Law and the freeing of more than 4 million African

Americans. Taken within its historical and financial context, the monument represented the views of millions of post–Civil War African Americans regarding Lincoln's actions to end slavery.

Gaining funds to erect the monument began with a call from a formerly enslaved Black woman named Charlotte Scott (1805–1891) from Covington, Virginia. Margaret (Meg) Scott's parents had given the enslaved Charlotte to Meg as a wedding gift upon her marriage to Dr. William Parks Rucker (1831–1905). Rucker, born into a distinguished military family, enlisted in the Union army during the Civil War. He served under General Crook and John Frémont until he was captured in 1862 by Confederate forces. Following the war, Rucker relocated to Keytesville, Missouri, where he died at the home of his son in January 1905.[4] Many years before the war, though, in 1855, Rucker had established a medical practice in Marietta, Ohio, granted Charlotte her freedom, and then paid her a salary to continue working for his family. Charlotte was moved to action by Lincoln's assassination in 1865, when she gave her entire life savings, $5, to Dr. Rucker to establish a memorial to honor the fallen president.[5] Utilizing her connections to members of Marietta society, such as Frances D. Gage, Charlotte began her fund-raising efforts. Frances Gage was a leader in the women's, antislavery, temperance, and Underground Railroad social movements in Marietta, served as a Marietta Underground Railroad station master, and counted among her many friends Sojourner Truth, Elizabeth Cady Stanton, and Susan B. Anthony. As an employee of the Western Sanitary Commission from 1863 to 1864, Gage was also superintendent in charge of the Parris Island, South Carolina, refugee camp that cared for more than five hundred freed slaves.[6]

To honor Charlotte's request, Dr. Rucker published her fund-raising plea in the *Marietta Register*. He then sent her financial contribution to an associate in St. Louis, Missouri, James Earl Yeatman, president of the Western Sanitary Commission. Moved by Scott's compassionate plea, Yeatman made it possible for all memorial funds to be collected at the Western Sanitary Commission offices. He expanded circulation of Charlotte's request nationally by republicizing her message in St. Louis, Missouri, newspapers and Western Sanitary Commission offices. Rucker's ad read:

A Noble Offering By a Grateful Heart

Charlotte Scott, a colored woman living at Dr. Rucker's on Putnam Street, Marietta, wishes to show, in a substantial manner, her profound regard and high veneration for Hon. Abraham Lincoln, especially in his proclamation of freedom to the slaves. She has handed me five dollars to be applied towards rearing a monument in memory of the greatest man, in her estimation, that ever lived on earth. This noble thought, so far as I know, originated with herself. She thinks many colored persons would love to contribute for this purpose, in this region. She wishes me to act as their agent and receive their contributions and hand over the same to such agents as the government may hereafter appoint to rear said monument. I consent, and will keep a faithful record of all such contributions.

C. D. Battelle (Marietta *First Unitarian Church*)

[This $5 is to be the foundation of a fund to be applied toward the erection of the Monument to Abraham Lincoln, for which Rev. Mr. Battelle— a suitable person for the purpose—will receive further contributions, depositing the same in bank as received, until the time for its applications shall arrive.—Ed. Reg.][7]

The Western Sanitary Commission was first established in Louisville, Kentucky, as a Civil War measure. Major-General John C. Frémont created the commission at the urging of his wife, Jessie Benton Frémont. Under military authority granted by Lincoln, the commission aided wounded Union soldiers on the western frontier. It was later confirmed by the US secretary of war, Edwin M. Stanton, and empowered to provide medical care for all Union soldiers and veterans.[8] Appointed members of the commission met in Washington, DC, on June 12, 1861, to formulate plans for conducting its work. At that meeting, Dr. Elisha Harris and Dr. Cornelius R. Agnew were added to the organizational membership. The Unitarian minister Reverend Henry W. Bellows was elected president,[9] and Frederick Law Olmsted secretary. As secretary, Olmsted served as the chief executive officer responsible for the commission's day-to-day work. At that time, Olmsted's "appointment was universally regarded as a guarantee of the success of the Commission's plans."[10] Headquarters were relocated from Louisville to Washington.

William Eliot and members of the Western Sanitary Commission chose Archer Alexander to serve as the model for the face and body of the monument's symbol of America's newly freed slaves. We know of Archer Alexander and the monument's prescient history primarily through the firsthand account provided by the Unitarian minister Reverend William Greenleaf Eliot (1811–1887), Archer's rescuer and self-appointed biographer.

Despite Eliot's attempt to apply a specific level of detail regarding Archer's life and actions, today's historians view many of Eliot's statements as inaccurate and often self-serving. Yet, despite its obvious flaws, Eliot's account continues to be one of the best sources of primary information on Alexander and the memorial.

Archer Alexander was born sometime between 1806 and 1816 near Richmond, Virginia. As a runaway slave, he is considered the last slave captured under the Fugitive Slave Law of 1850. The Fugitive Slave Law was part of a collection of bills authored by the Kentucky senator Henry Clay to stave off the start of a civil war and generally referred to as the Compromise of 1850. Clay's efforts were successful for a time. Provisions of the law forcibly compelled free states to return runaway slaves. It required citizens to assist in the capture and rendition of runaways to their former slave owners and levied harsh fines and punishments against those who resisted or interfered with federal marshals enacting slave captures. The law denied enslaved people the right to a jury trial and imposed up to a $1,000 fine and a six-month jail sentence for any citizen interfering with federal authorities. Concerned that free states would become safe havens for runaways, Southern politicians took advantage of the Fugitive Slave Clause in the US Constitution (Article 4, section 2, clause 3), which stipulated that "no person held to service or labor" would be released from bondage in the event they escaped to a free state. The Fugitive Slave Law was unpopular and widely resisted by many Americans. Opposition to the law made it virtually unenforceable, and by 1860 only an estimated 330 slaves had been successfully returned to slave owners.[11]

In 1883, Eliot published his firsthand account of Archer's life, *The Story of Archer Alexander from Slavery to Freedom,* three years following Archer's death. As a minister, educator, abolitionist, and rescuer, Eliot had befriended Archer in St. Louis following Archer's escape from the enslaver James Hollman. Born sometime between 1808 and 1810 on the Kalorama Plantation located approximately thirty miles from Richmond, Virginia, Archer was the son of Aleck and Chloe Alexander, the enslaved property of the Presbyterian minister Dr. Delaney (Dulaney) of Fairfax, Virginia.[12] The facts that Eliot relates regarding Archer's Virginia life closely suggest the life of the Presbyterian minister Dr. Archibald Alexander or John Alexander, both of Rockbridge County, Virginia.[13]

Archer's father, Aleck, acquired the ability to read, and of him Eliot writes:

[Aleck] was . . . a full black, forty-five years old, strong, stalwart, intelligent; in fact, his [Dr. Delaney's] very best "hand." Somehow or other, this fellow had learned to read. Nobody knew how, but probably from the children and by chance opportunities. A good deal of discussion about slavery was going on at the time, which was not very far from the Missouri compromise days; and Aleck had got some advanced notions of which he was rather proud, talking them out rather freely among his fellows. In fact, "he made himself altogether too smart." At a colored prayer-meeting he had gone so far as to say that "by the 'Claration of 'Dependence all men was ekal," and that "to trade in men and women, jess like hogs and hosses, wasn't 'cordin' to gospel, nohow."[14]

Neighborhood accusations that Delaney was "too soft on his slaves" resulted in a lawsuit and judgment against him in the amount of $1,500. Aleck's talk of Black freedom and God's purpose for Black people generated fear among Delaney's slaveholding neighbors, and, as a result, Aleck was sold away from the Kalorama Plantation to "Colonel Jones" in Richmond, Virginia, when Archer was still a child "too young to remember his father."[15] Delaney owed money to Colonel Jones, a well-known slave merchant who routinely bought and sold slaves from his Grace Street offices in Richmond. In settlement of Delany's debt and civil judgment, Colonel Jones purchased Aleck for $1,500 and immediately resold him to the slave trader Jim Buckner, who was gathering slaves for sale in the South Carolina slave market.[16] During this time, the slave trade was Virginia's largest industry, and Richmond was the location of its most heavily trafficked slave sales. It is estimated that during the 1850s more than 80,000 men, women, and children were forced from the state each year, down from the estimated 120,000 slave sales per year during the 1830s and 1840s. Virginia sent across state lines nearly half of all enslaved people in the United States. Richmond's share of these total sales is difficult to measure, however; a ledger from just one slave trader indicated that during the 1840s he sold an estimated 2,000 slaves per year.[17]

Financial loss continued to plague Delaney until his death, thought to be around 1828. Upon his death, Delaney's estate contained about fourteen slaves. His holdings were further reduced by creditors, who acquired half his lands and auctioned off two-thirds of his remaining slaves. The remaining slaves, including Archer, were divided among Delaney's widow and children. Reportedly, Mrs. Delaney retained ownership of Archer's mother, Chloe, while Delaney's oldest son, James, inherited ownership of young Archer, estimated as age eighteen at the time.[18] In 1829, James Harvey Alexander and his wife, Jane McClure, were more than likely Archer's owners. The Alexanders joined other Lexington, Rockbridge County, Virginia, families in migrating to Dardenne Township, St. Charles County, Missouri, where James eventually purchased his own farm. James's wife, Jane McClure, was also the owner of Archer's wife and companion traveler, Louisa, whom she inherited upon the death of her father, John B. McClure (1750–1822). Six months following Archer's departure from Virginia, circa 1829, his mother, Chloe, died. Both James and Jane Alexander died in St. Louis during the cholera epidemic of 1834, following which their minor children—John McClure, William Archibald, Agnes Jane, and Sarah Elizabeth Alexander—were put in the custody of their uncle Alexander B. Stuart (1797–1886) in Rockbridge, Virginia. James and Jane's slaves were then hired out to pay the expense of raising their orphaned children.[19] Archer was hired out to the St. Louis brickyard of Letcher & Bobbs. By 1844, seven of Louisa and Archer's ten children—Eliza, Mary Ann, Archer, James, Alexander, Lucinda, and John—were leased to James and Jane Alexander's estate to support their surviving children. When the white Alexander children came of age, Louisa and Archer's enslaved children were divided and sold to settle the estate. Archer and Louisa's sons Ralph and Wesley were also sold from the James Naylor Plantation in St. Louis, where Louisa had remained an enslaved resident.[20] Archer and Louisa were trusted workers on the Naylor Plantation, where they remained for the next thirty years, approximately 1833 to 1863, but Archer experienced very little physical contact with his children until well after the Civil War.[21]

The majority of slave owners in Missouri, such as James Alexander, arrived from worn-out agricultural fields in North Carolina, Tennessee, Kentucky, and Virginia. Upon their arrival in the "West," settlers concentrated their agricultural efforts on the production of tobacco, hemp, grain, and livestock. A number of slaves imported to the region were leased out as stevedores, cabin boys, and deckhands on Mississippi River ferries. The border states Kentucky and Missouri were exempt from the Emancipation Proclamation because they had remained part of the United States instead of seceding, and both rejected the Thirteenth Amendment at the conclusion of the war. Missouri officially abolished slavery on January 11, 1865, by a vote of sixty to four in the state legislature.[22] The Kentucky Legislature considered a conditional ratification of the Thirteenth Amendment, which would deny freedmen and other Blacks their constitutional rights and would require them to leave the state within ten years of gaining their freedom. The state's reticence allowed the regional holding and trading of enslaved people throughout 1865 and beyond. The Kentucky Legislature did not officially vote to ratify the Thirteenth Amendment until March 18, 1976, by a vote of seventy-seven to zero. To avoid losing money on their investments in human property, upon outbreak of the Civil War many Kentucky and Missouri slave owners attempted to recoup their losses by continuing to sell their slaves South to Texas, where there remained a lucrative slave market.

As a border state and Civil War battleground, Missouri was home to a number of Confederate supporters, including Louisa's owner, James Naylor. On July 1, 1861, in an attempt to root out Southern secessionists, Lincoln appointed Major General John Frémont commander of the Department of the West. Upon Frémont's arrival in Washington, he, Lincoln, and Commanding General Winfield Scott devised a plan to clear all Confederates from Missouri in a military campaign down the Mississippi River in an advance on Memphis.[23] Lincoln gave Frémont carte blanche authority to conduct this western war campaign. Frémont exercised this authority to create the Western Sanitary Commission. He was aided in those efforts by his friend and former Kentuckian Benjamin Gratz Brown (1826–1885), then a US senator representing Missouri.

Born in Frankfort, Kentucky, the son of Mason Brown and Judith Ann Bledsoe, the grandson of John Mason Brown and Jesse Bledsoe, and the great-grandson of Margaret Wickliffe, Brown began his professional and political career as a Frankfort attorney after his graduation from Yale Law School in 1847.[24] Brown moved to St. Louis in 1849, where he joined the law firm of his politically active cousins Frank and Montgomery Blair. Brown won election to the Missouri House of Representatives in 1852 and 1858, was a founder of the Free Soil Party, was a successful candidate for governor, and served in that office from 1871 to 1873. As an ally of Thomas Hart Benton, the father of John Frémont's wife, Jessie Hart Benton, Brown struggled with Benton to gain control over Missouri's pro-slavery forces. Brown was a founder of Missouri's Republican Party, which worked to keep Missouri in the Union. During the Civil War, Brown served as a colonel in the Union army, raising a regiment (Fourth US Reserves) of more than 1,100 soldiers, many of whom were German Americans stationed near his St. Louis neighbor William Eliot.[25] Brown's volunteer regiment became his political constituency following the Civil War.[26] As the 1860s progressed,

Brown continued to speak against slavery. He supported John C. Frémont over the reelection of Lincoln in 1864, campaigning against Lincoln, accusing him of being a moderate, and opposing the Emancipation Proclamation because it did not free slaves in Missouri and other loyal border states. He ran as the vice presidential candidate of Horace Greeley in 1872 after losing the presidential bid to Greeley in the primary. Brown strongly opposed President Andrew Johnson's Reconstruction policies and fully supported the legislative initiatives of the Freedmen's Bureau.[27]

As a forceful political figure, Brown had moved quickly to aid in the protection of Missouri's escaping slaves, in particular those enslaved by Confederates. During the Civil War, tensions were high in Missouri, and in February 1863 Archer's owner, James Hollman, in the company of fellow pro-slavery conspirators, cut the wooden timbers of a bridge expected to bear the weight of a trainload of Union soldiers near O'Fallon, Missouri.

When Archer learned of the sabotage, he walked five miles in the middle of the night to alert those he knew were sympathetic to the Union cause. Because of his efforts, the bridge was repaired before any injury or damage occurred, and in June 2018, St. Charles County, Missouri, officials recognized Archer's heroic act by changing the name of the identified creek to "Archer Alexander Creek."[28] St. Louis Confederates suspected Archer as the informant and made plans to brutally question him. Realizing he had nothing to gain by returning to his owner's property, where he would in all likelihood be killed, Archer fled, leaving behind his wife and children. Upon fleeing, he met other escaping slaves and joined them in crossing the Missouri River in the search for freedom. They all were captured by slave hunters and returned to a tavern on the south side of the Missouri River for the night to await the next morning's ferry downriver to a Kentucky slave jail.[29] Certain of their ability to restrain their captives, the bounty hunters locked them in an upstairs room of the tavern and spent the remainder of the night drinking. Archer managed a solo escape from the second-floor window of the tavern when the guard dog stationed below became distracted. He then made his way to St. Louis, where a Dutch immigrant introduced Archer (who initially identified himself as "Aleck") to the wife of William Eliot, Abigail Adams (Cranch) Eliot (1817–1908). Abigail Eliot was also the grandniece of First Lady Abigail Adams, the wife of former president John Adams.[30]

Introduced to Archer by his wife, William Greenleaf Eliot became a lifelong friend to Archer. Born in New Bedford, Massachusetts, Eliot came from a prominent New England family. He entered Harvard Divinity School in 1831, where he developed a religious belief in Unitarianism. He arrived in St. Louis in 1834 as a Unitarian missionary and by 1837 had built his first church, the Church of the Messiah, where Archer became a regular attendant and faithful member. As his church congregation grew, so did Eliot's stature as a civic leader, serving as president of the St. Louis school board and founder of the Academy of Sciences of St. Louis as well as an early supporter of temperance and women's suffrage.[31] As a St. Louis resident and minister, Eliot, along with the Missouri senator Wayman Crow, spearheaded the establishment of St. Louis's Washington University in 1853, of which Eliot became the chancellor. He was also the grandfather of the Nobel Prize laureate poet T. S. Eliot.[32]

After several weeks of Archer working in service to Eliot in 1863, Eliot sought the advice of the St. Louis provost marshal general about ways to protect Archer from capture and reenslavement. To accomplish this goal, the provost issued Eliot a thirty-day permit that allowed Archer to legally stay in Eliot's home and in his employ. Expressing a desire to pay the full purchase price for Archer's freedom (an estimated $600), Eliot interviewed Archer concerning the best way to proceed. Archer informed Eliot that the St. Louis judge Barton Bates knew his former owner. Judge Bates served as one of three Missouri Supreme Court judges appointed in 1862 to fill seats vacated by judges who had refused to sign Union loyalty oaths. Eliot proceeded to send what he hoped was an anonymous letter of purchase through Bates to James Hollman. Eliot never received a response regarding his request. However, the letter did alert Hollman as to Archer's whereabouts. At the end of thirty days, Archer was viciously beaten by slave hunters in front of Eliot's children and forcibly taken from Eliot's property. Under Missouri martial law, slaves were not to be returned to slave owners or exported from the state but rather to be handed over to Union authorities for protection. Realizing the provost marshal's laws had been violated, Eliot made an immediate request to Benjamin Gratz Brown for aid in locating Archer. Upon finding that Archer was being held in a local police station, Brown utilized his connections to return Archer to Eliot's personal protection and the safety of Western Sanitary Commission offices. Made aware Hollman had no intention of ever freeing Archer, Eliot sent Archer to live and work with his friend and associate William Smith in Alton, Illinois, where Archer remained until January 1865, when all slaves in Missouri were manumitted.

Later in 1863, with the aid of those familiar to Archer and a $20 payment, Archer—still considered a fugitive slave—secured the freedom of his wife, Louisa, and their youngest daughter, thirteen-year-old Nellie, from the Naylor Plantation. Louisa lived for only one year after gaining her freedom. She died mysteriously at Naylor's home after returning at Naylor's invitation to collect her possessions. In addition to Nellie, three of Archer's children, including his married thirty-year-old daughter, found their way to a life of freedom in St. Louis before the end of the Civil War. These four are the only children Eliot accounts for in his record of Archer's life. Following the Civil War, many of Archer's other children came forward to claim a relationship with him in his old age, including his son, James Alexander, named for Archer's former enslaver, James Alexander. Eliot states that during the Civil War Archer's son Thomas enlisted in the United States Colored Troops and was killed at Hilton Head, South Carolina, while storming Fort Wagner.[33] It is believed Thomas was a member of the Thirty-Second Regiment, the only USCT regiment to list several Thomas Alexanders. The regiment was organized at Camp William Penn in Pennsylvania during the spring of 1864. The Thirty-Second was immediately ordered to Hilton Head upon completion of their military training, arriving there on April 27, 1864. Stationed on Morris Island, the regiment joined operations against Charleston and other points along the South Carolina coastline throughout its term of service. Losing more than 115 soldiers during its tour of duty, it was mustered out of service on August 22, 1865. Archer continued to receive a small pension for his son's military service until his death on December 8, 1880.[34]

A year following Louisa's death, apparently about the same time Archer returned to Missouri from Illinois, Archer took a new wife, referred to by Eliot as "Judy." Upon his second marriage, Archer departed the Eliots' home to establish his own home in Jefferson County, Missouri. The US census of 1870 indicates the presence of an Archer Alexander living as a resident of Joachim, Jefferson County, Missouri, an area approximately thirty-three miles south of St. Louis along the Missouri River. This area was home to residents from Licking County, Kentucky (Ohio), who had begun to settle the area near Bailey Station beginning in 1799.[35] The census lists a fifty-four-year-old mulatto and farm laborer named "Archer Alexander," born in Virginia around 1816, possessing real estate valued at $1,200. In addition to Archer, the census listed the children dwelling in the household as James Alexander, age fourteen; Ellen Alexander, age seventeen; and Archer's white wife, Julia Alexander, age thirty. Others living in the house were Dora White, age fourteen, and Alfred White, age twelve, both listed as white.[36]

In 1880, Archer was taken to St. Louis for medical care, where he later died. Eliot states that he preached at Archer's funeral service at St. Paul African Methodist Episcopal Church and followed, along "with many friends," the body to its "resting place" at the Methodist Centenary Burial Ground near Clayton Court House.[37] According to Eliot, Archer Alexander's body was laid to rest immediately following the St. Paul funeral service. Both Keith Winstead and the researcher Dorris Keeven-Franke seem to agree with Eliot that Archer's body is buried in what is now referred to as the Common Field burying ground of St. Peter's United Church of Christ Cemetery (2101 Lucas and Hunt Road) without benefit of a headstone.[38]

Major contributors in support of Charlotte Scott's call for a monument to Lincoln were soldiers with the USCT, in particular those under the command of West Point graduate Brigadier-General John Wynn Davidson (1824–1881).[39] Black troops in the USCT had battled the Civil War on two fronts: against Union soldiers who felt that the presence of Black troops demeaned their ranks and against Confederate soldiers personally offended by a Black man in uniform. The combined fund-raising efforts by Black veterans totaled $16,242, with $12,000 contributed by newly freed slaves.

Following the assassination of Lincoln, Vice President Andrew Johnson was sworn in as the seventeenth president of the United States. As president, Johnson ordered a halt to all federally supported fund-raising efforts for the monument, in particular those undertaken by Black soldiers. These fund-raising efforts were never renewed. Realizing that the collected funds were not sufficient to construct the desired monument, William Eliot and James Yeatman placed them in a bank to gather interest while awaiting more favorable political conditions, which presented themselves under the presidency of Ulysses Grant. As the political climate remained frozen, the Ku Klux Klan rose, and African Americans were lynched in high numbers, the funds collected grew to an estimated $50,000 by 1876. And while awaiting the "opportune moment" to proceed with plans for the monument, Western Sanitary Commission members spearheaded by William Eliot reviewed several proposed monument designs and designers as well as the proper location to install the anticipated monument.[40]

Ten years earlier, upon hearing of Lincoln's assassination, Thomas Ball (1819–1911), a self-taught musician, painter, and sculptor, had immediately begun to craft a half-life-size work of Lincoln in Italian marble. His initial work to honor Lincoln was eventually transformed into today's Emancipation Memorial. Ball clearly stated the intent of his work was to honor Lincoln's "noble act" of emancipating the slaves, ideas readily apparent in the final version of his work. Upon completion of the memorial image, Ball placed the model in his studio in Italy for local artists and friends to admire.[41] Earlier in his life, as an artist Ball had worked on Tremont Row, a notorious abolitionist location in Boston. In this liberal Boston community, he was a friend and supporter of several Massachusetts abolitionists, including John A. Andrew, the attorney for William Lloyd Garrison's American Anti-Slavery Society. Ball studied in Florence, Italy, where he remained until 1897. It was in Italy that William Eliot engaged Ball as the designer of the Emancipation Memorial on behalf of the Western Sanitary Commission. Though Ball had gained national attention as a performing American violinist and singer, he is best known as a sculptor who produced some of the nation's best-known monuments to memorialize notable American figures, such as Daniel Webster at Dartmouth College, the New Hampshire State House, and New York's Central Park; Benjamin Franklin at Boston City Hall; Henry Clay in the US Capitol; George Washington at the Boston Public Garden; Governor John A. Andrew in Boston; St. John the Evangelist in Boston; and P. T. Barnum in Bridgeport, Connecticut.[42]

Ball's major competition in earning the Lincoln Square commission came from another Massachusetts sculptor, Harriet Goodhue Hosmer (1830–1908), a member of a Rome artist colony. Although Hosmer's work was preferred by members of the African American community, Eliot, and the commission, it was ultimately rejected as too expensive for the commission's available funds.[43] Another factor that may have influenced the commission's decision was Hosmer's insistence upon making armed Black troops and women a major focus of her work rather than Lincoln, as originally requested by Charlotte Scott.

During the summer of 1869, William Eliot toured the artist studios of Thomas Ball and Harriet Hosmer, where he saw Ball's half-sculpted, marble tribute to the fallen Lincoln. It was there Ball informed Eliot that his work had begun "with no special end in view, except to express the magnificent act which had given new birth to his country, and for which the beloved and heroic leader had suffered martyrdom."[44] Following a review of Hosmer's work, Eliot, members of the Western Sanitary Commission, and the Freedmen's Bureau Memorial Association selected Ball's design, with certain alterations, to complete the new Lincoln Park group of proposed "Emancipation" monuments.[45] Ball did not charge for his artistic labor, only for the cost of recasting the monument in bronze at a Munich, Germany, foundry.[46]

Ball's revised monument depicts Kentucky-born President Lincoln holding his hand above the body of a Black man rising to his feet after breaking the chains of slavery. Lincoln's right hand holds an unfurled copy of the Emancipation Proclamation, which freed slaves in rebelling states and opened the door for Black military enlistment. The monument portrays a Black man rising to a standing position to accept the gift of freedom from Lincoln's presidential hand. As a lifelong friend to Archer Alexander, Eliot provided Ball with photographs of Archer for use in the recast bronze work. Both Archer and Lincoln are surrounded by the emblems of American freedom, including a profile of George Washington; the fasces of the US republic; a shield bearing the American Stars and Stripes; a slave whipping post covered in cloth; and a growing vine retracing the path of the slave chain. Cast in Munich in 1875, the monument was shipped directly to Washington and accepted by Congress as a gift from the "colored citizens of the United States" in 1876. To facilitate placement of the monument, Congress allocated $3,000 for construction of a pedestal.

Soon after the Washington monument installation ceremonies, William Eliot showed Archer photographs of the newly installed Emancipation Memorial, which utilized Archer's image to honor Lincoln and issuance of the Emancipation Proclamation. Eliot explained to Archer that this monument would forever link him with the deeds of Abraham Lincoln, a connection that, Eliot stated, seemed to please Archer.[47]

At the time of its installation, the Emancipation Memorial represented the first and only national monument to Lincoln and the only one paid for by African Americans. The Western Sanitary Commission chose to erect the Emancipation Memorial on the site of the former Lincoln Hospital and Contraband Hospital and Camp. At this former site, Black troops lucky enough to receive any form of medical treatment had lain injured, bleeding, and dying for the cause of Black freedom. The treatment of wounded

Black men at this location and on many other Civil War battlefields was rendered primarily by Black women, dedicated to the care of their families and their communities. The government commissioned Black Civil War doctors to care for Black soldiers at the Contraband Hospital near Lincoln Hospital.[48]

It was from this location while touring Washington military hospitals that New York author, poet, and abolitionist Julia Ward Howe first heard Union troops singing the words to "John Brown's Body." The song contained the provocative words "John Brown's body lies-a-mouldering in the ground. . . . His soul is marching on" as a tribute to the executed John Brown and his failed attempt to free enslaved African Americans during his attack on Harpers Ferry. Howe reframed the words into what is now an American national anthem, the "Battle Hymn of the Republic," first published in the *Atlantic Monthly* in 1862.[49] For members of the Western Sanitary Commission, it seemed the only appropriate location for the Emancipation Memorial, which also honored the ground where African American soldiers had bled and died in service to the country and the quest for freedom.

In 1861–1862, the Western Sanitary Commission had urged the importance of building pavilion-style hospitals rather than renting buildings that were ill equipped to serve as military hospitals. Lincoln Park is the largest urban park in Washington. Known historically as Lincoln Square, the Washington site served from 1862 to 1865 as the location of Lincoln Hospital and Contraband Hospital and Camp, equipped to accept wounded Black soldiers as well as freed and escaping slaves.[50] The encampment included twenty pavilions arranged in a V formation. Twenty-five tent wards provided beds for 2,575 wounded soldiers. Other buildings on site included quarters for the Sisters of Mercy,[51] who provided nursing care to white wounded regular army soldiers. Separate medical quarters were provided for the nursing care of military "contraband" (that is, former slaves and Black soldiers). In 1867, Congress authorized the grounds to be called Lincoln Square as a memorial to the former president so that it became the first public park in America to bear his name.[52]

While Sisters of Mercy provided medical care for wounded white soldiers within the segregated wards of Lincoln Hospital, wounded members of the USCT, runaways, and newly freed slaves (contraband) were cared for at the Contraband Camp and Hospital by Black doctors and nurses trained for that purpose at the camp. The Black medical facility was initially established on swampy Washington land bounded by Twelfth, Thirteenth, R Street, and S Street, Northwest. The camp and hospital aided more than 40,000 escaped slaves and Black soldiers who sought freedom, refuge, and medical treatment in the District of Columbia.[53] Constructed as a one-story frame building with additional tented structures added by the Union army, the Contraband Hospital and Camp provided less than favorable housing and hospital wards for Black civilians and soldiers.[54]

The Contraband Camp survived for more than a year before being disbanded in December 1863. The US Sanitary Commission relocated the hospital and continued to provide medical care to Black civilians and soldiers. By late 1864, the facility had moved several times from its original location in Lincoln Square, eventually establishing itself on the site of the former Campbell Army Hospital. In 1865, no longer under control of the US Army, the Contraband Hospital became known as the Freedmen's Hospital, an official part of the Freedmen's Bureau. With its move to Campbell Army Hospital, Freedmen's Hospital offered improved facilities for its patients, which included a better water supply and waste-disposal system as well as a six-hundred-bed treatment capacity. The hospital continued to serve as a medical facility for Washington's African American community following the war. It eventually moved to the site of Howard University in 1868, where it became the teaching hospital for Howard's newly formed Medical Department.[55] In March 1967, President Lyndon B. Johnson officially transferred Freedmen's Hospital to Howard University, renaming it Howard University Hospital.

Archer Alexander's death and the installation of the Emancipation Memorial did not end the far-reaching impact of his story on Kentucky and American history. A story by Ben Strauss in the *Washington Post* on October 2, 2018, linked Archer Alexander's DNA to that of the world heavyweight champion Muhammad Ali. Ali's third cousin Keith Winstead used DNA testing to discover the family's connection to Archer Alexander. Winstead stated that Muhammad Ali had always expressed an interest in learning more about his ancestors.[56]

DNA lineage connecting Muhammad Ali to that of Archer and Louisa Alexander was traced to their sold-away son Wesley (1829–1888). No doubt sold to a Kentucky owner, at some point Wesley married Kentucky-born Patsy (Daisy) Fry in Louisville. The US census of 1900 indicates that a widowed Patsy Alexander lived at 1231 Oldham Street in Louisville's

Tenth Ward. At 1219 Oldham lived forty-four-year-old John Alexander (b. 1855), possibly Wesley's brother. John stated he was born in Kentucky, and the census indicated that he lived with his wife, Tillie, age thirty-four, also born in Kentucky, and their children Emma, age nine; Patsy, age six; Ner, age three; and Malinda, age four months.[57]

Patsy was listed as the sixty-nine-year-old widow of Wesley Alexander and a colored laundress born in January 1831. News reports state that her husband, Wesley, had died January 9, 1888, after sustaining an accidental gunshot wound.[58] Patsy owned her own home and was listed as head of household. She was the mother of eleven living children. Residing in her home at the time of the census were her son Philip, age twenty-one; Gertrude, age twenty-four; Eva, age twenty-two; and Lelah Alexander, age twenty-six. The census also confirmed the presence of Montgomery Greathouse, fifty-one, and Betsy Jane Alexander Greathouse, thirty-four, as residents of Oldham Street. The Greathouses were listed as the parents of a nine-year-old Black female named Edith. On April 28, 1888, Wesley and Patsy's daughter Betsy Jane Alexander (1864–1964) had married former USCT soldier Montgomery Greathouse (1849–1914) in Louisville. They had three children: Edith Edean (Clay); James M. Greathouse; and Coretta (Brooks).[59] A graduate of Louisville's Central High School, Edith Greathouse married Herman Heaton Clay (1876–1954) on December 30, 1909, and they became the parents of Muhammad Ali's father, Cassius M. Clay Sr. (1913–1990). And thus was the direct line from Archer Alexander to Cassius Clay Jr. (Muhammad Ali) established.

Paul Shackel makes us aware of the difficulty that local, regional, and national museums and history organizations face in addressing the changing meaning, dynamics, and focus of static commemorative efforts such as monuments.[60] The contributions and sacrifices of African Americans, a moment that the Emancipation Monument seeks to honor, lifted America to a higher standard of humanity and inclusion. We now view this monument through a modern lens of what we would like to see, not as a statement made by newly freed nineteenth-century African Americans. As America seeks to provide a more accurate and inclusive retelling of the "American Story," the need for change often confronts resistance. A scratching of the surface of the underrepresented history of the Emancipation Memorial exposes a connection to an American icon, Muhammad Ali, but it also reveals the painful history of African Americans' status and treatment in the United States. When viewing the monument, many focus on Lincoln as the "emancipator," while the name "Archer Alexander" remains virtually unknown in the public and historic record. The modern eye is offended by the image of Archer Alexander, who appears to be placed in a position of weakness. If we look closer, though, we see Archer's raised eyes fixed on the Emancipation Proclamation, not on Lincoln. Archer's gaze indicates the importance of this presidential legislation in *beginning* the struggle for Black freedom in America. It is this modern understanding of America that football player Colin Kaepernick's bended knee during the playing of the national anthem continues to emphasize in today's struggle.

Notes

1. Natalie O'Neill, "Barrier Installed to Protect DC Emancipation Memorial from Protesters," *New York Post,* June 26, 2020.

2. Tom Fitzgerald, "DC Lincoln Park 'Emancipation' Statue among Monuments Drawing Scrutiny," news report, Fox 5, Washington, DC.

3. In the nation's capital, five monuments associated with the lives of African Americans include the Emancipation Memorial (1876), commissioned by the Western Sanitary Commission of St. Louis, Missouri; the Mary McLeod Bethune Monument (1974), commissioned by National Council of Negro Women; the Martin Luther King Jr. Monument (2011), commissioned by the US Congress; the Frederick Douglass Monument (2013), commissioned by the District of Columbia; and the Rosa Parks Monument (2013), commissioned by the US Congress.

4. "Obituary of William P. Rucker," *Chariton Courier* (Keytesville, MO), January 13, 1905, 1. Margaret and William Rucker had four sons: William Waller Rucker (1855–1936) served in the US House of Representatives from Missouri's Second District from 1899 to 1923 (Waller's biography states he attended common schools and moved to Chariton County, Missouri, with his parents in 1873); H. S. Rucker was an attorney-at-law; James T. Rucker was principal for Missouri's State School for the Deaf, Dumb, and Blind; and Edgar P. Rucker was the county attorney for Welch and McDowell Counties, Missouri.

5. William G. Eliot, *The Story of Archer Alexander: From Slavery to Freedom* (Boston: Cupples, Upham, 1885), 12; Henry Burke, "A Friend of Lincoln," n.d., in "Charlotte Scott, a Friend of Lincoln," posted by David Baker, Early Marietta, February 17, 2015, at https://earlymarietta.blogspot.com/2015/02/charlotte-scott-friend-of-lincoln.html. Charlotte's gift of $5 in 1865 would total $175 in today's currency market.

6. "Frances D. Gage," n.d., Iowa State University Archives of Women's Political Communications, at https://awpc.cattcenter.iastate.edu/directory/frances-d-gage/.

7. This letter is included in "Charlotte Scott and the Emancipation Memorial," Historical Marietta, Ohio, July 2, 2020, at http://historicalmarietta.blogspot.com/2020/07/charlotte-scott-and-emancipation.html.

8. Eliot, *The Story of Archer Alexander*, 120–22.

9. "Bellows, Henry Whitney," in *Encyclopædia Britannica*, 11th ed., ed. Hugh Chisholm (Cambridge: Cambridge University Press, 1911), 705. Henry W. Bellows (1814–1882) was born in Boston, Massachusetts, was a graduate of Harvard Divinity School, and held a brief pastorate (1837–1838) at Mobile, Alabama. In 1839, he became pastor of the First Congregational (Unitarian) Church in New York City (renamed All Souls Church) until his death.

10. Charles, J. Stille, *History of the United States Sanitary Commission, Being the General Report of Its Work during the War of the Rebellion* (Philadelphia: J. B. Lippincott, 1866), 76. As a Louisville resident, Olmsted had also actively designed several of the city's now famous parks.

11. "Fugitive Slave Acts," History.com, n.d., at https://www.history.com/topics/black-history/fugitive-slave-acts. Henry Clay had negotiated the Missouri Compromise of 1820, which admitted Missouri into the union as a slaveholding state while limiting the expansion of slavery above the thirty-sixth parallel.

12. Archer was more than likely the inherited property of James Harvey Alexander (1789–1834) and Jane McClure, initial residents of Rockbridge County, Virginia. In her research, Dorris Keeven-Franke disputes many elements of Eliot's original writing (see Dorris Keeven-Franke, "Archer Alexander's Untold Story," n.d., at https://archeralexander.wordpress.com, where Keeven-Franke references Archer Alexander's descendant Keith Winstead; and Dorris Keeven-Frank, "Never Say Never! With Dorris Keeven-Franke and Keith Winstead," May 13, 2020, at https://www.blogtalkradio.com/bernicebennett/2020/05/13/never-say-never-with-dorris-keeven-franke-and-keith-winstead). Despite any possible flaws, Eliot's account historically remains the closest thing to a firsthand account of Alexander's life. Keeven-Franke's account of events may not take into consideration that both Archer and his wife, Louisa, may have been sold to other owners upon settlement of James and Jane Alexander's estate and possibly other times following that.

13. Information regarding the life of Archibald Alexander comes from Archibald Alexander Papers, 1815–1851, ArchiveGrid, Presbyterian Historical Society, Philadelphia, at https://researchworks.oclc.org/archivegrid/collection/data/48206505; and "The Death of Archibald Alexander, October 22, 1851," at https://landmarkevents.org/the-death-of-archibald-alexander-1851/. Archibald

Alexander's father was also a Presbyterian minister in Rockbridge and a founder of the College of Washington and Lee University. More than likely, it was Archibald Sr. who owned Archer Alexander's family. Eliot's written description seems to fit more closely with this description of Archer Alexander's early life in Virginia. Both Archibald Alexander Senior and Junior were born in South River, Rockbridge County, Virginia. Archibald Jr. was born into a family of means. A graduate of Washington and Lee University, where his father taught, Alexander was ordained as a minister of the Presbyterian Church in 1791 and served as an itinerant Presbyterian minister in Virginia's Charlotte and Prince Edward Counties from 1791 to 1794. He was appointed president of Hampden-Sydney College from 1797 to 1806 and later served as a professor at Princeton from 1812 to 1843. He married Janetta Wadell in 1802, and they had three children: James (possibly Archer Alexander's owner), William Cowper, and Joseph Addison. The US census of 1850 also lists a sixty-one-year-old James Alexander (1821–1899), with wives Rachel Shannon Alexander (1831–1854) and Mary Louise Holt Alexander (1841–1903), as a farmer and resident of Anderson County, Kentucky, where there is also a Delaney Road. This James Alexander (the son of Archibald Alexander Jr.) died on December 25, 1899, and is buried in Reid Cemetery, Lincoln County, Missouri, a county adjacent to St. Charles County. See "James Harvey Alexander," US census, 1850, Ancestry.com, at https://www.ancestry.com/discoveryui-content/view/81679250:60525?tid=&pid=&queryId=94e55ac452cca594dcef1e6eca895191&_phsrc=Yat112&_phstart=successSource.

14. Eliot, *The Story of Archer Alexander,* 19. Keith Winstead, an Archer Alexander descendant, also lists Archer's parents as Aleck Prince (circa 1783) and Chloe Prince, in keeping with Eliot's reference. Winstead lists Archer's wives as Louisa McCluer Alexander (1811–1866) and Julia Alexander (1840–1879). He also lists two of Archer's children sold away from the Pitman plantation, Ralph (1828–1864) and Wesley Alexander (1829–1888), which occurred while Louisa and Archer were residents on the Pitman farm. Winstead's family research is gathered in Tami Glock, "Archer Alexander," Find a Grave, updated March 28, 2012, at https://www.findagrave.com/memorial/190147492/archer-alexander.

15. Eliot, *The Story of Archer Alexander,* 25.

16. Eliot, *The Story of Archer Alexander,* 20, 21. East Grace Street dates back to Richmond's original street grid of 1737 and in the course of the nineteenth century evolved into one of the city's two most prestigious residential streets. See Doug Childers, "West Grace Street: From Antebellum Architecture to Midcentury Subdivisions," *Richmond (VA) Dispatch,* November 5, 2016.

17. Scott Nesbit, Robert K. Nelson, and Maurie McInnis, "Visualizing the Richmond Slave Trade," American Studies Association, University of Richmond,

Richmond, VA, November 2010. Aleck was possibly sold to Richmond slave dealers Jones & Slater at Locust Alley between Exchange Place and Franklin. See Elizabeth Kambourian, comp., "Slave Traders in Richmond," *Richmond (VA) Times Dispatch,* February 24, 2014, at https://richmond.com/slave-traders-in-richmond/table_52a32a98-9d56-11e3-806a-0017a43b2370.html.

18. Eliot, *The Story of Archer Alexander,* 26.

19. Eliot, *The Story of Archer Alexander,* 29.

20. Eliot, *The Story of Archer Alexander,* 40; Keeven-Franke, "Archer Alexander's Untold Story." It is suspected that Ralph and Wesley were sold to Kentucky slave owners.

21. Eliot, *The Story of Archer Alexander,* 40. Slaves were first imported into Missouri by the French merchant Philippe François Renault in 1720, when Renault brought an estimated five hundred enslaved Black people from Saint-Domingue to work in the southeastern Missouri and southern Illinois lead mines. The institution of slavery became more prominent in Missouri with the invention of the cotton gin and completion of the Louisiana Purchase. Both of these events led to increased westward expansion and migration of slave-owning settlers into present-day Missouri and Arkansas, then known as Upper Louisiana.

22. Thomas C. Fletcher, *Missouri's Jubilee* (Jefferson City, MO: W. A. Curry, 1865); Aaron Astor, *Rebels on the Border: Civil War, Emancipation, and the Reconstruction of Kentucky and Missouri* (Baton Rouge: Louisiana State University Press, 2012).

23. "Frémont, John Charles," in *Dictionary of American Biography,* ed. Allan Nevins, Allen Johnson, and Dumas Malone (New York: Scribner's, 1931), 19–23.

24. The Kentucky politician and attorney John Mason Brown (1757–1837), the son of Reverend John Brown and Margaret Preston Brown, represented the Continental Congress and the US Congress, where he introduced bills that Kentucky be granted statehood. In 1812, Brown was appointed to oversee construction of a public house of worship on the Frankfort Public Square and oversaw construction of the brick Capitol Building and the limestone one that replaced it. In 1836, he presided over the organizational meeting of the Kentucky Historical Society. His home became Frankfort's historic Liberty Hall.

25. Daniel M. Grissom, "Personal Recollections of Distinguished Missourians: B. Gratz Brown," *Missouri Historical Society* 19, no. 3 (1925): 423–26; Eliot, *The Story of Archer Alexander,* 55.

26. "Missouri's Civil War," Missouri's Civil War Heritage Foundation, n.d., at http://www.mocivilwar.org/portfolio/brown-benjamin-gratz/.

27. The Freedmen's Bureau was established on March 3, 1865, as a Lincoln initiative to last through the Civil War and no longer than one year following the

end of the war. The bureau was created to assist newly freed slaves in obtaining housing, education, citizenship rights, and employment. President Lincoln appointed the Medal of Honor recipient General Oliver Otis Howard (1830–1909) to lead the efforts of the Bureau of Refugees, Freedmen, and Abandoned Lands (Freedmen's Bureau). Howard spearheaded efforts to honor the fallen president's wishes, extending his work to include the establishment of Lincoln Square. However, because President Johnson considered Howard a religious and political "fanatic," Howard's restorative efforts proved only partially successful. He was known as the "Christian general" because his reform policies attempted to adhere to decisions based in evangelical piety. Johnson's determination not to provide funding or staff support for Howard's Freedmen's Bureau initiatives stymied monument fund-raising efforts. Despite Johnson's fierce opposition, Howard did establish Howard Normal and Theological Institute for the Education of Preachers and Teachers, later renamed Howard University. As a reformist, Howard led promotion of higher-education opportunities for freedmen, becoming the founder and first president of Howard University from 1867 to 1873. He also supported post–Civil War funding for Berea College, which aided the college in recruiting and educating former members of the USCT. Howard was quoted as saying, "The opposition to Negro education made itself felt everywhere in a combination not to allow the freed men any room or building in which a school might be taught." After 1874, Howard joined military leaders such as J. W. Davidson in commanding Buffalo Soldiers against Indians in the West, conducting a famous campaign against the Nez Percé, who dwelled primarily in the region that became Washington, Oregon, and Idaho, in 1877 and negotiating a treaty with Cochise in 1872. See *Annual Report of the Secretary of War for the Year 1869* (Washington, DC: US Government Printing Office, 1869), 499, 504; and David Thomson, "Oliver Otis Howard: Reassessing the Legacy of the 'Christian General,'" *American Nineteenth Century History* 10 (September 2009): 273–98.

28. Brett Auten, "St. Charles County Creek Renamed," *St. Charles County Community News,* July 11, 2018, at https://mycnews.com/st-charles-county-creek-renamed/. The creek is 2.5 miles long, with its head in the city of O'Fallon. It flows generally south through the city of Cottleville to enter Dardenne Creek 3.9 miles north-northwest of Weldon Spring.

29. Eliot, *The Story of Archer Alexander,* 48.

30. Eliot, *The Story of Archer Alexander,* 56; "Abigail Adams Cranch Eliot," Ancestry.com, n.d., at https://www.findagrave.com/memorial/11827225/abigail-adams-eliot.

31. "William Greenleaf Eliot," Washington University in St. Louis, n.d., at https://wustl.edu/about/history-traditions/chancellors/eliot/.

32. Candace O'Connor, "The Founding of Washington University," *Washington University in St. Louis Magazine,* Summer 2003, at FreedomsMemorial/ArcherAlexander/Washington%20University%20in%20St.%20Louis%20Magazine.html. Eliot was born in New Bedford, Massachusetts, where he attended the Friends Academy in New Bedford; he then attended Columbian College (now the George Washington University) in Washington, DC, graduating in 1831, and completed graduate work at Harvard Divinity School in 1834. He was ordained a minister of the Unitarian Church on August 17, 1834.

33. Eliot, *The Story of Archer Alexander,* 82.

34. Information on the military activity of Thomas Alexander was compiled from the National Parks Service Soldiers and Sailors Database at https://www.nps.gov/civilwar/search-soldiers.htm#sort=score+desc&q=Alexander,+Thomas&fq%5B%5D=State%3A%22United+States+Colored+Troops%22; and "32nd USCT Regiment," African American Patriots of Pennsylvania, Civil War to Civil Rights, n.d., at https://housedivided.dickinson.edu/sites/patriots/2010/04/30/32nd-usct-regiment-2/.

35. "Joachim Township," Jefferson County (Missouri) Genealogical Society, n.d., quoted from *An Illustrated Historical Atlas Map: Jefferson County, MO* (Brink, McDonough, 1876), 18, at http://www.jcgsmo.org/resources/maps/Joachim.html; Debra Alderson McClane, *Botetourt County* (Charleston, SC: Arcadia, 2007). There is no Licking County, Kentucky, so this may have been a reference to settlers from the area of eastern Kentucky's Licking River; in particular, John Bailey, a former Garrard County resident, is listed as one of Joachim's early settlers. Keith Winstead says that Botetourt County, Virginia, is Archer Alexander's birthplace (Keith Winstead, telephone interview by Alicestyne Turley, September 21, 2021). In 1770, when Virginia claimed most of the Northwest Territory, the territory identified initially as Botetourt County divided to create Botetourt County and Augusta County, Virginia. The territory that eventually became Kentucky was removed from Botetourt and became Fincastle County in 1772 and Kentucky County in 1776 (see "History of Botetourt County," n.d., at https://www.visitroanokeva.com/region/cities-and-counties/botetourt-county/history/). Mr. Winstead has taken much of the information he cites regarding Archer Alexander's early Virginia history from research conducted by the St. Louis, Missouri, author, public historian, educator, and professional genealogist Dorris Keeven-Franke, who was working on a book about Archer Alexander. See Keeven-Franke, "Never Say Never! With Dorris Keeven-Franke and Keith Winstead." (I do question many of her conclusions.)

36. US census, 1870, Joachim, Jefferson County, Missouri, Ancestry.com, at https://www.ancestry.com/search/collections/7163/?name=Archer_Alexander&birth=_joachim-jefferson-missouri-usa_49043.

37. Eliot, *The Story of Archer Alexander,* 86–89. St. Paul African Methodist Episcopal (AME) Church was organized by Reverend William Paul Quinn in 1841 and is described as the oldest AME church west of the Mississippi River. The original AME church congregation met in a log cabin at the end of Main Street but soon moved to an old Presbyterian mission at Seventh and Washington Streets. The congregation also occupied a new church at Eleventh and Green (now Lucas Street) in 1852; a brick structure replaced this church in 1871, and then a new church was dedicated at Lawton and Leffingwell. St. Paul AME Church also occupied the former Christian Church building at Hamilton and Julian until 1962. In 1883, St. Paul was considered the largest African American Methodist congregation in St. Louis, with more than twelve hundred communicants. See David A. Lossos, "Early (Pre-1900) St. Louis Places of Worship," September 12, 2007, at https://stpaulamestl.net/church-history/.

38. Glock, "Archer Alexander." The cemetery described by both Eliot and Keeven-Franke is located four miles south of Ferguson in Normandy, St. Louis County, Missouri.

39. J. W. "Black Jack" Davidson had served in the Union army as an Indian fighter prior to being offered a commission in the Confederate army, which he rejected. He was transferred to the Civil War Trans-Mississippi Theater, where he was placed in command of the District of St. Louis from December 3, 1862, to March 26, 1863. Much of his army was later transferred to Ulysses Grant in preparation for the Vicksburg Campaign. Following the Civil War, Davidson was again posted in the West, this time as a lieutenant colonel for the Buffalo Soldiers Tenth Cavalry organized at Fort Leavenworth, Kansas. The Buffalo Soldiers were created by an act of Congress on June 28, 1866. Congressional legislation authorized the establishment of two cavalry and four infantry regiments, organized as the Ninth and Tenth Cavalry and the Thirty-Eighth through Forty-First Infantry. All former USCT cavalry and infantry units, including members of Kentucky's Fifth and Seventh Cavalry and remaining USCT infantry units, were folded into segregated Buffalo Soldier US Army units. As segregated regular army units, Buffalo Soldiers fought the Indian Wars in the West, the Spanish-American War in Cuba, and the Philippine-American War. See Will Gorenfeld, "The Battle of Cieneguilla," *Wild West Magazine,* February 2008, at https://www.chargeofthedragoons.com/2006/11/dragoons-v-jicarilla-apache-the-battle-of-cieneguilla/; American Battlefield Trust, at https://www.battlefields.org/learn/articles/united-states-colored-troops; and Lieutenant John Bigelow Jr., "The Tenth Regiment of Cavalry," in *The Army of the United States: Historical Sketches of Staff and Line with Portraits of Generals-in-Chief,* ed. Theophilus Francis Rodenbough and William L. Haskin (New York: Maynard, Merrill, 1896), at https://history.army.mil/books/R&H/R&H-10CV.htm.

40. Eliot, *The Story of Archer Alexander,* 11–13.

41. Burke, "A Friend of Lincoln."

42. "Thomas Ball," Smithsonian Art Museum, n.d., at https://americanart
.si.edu/artist/thomas-ball-218; "Ball, Thomas," Encyclopedia.com (*Columbia Ency-clopedia*, 6th ed.), n.d., at https://www.encyclopedia.com/reference/encyclopedias-almanacs-transcripts-and-maps/ball-thomas.

43. Friends within Harriet Hosmer's (1830–1908) artist colony included the American artists and writers Nathaniel Hawthorne, William Makepeace Thackery, Elizabeth Barrett and Robert Browning, Anne Whitney, Edmonia Lewis, Emma Stebbins, Louisa Lander, Margaret Foley, Florence Freeman, and Vinnie Ream. See Priscilla Frank, "The 19th Century American Women Artists You Don't Know, but Should," *Huff Post*, May 29, 2015, at https://www.huffpost
.com/entry/19th-century-american-wom_n_7453748; "Hosmer, Harriet," in *Appletons' Cyclopædia of American Biography*, ed. J. G. Wilson and J. Fiske (New York: D. Appleton, 1892), 5.

44. Eliot, *The Story of Archer Alexander*, 13.

45. Laid out in L'Enfant's plan for Washington as a square to hold a monumental column from which point all distances on the continent would be measured, Lincoln Park was slow to develop and in fact was used for years as a dumping ground. During the Civil War, it was the site of Lincoln Hospital, named after the president. The name apparently stuck, and in 1867 Congress authorized that the park be called Lincoln Square as a memorial to the martyred leader, the first site to bear his name (US National Park Service, "Lincoln Park," n.d., at https://www.nps.gov/cahi/learn/historyculture/cahi_lincoln.htm).

46. Eliot, *The Story of Archer Alexander*, 13.

47. Eliot, *The Story of Archer Alexander*, 86–89.

48. African American surgeons were commissioned as military officers or private physicians under contract with the US Army to care for Black soldiers. They were the first Black physicians to serve in positions of authority at any hospital in the United States. Doctors enlisted to care for soldiers and contrabands included Alexander T. Augusta, Anderson R. Abbott, John H. Rapier Jr., William P. Powell Jr., William B. Ellis, Charles B. Purvis, and Alpheus W. Tucker. Federal records indicate surgeons received their medical assignments based on race. Work assignments of Black surgeons took them to duty stations at facilities treating only African Americans. No Black surgeons were ever assigned to white-only hospitals or wards.

49. "It was from this background that Julia Ward Howe had been inspired to write the lyrics to her 'Battle Hymn of the Republic,' the previous day, while picnicking with her husband and others as they watched a review of Massachusetts troops, just outside of Washington City. During the review she was captivated by

Massachusetts soldiers singing 'John Brown's Body' to a lovely tune that had been composed by South Carolinian William Steffe as a Methodist Sunday school and camp meeting song about 5 years earlier. But, it seems the review of troops was disturbed by some Confederate soldiers who opened fire on outlying pickets and sent the picnickers 'scurrying back to the capital'" (Howard Ray White, "Understanding the 'Battle Hymn of the Republic,'" July 14, 2014, at https://www.abbevilleinstitute.org/understanding-the-battle-hymn-of-the-republic/).

50. Stephen M. Forman, *A Guide to Civil War Washington* (Washington, DC: Elliott & Clark, 1995), 50–51.

51. Grant Gerlich, archivist, "Civil War Sisters Healing the Wounds of the Nation," Sisters of Mercy, January 29, 2015, at http://www.sistersofmercy.org/blog/2015/01/29/civil-war-sisters-healing-the-wounds-of-the-nation/. The Sisters of Mercy were an order of Catholic women founded in 1831 in Dublin, Ireland, by Catherine McAuley (1778–1841). The order arrived in the United States in 1843, settling in Pittsburgh, Pennsylvania. Within four years, they had opened the first Mercy Hospital in the world. They soon established nursing communities across the county, operated hospitals, and opened nursing schools in the District of Columbia. The sisters' actions included nursing the wounded, organizing housekeeping, cooking, distributing food, and providing laundry services. They cared for Union and Confederate soldiers alike: officers and enlisted men, rich and poor, no matter their religion or heritage.

52. "Lincoln Park," Capitol Hill Parks, District of Columbia, US National Park Service, n.d., at https://www.nps.gov/cahi/learn/historyculture/cahi_lincoln.htm; "Historic Medical Sites Near Washington, DC," National Library of Medicine, National Institutes of Health, n.d., at https://www.nlm.nih.gov/hmd/historic-medical-sites/area-sites.html#!.

53. Jill Newmark, "Contraband Hospital, 1862–1863: Health Care for the First Freedpeople," BlackPast, March 28, 2012, at https://www.blackpast.org/african-american-history/contraband-hospital-1862–1863-heath-care-first-freedpeople/.

54. Newmark, "Contraband Hospital."

55. Newmark, "Contraband Hospital."

56. Ben Strauss, "DNA Evidence Links Muhammad Ali to Heroic Slave, Family Says," *Washington Post,* October 2, 2018, at https://www.washingtonpost.com/sports/2018/10/02/dna-evidence-links-muhammad-ali-heroic-slave-family-says/.

57. US census, 1900, Louisville Ward 10, Jefferson County, KY, p. 9, Enumeration District: 0097, microfilm: 1240531, Family History Library, Salt Lake City, Utah.

58. Birth and Death Records, Film 7007128: Louisville, Books 7–8, Kentucky Department for Libraries and Archives, Frankfort.

59. US census, 1910, Louisville, Jefferson County, Kentucky, Ancestry.com, at https://www.ancestry.comsearch/collections/7884/?name=Edith_Clay&birth=_louisville-jefferson-kentucky-usa_32672&residence=_louisville-jefferson-kentucky-usa_32672.

60. Paul A. Shackel, *Memory in Black and White: Race, Commemoration, and the Post-bellum Landscape* (Walnut Creek, CA: AltaMira Press, 2003), epilogue.

Acknowledgments

More than fifteen years ago, I began offering a course at the University of Kentucky titled "The Kentucky African American Experience." Using primary and secondary sources, I introduced my students to myriad topics and themes that explored the intersections of race, class, and gender. Each semester I taught the course, it became a challenge to identify new scholarship for our classroom discussion. I was able to begin addressing this concern when I served as guest editor for a special edition of the *Register of the Kentucky Historical Society* in 2011. This publication included essays on selected topics on Black people in Kentucky.

Four years later, I wrote an essay titled "'Straining to Hear Their Thoughts and Desires': Researching and Writing the African American Experience in Kentucky" for another special edition of the *Register*, titled "Building a History of Twentieth-Century Kentucky" (vol. 113, nos. 2–3 [Spring–Summer 2015], guest edited by Thomas Kiffmeyer and Robert S. Weise). In this work, I pressed my case for expanding research on Black Kentuckians. I pointed out that "African Americans in Kentucky experienced similar forms of racism and discrimination as those living farther south. Yet, within this context, Kentucky African Americans had varied experiences that were determined by time, place, and circumstances" (510). More importantly, I explained that "the black experience *cannot* be divided into two parts, 'Louisville and the rest of the state.' It should not be examined in merely an urban versus rural context or in a confined setting of 'polite racism' to an environment rooted in racial violence. This kind of paradigm," I wrote, "leaves little room for exploring the complexities, challenges, and changes Kentucky African Americans witnessed and experienced during the twentieth century" (511). These two publications planted the seeds for this current volume.

I have always believed Kentucky Blacks have a deep and rich story that has been overlooked far too long. Names, events, and subject matter have been either lost or hidden or ignored in the traditional narratives of

Kentucky and southern history. This book is further proof of this fact. It seeks to remove African Americans from the margins of history and place them at the center of the Kentucky experience. This effort has been made possible by noteworthy contributions by students, colleagues, archivists, and friends. Each in some way has helped shape this book in meaningful ways from idea to completion.

I thank Director Ashley Runyon, Acquisitions Editor Patrick O'Dowd, and Managing Editor David Cobb at the University Press of Kentucky for their unwavering support of this project. They saw the lasting value of this work and thereby challenged me to seek fresh new studies that could make a difference in shaping our understanding of Kentucky history. Likewise, the anonymous readers of the manuscript provided salient comments that enhanced its cohesiveness. Special thanks to copyeditor Annie Barva.

I am especially grateful for the tremendous research and writings of the contributors, who willingly shared their work for this volume. The immense value of their individual contributions cannot be overstated. Each author was timely and efficient in producing rounds of drafted essays, responding to emails, and meeting deadlines to finish the book on schedule. Because of their hard work and profound scholarship, this book gives new understanding to race and history in Kentucky.

This work clearly would not have been finished had it not been for the assistance provided by other scholars. When I began soliciting essays in spring 2020, my colleague Amy Murrell Taylor was especially helpful in connecting me with possible contributors. She and Vanessa Holden, another colleague in the Department of History at the University of Kentucky, read selected chapters authored by Brandon Wilson, Charles Welsko, and Guiliana Perrone. To be sure, Amy and Vanessa's vast knowledge of slavery and reconstruction as well as their sharp analytical skills enhanced the intellectual arguments made in these chapters. I am also appreciative of the historian Kenneth W. Goings's reading of the introduction. He provided strong feedback that prompted me to think even more critically about the volume's meaning and purpose. I also wish to express my appreciation for former students who assisted me with research included in the introduction and chapter 10. Anthony Hartsfield Jr. was an undergraduate research assistant who traveled with me to give a presentation in Bardstown, Kentucky, and joined me as a tourist at My Old Kentucky Home (Federal Hill). Former Kentucky State Parks commissioner

Gerry van der Meer and Kentucky archaeologist Philip B. Mink II provided helpful information about the enslaved burial ground on the My Old Kentucky Home historical site. Lametta Johnson and Theda Wigglesworth mined primary sources and found newspaper articles that were extremely helpful. Sally Powell and Joshua Farrington found important nuggets of information while we were working on *The Kentucky African American Encyclopedia* (University Press of Kentucky, 2015). Their searches through archives and newspapers were indispensable, as were the encouraging insights of the historian John A. Hardin. I am thankful for the support of the Kentucky African American Heritage Commission, which I chaired (2014–2018). The commissioners played an important role in seeking to elevate the history of enslaved Blacks at My Old Kentucky Home.

I would also like to recognize Jason Flahardy, photographic archivist, and Jennifer Bartlett, oral historian, at the University of Kentucky Libraries; Doug Boyd and Kopana Terry in the Louie B. Nunn Center for Oral History at the University of Kentucky Libraries; Amy Hanaford Purcell and Cassidy Meurer in Archives and Special Collections at the University of Louisville; Emma Johansen and Heather Potter at the Filson Historical Society; and Teresa Searcy, chair of the Robert H. Williams Cultural Center. I also want to convey my appreciation to Rufus Friday, who read the introduction and my chapter in the book and made helpful edits. My family friend Camille Lucas provided valuable technical support during critical junctures in the preparation of the book.

In the end, putting this book together has been a collaborative effort. However, I am especially grateful to my wife, Teresa; my children, Elizabeth and Sarah; and my mother, Mary Crawford. I am blessed to have them in my life.

Contributors

Charlene J. Fletcher serves as affiliate faculty in the Center for Africana Studies and Culture at Indiana University–Purdue University, Indianapolis (IUPUI). Before working as a historian, she led a large prison reentry initiative and served as a lecturer on criminal justice in New York City. She is completing her first book, which explores the experiences of incarcerated Black women from Reconstruction to the Progressive Era.

Erin Wiggins Gilliam formerly served as associate professor of history and dean of the Whitney Young Honors Collegium at Kentucky State University. She is currently assistant vice president of Student Retention and Matriculation Success at Texas Southern University. Her research interests include the importance and continued relevancy of historically Black colleges and universities.

Jacob A. Glover is former director of public programs and education at Shaker Village of Pleasant Hill. His doctoral research focused on everyday racial violence in Kentucky and Louisiana after the Civil War, and he is currently revising his dissertation for publication.

Melanie Beals Goan is professor of history at the University of Kentucky. Her research interests and teaching focuses include twentieth-century US history, Kentucky history, gender, and the history of health care. She is the author of *Mary Breckinridge: The Frontier Nursing Service and Rural Health in Appalachia* (2008) and *A Simple Justice: Kentucky Women Fight for the Vote* (University Press of Kentucky, 2020).

Le Datta Denise Grimes is an oral historian at Clemson University. She is a trained historian and journalist who has taught history at the University of Kentucky and Kentucky State University. Her research centers on

Rosenwald Schools built both by and for rural southern Blacks from 1912 to 1932. She is the coproducer and cowriter of *Invented Before You Were Born* (2022), a film that chronicles the lives of three free Black communities in western Kentucky prior to the Civil War.

Giuliana Perrone is assistant professor of history at the University of California, Santa Barbara. She is currently finishing her first book, which explores the legal history of slavery and abolition in Reconstruction-era state courts.

James M. Prichard supervised the Research Room at the Kentucky Department for Libraries and Archives from 1985 to 2008. He is the author of *Embattled Capital: Frankfort, Kentucky, in the Civil War* (Frankfort Heritage Press, 2014). He is currently a member of the Special Collections Department at the Filson Historical Society in Louisville, Kentucky.

Gerald L. Smith is professor of history at the University of Kentucky and pastor of Pilgrim Baptist Church in Lexington, Kentucky. He is the author of *A Black Educator in the Segregated South: Kentucky's Rufus B. Atwood* (University Press of Kentucky, 1994), coeditor of *The Kentucky African American Encyclopedia* (University Press of Kentucky, 2015), and author of other publications on Black Kentuckians.

Alicestyne Turley is the program director for the International Storytelling Center in Jonesborough, Tennessee, a member of the Kentucky Historical Society board of directors and the Kentucky African American Heritage Commission, and an eastern Kentucky resident. She is the author of *The Gospel of Freedom: Black Evangelicals and the Underground Railroad* (University Press of Kentucky, 2022).

Charles R. Welsko is the project director of the *Civil War Governors of Kentucky Digital Documentary Edition* at the Kentucky Historical Society. He is a cultural, social, and political historian of the long Civil War era, with a focus on borderlands and national identities. He has published in *West Virginia History: A Journal of Regional Studies* and has an essay in *Playing at War: Identity and Memory in American Civil War Era Video Games,* edited by Patrick A. Lewis and James Welborn III (forthcoming).

Brandon R. Wilson is a Lyman T. Johnson Postdoctoral Fellow at the University of Kentucky whose research uncovers the early American prison system and its interdependent relationship with the domestic slave trade. He analyzes the political and economic foundations of jails and penitentiaries as sites of containment and extraction that become necessary functions of racial capitalism. This work, which stems from his doctoral dissertation at Washington University in St. Louis, expands the discourse beyond the academic sphere into arenas of public history and education. With experience teaching labor-history courses in the Missouri Prison Education Program, Wilson is deeply committed to the accessibility and democratization of knowledge.

Index